British Culture and Society in the 1970s

British Culture and Society in the 1970s:
The Lost Decade

Edited by

Laurel Forster and Sue Harper

CAMBRIDGE
SCHOLARS

P U B L I S H I N G

British Culture and Society in the 1970s: The Lost Decade,
Edited by Laurel Forster and Sue Harper

This book first published 2010

Cambridge Scholars Publishing

12 Back Chapman Street, Newcastle upon Tyne, NE6 2XX, UK

British Library Cataloguing in Publication Data
A catalogue record for this book is available from the British Library

ISBN (10): 1-4438-1734-1, ISBN (13): 978-1-4438-1734-9

TABLE OF CONTENTS

LIST OF ILLUSTRATIONS

ACKNOWLEDGEMENTS

We should like to acknowledge the support of the Arts and Humanities Research Council (AHRC), under whose aegis the Portsmouth project on 1970s British Cinema was carried out. Their advice was invaluable throughout. We also profited from the support of the Centre For European and International Studies (CEISR) at the University of Portsmouth. Our Faculty of Cultural and Creative Industries (CCI) and our School of Creative Arts, Film and Media (SCAFM) both provided substantial support.

Colleagues in the 1970s group at Portsmouth have been unfailingly encouraging, and have been both a stimulus and a resource. We should like to thank Dave Allen, Laurie Ede, Vincent Porter, Justin Smith and PhD students Sian Barber, Patti Gaal-Holmes and Sally Shaw. Special thanks must go to Peri Bradley for her tremendous input into the conference. Maria Fritsche coped with great good humour with our many "final" versions of the book. Thanks also to Verena Wright for her work on the index.

We should also like to acknowledge the support from our Head of School, Esther Sonnet, and our Associate Dean of Research, Paul McDonald.

We are grateful to Daniel Meadows, Norman J. Warren and Tony Klinger for permissions to reproduce photographs, and to James Woodward for allowing us to reproduce his drawing.

Finally, Laurel would like to thank Nick, Florine, Eden, Pierre and Hugo just for being themselves and making it all possible. Special thanks too to Janet Floyd for her consistently good advice. And Sue would like to thank Walter and Ted for putting up with the domestic chaos occasioned by this book.

PREFACE

We are most grateful to the Arts and Humanities Research Council for granting a major award to the University of Portsmouth, School of Film, Media and Creative Arts. This was to support a three-year project, led by Professor Sue Harper, to draw the map of British cinema in the 1970s. One of the designated outcomes of that project was a conference, but in order not to overlap with the conference on British cinema of the 1970s called "Don't Look Now" at the University of Exeter 2007, we decided that a conference with a broader remit was appropriate both for the Portsmouth project and for the study of the 1970s as a whole. Accordingly we organised a large conference at the University of Portsmouth in July 2008, entitled "British Culture and Society in the 1970s".

The conference had an array of panels and papers on a wide range of aspects of British culture and society of the decade: television, novels, drama, music, critical theory, film, journalism, political activism and radical culture. There were also showings of rare films, and plenary sessions with Sandy Lieberson, David Edgar, Richard Weight, Mark Kermode and Ken Russell. This collection had its inception in that wide-ranging conference. It provides a selection of those discussions to form an original and broad-based commentary on the decade. We wanted to produce sustained and coherent meditations on themes of specific significance to the 1970s in Britain. Alas, this meant it was necessary to be highly selective, and had to sacrifice many excellent papers. We have produced a volume with clear sections on: politics and art; media and social change; youth cultures; film production contexts; and social spaces. The essays set up dialogues and synergies with each other, interrogating some of the multifarious cultural interventions, social experiments and developments of this most exciting moment in British recent history: the 1970s.

Arts & Humanities
Research Council

INTRODUCTION

For a long time, the 1970s only existed in popular memory as a decade of embarrassing kitsch and tastelessness, and this has concealed many other important aspects of the culture of the decade. Until recently, the decade has been recalled only with uncomfortable humour and irony, and with only a few enduring but empty motifs such as flared trousers, the pop group ABBA, sexploitation movies and angry feminists in dungarees. These epitomise the ways in which this whole decade has been despised and misremembered. For example, a popular 'talking heads' style television programme, *I Love the '70s* (BBC1, 2000) follows a recognisable format, and led viewers down a media "memory lane" hour for ten weeks. Each episode covered popular culture year by year, and was hosted by different "personalities" of the 1970s, emphasising television programmes, music and ephemera. Dave Haslam's book *Not Abba: The Real Story of the 1970s* (2005) comments on the blandness and repetitiveness of history remembered through television, as a result of the limited range of material available in television archives, recycled endlessly in such formulaic presentations of culture. The film *Mamma Mia!* (2008, Dir. Phyllida Lloyd), based on a popular theatre musical, is an important index of the enduring but powerful nature of these cultural topoi, and the enormous success of the film indicates that cultural memory of the 1970s still has considerable currency. The film brings the 1970s "alive" by performing a series of ABBA hits anew and weaving a fresh story round them, which can be performed in turn by the audience in sing-along mode. The finale of the film repays attention. The actors, gorgeously arrayed in 1970s glitter and platforms, provide an ironic, even camp, performance of themselves as members of the band. They seem to mock, yet hugely enjoy, the supposedly tasteless excesses of the decade. What is evoked is a sense of fun: the 1970s is powerfully presented not as a period of repression and difficulty but as one of expressiveness and spontaneity. This has been an incredibly persistent way of relating to and remembering the 1970s.

This volume seeks to present an alternative view of 1970s culture. If we conceptualise the period as "The Lost Decade," this provides a useful framework for more rigorous discussions of the period. The 1970s may be considered 'lost' in a number of ways. Firstly, intense feelings were produced by the radical social changes of the period, and such social and emotional trauma is often unsettling to reproduce or recall. The media deal unevenly with the subtleties of emotional response to social change. Secondly, the personal hardships endured make it a decade which many people would prefer to forget. Indeed 1970s television was awash with varieties of escapism from its disturbed present, with Edwardianism and nostalgic heritage dramas which allude to so-called "halcyon days". And thirdly, the essence of the 1970s is more difficult to distil than that of the preceding 1960s and the subsequent 1980s. The 1960s seem easily recalled as the decade of hippies and youth cultures, where free love, music and pop art glamorously take priority in general recollection over the less palatable actualities of that time. The 1980s, in stark contrast, is remembered for 'yuppie' materialistic ostentation, as well as high levels of conflict and unemployment. This potentially leaves the 1970s open to the accusation of being a cultural vacuum, or merely the transitional moment when the youthful optimism of the 1960s degenerated into the socio-political rigidity and complacency of the 1980s. The breadth and range of cultural production illustrated in this volume points to a different story of the 1970s.

This collection appears at a time when a retrospective recovery of the 1970s is taking place through a number of popular television dramas. As those whose childhoods were most influenced by the 1970s now reach their mid-forties and the height of their influence in cultural production, so a less inhibited and perhaps more accurate recovery of the decade can become more likely, interrogating the 1970s in a more dispassionate way. One example is the highly successful police drama *Life on Mars* (BBC1 Jan 2006-Apr 2007), a two-series-long immersion in the 1970s, and indeed it owes much to the 1970s police procedural, *The Sweeney* (ITV, 1975-1978). *Life on Mars* revisits some uncomfortable aspects of the decade such as unprincipled policing methods, sexism in the workplace, and hierarchical social exploitation. Through well-crafted narrative structure and the devices of flashback and flashforward, *Life on Mars* cleverly, albeit patchily, reflects back to us just how far Britain has, and simultaneously has not, moved on since that decade. Less explicit about historical distance but more hard-hitting was *Red Riding* (Channel 4 2009), a series of three films for television. These films gradually and complexly reveal the underworld of a Northern community in the 1970s and 1980s beset by corruption and lawlessness. Involving and including the West Yorkshire Police Force, a tough, mean Britain is convincingly portrayed, where hypocrisy and racketeering are rife, and the ordinary, honest citizen is almost totally disempowered. In *Red Riding*, the 1970s is again being raided for a message about the way we were: the series presents the past as a corrosive, bleak and smoke-filled dive, in which dreadful things were done and little could be redeemed.

Another example is *Survivors* (BBC 2008), which also demonstrates the continuing relevance of 1970s issues. Here the central apocalyptic premise of the programme—the human race all but wiping itself out—remains identical to the series of the same name three decades earlier (BBC 1975-1977). The underlying question of rebuilding our society remains compelling but unanswered, and offers the opportunity to imagine our world radically anew. This sense of the controlling centre of society being in flux, if not totally dysfunctional, was a prevalent theme in 1970s culture. However, in the 1970s series, the survivors' vision largely leans towards a utopian optimism, whereas in the 2008 version, the outlook is much less secure. These three recent series offer a much more nuanced view of 1970s Britain than previously available on the television. The time, it would seem, has finally come to reappraise cultural output of the period.

This volume, as a work of recovery and reappraisal, argues in favour of presenting the 1970s as a period of cultural exuberance and plenitude. We suggest that the essays in this volume prove that demands for change were made, forcefully and creatively, in a wide variety of ways through political, cultural and artistic routes. The range of material presented in these essays makes it clear that it is no longer adequate to conceptualise the period in a simplified or parodied manner. The depth of both protest and innovation has to be assessed if we want to engage with the decade in a meaningful way. It was, we suggest, a moment when artistic endeavour was considered to have true political purchase, and many of the essays in this volume, selected from different disciplines, reflect this combination of creativity and commitment. It is hoped that this collection will bring some of these lost causes and complex ideas back to centre stage.

The 1970s in Britain was a decade of immense complexity in almost every sphere. There were numerous contradictions which were, socially and politically speaking, born out of concerns about gender, race, class, living conditions and the workplace. It was a decade of great early optimism, which slid into a general sense of decline; changes were anticipated, worked towards, and sometimes unevenly achieved: it was a decade in flux. Most interestingly for our purposes here, it was a decade when there were significant, varied, and often highly politicised cultural responses to changes in the past, present and future.

The fluctuations in the political parties elected by the British public are one way of understanding the changing Britain of the 1970s. The decade started with Wilson's Labour government which had been elected in 1964, but this was brought to a halt in 1970 when Edward Heath and the Conservatives came to power.   Four years later in 1974, after much-publicised miners' strikes, Wilson was returned, only to give up the leadership to Callaghan after two years. Callaghan ran a competent government, but unemployment, racial tensions, the "troubles" in Northern Ireland and a wave of strikes in the 1978 "Winter of Discontent" led to a no-confidence motion being carried in the House of Commons, which then led to electoral defeat. In 1979, the Conservatives with Margaret Thatcher as their leader came to office, and the shape of British society changed utterly thereafter.

Despite fluctuating political parties in government, there was a consistently liberal direction in legislation during the decade, although the changes intended did not always have an immediate or straightforward impact.   For example for women, the 1970 Equal Pay Act was an important first step, although it did not come into full force until 1975. It was followed by the 1975 Sex Discrimination Act, a comprehensive anti-discrimination law; and the 1975 Employment Protection Act, which outlawed dismissal on grounds of pregnancy and introduced maternity pay. However, evasion by bureaucracy and cautious employers made real change a very slow process for many women.   Other legislative changes, such as the 1971 Industrial Relations Bill, designed to regulate trade union activity, did not always have the desired effect.   And the 1976 Race Relations Act, intended to make racial discrimination and segregation illegal, was widely seen to be ineffectual.   Nonetheless, despite poor enforcement, there could be little doubt that in this decade quite radical legal change was afoot.

In many other ways too, the 1970s was a radical decade. We have found it curious that British popular cultural memory chooses to think of the 1960s as the radical decade, a time of renewal and rebirth, the "Age of Aquarius", and that it conceives of the 1970s as an age of cultural stagnation and decline. Our research leads us to the opposite view: that the 1960s was the decade of dreams, and that the 1970s was the decade where real effort, energy and creativity were engaged in ambitious projects which tried to harness those dreams into reality. The Women's Liberation Movement formed the now-called "second wave" of feminism in the 1970s and women organised themselves into petitioning, activist groups, at times radical and revolutionary, to lobby and gain publicity and support for equal rights and status for women.   Another radical movement focussed on environmentalism, and aimed to gain entry into British politics as well as to educate the public away from consumerism. The Gay Liberation Front marched and demonstrated for the rights of homosexuals against a persistent oppression, aiming to increase public awareness of homophobia. There were also movements which made pop festivals into politicised events, and others which advocated communal lifestyles, free from the nuclear family and with greater civil liberties. By the end of the decade, many of these groups had been assimilated into the mainstream culture in one way or another. Nonetheless, the 70s was a decade when different groups attempted, in their different ways, to effect change for the better.

We want to argue that there was a revolution in consciousness in the 1970s, as sub-cultural groups of the 1960s became more vociferously counter-cultural. This revolution in consciousness meant that social change was seen as necessary by a large part of the population, and this was an important driver for much of the political and personal activity in the 1970s. It became widely accepted that change was necessary, because the early 70s were tough times for many people with strikes, threatened food shortages, financial hardship and blatant inequalities for various sectors of society. There was high inflation, and from 1974 standards of living started to decrease. Despite there being greater social equality in the mid-70s, all sorts of conflicts arose which highlighted differences in class and education, religion and political allegiance. This tumultuous decade, with swings to the political Left and Right, with trade union strikes affecting the whole country, and with general uncertainty for the ordinary individual, has been difficult to document. For a long time, the 1970s has been a sort of "Bermuda Triangle" of historical analysis.

Recently however, some illuminating studies of the 1970s have been written, and these have very much helped with the serious recovery of the social and cultural history of this "lost" decade. Some have concentrated solely on the 1970s such as: Andy Beckett's *When the Lights Went Out: Britain in the Seventies* (2009). Beckett intersperses his account with a series of interviews of people, both famous and ordinary, who identified strongly with Britain in the 1970s. He offers an interpretation which elides the massive political upheavals with subjective experiences. Other texts have taken a longer historical view: Richard Weight's *Patriots: National Identity in Britain 1940-2000* (2002) looks at the countries which comprise Britain, their economic and social histories. In his discussion of the 1970s he comments on the very divided nature of Britain at the time with a series of fractured perceptions contingent upon EEC membership, striking workers, Ireland, and shifting class ascription. Mark Garnett's *From Anger to Apathy: The British Experience since 1975* (2007) divides the decade in half in order to tell a longer story about British consciousness up to the end of the twentieth century. The first portion of his book takes a close look at what it felt like to be British in the second half of the 1970s, using cultural and political histories. In taking the emotional temperature of the nation, he diagnoses disillusionment with democracy, government and other agencies; concern at levels of lawlessness, sexual excesses, terrorism, and riots. In all, he notes high levels of anger, insecurity and loss of confidence.

In addition to work done on the social changes in the decade, there has been some on its cultural practices. A number of studies have addressed this, and influenced the ways in which we have reflected on the decade and conceived this volume. Robert Hewison's *Too Much: Art and Society in the Sixties* (1986) dispenses with the idea of periodising cultural history through discrete decades, and instead interprets the early 1970s as a logical consequence of the cultural ferments of the 1960s. This is a fruitful approach, since it provides a way of locating the long and the short roots of artistic innovation. But Hewison's view is that 1970s culture provides us with evidence about the dissipation of the energies of 1968, and this inevitably colours his views on the achievements of the latter decade. We want to argue that the cultural output of the 1970s, as well as following on from the 1960s, developed its own discrete identity and energy. We take the "long 1970s" view: that is, that it is not a separate period, but can be interpreted as beginning with the so-called revolutions of 1968 and ending with the rise of Thatcher in 1979.

Bart Moore-Gilbert's *The Arts in the 1970s: Cultural Closure?* which came out in 1994, remains one of the most competent analyses of the period. The essays in the collection are divided up strictly by medium: film, radio and so on, and are of a uniformly high quality. Moore-Gilbert's Introduction provides us with some useful pointers, as it does try to link political and artistic crises. The problem with Moore-Gilbert's essay is that, like many others, it concentrates exclusively on highbrow culture. It uses the explanatory model of "post-avantgardism" to characterise the culture of the period, interpreting the artistic production of marginal groups as an exasperated response to the higher reaches of Modernism. But the book does not interrogate low or middle-brow culture, and is hampered by the way that the articles remain strictly within their individual terrain. By adopting an interdisciplinary approach and a broad view of culture as a whole, we hope that our book will help to see connections between different cultural forms in a more comprehensive way.

In a sense, all the extant accounts of 1970s British culture concentrate on one aspect, and that exclusivity hampers them from coming to a full explanation of the culture. Moore-Gilbert's collection is highbrow in its focus; Leon Hunt's book, *British Low Culture: From Safari Suits to Sexploitation* (1998) looks only at the lowbrow, as its title suggests, and it is poised between ruefulness and nostalgia. It is a lively interpretation of those cultural texts which are entirely without status and "hail" us loudly, reminding us of what it was to *be there*. And yet 1970s culture was characterised by the unusually permeable membranes between different cultural forms and works of different status and value. We see it as part of our task to allude to, and to account for, those "permeable membranes" which facilitate shifts between high and low culture; in the 1970s, these shifts occur in an unusually intense way.

The real issue is how to write a history of the culture—how to structure or proportion it. John A. Walker's *Left Shift: Radical Art in 1970s Britain* (2002) was very important historiographically. It used a chronological approach, highlighting key cultural developments on a year-by-year basis. This could have ended up as a list of unrelated events, but the strength of Walker's book was that the spread of attention was broad, looking at a comprehensive range of avant-garde practices and media that hinted at the level of cultural exchange taking place between radical and mainstream art. Of course, the rationale of the book proscribes detailed engagement with the popular culture of the 1970s, but it does offer an analysis of the conditions for innovation in the decade.

Another way of writing the history of the 1970s is to use a kind of "snapshot" approach, in which discrete events are located in their social and ideological context. This is what drives Francis Wheen's *Strange Days Indeed: the Golden Age of Paranoia* (2009), and is a useful method, but the book presents the cultural as a logical consequence of the political, and we hope to produce a more nuanced account.

Some recent work on 1970s culture has shown partiality and undue selectivity. Alwyn Turner's *Crisis? What Crisis?* (2008) tends to focus on popular forms such as football and pop music, but does not construct an argument about the relationship between high and low cultural forms in the 1970s. In a sense the title of Howard Sounes' *Seventies: the Sights, Sounds and Ideas of a Brilliant Decade* (2006) says it all; it uses a case-study approach whose rationale tends to be personal, and the recollections range from the Isle of Wight Festival to memories of Diane Arbus and to the *aperçu* that several 1970s alumni died at the age of 27. The most intense "case-study" approach is Michael Bracewell's *Re-make/Re-Model: Art, Pop, Fashion and the Making of Roxy Music* (2007), which, in a painstaking way, disinters the cultural and biographical hinterland of a particularly eclectic group. Our collection provides a more diverse and less personalized approach.

We hope that our book will build on some of the existing scholarship, and take it a step further. We want to argue that the culture of the 1970s contributes an enormous amount to the history of consciousness of the decade, and that it should be given major currency in any debates about culture and society. The uncertainty and radical change at the social level shook free and gave permission to an astonishingly wide range of cultural forms. These both consolidated and experimented at the formal level.

Even if there could be such a thing as the *Zeitgeist*, it would be particularly difficult to define it for such a varied and fragmented period as the 1970s. We might playfully argue that the "spirit of the age" inheres in its cultural texts. But what is needed is a *materialist* and *detailed* interrogation of those texts, and that entails asking about their structure, sponsorship, their conditions of production, and the cultural competence required to decode them. The articles in this book begin that task, and adumbrate a culture which is allusive and risk-taking, and which embraces and transcends the notion of chaos.

We are addressing culture not as a "whole way of life" in the broadest sense of Cultural Studies. Rather, in this book we are giving attention to forms which are the result of creative endeavour, or political strife. All the essays in the book are studies of artifacts, media forms or cultural policies of one sort or another, which have authors, audiences and discourses. Accordingly, all our essays pay attention to *agency*, *style* and *intention*. Works of journalism, television programmes, novels, "happenings", films, buildings, and plays are considered with regard to their sponsorship, the autonomy of their producers, their effect upon various groups and society in general, and the way in which their intentions were challenged or achieved within the constraints of the period.

The 1970s was, as we hope this volume will demonstrate, a period of extraordinary cultural ferment. In virtually every type of artistic production, new parameters were established, and there was a restless push against old boundaries and limitations. Even in cultural forms with minimal status, such as the *Confessions...* films or pornography, there was a qualitative shift, due in part to the shifting boundaries of taste and permission. In middle-brow or high-brow art forms, the transformation is even more marked. It is a period in which the old certainties abut mood and form are called into question in the majority of cultural forms. Certainly, 1970s culture owed much to the fêted revolutions of the 1960s. But the decade has its own intrinsic messages too. Many 1970s art forms, including poetry and the novel, exhibit a sense of fracture far more acute than that which obtained in the 1960s. Many artistic texts broke down common assumptions about society and the self.

A metaphor which is commonly used for thinking through the relationship between culture and society is that of a "reflection"—that art offers a straightforward and predictable index of the social "background." In this instance, this does not help us to account for the richness and variety of 1970s culture. The transformations which took place in the political, social and sexual arenas, through legislation and the increasing visibility of radical groups, did not appear *directly* in cultural forms. In the first place, media-specific but spasmodic attempts were made to allow more permeable boundaries between media forms. In the second place, in virtually every area of artistic production, previous organisational structures were in flux, and this gave a degree of autonomy to individuals who wanted to take risks. In the third place, new artists were coming to maturity, and came to their peak precisely when everything looked as though it was in meltdown. This seeming chaos led to a sort of over-stimulus in artistic production, and a sense that everything was up for grabs. Many cultural forms exhibit a playful, self-referential manner, which evinces a profound sense of disquiet.

Another metaphor which is often used as a way of accounting for culture is the Marxist one of the economic base determining and predicting the cultural superstructure. This may work well for other periods, but certainly not for the 1970s. In that period, there was a profound disjunction between economic provision and levels of artistic production. Some art-forms, such as community arts, experienced something of a bonanza in the decade. Others, the cinema for example, experienced penury and crisis. But all the cultural forms exhibit a sort of reckless, risk-taking, might-as-well-as-not attitude. This is the politics of emergency: and it leads to art which may be messy and inconsistent, but whose vitality is beyond doubt.

***

We have tried to provide ways of thinking about such diversity and complexity by grouping essays into spheres of cultural activity. Our first theme, **Narratives of Politics and Art** looks at the spread and intensity of Marxist ideas in social and cultural practice. The 1970s was a period in which some parts of society expressed intensified interest in varieties of Marxism: the unions and the universities, for example. Marxism told silently on the minds of a whole generation, and extreme change in the political arena—varieties of Labour administrations, Heath's governmental style, and the rise of Thatcherism—had unpredictable impacts on the cultural level. Rochelle Simmons' essay on John Berger provides a precise focus on the work on a particular artist of the period, and asks how

Berger's radical ideas on visual perception and subjectivity filtered through into his creative writing. Anthony Dunn looks at the rise of Marxism in British academic and intellectual life and traces its roots in, and in turn its influence on, American and European Marxist theories. Dunn's approach is a broad and theoretical one, whereas the other essays focus on the interface between Marxist ideas and specific cultural practices. Gillian Whiteley's piece on Welfare State International captures the nomadic, eclectic nature of much 1970s cultural expression, and, based on new primary source material, demonstrates the capacity for innovation which characterises much avant-garde work in the period. Kirsten Forkert's essay on the Artists' Union—an attempt to set up a union for artists akin to the TUC—considers its work in relation to the labour movement of the 1970s. Finally, Sean Tunney examines the complex link between various Labour administrations and the newspaper industry, and he outlines the developments of a coherent "left current" in the Party. His analysis demonstrates the problems of political representation in the decade, showing the difficulty of achieving consensus and sustained momentum.

Our second section, **The Media and Social Change** raises the issue of the ways in which various media forms responded to social change. The relationship between the media and society is often damagingly oversimplified, and the old model of the "injection method" of media effects is still hoisted into use. What we wanted to do was to use a modified uses-and-gratifications model, and to show the *means whereby* innovative ideas about society were both inserted into, and developed by, media texts. 1970s television and journalism showed a sophisticated and selective awareness of innovation, and fashioned it to appear in a form which audiences would accept and internalise. All the essays in this section show how complex a procedure this was. David McQueen indicates the way in which current affairs programmes engaged urgently and deeply with political crisis and change, and had a clear understanding of the regulatory challenges they faced. The other essays in this section deal with the ways in which the media responded to minority or emergent issues—women's and gay liberation, racialised politics and the ecological movement. Laurel Forster's essay on women's magazines and second-wave feminism demonstrates how varied journalistic response was, and how carefully it was modified to fit the needs of readers from different backgrounds and cultural competence. *Till Death Us Do Part* is the focus of Gavin Schaffer's article, and he maps the way the series and its author Johnny Speight have an ambivalent attitude to racial politics and identity. The 1970s was a period in which discourses surrounding homosexuality emerged more frequently in the public domain, and Peri Bradley's article examines the idea of "camp" and the way it was critically deployed in a range of television comedies of the period. The self-sufficiency movement was one which had long historical roots and came of age in the 1970s, and Gwilym Thear's essay demonstrates its complexity and shows how television dealt selectively with it. All the essays in this section show that the media recognised the intensity of social change that was afoot, and played an important role in making the personal political.

Our third section is entitled **Youth Cultures**, and we hope goes some way to establishing the radical nature of generational transformation in the 1970s. The new youth culture was increasingly splintering in the period, and there was an increase in cultural texts which were *about* the young, as well as those which were *for* them. It was not just a matter of appearance: the uniforms of Punk and the moral panics which it engendered. Rather, the media in the 1970s made a serious attempt to provide entertainment for youth groups, and represented it in a more nuanced way than is often thought. Dave Allen takes *Quadrophenia* as a point of departure for thinking through the ways in which we conceptualise the past, and suggests that such cultural texts can conceal an understanding of the complexity of youth movements. Other essays in this section look at the new types of cultural provision for young people. Keith Johnson's piece on the phenomenon of The Wombles shows how permeable it was to social influences, and that the furry creatures encompassed both conservative and liberal attitudes. Julian Matthews considers *John Craven's Newsround*, a current affairs programme specially for the young, and shows what a major innovation it was in terms of material and approach. And Stephen Hill's essay on the pop music magazine *Smash Hits* shows how it transformed its audience's understanding of popular music throughout the decade, and exerted a modernising influence in terms of format and discourse. All these articles provide evidence for a change in media provision and media representation which cannot simply be accounted for by the desire for profit.

Section Four, **Film Production Contexts**, focuses on the film industry. 1970s British cinema is often neglected or demonised, and frequently misunderstood. There is one recent edited collection on *Seventies British Cinema*, Robert Shail (2008) and one forthcoming from the Portsmouth project, but the essays in the present volume represent substantially new work. The essays in Section Four are based on hitherto unused material—archives, interviews and diaries—and by using material close to the source, unearth a new understanding of British 1970s film. The essays provide important evidence about the industry and the way genres, authorship and funding were transformed in the decade. Andrew Spicer's piece on Michael Klinger studies him as an innovatory entrepreneur in the period, and fills in an important gap in our knowledge about mainstream producers. The other essays focus on directors. John Izod and his colleagues at Stirling use Lindsay Anderson's diaries as a source for a re-evaluation of *O Lucky Man!* and its motifs from popular culture. Adam Locks uses his interview with the "forgotten" director Norman J. Warren to develop an argument about the way in which British cinema of the period redeploys images of the rural and the gothic, and Adrian Garvey re-evaluates the work of Ken Russell. His *The Boy Friend* deploys a characteristically 1970s type of nostalgia which is located in its cultural context.

Section Five, **Social Spaces** focuses on urban and domestic experience, and examines the real, imagined and constructed spaces which were available for habitation by Britons of the 1970s. Tim Gough's article looks at a "real place", the Alexandra Road project, and locates it in relation to the concepts of brutalism and modernism. Sue Evans develops the idea of the concrete landscape and shows its importance for certain theatrical productions in the 1970s, having such currency that it is frequently recycled. Jo Turney's essay moves from the idea of the buildings themselves to the decoration within them, and she analyses the influences on 1970s interior design, accounting for the nostalgic, tactile and sexualised aspects of its mise en scène.

Much remains to be done. We have tried to indicate something of the complexity of 1970s culture and show how it responded, in faltering and unpredictable ways, to the social changes taking place. A further edited collection might include more work on the novel of the period (to show how types of experiment persisted across a range of novels), and would analyse developments in poetry and show how the idea of a "national" poetry was disrupted by a growing internationalism. It would be good, too, to examine the powerful links between the visual arts and other media, and to ask how far political debates about materiality extended into painting and sculpture. More work could be done on the way in which 1970s culture tried to narrow the gap between high and low art. And a consistent examination of the relationship between popular and classical music in the 1970s is long overdue.

But such an enterprise must be postponed for another time. For the moment, we hope we have produced a thought-provoking volume which stimulates debate about the connections, contradictions and (sometimes) confusions in a fascinating and under-researched period in British cultural history.

PART I:

NARRATIVES OF POLITICS AND ART

JOHN BERGER'S REVOLUTIONARY NARRATIVES

ROCHELLE SIMMONS

Many people's most vivid memories of John Berger in the 1970s no doubt derive from the collaborative television series that he presented on BBC2, *Ways of Seeing* (1970), and the book that developed out of the series (1972), in which he presented a provocative Marxist critique of the relationship between art, class, and property. In the opening sequence of *Ways of Seeing*, the image of a long-haired Berger dressed in an exuberantly-patterned print shirt appearing to hack at Botticelli's *Venus and Mars* (1483) with a knife while it is hanging in the National Gallery testifies to his iconoclasm. It might also be said to offer a visual depiction of the barbarism Sir Kenneth Clark railed against in his television series *Civilization* (1969-70), in which the patrician Clark traced the rise of civilization through "great works by Western man." Indeed, *Ways of Seeing* provides a Marxist response to *Civilization*. But Berger's actions do not merely overturn traditional beliefs about art, for they arise out of a revolutionary impulse that lies behind much of Berger's cultural production over a thirty-year period.

Teasing out connections between Berger's art criticism of the 1960s and his television, fiction, and film of the 1970s reveals some of the ways in which intellectual and aesthetic innovations of the 1960s permeated British film culture of the 1970s, since, from the 1950s until the 1970s, Berger was engaged in various efforts to formulate a revolutionary aesthetic across these domains. My argument implicitly contradicts Robert Hewison's view of the 1970s as an era of "cultural closure"[1] and is in agreement with Bart Moore-Gilbert's counter-claim that "the mainstream was significantly changed by the legacy of the previous decade's experimental energy."[2]

---

[1] Robert Hewison, *Too Much: Art and Society in the Sixties 1960–75* (London: Methuen, 1986), 230.
[2] Bart Moore-Gilbert, *The Arts in the 1970s: Cultural Closure?* (London: Routledge, 1994), 15.

Berger's categorisation as a British writer requires some explanation. Although Berger has lived in Europe since 1960, and was therefore not resident in Britain during the 1970s, Berger's work was, and is, in dialogue with British culture. For example, *G.* (1972) is classified as an experimental British novel.[3] The two contemporaneous novels with which *G.* has most in common are B.S. Johnson's *Travelling People* (1963) and John Fowles's *The French Lieutenant's Woman* (1969). Johnson's novel shares *G.*'s self-conscious narration and stylistic experimentation, but these derive from eighteenth-century rather than Brechtian sources. Similarly, both Fowles's and Berger's novels exhibit features of the *nouveau roman*. Yet, if *G.* is considered within a British context, it is more by way of contrast than comparison, because, from the 1950s onwards, Berger's espousal of Sartrean commitment set him apart from most of his fellow writers. However, it allied him with left-wing filmmakers, like the French-Swiss director Alain Tanner (who worked briefly in London) and Lindsay Anderson. Only David Caute produced a comparably modernist, dialectical novel called *The Occupation* (1971).

Berger's efforts to formulate a revolutionary aesthetic over a thirty-year period demonstrate a consistent belief in the need for radical political action. For most of his career Berger has identified himself as a Marxist, and has campaigned against the inequalities of capitalism. But if Berger's political beliefs remain constant, the same could not be said for his sense of which kind of art best served his political ends. As art critic for the *New Statesman* in the 1950s, Berger worked tirelessly to bring about a realist revival in British painting, by advocating a social realism that adapts some of Georg Lukács's philosophical theories to the visual arts, since he believed that social realism provided the only radical alternative to the dominant formalist abstraction.[4] In his first novel, *A Painter of our Time* (1957), the work of its artist-hero, Janos Lavin, is based on that of the socialist painter Fernand Léger. Berger ultimately suggests that Lavin's attempts to bring about a socialist state by revolutionary means, as a

---

[3] For a discussion of *G.* as an experimental novel, see Randall Stevenson, *The British Novel Since the Thirties: An Introduction* (Athens: University of Georgia Press, 1986), 216, and Moore-Gilbert, *The Arts in the 1970s*, 169–71.

[4] Berger's espousal of social realism is discussed by Geoff Dyer in *Ways of Telling: The Work of John Berger* (London: Pluto Press, 1986) and by James Hyman in *The Battle for Realism: Figurative Art in Britain During the Cold War 1945–60* (New Haven: Yale University Press, 2001). Berger pays tribute to Lukács's theories in *Art and Revolution: Ernst Neizvestny and the Role of the Artist in the U.S.S.R.* (London: Weidenfeld & Nicolson, 1969).

painter, are equivalent to his activities as a political activist. Thus, both artist and activist are united in a revolutionary cause.

As a freelance art critic in the 1960s, Berger replaced his earlier ideas about social realism with theories about the revolutionary nature of modernist Cubist art.[5] These theories are set out in *The Success and Failure of Picasso* (1965) and "The Moment of Cubism" (1967). It is, of course, an art-history commonplace to assert that the Cubist painting of Pablo Picasso and Georges Braque brought about a revolution in visual representation, by replacing the linear, one-point perspective, which had dominated Western art for five centuries, with simultaneous, multiple perspectives. Yet Berger ascribes political as well as stylistic significance to the revolutionary nature of Cubism, by emphasising the ideological aspects of the Cubist historical moment, during which the world underwent unprecedented philosophical and material change. According to Berger, many of these developments appeared to offer the possibility of a transformed world, and Cubism reflected this possibility, by altering "the nature of the relationship between the painted image and reality."[6] However, these paintings do not constitute a social or political blueprint. Berger states: "The content of these works is the relation between the seer and the seen. [...] They do not illustrate a human or social situation, they posit it."[7]

In writing *G.*, Berger draws upon his art critical writings to create an experimental Cubist narrative that is conspicuously modernist in its use of language and form. This novel is also an attempt to formulate a revolutionary Marxist modernist aesthetic, at a time when Britain was dominated by a Marxist realist tradition.[8] But before I discuss the revolutionary aspects of *G.* in detail, I should indicate that the connections Berger was drawing between modernist aesthetic practices and Marxist

---

[5] In an article called "Cubism as Revolutionary Realism" (1983), David E. James takes a different position from the one that will be argued here, in that he approaches Berger's art criticism in general rather than specific terms, and defines Cubism as "[a] model of the artist's totalizing consciousness". David E. James, "Cubism as Revolutionary Realism: John Berger and *G,*" *Minnesota Review* 21 (1983): 98. My doctoral dissertation entitled *John Berger's G. as a Cubist Novel* (PhD thesis, University of Toronto, 1994) proposes a far more complex argument about Berger's theories than what I have presented in this chapter, since I argue that Berger exhibits—but does not reconcile—ideas of totality and heterogeneity within his dialectical writing in *G.*

[6] John Berger, "The Moment of Cubism," in: John Berger, *The Moment of Cubism and Other Essays* (London: Weidenfeld & Nicolson, 1969), 171.

[7] Ibid., 29.

[8] Dyer, *Ways of Telling*, 25, 83.

politics are in keeping with James Hay's succinct description of the formation of Film Studies in the in the 1960s and 1970s. He writes:

> Film Studies' emergence through post-structuralist literary criticism, particularly Marxist literary and film theory's shared valorization of a revolutionary and transformative aesthetic and, simultaneously, efforts to develop a Marxist critical theory of "film form" [...] occurred by recuperating the European avant-garde's discourse on modernity.[9]

Berger's participation in 1970s cinema culture will be discussed later, with respect to the films that he made with Tanner. However, the interest in revolutionary (and dialectical) form—which is evident in Berger's art criticism, fiction, television, and film from the late 1950s onwards—intersects with a larger development within film history and theory that includes ideological debate over films by Sergei Eisenstein, Jean-Luc Godard, and others in the journal *Cahiers du Cinéma* and *Cinéthique* during and following May '68.[10] Significantly, the texts that Hay cites as being central to a "progressive" or "counter-" cinema during the 1960s and 1970s—Russian constructivist montage theories, Bertold Brecht's theatrical devices, and Walter Benjamin's "The Work of Art in the Age of Mechanical Reproduction"—are all crucial to Berger's formulation of a revolutionary narrative within the above-cited domains. Thus, in relation to Berger's 1970s works, my use of the term "revolutionary" is informed by what I perceive to be Berger's interpretation of these debates and texts, as my following discussion of *Ways of Seeing* demonstrates in relation to Benjamin's essay.

Ways of Seeing manifests its revolutionary politics in a number of ways. By taking "The Work of Art in the Age of Mechanical Reproduction" (1936) as its starting point, it implicitly endorses Benjamin's revolutionary political agenda, since Benjamin begins his essay by invoking Marx's critique of capitalism and by anticipating the abolition of capitalism. Benjamin then discusses the transformative effects of mass media upon the work of art. He argues that mechanical reproduction results in a loss of aura, because, when the original is placed in inappropriate contexts, its presence is always depreciated.

---

[9] James Hay, "Piecing Together What Remains of the Cinematic City," in *The Cinematic City*, ed. David B. Clarke, 214–15 (London: Routledge, 1997).
[10] In *May '68 and Film Culture*, Harvey examines the debates over radical aesthetics and the construction of a materialist cinema within these journals.

The television series of *Ways of Seeing* puts many of Benjamin's ideas into practice.[11] For instance, Berger's literal selection of a "detail" from Botticelli's painting, to which I alluded earlier, serves to demonstrate Benjamin's point about how mass-produced images detract from the original. In addition, Benjamin's conception of the image has formed the basis for Berger's reconceived history of art, which augments the Western high art tradition with a history of images. Berger concludes the book of *Ways of Seeing* with a reproduction of René Margritte's painting *On the Threshold of Liberty* (1937) which shows a cannon aimed at a series of panels displaying a variety of figurative images, including a building façade, trees in a forest, and a naked female torso. Since *Ways of Seeing* takes aim at class supremacy based on property and wealth, this image functions as an obvious political revolutionary metaphor. The book's final words: "To be continued by the reader. . . " make this exhortation even more emphatic.[12]

As an aside, *Ways of Seeing*'s revolutionary message can also be seen in the way that this television series opposes all that *Civilization* stands for. Clark came from a wealthy background and was a member of the establishment: he was an Oxford-educated aesthete, art collector and scholar. By contrast, Berger is an anti-establishment Marxist, and an autodidact, who worked as a painter, art critic, journalist and writer, and who has remained outside institutions. Clark and Berger's manners of presentation are diametrically opposed, since the elderly Clark is a model of decorum and restraint, whereas the youthful Berger displays the kind of "passionate intensity" that Clark considers dangerous. While *Civilization* was abundantly resourced, *Ways of Seeing* was made on a meagre budget. Whereas Clark is photographed on location beside original works of art, Berger often has a blue screen backdrop and he comments on reproduced images. The series was partly filmed in Paris during May '68, and, from the opening credits onwards, Clark addresses the dangers of this revolutionary uprising: the triumphal procession of "great works of genius" includes a palace with a tank in front of it. Clark emphasizes the threat posed by barbarians from the Roman Empire onwards and he draws pointed comparisons between barbarians and rioting students, particularly in the episode entitled "The Fallacies of Hope," which takes revolution as its subject. In his conclusion to the series, he examines the "moral and

---

[11] Berger pays direct tribute to Benjamin in John Berger and others, *Ways of Seeing* (Harmondsworth: Penguin, 1972), 34.
[12] Ibid., 166.

intellectual failure of Marxism."[13] By contrast, Berger does not regret, but celebrates, the revolutionary spirit of May '68 in both *Ways of Seeing* and in his novel *G.*

With respect to the relationship between *G.* and Berger's theories about the revolutionary nature of Cubist painting, *G.* is extensively concerned with Cubist art. The book has a collage-like structure and it exhibits all the canonical generic features of a Literary Cubist novel.[14] However, it also draws on Berger's writings about Cubism on a conceptual and a verbal level. *G.* is set during the Cubist historical moment and the eponymous character G. is based on Berger's notion of Picasso, whom he considered a "Don Juan in relation to art,"[15] and whom he thought of in revolutionary terms.[16] Likewise, G. is a latent revolutionary, who eschews politics, but who attempts to destroy society in his own mind through his subversive sexual activity.[17]

Like the Cubists, Berger's protagonist is not involved in politics, but he does have a revolutionary consciousness.[18] The reader is never told what G.'s initial stands for, and, while he is most closely identified with Don Juan—or Don Giovanni—he is also linked with a number of political revolutionaries in the novel, who stand for some of the "possible selves" that G. might have become. The devastating looks G. bestows upon women that provide the clearest indication of his revolutionary significance. Yet, G.'s looks are only able to convey this meaning, because Berger locates his novel during the Cubist moment and G.'s span of maximum sexual activity coincides almost exactly with the Cubist years. Therefore, G.'s vision reflects the promise offered by his age.

In Berger's novel, too, G.'s revolutionary import rests upon "the relation between the seer and the seen." Berger introduces the significance of G.'s looks by providing some information on the split subjectivity of women. This discussion is almost identical to a sequence in "Ways of Seeing," which had a formative influence on theories of the male gaze.[19]

---

[13] See Robert Hewison, *Culture and Consensus: England, Art and Politics since 1940* (London: Methuen, 1995), 153–4.

[14] See Simmons, *John Berger's G.* , 93–130.

[15] Berger, cited in Dyer, *Ways of Telling*, 90.

[16] Berger, *The Success and Failure of Picasso* (London: Writers and Readers, 1980), 129–30.

[17] Berger, cited in Dyer, *Ways of Telling*, 91.

[18] R. Selden, "Commitment and Dialectic in Novels by David Caute and John Berger," *Forum for Modern Language Studies* 11 (1975): 116.

[19] *Ways of Seeing* predated Laura Mulvey's influential essay "Visual Pleasure and Narrative Cinema," which was written in 1973 and published in 1975 in *Screen*.

We are told that nineteenth century middle-class women lived in a socially conditioned, subjunctive world where each woman was divided within herself "between surveyor and surveyed".[20] G.'s looks enable the woman to gain a sense of her own singularity and they therefore provide her with a unified sense of self. It must be said, however, that for those with feminist sympathies, the revolutionary transformation that G. offers is heavily compromised by his being identified with Don Juan, whose seductions can be seen as the very embodiment of patriarchal oppression.

Berger provides us with a clue to G.'s Cubist consciousness, when, in a resonant gesture, G. dethrones an ornamental swan. This action is thematically depicted as a revolutionary transformation; it also occurs during a conversation that explores the transformative effects of looking, dancing, reciting, and swinging on a merry-go-round. This gesture follows on from Camille's recitation of some lines by the Symbolist poet Stéphane Mallarmé, from a sonnet commonly referred to as "The Swan." If G. is identified with Cubism, and, in this episode, Camille with Symbolism, when G. dethrones the ornamental swan, his action represents the Cubist displacement of Symbolism. We are told that: "On a low table near which they sat was a large glass statue of a swan, rose-coloured, and mounted on a silver turntable which revolved. It was neither art nor toy, but an ornament denoting wealth":[21]

> G. leant forward and pushed the glass swan quite forcefully so that its silver turntable began to revolve. It ceased to look like a swan and resembled a tall-necked, many-sided carafe of rosé wine.
>
> The swan is drunk, said a young man.[22]

Although the comment that "The swan is drunk" recalls Mallarmé's opening line of "Le vierge, le vivace et le bel aujourd' hui / Va-t-il nous déchirer avec un coup d'aile ivre",[23] the description of the revolving swan is as suggestive of Cubism as it is of Symbolism. A carafe is often depicted in Braque's and Picasso's still-lives from 1912-13 as a "many-

---

[20] John Berger, *G.* (Harmondsworth: Penguin, 1976), 167.
[21] Ibid., 182.
[22] Ibid., 183.
[23] MacIntyre translates these lines as: "The lively, lovely and virginal today / will its drunken wings tear for us with a blow...". See Stéphane Mallarmé, *Selected Poems*, trans. C.F. MacIntyre (Berkeley: University of California Press, 1957), 83.

sided," or multi-faceted, fragmented form.[24] The elaborate, rose-coloured glass swan, which could be said to stand for the natural object seen through the rose-coloured glasses of the Symbolist tradition, is transformed into an everyday object, seen within the Cubist tradition. Thus, the Symbolist emphasis upon a rarefied representation of reality gives way to a more analytical, complex view. Furthermore, G. effects this transformation by revolving the turntable, or bringing about a literal revolution. This image demonstrates how G.'s consciousness carries an intimation of a world transformed.

The revolving swan alerts us to the revolutionary process that provides a subtext for G's description of riders joining hands and "holding onto each other's chains" on a merry-go-round.[25] The sense of freedom the riders experience when they are in the air contrasts sharply with their careworn attitude when they are on the ground. The circular, swinging movements, the thrown-back hands and feet, and the cries of delight of men and women who are "free and abandoned in the air," connote sexual orgasm.[26] By thus associating the sexual act with revolutionary politics, Berger accentuates the subversiveness of G.'s single-minded pursuit of sex. The revolutionary transformation G. proposes in the sexual realm is metaphorically related to the theme of freedom from oppression in other areas. In dedicating this novel to "Anya and her sisters in Women's Liberation," Berger seems to suggest that the freedom claimed by the women in the 1970s feminist movement compares with the claims of other oppressed groups—the hungry Italians, the chained Moors, the subjugated Slavs—in an early expression of identity politics.

The above-mentioned description of riders on a merry-go-round also provides an image of the collective solidarity that occurs during a revolution, such as the 1898 mass demonstration in Milan, which Berger describes in G. But chains also obviously symbolize oppression in the novel, and are linked explicitly with racial oppression, as when Berger describes how four bronze figures of naked African slaves are chained to a statue of Archduke Ferdinand I.[27] Berger won the Booker Prize for G. in 1972 and he caused a scandal by announcing in his acceptance speech that he would give half the money to the London-based Black Panthers, because he attributed the poverty of the Caribbean to its exploitation by

---

[24] Picasso's mixed-media sketch *Glass and Bottle* (1913–14) provides one such example.
[25] Berger, *G.*, 185.
[26] Ibid.
[27] Ibid., 113.

McConnell and others.[28] Berger praised the Black Panthers for resisting oppression "both as black people and workers."[29] In a 1972 television interview, Berger claimed his aims as a writer and those of the Black Panther movement were shared and he referred to himself as a revolutionary writer for whom writing and politics were ultimately one activity.[30] Thus, not only does Berger affirm that the aesthetic and the political are integral to one another, but also he also suggests that, in this 1970s work, revolution presupposes sexual as well as political freedom.

In arguing that *G.* is a revolutionary narrative partly because it draws its conception of revolutionary or transformative aesthetics from 1970s debates about this subject, I am not implying that the book is revolutionary in terms of its impact upon other texts. Reviews of *G.* indicate a wide range of response to the work, varying from admiration to outrage.[31] Furthermore, despite its unusual combination of radical left-wing politics and experimental form, *G.* could not be called an avant-garde text, because it was written some fifty years after its high modernist predecessors. However, it could be said to transfer aspects of Berger's art criticism in the 1960s into the literary—and, as we shall see, cinematic—culture of the 1970s.

It is not known whether Berger attended the Dialectics of Liberation congress in London, 1967, but some of the ideas discussed there are relevant to his revolutionary narratives of the early 1970s. In particular, American Black Panther Stokely Carmichael's address entitled "Black Power" would have resonated, despite Carmichael's separatist tendencies.[32] Moreover, Herbert Marcuse's invocation of Benjamin's description of people shooting at clocks during the Paris Commune, in order to convey a sense of rupture between the new and the old order—which was repeated by congress organizer, David Cooper, as a rallying cry—has echoes in

---

[28] Dyer, *Ways of Telling*, 93.

[29] Ibid., 94.

[30] Nicholas Harman, "John Berger Interview," in *Midweek* [Television Broadcast] (London: British Broadcasting Corporation, 1972).

[31] Whereas Green praised *G.* for being "brilliantly radical in every sense—politically, sexually, and in literary technique", Waugh wrote: "it is the general climate which explains how a sane commercial publisher like Weidenfeld can be led to produce something like *G.* and expect the public to take it seriously." Martin Green, "Nostalgia Politics," Review of *Ragtime*, *The American Scholar* 45 (1976): 842; Auberon Waugh, "Critical Questions of Utmost Importance," Review of G., *Spectator*, June 10, 1972, 892.

[32] Stokely Carmichael, "Black Power," in *The Dialectics of Liberation,* ed. David Cooper, 150–174 (Harmondsworth: Penguin, 1968).

Berger's work.[33] For example, in *G.*, the boy's dream of smashing the face of the grandfather clock has revolutionary import. I am not suggesting that this idea necessarily came from the congress, since Berger knew Benjamin's "Theses on the Philosophy of History," whence the clock image derives, to the extent that he based *G.*'s discontinuous structures on Benjamin's method.[34] But, clearly, *G.*'s political radicalism chimed with other events that were taking place within 1970s British culture.

The revolutionary fervor of France in May '68 provides the impetus for the three feature film scripts Berger wrote in collaboration with Tanner during and following the completion of *G.*: *The Salamander* (1971); *The Middle of the World* (1974) and *Jonah Who Will be 25 in the Year 2,000* (1976). Not only are the individual films dialectical in structure, but Tanner's and Berger's films of the early seventies also trace a dialectical pattern of development, from the beguiling *Salamander,* to the austere *Middle of the World*, to *Jonah*, which enlists empathy and analysis and can therefore be seen as a synthesis of the two earlier films. In particular, *Jonah* explores revolutionary themes, since it addresses both the failed revolution in '68 and possibilities for an alternative future. In this film, as in *G.*, the treatment of time is dialectical, in that various characters adopt contradictory positions on the subject, so as to elicit an antagonistic or a synthetic response from the viewer. The treatment of time is also revolutionary, as we see when Max, a disillusioned ex-combatant in May '68, mimes the action of firing at a clock in the mirror, thereby asserting his status as a would-be revolutionary.

The continuity between *The Moment of Cubism* and *G.*, which includes ideological and stylistic interpretations of the revolutionary nature of Cubism, can therefore be extended to thematic and formal aspects of *Jonah*. There are many other ways in which these art critical, fictional and cinematic works intersect, which the pressure of space does not allow me to discuss. However, what I have outlined should provide evidence of the many connections between Berger's art criticism of the 1960s and his television, fiction and film of the 1970s. These indicate some ways in which intellectual and aesthetic innovations of the 1960s could be said to have permeated British (and European) film culture of the 1970s.

---

[33] See Herbert Marcuse, "Liberation from the Affluent Society," in *The Dialectics of Liberation*, ed. Cooper, 178; David Cooper, "Beyond Words," in ibid., 202.
[34] Selden, "Commitment and Dialectic in Novels," 116–18.

AESTHETICS AND POLITICS:
THE CASE OF RAYMOND WILLIAMS
AND HERBERT MARCUSE

ANTHONY DUNN

Part One

From January 1969 the educational publication *Screen* became a journal devoted to the academic study of film and television. By the mid-1970s it had established itself as the forum for debating and applying new ways of seeing visual mass media, particularly those drawing upon semiotics and Lacanian psychoanalysis. *Screen*'s emphasis was on theory as well as practice and, as with the heterodox Marxism of John Berger's very popular *Ways of Seeing* (TV series and Pelican Original 1972) and the mating of sociology and literary criticism to produce new ways of reading at the Essex University annual conferences from 1976, its focus was as much on theorising the viewer/reader as elucidating the text.

Geoffrey Nowell-Smith, a member of *Screen*'s editorial board and an acknowledged expert on the prison writings of the Italian communist Antonio Gramsci, edited the four numbers of *Screen* for 1977. His selection of contents and his editorials are representative of his generation of left-wing intellectuals, too young to fight in the war but old enough to be conscious of Khrushchev's denunciation of Stalin's tyranny and the Soviet invasion of Hungary in 1956. His Italian interests incline him towards privileging concepts over facts and recognising aesthetics as a legitimate branch of philosophical enquiry. When he writes, in his editorial to the Spring number, of the journal's consistent discussion of "the epistemology of representation" and its use of "the three discourses of historical materialism, semiotics and psychoanalysis" to that end, he could as well be writing for a journal of literary criticism or radical sociology. The main theme of the Spring number was Realism but, in a characteristic inflection, the editor prefers to pose the question of "realisms". The pluralisation of the concept allows for democratic debate of a kind incompatible with the top-down command and control structure of Soviet cultural criticism. Raymond Williams is from the generation preceding Nowell-Smith, but his article is a finely-tuned series of discriminations between naturalism and realism as applied to a reading of the BBC Television play *The Big Flame*, thus showing there is still a place, among the more abstract theoretical approaches, for firmly grounded historical studies. Elsewhere, Rosalind Coward suggests that in the post-68 period, new political movements such as the women's movement, entail a redefinition of concepts such as representation and ideology.[1] The political question, we could deduce, is therefore twofold: what is representation and who is to be represented?

In his editorial for the Winter number of *Screen*, Nowell-Smith alludes to another debate on the Left, the role of subjectivity in theories of revolution. The 1960s had witnessed the coming into being of peoples and groups, whether students, peasants or American urban blacks, as subjects in their own right. Nowell-Smith's comments arise specifically out of fiercely-argued exchanges, reproduced in the journal, between Rosalind Coward and the Centre for Contemporary Cultural Studies at Birmingham University about redefinitions of culture and class. He accepts that this exchange is part of a larger debate, the somewhat "uneasy fit between classical Marxism and contemporary theories of discourse and the subject" but, as with the notion of "realisms", he provides for a catholicity of approaches. "The problem comes when Procrustean attempts are made, on whichever side, to compress one set of problems into another".[2] He practises what he preaches and the rest of the number comprises an article on History and the production of memories, and an English translation of a densely-argued article on the concept of "suture" as applied to Robert Bresson's *Joan of Arc*.

It is not, therefore, that these new ways of seeing, reading and understanding were exclusively Marxist. Class struggle and surplus value played minor roles in the historical analyses of Michel Foucault and the semiotic analyses of Roland Barthes. Sartre's immense *oeuvre* of philosophical and literary writings, which only became available in paperback to students and the general reader from the early 1960s, was one long contestation with the impersonal "forces and relations of production" of classical Marxism.[3] Lacanian psychoanalysis had only a

---

[1] Geoffrey Nowell-Smith, "Editorial," *Screen* 18, no. 1 (1977): 5–6.
[2] Geoffrey Nowell-Smith, "Editorial," *Screen* 18, no. 4 (1977): 7.
[3] Editor Tony Godwin and designer Germano Facetti established the Penguin Modern Classics series in 1961. They commissioned new translations and designed the covers with relevant and striking reproductions of paintings. The cover, for example, for Sartre's *Nausea* (*La Nausée*), published in 1965, was a section of

tangential relationship with Marxism; and Jean Baudrillard, by the late 1970s, had abandoned the productivist metaphor in Marxism as "inappropriate for comprehending the status of commodities in the post-war era".[4]

It is in the immediate post-war period that Sartre began to construct his reputation as a public intellectual, followed by Lacan and Barthes in the 1950s and Foucault in the 1960s. With whatever political differences, all these figures were products of the French tradition of rationalism and deductive method; and as public intellectuals at a time when the French Communist Party was powerful and respected, their revisionist or heterodox readings of Marx were bound to provoke controversy across the political spectrum. Marx and Freud were active schools of thought in the larger bodies politic of continental Europe in ways that did not obtain in Britain.   Britain's communist presence was small; its dominant philosophical tradition was empirical and inductive; and no fascist occupation had forced its population to make clear ideological choices. It is onto this unpromising terrain that, as we shall see, the editorial board of the journal *New Left Review* attempted, from the early 1960s, to graft European revisionist accounts of Marx.

Part Two

The title of this essay, "Aesthetics and Politics", echoes the title of a collection of edited writings by such as Bertolt Brecht, Walter Benjamin, Theodore Adorno and others, published in 1977 by New Left Books, sister publishing-house to *New Left Review*. Two books also published in 1977, Raymond Williams's *Marxism and Literature* (OUP) and Herbert Marcuse's *The Aesthetic Dimension* (German ed. 1977, English translation for Macmillan 1979) debate, from different intellectual traditions, the vexed relationship for Marxists between aesthetics and politics and enable us to focus more precisely on the issues raised above. Marcuse's book appeared as part of Macmillan's *Communications and Culture* series and members of its Editorial Board included Richard Hoggart, Stuart Hall and Raymond Williams. All three had expanded their initial training in literary criticism into a concern for the procedures and politics of mass communications, a terrain in need, if ever, of a new epistemology of

---

Salvador Dali's *The Triangular Hour.* Penguin Modern Classics and Pelican Books were a significant formative influence on the new generation of humanities and social science lecturers in the early 1970s.

[4] Mark Poster, "Introduction," in *Jean Baudrillard: Selected Writings*, ed. and intr. Mark Poster, 1 (Oxford and Cambridge: Polity Press, 1988).

representation. The OUP series in which Williams's book appeared was *Marxist Introductions* and its General Editors were Williams himself and Steven Lukes.

Just as Penguin a decade before had sensed there was a new public for the classics of modern European literature, so publishing houses perceived that there was now an Anglo-American readership for a new mating of Marxism and, in a broad sense, "culture". All the writers presented in the *Aesthetics and Politics* collection had been active from the inter-war years onwards. Several were already known for their achievements in distinct cultural fields: Brecht as a playwright championed by the Royal Court from the mid-1950s, and Lukács as a literary historian. Others, such as Walter Benjamin, had, in effect, been "discovered" for an English-speaking public by *New Left Review*. The journal's publication in 1968 of Benjamin's "Paris—Capital of the Nineteenth Century", an extract from his much longer *Arcades* project, was a revelation to English readers of how the dialectical method, which called into question accepted boundaries between high and popular culture, could elicit new configurations of meaning from such a familiar object of study.[5] Benjamin's writing was, in effect, a model in action of what the 1970s academic degrees in British Cultural Studies would strive to become. None of the writers in this collection, however, was a native writer in English. They wrote in German, so they inherited and refined upon the German debate between the idealism of Hegel and the materialism of Marx. Their mode of procedure was, accordingly, dialectical and their central concept was contradiction.

Perry Anderson had been appointed editor of *New Left Review* in 1962. He was born in 1938 and his father was employed by the Chinese Imperial Maritime Customs. He came up to Worcester College, Oxford in 1956, the year of Suez and the Soviet invasion of Hungary. He thus had an international background and had to position himself ideologically at an early age with regard to "imperialisms" of West and East. The Editorial Board's brief, as they saw it, was to introduce to the English-speaking world the inheritance of what they called "Western Marxism". This was considered, according to Robin Blackburn, a member of the Board, "a vital resource in rejecting alike the authorised catechism of official Communism and the bland philistinism of social democracy."[6] In the July-August number of the *Review* Anderson published a lengthy article

---

[5] Walter Benjamin, "Paris, Capital of the 19th Century," *New Left Review* 48 (March–April 1968): 77–88.
[6] Robin Blackburn, "A Brief History of New Left Review," *New Left Review,* http://www.newleftreview.org/?page=history.

entitled "Components of the National Culture". His thesis was that English
intellectual life had suffered from the lack of a classical sociology and a
developed Marxism. The necessary concepts were, therefore, not present
to construct a revolutionary class-consciousness such as had been
evidenced by the recent May/June *évènements* in France and student/worker
contestation of state repression in Italy, Czechoslovakia, Japan and the
USA. It was English departments in the UK that had assumed the task of
social and cultural critique. F. R. Leavis and his Cambridge-based journal
Scrutiny had waged war against linguistic degeneration and the baleful
influence of metropolitan culture for twenty years. Anderson paid tribute
to Leavis's principled stands and acknowledged that his vision of a
technologico-Benthamite society had been confirmed by the rise of mass-
media consumer society. But he pointed out that while literature and art
certainly dealt with man and society they did not "provide us with their
concepts".[7]

By the mid-1970s, however, Anderson was critical of "culturalist"
approaches to state power and a capitalist economy. In *Considerations on
Western Marxism* he noted that Western Marxism had nothing to say about
"the economic laws of motion of capitalism as a mode of production" nor
did it have any extended analysis of "the political machinery of the
bourgeois state."[8] Only Antonio Gramsci had attempted a detailed analysis
of the latter, but his prison conditions had imposed a fragmentary, if
brilliant, mode of exposition. Culture, not economics or politics, had been
the central focus for Western Marxists; and, within culture, art and in
particular literature, had provoked its most sophisticated readings.
"Aesthetics, since the Enlightenment the closest bridge of philosophy to
the concrete world", he concluded, "has exercised a special and constant
attraction for its [Western Marxism's] theorists."[9] It is within this context,
one of defeat for a Marxist reading of capitalism and the state, but one of
growing influence for Western Marxist readings of culture, in publishing
and academe, that we should situate the two titles by Raymond Williams
and Herbert Marcuse cited above.

---

[7] Perry Anderson, "Components of the National Culture," *New Left Review* 50
(July–August 1968): 5–6.
[8] Perry Anderson, *Considerations on Western Marxism* (London: Verso Books,
1979), 44–45.
[9] Ibid., 78.

Part Three

Anderson observes, in *Considerations*, that "a remarkable amount of the corpus of Western Marxism became a prolonged and intricate Discourse on Method."[10] Williams's book, written in his own dogged, hesitant and painfully qualificatory style, could be called a Discourse on Methods. The chapter headings summarise, with balance and objectivity, the approaches to art of classical Marxism ("Base and Superstructure"), structuralism ("Signs and Notations"), the Frankfurt School ("Mediations") and Gramsci ("Hegemony"). He also gives space to his own very important conceptual contributions to this field: "Structures of Feeling" and "Dominant, Residual and Emergent Cultures". The first section is devoted to "Culture", a term that Williams had interrogated and redefined throughout his early career. Whether discussing film (*Preface to Film*, 1954), literature and politics (*Culture and Society: 1780-1950*, 1958) or everyday life ("Culture is Ordinary" 1958), Williams insisted always on culture's material presence in social life, its inescapable linkages to class and status, and the ideological specificity of the media that produced it. If peoples and concepts had histories so did cultures. Williams therefore represented the generation of intellectuals before Anderson and *New Left Review*. He had seen war service and come up to Cambridge from a Welsh working-class background. He was enthused by the radical populism of the Marxism he encountered at Cambridge in the early post-war years, a period when the Soviet Union was seen as the triumph of socialism over fascism and a reforming Labour Government was constructing the Welfare State. For Williams, as for his colleagues in the Communist Party Historians Group such as Edward Thompson and Christopher Hill, the immediate intellectual task was not to produce a new concept but to revalue one of the country's oldest: "the people".

Twenty years later, with *Marxism and Literature*, Williams undertook to map onto his radical populism the esoteric and concept-based Western Marxism of Adorno and company. The result is a precarious syncretism between old and new. Literature and art, he allows, have their specific rhythms and conventions, but we have always to find "ways of recognising their specific kinds of sociality". Language is "a constitutive faculty" of reality, one of the "indissoluble elements of the material social process itself", but reality is constituted of more than language. The recent and influential attempt to mate Marxism and structural linguistics risks the expulsion of language from history and the reaffirmation of such divisive

---

[10] Ibid., 53.

bourgeois categories as the distinction between the "individual" and the "social". Literature and art have meaning, but that meaning is "always *produced*; it is never simply expressed".[11]

There is a sense of give-and-take in these presentations, an interested accommodation of these new concepts to an already-formed critical approach. Williams' tone sharpens, however, when he reviews the history and influence of one particular concept: "the Aesthetic". He traces the late eighteenth century shift in its meaning from a sense of general perception to a specialised category to define what is considered artistic and beautiful. He admits its power as one of "the two great modern ideological systems—the 'aesthetic' and the 'psychological'".[12] He allows that the new method of semiotics, as applied to both traditional (books and paintings) and popular (photography, film and TV) media offers a mode of analysis that combines a "sociology" with an "aesthetics". But he worries away at its asociality, the removal by what he calls bourgeois aesthetic theory of the art object from its relations of production. His tone of measured accommodation shifts into one of rhetorical confrontation. An unidentified "we", he claims, will eventually turn away from the proposition that "all literature is 'aesthetic', in the crude sense that its dominant intention (and then our only response) is the language of beauty or form..." The aesthetic effect, he contends, has malign intentions upon us – to make us forget that we live in a divided and dividing society through "the dulling, the lulling, the chiming, the overbearing" of its techniques and subject matter.[13]

It is precisely the aesthetic dimension of art that Marcuse, with his Western Marxist synthesis of Hegel, Marx and Freud, revalues as revolutionary. He subtitles his book "Toward a Critique of Marxist Aesthetics" and announces his argument on the first page of the Preface: "I see the political potential of art in art itself, in the aesthetic form as such." He considers art to be largely autonomous of social relations and in this autonomy "art both protests these relations and at the same time transcends them". The dominant consciousness, which for him is the same as ordinary experience, is thereby subverted. [14] Marcuse, for his part, lauds the asociality of art as a weapon against "aggressive and exploitative socialization". He had already proposed a version of Freud's Eros (*Eros*

---

[11] Raymond Williams, *Marxism and Literature* (Oxford: Oxford University Press, 1977), 133, 24, 99, 166.

[12] Ibid., 129.

[13] Ibid., 155–56.

[14] Herbert Marcuse, *The Aesthetic Dimension* (London and Basingstoke: Macmillan, 1979), ix.

and Civilization, 1955) as a counter to the puritan work-ethic in America, and had analysed, in *One-Dimensional Man* (1964), the pressures towards conformity in post-war Soviet Russia and corporate America, where he had lived since 1935, when the Frankfurt Institute for Social Research relocated to the USA. Citizens of both West and East are, in Marcuse's analysis, socialised into mass production, of goods and of themselves. He argues that: "Art's separation from the process of material production has enabled it to demystify the reality reproduced in this process."[15] Beauty, through the individualism of its techniques, can recover the repressed individualism of its participants, enact an image of what might be, and define by its criteria what is real. The sensuousness of beauty proffers fictions of pleasure which restore Eros to lives of alienated labour, but these fictions are representations through estrangement. They are critical mimeses which span the spectrum of techniques and subject-matter from Brecht to Beckett to Leni Riefenstahl. Marcuse admits that it is difficult for a Marxist to acknowledge "the beauty of the fascist feast" when he cites the pro-Nazi films of Riefenstahl, but he argues that the speed and immediacy of the medium pre-empt critical analysis. Fascism in literature, however, "carries freely the recognition and the indictment" of its monstrous deeds in politics. Literary stylization "petrifies the lords of the terror into monuments that survive—blocks of memory not to be surrendered to oblivion."[16]

Marcuse, though enthused by youth's, particularly American youth's, challenges to political and social norms in the 1960s, is no naïve utopian. The possible "other" which appears in art may be transhistorical, but the other history, of mass alienation, always drags it down. Beauty as political Eros may be represented in committed works of the Left, but there is always an inevitable conflict between art and political praxis. The liberation promised in the beautiful image is a liberation of the moment, "the remembrance of things past", a phrase which reverberates throughout the book. It is as if political Eros is in constant rehearsal for a play that never gets beyond the first scene: "The authentic utopia is grounded in recollection, but the joy of memory is overshadowed by pain."[17]

---

[15] Ibid., 5, 22.
[16] Ibid., 63.
[17] Ibid., 73.

Part Four

Jean Baudrillard, as noted earlier, had, by the late 1970s, exhausted for his purposes the Marxist conceptual inheritance of "production", "commodity" and "alienation". He began his academic career as a younger associate and admirer of the distinguished Marxist sociologist and philosopher Henri Lefebvre. From 1947 Lefebvre's main academic interest was the description and theorisation of that eminently democratic topic: "everyday life" ("le quotidien"). His analysis focussed on the alienating effects of the incipient consumer society on traditional structures of communal life in, above all, urban environments. Perry Anderson notes in *Considerations* that Lefebvre made the first French translation in 1933 of Marx's *Economic and Philosophic Manuscripts of 1844*, where the concept of "alienation" is pivotal to Marx's dialectical reading of the relationship between the worker and what he produces. He also notes that the full impact of these early writings of the "humanist" Marx did not register in Left circles in Europe until the late 1950s, but from then on their main themes were widely diffused throughout Western Europe.

Baudrillard, using both Marxist and semiotic techniques of analysis, dutifully tried to comprehend and critique the booming consumer society which was 1960s and 1970s France. But neither Marx nor Saussure had any relevant experience of the developed power of the electronic image in late twentieth century society. This, for Baudrillard, was the mediator between product and people, aesthetics and politics, beauty and power. Ways of seeing, reading and understanding had all to be reconceptualised in this new era. Representation, of objects and people, seemed increasingly self-referential. The image was not only not a reflection of basic reality; it bore no relation to any reality whatever. In his long essay *Simulacres et Simulation*, published in France in 1981, Baudrillard proposes that this new world is one "in which there is no longer any God to recognise his own, nor any last judgement to separate truth from false." It is a world of "hyperreality" whose Seventh Wonder is Disneyland. With the erasure of any tradition of objective evaluation, the past is rendered as nostalgia or myths of origin. He argues that: "There is an escalation of the true, of the lived experience; a resurrection of the figurative where the object and substance have disappeared."[18]

Baudrillard spent much of the latter part of his career in the USA. The first English translators of his early writings were his editors at the small Left-wing publishing house of Semiotext(e) Inc. in New York and

---

[18] Poster, *Jean Baudrillard*, 170–171.

Baudrillard's later writings were a series of reports by a European intellectual on the USA as the country which had most efficiently created and exported the "hyperreal" existence. He quoted Marshall McLuhan extensively on the effects of the new media, and his fascination with America was in a tradition of such French post-war assimilations of its culture as Sartre's eulogies of New York and the *Nouvelle Vague's* debt to American "B" movies and Alfred Hitchcock. The British New Left, by contrast, paid little attention to American culture. This is an odd omission, since by constitution and history the concept of "the people" was democratic in a way that it had never been in Britain.

Baudrillard, however, found in the career of Andy Warhol the aesthetics and politics of the future. While still a fine art student in 1948 at Pittsburgh's Carnegie Institute of Technology, Warhol speculated that window-dressing, an occasion in "everyday life", could be considered a kind of art-form. He saw a shop-window as a huge frame enclosing a variety of objects, like a Dutch still-life. Warhol would also have been attracted by the inanimacy, the very stillness of the objects, particularly the mannequins, simulacra of human beings. In 1963, on the occasion of his first one-man show on the West Coast, he observed, of the ubiquitous public adverts in Los Angeles: "I'm going to make their language the language of art".[19] In the same year he opened his studio which he named The Factory and where he developed his trademark aesthetic; flat, affectless, serial representations of the unique stars (Marilyn Monroe) and banal objects (100 Coke Bottles) of popular culture. They only needed his frame to make them our Art.

Baudrillard cites in his essay, "Transeconomics", Warhol's statement that he wished he were a machine and declares "all the industrial machinery in the world has acquired an aesthetic dimension". This is not Marcuse's sensuous beauty that may redeem the alienation of labour. It is rather "a *materialization* of aesthetics everywhere under an operational form", beauty as value-added rather than intrinsically other. "Materialism", for Williams, is a grounding concept, anchoring art and culture in the sociality of everyday life: for Baudrillard, whose essay evinces everywhere a nostalgia for art as transcendent other, it is a limiting concept which forces art to "minimalize itself, to mime its own disappearance".[20] The only transcendence Baudrillard detects in our society is what he calls, in a companion essay, the weightlessness of "Loan, finance, the technosphere

---

[19] Cited in part One of Chris Rodley, dir., *Andy Warhol: The Complete Picture* [Three-part Television Series] (London: Channel 4, 2002).
[20] Jean Baudrillard, "Transaesthetics," in *Jean Baudrillard: The Transparency of Evil: Essays on Extreme Phenomena,* 16 (London: Verso Books, 1993).

[and] communications". [21] With value ephemeral and aesthetic criteria archaic, Warhol re-appears, for Baudrillard, as the avatar of our taste today:

> The only benefit of a Campbell's soup can by Andy Warhol (and it is an immense benefit) is that it releases us from the need to decide between beautiful and ugly, between real and unreal, between transcendence and immanence. Just as the Byzantine icons made it possible to stop asking whether God existed— without, for all that, ceasing to believe in him. [22]

Walter Benjamin's most popular essay for 1970s students and teachers was "The Work of Art in the Age of Mechanical Reproduction". The Epilogue firmly locates this historical discussion within the agonistic politics of the inter-war period. Referring to Hitler's carefully choreographed Nuremberg rallies and Mussolini's utilization of the Futurist exaltation of war in literature and the visual arts, he proposes that the "logical result of Fascism is the introduction of aesthetics into politics" and argues: "This is the situation of politics which Fascism is rendering aesthetic. Communism responds by politicizing art." [23] This conclusion also held good for many Left discussion in the 1970s about aesthetics and politics. We live in a more nuanced age now. Benjamin's near-epigram is in fact a figure from classical rhetoric known as a chiasmus, where outer and inner grammatical structures correspond. Thus his sentences can be summed up as "aestheticization of politics: politicization of art" or ap:pa. A chiasmus, however, is a locked statement. It is either all true or all false. Baudrillard's post-modernity, at least, has taught us to be cautious about agonistic dogmatism. It may turn out that aesthetics and politics have no relationship at all.

---

[21] Jean Baudrillard, "Transeconomics", in ibid., 31.
[22] Jean Baudrillard, "Transaesthetics," 17.
[23] Walter Benjamin, "The Work of Art in the Age of Mechanical Reproduction," in *Illuminations*, ed. and intr. Hannah Arendt, transl. Harry Zohn, 243–244 (London: Collins/Fontana, 1973).

"NEW AGE" RADICALISM
AND THE SOCIAL IMAGINATION:
WELFARE STATE INTERNATIONAL
IN THE SEVENTIES

GILLIAN WHITELEY

Introduction: aesthetic, visceral and political

Lancelot Quail, Britain's new folk hero (a working-class hermaphrodite strong man) was presumed lost on Her Majesty's submarine Andrew...after following a mermaid on a ley line trail across SW England last September...Lancelot Quail is living on a rubbish tip in NW Lancs. Rebuffed by the Department of the Environment, he is trapped in a labyrinth, but is constructing home-made wings and an elaborate radio telescope. Although Lancelot has lost the mermaid for ever, he is still seeking Beauty. The Beast and the Winter Tree King are hunting him down, but with luck on Spring Bank Holiday Monday, he will escape in one time or another.[1]

In 1973, Welfare State International (WSI), a nomadic collective of artists, musicians, poets, performers and engineers, set up their touring caravans and lorries on a reclaimed rubbish tip at Heasandford quarry in Burnley in Lancashire. They ended up staying five years as part of the Mid Pennine Association for the Arts' (MPA) innovative community programme, which included people such as the social-documentary photographer Daniel Meadows who toured England in his Free

---

This paper emerges from extensive primary research and interviews conducted for a retrospective exhibition, *Radical Mayhem: Welfare State International and its Followers* which I curated for Mid Pennine Gallery, Burnley, 26 April to 7 June 2008. I am currently planning a major AHRC research project in collaboration with the Theatre Collection at the University of Bristol which holds an extensive WSI archive.
[1] Welfare State, "Beauty and the Beast" (leaflet), Burnley, May 19–28, 1973.

Photographic Omnibus from 1973-74.[2] In one of their first performances, *Beauty and The Beast*, WSI created a labyrinthine junk environment through which the audience were invited to roam. MPA's press release of the time made no attempt to hide the incongruities of locating this New Age vision amidst the industrial dystopia of Lancashire:

> On a plateau above a polluted river skirting green houses, allotments, new factories and NCB sludge, the Welfare State settlement—a cross between a Bolivian tinmine, TS Eliot's 'wasteland' and an Inca stilt village—is growing and extended through scarecrows, subterranean tunnels and living vans decorated with mythical paintings of *Beauty and the Beast.*[3]

Emerging from the radical politics and culture of 1968, WSI was largely the creative project of its founder and artistic director, John Fox, then a lecturer-librarian at Bradford College of Art. The collective's adopted name, Welfare State, represented their dedication to "the assistance of the national imagination rather than agitprop."[4] With their commitment to the need for ceremony and theatrical celebration in everyday life, they were part of a range of alternative experimental UK-based performance practices in the 1970s which included groups such as the Yorkshire Gnomes, John Bull Puncture Repair Kit and the People Show. Active for almost forty years, WSI was particularly important, however, because they pioneered the idea of temporary *site-specific* multi-media performance, celebratory feasting and new forms of processional art using fire, ice, sound and light as raw materials for transient installations and events.

As Tony Coult commented in 1976:

> in many ways, Welfare State are the most daring of the Alternative Theatre companies because they are in the business of yoking together the aesthetic and visceral nature of theatre with a developing political analysis and at the same time of making that powerful conjunction available to people who have no interest in theatres or plays.[5]

---

[2] See Daniel Meadows, *Living Like This: Around Britain In The Seventies* (1975) and *How We Are. Photographing Britain*, Tate Britain, 2007.
[3] Mid Pennine Association for the Arts, press release, March 1973
[4] Welfare State, "The Tenth Anniversary of Welfare State" (booklet), Burnley,1978.
[5] Tony Coult in *Plays and Players*, May 1976, 20–23.

Fig. 3-1. *Parliament in Flames,* Burnley, November 1976. Directed by Boris Howarth, designer Maggy Howarth, Ali Wood, Andy Plant, Tim Hunkin, Tony Lewery with pyrotechnics by David Clough.
Photo by kind permission of Daniel Meadows.

Over the decades, they made community films such as *King Real and the Hoodlums* (1983) and created large-scale pyrotechnic spectacles such as *Parliament in Flames,* ran educational workshops and engaged with ordinary people on housing estates, in workplaces and schools.

This paper is part of a major research project which will explore the legacies and networks of influence of WSI's extensive activities. That project aims to situate their practices within the context of recent communitarian discourses, a post-politics ethical turn and the focus on participation, collaboration and collectives which emerged as key critical debates in the 1990s. The writings of Nicholas Bourriaud, Grant Kester and Claire Bishop[6] on issues to do with participation, in conjunction with

---

[6] See Claire Bishop, "The Social Turn: Collaboration and its Discontents," *Artforum,* http://findarticles.com/p/articles/mi_m0268/is_6_44/ai_n26767773; Claire Bishop, ed., *Participation, Documents of Contemporary Art* (London: Whitechapel/MIT Press, 2006.)

the ideas of Jacques Rancière, Giorgio Agambon and Jean-Luc Nancy[7] on politics, aesthetics and community, offer significant insights for re-framing WSI, which continued to develop alternative models of participative art amongst a diverse range of communities and international locations.

Here though, I specifically want to examine the radicalism of WSI's practices and artforms and, specifically if tentatively, consider some of the social, political and cultural questions raised by their artistic residency in Burnley between 1973 and 1978. How did WSI's participative events operate with and within communities? What were (and are) the aesthetic, ethical, political and social aspects and implications of such collaborative practices? Did WSI's ephemeral performances and events acquire a place in the social imagination and cultural memory? Indeed, how, if at all, was WSI an agent of radical social and political transformation and how did they effect and affect social and cultural relations?

1968 and the Seventies

WSI was founded in 1968, a moment currently undergoing reassessment, forty years on.[8] The significance of 1968 sits uneasily in the popular imagination, bound by myth and cliché yet profoundly marked by liberationary discourses and revolutionary politics. Kristin Ross has iterated the "moment" of May 1968 as a "discursive and syntactic jumble" which has come to incorporate "everything and therefore nothing".[9] Ross discusses sociological interpretations of May 1968 which verge on the tautological: answering the charge that "nothing happened", she comments that "everything happened". Undoubtedly, the apparent failure of 1968 had considerable repercussions and ramifications for social, cultural and political imaginaries.

Most importantly for our purposes here though, it was the following decade, the 1970s, which was profoundly marked by the confusions and

---

[7] See Bishop, 2006; Jacques Rancière, *The Politics of Aesthetics*, trans. and intro. Gabriel Rockhill (London, New York: Continuum, 2006); Giorgio Agamben, *The Coming Community,* trans. Michael Hardt (Minneapolis: University of Minnesota Press, 1993); Jean-Luc Nancy, *The Inoperative Community,* ed. Peter Connor (Minneapolis: University of Minnesota Press, 1991).
[8] Forty years on, the phenomenon of '1968' was revisited both academically and in terms of popular culture. see, for example, the inter-disciplinary conference *1968: A Global Perspective*, University of Austin, Texas, October 10–12, 2008.
[9] See Kristin Ross, *May 68 and its Afterlives* (Chicago: University of Chicago Press, 2002) for a discussion of the social, political and institutional impact of 1968.

disappointments, reversals and desertions of 1968. Despite the extensive attention paid to it, rather than in 1968 itself, real politics came in the aftermath of the failed revolution—in the neglected *undecade* of the 1970s.[10] Certainly, a range of art practices in Britain in the 1970s were highly politicised, as John A. Walker has outlined in some detail in one of the few surveys of this period.[11] John Hilliard commented in 1981:

> It was a decade of austerely radical art, severely ascetic in its uncompromising purity, the product of a cultural moment when a generation of young artists genuinely seized the time, exerting seminal influence in an international arena … what remained consistent was a determined commitment to the present, an egalitarian spirit and an almost cavalier disinterest in money.[12]

Marxist writings, Althusserian revisions and Maoism were particularly influential and informed cultural practice. Art itself became, to cite a clichéd but contemporaneously pertinent phrase, a site of struggle. Revolutionary politics was sectarian and divisive in the 1970s but some activists asserted that art did have a role in initiating or executing social change: Victor Burgin put up posters on housing estates in Newcastle; David Medalla, John Dugger and others started The Artists' Liberation Front in London, unfurling banners with Marxist-Leninist slogans.[13] For others, the ultimate political weapon was to make no art at all: in 1974, Gustav Metzger called for an art strike to take place 1977-80 with the aim of "crippling the capitalist system". A special 1976 issue of *Studio International,* devoted to "Art and Social Purpose", reflected the range of political positions adopted. The editorial warned that artists could not afford to operate in a "vacuum of specialised discourse without considering their function in wider and more utilitarian terms", arguing:

> never, ever forget that means must have an *end* and that this end is inextricably bound up with art's responsibility to contact and nourish the wider audience it now ignores at its peril … the short-winded, rootless

---

[10] See Introduction in John A Walker, *Left Shift:Radical Art in 1970s Britain* (London: IB Tauris, 2002), 1.
[11] See Walker, ibid. for a year-by-year account of practices and events.
[12] Hilliard, quoted by Walker, ibid., 2.
[13] In the summer of 1976, Victor Burgin put up his posters, *What does possession mean to you,* around Newcastle upon Tyne; David Medalla and others showed at Gallery House an experimental space run by Sigi Krauss, 1972–73. On Medalla, see Guy Brett, *Exploding Galaxie: The Art of David Medalla* (London: Kala, 1995).

history of modernism's attempts to evolve an art directly expressive of its own zeitgeist will terminate in a cul-de-sac overpopulated by myopic, self-obsessed artists with nowhere, finally, to go.[14]

Whether this was political engagement or dilettantism is not my concern here, but it does provide plenty of evidence of emergent political avant-gardes and artistic activism, much of it reflecting and responding to industrial strife and political violence on an international scale, exacerbated, for example, by the struggles for civil rights in Northern Ireland and the campaigns of the Angry Brigade in the UK.[15] The aftermath of 1968 provided an intensified political context in Britain, with the 1970s characterised by increasing working class militancy.[16] In a short article published in 1979, David Widgery pondered the political legacies of 1968.[17] By 1979, revolutionary fervour had dissipated into the "winter of discontent": the miners' strikes in 1972 and 1974, along with waves of industrial action by dockers and engineers, had brought down the Heath government and Labour had been installed in 1974 with their most radical post-war election manifesto. This provoked Widgery to comment that "revolution did seem in the air somewhere."[18] All this had achieved little but mass unemployment and, with whole regions "slipping off the industrial map", he remarked that:

> Go to Liverpool Wigan or Skelmserdale and see the bleakness in the streets and the despair in the faces ... jobs gone for good, skills made useless, redundancy pay that melts away ... now the cuts are a codeword for a social counter-revolution [...] One doesn't have to be a punk or gay to feel that the UK in 1979 has turned out rather less appetising than the menu promised in 1974 of Social Contract flambéd in "the red flame of socialist outrage". Our new Jerusalem has turned out a harsher meaner poorer Britain.[19]

---

[14] "Editorial," *Studio International: Art and Social Purpose*, March/April 1976, 94.
[15] See Jean Weir, *The Angry Brigade 1967-198: Documents and Chronology* (London: Elephant Editions, 1985).
[16] For general social and cultural histories of the period see Robert Hewison, *Culture and Consensus: England, Art and Politics* (London: Methuen, 1997); Richard Weight, *Patriots: National Identity in Britain 1940-2000*, (London: Pan/MacMillan, 2003).
[17] See David Widgery, "The Winter of 1979," in David Widgery, *Preserving Disorder*, 162–71 (London: Pluto Press, 1989).
[18] Ibid., 162.
[19] Ibid., 163.

And, reiterating the bleak lyrics from a track on Tom Robinson's album, *The Winter of 79*:

Consternation in Mayfair
Rioting in Notting Hill Gate
Fascists marching up the High Street
Carving up the Welfare State [20]

Welfare State International in Burnley

Late 1960s activism, anarchism and 1970s militancy provided key British contexts for WSI but the creative techniques and aesthetic vision which they adopted were rooted in the radical political ethos of international groups such as el Teatro Campesino, San Francisco Mime Troupe and the US-based Bread and Puppet Theatre.[21] WSI proclaimed an "alternative aesthetics", a hybrid approach which brought together Jungian archetypal myth-making, a Blakeian vision typically reflected in 1960s Pop and English counterculture along with a "New Age" rhetoric of magic and ritual, as seen here in their 1972 manifesto:

The Welfare State make images, invent rituals, devise ceremonies, objectify the unpredictable, establish and enhance atmospheres for particular places, times, situations and people [...].

We will continue to analyse the relationship between performance and living, acting and identity, theatre and reality, entertainment and product, archetype and need.

We will react to new stimulus and situations spontaneously and dramatically and continue to fake unbelievable art as a necessary way of offering cultural and organic death. [22]

The WSI, were variously described as "dream-weavers, purveyors of images, sculptors of visual poetry, civic magicians and engineers of the

---

[20] Lyrics from Tom Robinson's *Up Against the Wall*, cited in Widgery, ibid.
[21] On San Francisco Mime Troupe see James Brook, Chris Carlsson and Nancy J. Peters, eds., *Reclaiming San Francisco: History, Politics, Culture* (San Francisco: City Lights, 1998). Founded in 1962/63, Bread and Puppet Theatre was primarily active in the anti-Vietnam war protest movement around New York and moved to Vermont in 1970 where it is still based. See http://www.breadandpuppet.org/
[22] From *The Welfare State Manifesto*, 1972.

imagination",[23] and their activities were an amalgam of feasting, music-making and performance which resonate with the amorphous notion of New Ageism, a cultural phenomenon particularly, though not exclusively, associated with the 1970s—and one yet to be extensively researched and theorised.[24] The eclectic set of activities and practices which constitute the New Age—or the Age of Aquarius, as it was labelled—does not lend itself to precise definition and tends to be used as an umbrella term. For Paul Heelas, a fundamental characteristic of New Ageism is a shared *lingua franca* to do with self-spirituality, and he outlines and explores a resurgence of teachings and practices associated with "the mystic, magician and shaman." He suggests this was partly a response to a cultural loss of certainty but, paradoxically, was also "a product of established orders of modernity."[25] Despite the slipperiness of the term and the spectrum of practices which it can incorporate—from "wilderness events" and Zen meditation to "enlightenment intensive seminars" and management training events—Heelas asserts that:

> in large measure, New Age is a *radicalised* rendering of more familiar assumptions and values .... The prosperity wing aside, the New Age provides a spiritual—and thus radicalised—rendering of the assumptions and values of humanistic expressivism.[26]

The imagery and narratives used by WSI certainly resonated with traits and values associated with the radicalised wing of New Age culture outlined by Heelas. In 1973, a reviewer for *Theatre Quarterly* wrote:

> The Welfare State is in many ways the most mind-blowing group of all. It contains many elements ... art school, rock culture, music, pagan ritual ... all fused into a poetic, Dyonisian vision of man liberated by revolution. [27]

---

[23] Welfare State, "The Tenth Anniversary of Welfare State." See also Tony Coult and Baz Kershaw, *Engineers of the Imagination: The Welfare State Handbook* (London: Methuen,1990).

[24] There is a wealth of literature on Sixties' 'counterculture' but little in-depth analysis of the intellectual and ideological roots and development of the eclectic cultural 'New Age' phenomenon of the 1970s. However, useful are Mark Ivor Satin's contemporaneous *New Age Politics* (New York: Delta Books, 1976) and more recently Paul Heelas, *The New Age Movement* (London: Blackwell, 1996), which focuses on 'popular' values, aspirations and practices, and Daren Kemp, *New Age: A Guide* (Edinburgh University Press, 2004).

[25] Heelas, *The New Age Movement,* 3.

[26] Ibid., 115.

[27] J. Hammond in *Theatre Quarterly*, October 1973.

Despite the references to ritual, myth and magic, it is evident from their early statements and activities that WSI was rooted in the revolutionary politics and emancipatory ideals of 1968. Herbert Marcuse's writings on cultural impoverishment and the ideas of the Situationists, with the primacy they gave to the role of *play* in social life and the idea of the urban environment as a space for participative performance,[28] were particularly influential on WSI's founder. Although WSI used the political form of the *manifesto* to explain their aims through the 1970s, they had a whole range of activities dedicated to play and emancipation through self-expression and creativity.

WSI's repertoire was extensive, but the kinds of multimedia practices they adopted were well established by the start of the 1970s. Besides drawing on popular traditions such as mummery and pantomime, WSI also incorporated the avant-gardism of Fluxus, Joseph Beuys and John Cage. WSI's happenings, events and assembled environments involved acrobats, wrestlers, musicians, fire-eaters and dancers with performances often improvising and expanding on a basis of rehearsed material. In 1972, Jamie Proud's alter-ego, Lancelot Quail, later billed as "Britain's new folk hero (a working-class hermaphrodite strong-man)" appeared at Surrey Hall in Brixton and became a recurring reference point for the company.[29] In September 1972, the company spent a month conducting the *Travels of Lancelot Quail*, a kind of processional theatrical event which roved from Glastonbury through Somerset, Devon and Cornwall, to end on a submarine off Land's End. A year later, after an aborted plan to hold an exhibition and event at the Serpentine Gallery in London,[30] WSI drove their entourage of vehicles into Burnley, a Northern working-class mill-town with a rapidly growing Asian population and a rapidly declining industrial base. This initiated their five-year residency as artists in the community.[31]

---

[28] See, for example, Sadie Plant, *The Most Radical Gesture: Situationist International in a Postmodern Age* (London: Routledge, 1992).

[29] See Welfare State, *Beauty and the Beast*.

[30] It failed to materialise when the Department of the Environment refused to allow performances and moving sculptures in the gardens at the Serpentine Gallery.

[31] The collective of various artists and musicians included Boris Howarth as Associate Artistic Director and Lol Coxhill, improvising jazz musician and composer, as WSI's Musical Director.

Fig. 3-2. *Brookhouse Summer Festival*, Blackburn, August 1977.
Photo by kind permission of Daniel Meadows.

In the 1970s, Burnley was a community in transition, in a state of becoming.[32] As Jean-Luc Nancy has noted, "community is always coming, endlessly, at the heart of every collectivity."[33] Into this, WSI took its own nomadic community of artists, musicians and performers—a self-contained and self-sustaining community of growing families. Symptomatic of this communitarian ethos and with a commitment to contemporary ideas about 1970s progressive education and the burgeoning Free School movement, WSI set up its own school. Some members of the collective registered as home teachers and the company opened its own school in April 1975.[34]

---

[32] In the mid-19th century, Burnley was the largest producer of cotton cloth in the world. Its industrial strength attracted a large immigrant population in the 1960s and early 70s and today Bangladeshi and Pakistani communities make up approximately 9% of its 88,000 inhabitants.
[33] Nancy, *The Inoperative Community,* 71.
[34] The company itself was used as a primary educational resource and the ethos was based around providing a well-structured child-centred educational experience that developed creativity and imagination. One of the troupe, Catherine Kiddle,

In November 1973, WSI created its first large-scale bonfire installation which later evolved into *Parliament in Flames,* staged in Burnley in 1976 with an audience of 10,000 people and then restaged in various other towns through the 1970s (see Fig. 1).[35] Whilst at Burnley, in 1974 WSI also made their first permanent earthwork at Gawthorpe Hall and their first giant icework at Wath-upon-Dearne. The following year, they created *Harbinger,* a large-scale sculpture from scrapyard junk and rusty cars, for the International Performance Festival in Birmingham city centre. Besides outdoor site-specific projects, they also worked in galleries. For example, with Bob Frith of Horse and Bamboo Theatre, they constructed a fully operative *Ghost Train* at the Mid Pennine gallery in Burnley in January 1977.

One of the major processional performances staged in Burnley, *Alien,* was filmed by Michael Kustow for London Weekend TV's flagship arts programme *Aquarius* (1970-77). Kustow's documentary-style film is particularly evocative: the narrator gives a brief history of WSI, the camera scans the town and focuses in on the encampment at Stoneyholme, a particularly socially-deprived area of Burnley. Subsequently, the production team film the instigation and development of *Alien,* following WSI's "blood-soaked colonial band" through the terraced streets at dusk to the finale, the ritualistic burning of an ice-figure (containing Lancelot Quail's lost spirit) and a scene which incites the swarming local crowd to destroy a giant slug representing the capitalist "forces of oppression". An interesting scene shows a group of local children on the WSI site, enthusiastically and imaginatively engrossed in making props, building a tower and flying kites. The group giggle self-consciously as the well-spoken interviewer quizzes them about their activities. With natural spontaneity, one of the young boys suddenly becomes quite serious; he looks up into the sky and says he would love to fly up with the kite and feels sure that, if he did, he would be able to see Blackpool. It is a moment of penetrating poignancy.

The Burnley residency culminated in *Barrabas,* a six-week project, described as a "total theatrical environment" in which daily performances included film, sideshows, processions and the "ritual disembowelling of The Dead Man (and his culture)."[36] By 1978, a series of aesthetic and directional differences developed within the group and a number of

---

recounted the school's history and educational roots in Catherine Kiddle, *What Shall We Do With the Children?* (Devon: Spindlewood, 1981), 25, 32.

[35] It was also staged at Milton Keynes (1978), Ackworth (1979), Tamworth (1980) and, finally, Catford (1981) with 15,000 spectators.

[36] Coult and Kershaw, *Engineers of the Imagination,* 245.

individuals split off to form the multi-media experimental theatre company, IOU. Subsequently, the nomadic school folded, the Burnley base was dismantled and, eventually, WSI moved on to develop a more permanent base in Cumbria. WSI passed through and into the space of cultural memory.[37] These hybrid multimedia performances and improvisational events brought together a New Age miscellany of ancient mythologies, traditional folk and contemporary popular and avant-garde cultural forms. Ascertaining its impact on the cultural and collective memory of participants and audiences will be a complex task and further research will address this. But what exactly was radical or political about WSI's activities?

A nomadic space of possibility

Although myth is often seen as a reactionary, conservative form, in the 1930s, Georges Bataille and Roger Caillois developed a discourse around the revolutionary potential of myth. They shared George Sorel's understanding of myth as a form of activism. According to them, myth's stroking of "the primordial longings and conflicts of the individual condition transposed to the social dimension" could move subjects to action.[38] They argued it could initiate a "psychological activism" and facilitate what Gavin Grindon calls a "leap into the impossible", an idea to which I will return.[39]

The very practice of working collaboratively could be seen as a challenge to the political status quo and the primacy of the individual: WSI's collective ethos *was* part of what Baz Kershaw has alluded to as "a

---

[37] Initially, the Fox family went on a residency to Australia. WSI established itself first in Liverpool and then from 1983 onwards in Barrow-in-Furness and, finally, Ulverston where it had a long-term base, Lanternhouse. For further information on WSI's subsequent activities see "Radical Mayhem: Welfare State International and its Followers" (Exhibition catalogue. Burnley: Mid Pennine Gallery, Burnley, April 26–June 7, 2008) and Coult and Kershaw, *Engineers of the Imagination*. See also http://www.welfare-state.org/ and
http://www.bris.ac.uk/theatrecollection/welfarestate.html
[38] For Sorel's comments on myth and references to the Caillois 'college of sociology' (1937–39) see Gavin Grindon, "The Breath of the Possible," in *Constituent Imagination: Militant Investigations, Collective Theorizations*, eds. Erika Biddle, Stephen Shukaitis and David Graeber, 95–96 (Oakland, USA: AK Press, 2007).
[39] Ibid.

rare attempt to evolve an oppositional popular culture."[40] Collectivist tactics can be a political statement and there are plenty of historical incidences in which collectivism is employed as a strategy to purposefully combat individualism.[41] But some caveats are needed here: the radicalism of the collective is undergoing a fashionable reiteration currently in academic and critical circles, as Blake Stimpson and Gregory Shollette contend in their recent book on collectivist art, modernism and the social imagination.[42] In terms of contemporary practice, Grant Kester has written on the disparate network of artists and artists' collectives working at the intersection of art and cultural activism.[43] He also reminds us that artists hold a compromised position in society and that a healthy scepticism is needed about claims that aesthetic experience can transform consciousness. Nevertheless, Kester argues that there are still artists committed to the idea that culture has emancipatory potential: they seek to activate this potential through processes of dialogue and collaborative production. [44]

The collective, *per se*, then, is not intrinsically radical or revolutionary: communes in the 1970s were often isolating and regressive places, as inequities embedded within gender power relations often persisted despite a rhetoric of sexual liberation. WSI did not liberate the nuclear family unit within its own community. Nevertheless, it was much more than just an artists' collective, as it did represent an attempt to envision and enact new radical ways of living and relating.

With its commitment to self-sufficiency, the development of ecological and alternative rites of passage and a de-schooled emancipatory education it was as much a social as an artistic experiment. They created alternative prototypes for weddings and funerals: their first naming ceremony was in 1969, and they were investigating "green" funerals and working on an

---

[40] Baz Kershaw, *The Politics of Performance: Radical Theatre as Cultural Intervention* (London, New York: Routledge, 1992), 18.

[41] For example, in the 1960s, the San Francisco Diggers (an influence on Welfare State) with their hotch-potch philosophy of social anarchism and direct action, employed guerrilla theatre, argued for a 'university of the streets' and worked to erase the boundary between art and life through manifestoes and strategies such as bartering, 'liberating goods', the daily distribution of free food and burning money. See Emmett Grogan's memoir, *Ringolevio* (Edinburgh: Rebel Inc., 1999), 329.

[42] Blake Stimpson and Gregory Sholette, *Collectivism after Modernism: The Art of Social Imagination after 1945* (Minneapolis: University of Minnesota Press, 2007), 9.

[43] See Grant H. Kester, *Conversation Pieces, Community and Communication in Modern Art* (Berkeley: University of California Press, 2004).

[44] Ibid., 153.

alternative technology project on a residency at Machynlleth in 1978.[45] Certainly, many of WSI's ethical and ecological practices have become absorbed into mainstream culture.

For me, another primary site of Welfare State's radicalism was the framework which they provided for the exploration of the potentially insurgent and subversive power of the social imagination. As cultural catalysts, their activities highlighted the potential for art to emancipate individual human creativity and initiate or contribute to socio-political change. The idea of the radical imagination is connected to its potential for envisioning beyond one's current situation and circumstances, thereby opening up potentiality and possibility. By exposing audiences to sensations that go beyond everyday perceptions and opinions, art practices are able to open up new ways of thinking about and engaging with the world. They offer a space of "creative criticality", both for the individual and for a community of individuals, with all the caveats about what might constitute a "community". Of course, in the 1970s, these ideas resonated with the ideas about the liberation of the imagination in Herbert Marcuse's highly influential *One Dimensional Man* (1967). Although difficult to assess, WSI's transitory performances undoubtedly had a profound effect on particular participants, and there is evidence that it has remained in the cultural memory and popular imagination within and outside the communities they touched. They created environments in which anything seemed possible and constructed events which assaulted the senses. They produced *affect*, "a non-conscious experience of intensity ... a moment of unformed and unstructured potential" and, as Deleuze and Guattari have contended, an aspect of art which is potentially revolutionary.[46]

Grindon comments on these kinds of experiences in his essay *The Breath of the Possible*:

> The open nature of these vital moments of affect allows us to grasp the virtuality and possibility of the space of practical political engagement ... [they offer us] a way to navigate the space between bare-faced utopianism and blank impossibility.[47]

---

[45] See note 37 for sources and also John Fox and Sue Gill's website at www.deadgoodguides.com.
[46] Eric Shouse, "Feeling, Emotion, Affect," *M/C Journal* 8, no. 6 (2005), http://journal.media-culture.org.au/0512/03-shouse.php. See also Brian Massumi, "Translator's Forward: Pleasures of Philosophy," in Gilles Deleuze and Felix Guattari, *A Thousand Plateaus,* trans. Brian Massumi, ix-xvii (Minneapolis: University of Minnesota, 1987).
[47] Grindon, "The Breath of the Possible," 106.

Finally, and perhaps more controversially, there is the revolutionary power and merits of disorder. In his classic study of city life, *The Uses of Disorder*, Richard Sennett argued for the paradoxical fruitfulness of disorder and disruption in everyday life as a positive, energising and creative force.[48] WSI catalysed disorder with their processions, festivals and spontaneous performances. These were agents of, in Bhaktinian terms, and as Baz Kershaw has argued, "carnivalesque resistance."[49] Hence, the festival or carnival is viewed as operating as a form of resistance, it represents non-conformity, the dishevelling of order. It is worth being circumspect here though: this notion is susceptible to romanticisation, and nostalgia for alternative forms of historical oppositional activity must not suppress the possibility that these can act as safety valves to avoid any real social and political change being initiated.

Fig. 3-3. *The Loves, Lives and Murders of Lancelot Barrabas Quail*, Burnley, September 1977. Photo by kind permission of Daniel Meadows.

---

[48] See Richard Sennett, *The Uses of Disorder* (New York: Alfred A. Knopf, 1970).
[49] See discussion of alternative/community theatre as radical cultural intervention in Kershaw, *The Politics of Performance*.

That said, with their capacity to disrupt the everyday order of things, in my view, WSI created what Hakim Bey has described as a Temporary Autonomous Zone, or TAZ, a transitory pirate utopia,[50] a space which enables the fleeting suspension of usual rules and mores. For a brief moment, WSI provided not only a *space of creative criticality* but also a *nomadic space of possibility*, facilitating an alternative temporary zone of transformatory potential.

---

[50] Hakim Bey, "From TAZ: The Temporary Autonomous Zone," in *Cultural Resistance Reader*, ed. Stephen Duncombe, 113 (London: Verso, 2002).

ARTISTS AND THE LABOUR MOVEMENT

KIRSTEN FORKERT

This essay, which deals with the Artists' Union (AU), will begin by examining what at first might seem a truism: that artists and trade unions represent completely opposite values. One need only think of individualism and entrepreneurialism, conventionally associated with artists, and promoted by the last fifteen years of cultural policy.[1] We could also consider the celebrity status of artists such as Damien Hirst and the millions collectors pay for his work;[2] and the expansion of the market for contemporary art and the circuit of art fairs.

Trade unions, for their part, are caricatured by the media as irrelevant institutions, as anachronistic as the industrial jobs or traditional working class communities they supposedly represent and hopelessly out of touch, with an ageing, dwindling membership. To a certain extent, this is a stereotype with little relationship to reality; according to 2008 statistics, female union members have outnumbered male union members for the past seven years, and union density is highest amongst employees in education and public administration, and amongst black employees.[3] However, due in part to a lack of representation of women and minorities in union leadership, the stereotype of the white male industrial worker persists. Without doubt there has been a marked decline in union membership over the past thirty years. Particularly after Thatcher, unions seem to play a greatly diminished role in the media and in society in general.

Thanks to Conrad Atkinson, Peter Dunn, Loraine Leeson and Avis Saltsman for agreeing to be interviewed and for their contributions to this text.
[1] Anthony Davies, "The Surge to Merge Culture with the Economy" (paper presented at Copenhagen Free University, 2001), http://www.copenhagenfreeuniversity.dk/AD01.html.
[2] Hirst's diamond skull sold for £50m in 2007. See http://news.bbc.co.uk/1/hi/entertainment/6971116.stm.
[3] Department for Business, Enterprise and Regulatory Reform (BERR), "Trade Union Membership 2008," http://stats.berr.gov.uk/uksa/tu/TUM2008.pdf.

My interest in the 1970s, and specifically in the Artists' Union (AU) is an attempt to find out about a time when the role and purpose of the artist was being seriously questioned, and to discuss an experiment that did not see artists and trade unions as mutually exclusive bodies. The AU could be seen as an attempt to adapt trade unionism for the conditions of cultural production, with all the questions and contradictions this raises in terms of both the nature of creativity and the nature of work. On a more personal level, as a researcher and a trade unionist who was trained as an artist, and who was too young to be active during the 1970s, I am asking what we can learn from the AU's successes and failures. In this paper, I will discuss the artistic climate of the 1970s, the structure of the AU, its goals and its key activities, and end by reflecting on the implications for the present. I will be drawing on texts of the era, archival documents of the AU (currently at the Tate Britain), and interviews with four members of the AU: Conrad Atkinson, Peter Dunn, Loraine Leeson and Avis Saltsman.

The AU existed from 1972 to 1983. Like other trade unions, it had a membership, a dues system and a national executive. However, unlike other trade unions, there were "working groups", or "workshops", that dealt with various issues facing artists, notably the role of women in the arts and the role of the artist in society. These workshops dealt not only with trying to gain greater rights for artists, but with questioning the artist's role in society, with various contradictory implications. Can one want a special status for artist, and simultaneously also want artists to be like other workers? Another major difference between the AU and other trade unions was that artists do not have a "workplace" in the conventional sense. Because of this, the AU could not engage in more conventional workplace activism, so turned its attention to government agency.

Art in the 1970s

The 1970s were a time when artistic practices were also being radically questioned, particularly the autonomy of the art object and the traditional isolation of the artist. The 1960s saw the expansion of the field of art, to include practices such as live art, conceptual art, community art, site-specific art, correspondence art and various experiments with communications technology. Lucy Lippard's *Six Years: The Dematerialisation of the Art Object from 1966 to 1972* (1997) provides interesting and important documentation of this development.

In the 1970s, this experimentation was being questioned as a hermetic, specialist practice and discourse, as artists turned to questions of cultural democracy. For example, the exhibition *Art For Whom?* which took place at the Serpentine in 1978, began with a collective statement that started with the following phrase: "WE are increasingly dissatisfied with the failure of so much contemporary art to communicate with anyone outside a small circle of initiates."[4] The catalogue essay by Richard Cork, the exhibition's curator, included criticisms of "contemporary artists and their supporters ... in the position of laboratory researchers." He argued that they were involved in "narrowly absorbed experimentation with concerns too specialised for anyone beyond their profession to care about" and that artists had a "glaring lack of communication with society at large."[5]

As John Walker described in *Left Shift*, there were similar struggles over the function of art education in the late 1960s and early 1970s;[6] the "dematerialisation of the art object", as well as the role of theory, played a central role. In the 1960s, art history courses had been introduced into art colleges to raise the academic status of fine arts (to make them worthy of degree status), and to improve the students' academic writing skills. However, "what the reformers did not anticipate was that reading and analysis might prompt students to cease making art objects and to become politically active."[7] Conceptual artists got teaching jobs and put their ideas of art and pedagogy into practice, but in some cases were punished for this. For example, John Latham of Artist Placement Group lost his teaching position at Saint Martins (Central School of Art and Design) in 1967, due to an event he organised which involved the "partial destruction by chewing of Greenberg's book, *Art and Culture* borrowed from the art school library."[8] David Bainbridge and Michael Baldwin of Art and Language eventually lost their posts at Coventry College of Art in 1973, due to the Art Theory course they introduced in 1969 (along with Terry Atkinson).[9] Students on the Art Theory course students produced written papers instead of paintings, denying the "primacy of the visual", the conventional division between theory and practice, and more crucially, producing nothing for studio staff to aesthetically evaluate and mark.[10] This alarmed the college management. As mentioned, Bainbridge and Baldwin lost their jobs; Atkinson resigned shortly after, and the students

---

[4] Richard Cork and others, *Art for Whom?* (London: Arts Council of Great Britain, 1978), 3.
[5] Ibid., 5.
[6] John Walker, *Left Shift: Radical Art in 1970s Britain* (London: IB Tauris, 2002), 57–64.
[7] Ibid., 59.
[8] Ibid., 57.
[9] Ibid., 57–58.
[10] Ibid., 58.

were specifically instructed by the Dean to produce "tangible, visual art objects for assessment purposes."[11]

In *Art of the 1970s: Cultural Closure*? Bart-Moore Gilbert characterises the 1970s as a "culture of post-avant-gardism", which "implies a contestatory as well as a temporal relationship to the 1960s avant-garde."[12] In other words, the assumed connection between formal innovation and political radicalism, central to the avant-garde, came under question. Perhaps connected to this, it is not surprising that in the 1970s, artists tried to actively define and shape the *context* within which they worked, as much as the *content* of their work. One important aspect of this was the development of alternative spaces. For example, the late 1960s and early 1970s saw the proliferation of "arts labs" in squatted buildings, such as the Drury Lane Arts Lab, which "had a theatre, coffee shop, gallery and a cinema" and served as an important space for experimental theatre, music and film, with close ties to the film co-op movement.[13] The Community Arts movement was another important development during the 1970s, with organisations that were "organised on a co-operative rather than a hierarchical basis, challenged accepted canons and divisions between 'high' and 'low' forms, and cut across the professional/amateur divide."[14] Community Arts received some institutional legitimacy through the Community Arts Committee as part of the Arts Council of Great Britain (ACGB); however, it also challenged the principles of aesthetic quality on a fundamental level, as exemplified by the following statement by community artist Su Braden:

> [The] so-called cultural *heritage* which made Britain great—the Bachs and the Beethovens, the Shakespeares and Dantes, the Constables and Titians—is no longer communicating anything to the vast majority of Europe's population—it is a *bourgeois* culture and therefore is only meaningful to that group. The greatest artistic deception of the twentieth century has been to insist to *all people* that this was *their culture....* *People make culture* and it is in this continually developing movement that money should be invested, rather than the Arts Council's notion of trying to make people cultured.[15]

---

[11] Ibid.

[12] Bart Moore-Gilbert, "Introduction: Cultural Closure or Post-Avantgardism?," in *The Arts in the 1970s: Cultural Closure?,* ed. Bart Moore-Gilbert, 20 (London: Routledge, 1994).

[13] Peter Thomas, "The Struggle for Funding: Sponsorship, Competition and Pacification," *Screen* 47, no. 4 (2006): 462.

[14] Moore-Gilbert, "Introduction," 21.

[15] Su Braden, *Artists and People* (1978), cited by Stuart Laing, "The Politics of

Following Habermas's suggestion that "the 1960s avant-garde was a counter-culture rising from the centre of bourgeois society itself,"[16] Bart Moore-Gilbert argues that post-avant-gardism "may be understood as a phenomena of the margins, whether in a literal or geographical sense ... or ideologically, in terms of dominant discourses of sex and gender."[17] For example, another important aspect of 1970s art was the proliferation of feminist spaces and publications, including: The Women's Liberation Art Workshop (1970), the Bristol Women's Group (1970), the Women's Free Art Alliance, and the Women Artists' Slide Library; publications such as *Shrew*, *Spare Rib*, *Women's Report*, *Women's Voice*, *Red Rag* and *MaMa*, publishing houses such as Virago and Women's Press, and exhibitions such as *Portrait of the Artist as a Housewife*, *Women and Work*, *A Woman's Place*. These existed to both counter patriarchy in the art world and to develop alternative organisations structured along feminist principles.[18]

The tumultuous events of the time (which included the Vietnam war, South African apartheid, and the nuclear arms race) meant that the familiar argument that art was beyond politics became increasingly problematic. As a response, artists not only set up alternative organisations, but directly made art in support of labour and social struggles. Conrad Atkinson, one of the founding members of the AU, made projects in solidarity with particular labour struggles, such as *Strike at Brannans*, in support of the 1972 strike at Brannans' Thermometer Factory, or *Asbestos*, in connection with the campaign for compensation for iron ore workers afflicted with asbestosis. Atkinson also designed banners for the Northern Region of the General and Municipal Workers' Union, which would become the GMB.[19] Two key exhibitions in 1978 presented socially engaged art to the public: the previously mentioned *Art for Whom?* at the Serpentine and *Art for Society* at the Whitechapel. Another example of socially-engaged art was The Poster Film Collective: a group of artists, photographers and filmmakers who made posters in response to the miner's strike, the

orsegment

Culture: Institutional Change in the 1970s," in *The Arts in the 1970s: Cultural Closure?*, ed. Bart Moore-Gilbert, 46 (London: Routledge, 1994).
[16] Jürgen Habermas, *Legitimation Crisis* (London: Heinemann, 1976), 85.
[17] Ibid.
[18] For an important historical account see Rozsika Parker and Griselda Pollock, *Framing Feminism: Art and the Women's Movement 1970–1985* (London: Pandora, 1987).
[19] For documentation of Atkinsons' work in the 1970s see *Conrad Atkinson: Picturing the System,* ed. Sandy Nairne and Caroline Tisdall (London: Pluto, 1981).

Vietnam War and the situation in Northern Ireland.[20] In the early 1980s
the Docklands Community Poster Project was founded in response to the
concerns of local residents in the development scheme[21].

At the time, there was a significant gap between cultural production as
it was understood and practised by artists, and the way in which it was
supported by cultural policy. As the art market was generally weak in the
1970s and corporate sponsorship was limited, the ACGB was the most
significant source of support.[22] However, ACGB support for experimental
art practices was limited. Major institutional clients such as national
theatre and opera companies remained the primary recipients.[23] The New
Activities Committee had a total budget of £15, 000.[24] Small amounts of
money were allocated through the Experimental Projects Committee.[25] In
an interview, Atkinson mentioned that shortly after presenting an
exhibition at the ICA in 1972, he received a letter from the ACGB saying
that that they would not fund the work because it used video, followed by
another letter saying that video was now considered to be a legitimate art
form.[26] Other critiques were made about the unwillingness to recognise
the multicultural nature of British society, such as Naseem Khan's *The
Arts Britain Ignores* (1976). All this meant that in terms of cultural policy,
the struggles for artists were connected to the funding of new artistic
practices, the challenging of institutionalised sexism and racism. In
addition, their struggles were against narrow and elitist definitions of
"artistic quality", and in favour of greater representation for artists in
policy decisions.

The Artists' Union

Within this climate, the Artists Union formed in 1972 in London. As
mentioned, it resembled other trade unions in many ways.[27] However,

---

[20] "Poster Film Collective," http://poster-collective.org.uk/.
[21] "Docklands Community Poster Project 1981 – 1991," *Archive Docklands Community Poster Project*,
http://www.cspace.org.uk/cspace/archive/docklands/dock_arch.htm.
[22] Stuart Sillars, "Is it Possible for Me to Do Nothing as My Contribution? Visual Art in the 1970s," in *The Arts in the 1970s: Cultural Closure?*, ed. Bart Moore-Gilbert, 75 (London: Routledge, 1994)..
[23] Laing, "The Politics of Culture," 42.
[24] Sillars, "Is it Possible for Me to Do Nothing as My Contribution?," 75.
[25] Laing, "The Politics of Culture," 41.
[26] Interview with Conrad Atkinson, June 2008.
[27] Avis Saltsman, "What was the Artists Union?," *Notes by Avis Saltsman*,

there was also a degree of decentralisation, to allow for active participation of the members, especially those outside of London. According to Atkinson, meetings would rotate to different cities, so that members from those regions could participate.[28] The stated goals of the Artists Union were: to seek affiliation to the Trades Union Congress; to regulate relations between members and patrons; to participate in local government; to lobby for access to mass media; to democratise art education; to end sexual and racial discrimination in the arts; to build closer ties with the trade union movement; to provide members with information relating art to science, technology and industry; and, to examine the position of art and artists in society.[29]   There were also "working groups", or "workshops", defined in the initial working paper as: Artists' Role in Society; Media; Art. Patronage, Marketing and Money; Government Policy for the Arts; Policy within the Trades Union Movement; The Artist in Education; Art, Science, Technology and Industry; Women in Art; and Exhibitions.[30] The women's workshop was particularly important. Members of the workshop founded and participated in the other organisations mentioned earlier; they also supported political struggles such as the strike at Brannans thermometer factory and the night cleaners' campaign.[31] They also actively fought the lack of representation of women in exhibitions, in education and on Arts Council panels.[32]

The workshops were where many of the debates took place, but also where many of the political tensions emerged. Atkinson mentioned that questions of gender and race were not without controversy, particularly because the Women's workshop was separatist (men were not allowed to attend). According to Dunn, the AU was committed to representing ALL artists and promoting equality across class, race, gender and sexual orientation in its policies.[33] However, they were not seriously engaged in any campaigns directly around racism in any concrete way because—due to the art education system—very few black artists emerged who asserted their identities as such in a politicised sense, until the 1980s. After several meetings, the idea was developed for the Artists' Union to join the Trades

---

http://www.art-science.com/Avis/au/au3.html.
[28] Atkinson interview.
[29] Artists' Union, *Aims of the Artist Union,* 1974.
[30] Saltsman, "What was the Artists Union?".
[31] Margaret Harrison, "Notes on Feminist Art in Britain 1970–77," *Studio International* 193, no. 987 (1977): 214.
[32] Ibid., 214–16.
[33] Interview with Peter Dunn, June 2008

Union Congress.[34] The Artists' Union did not have enough members to count as an independent organisation for the TUC, although it was in contact with other unions, including TGWU (now UNITE) and the freelance branch of NUJ.[35] However, according to a 1972 membership campaign document, integration with the trade union movement was not just about legal or financial resources, but a reorientation of the arts away from bourgeois institutions such as museums and commercial galleries, and "identifying our aims ultimately with the working class movement as a whole."[36]

Because the ACGB was a strong supporter of the arts in the 1970s (both through grants and through the purchase of works for its collection), it became a primary target of the AU. The AU tried to lobby the ACGB to recognise a broader range of cultural expression, and also to be more transparent and publicly responsible.[37] According to Atkinson, the ACGB was actually banning controversial works with little explanation, and so freedom of expression was also an important issue. The AU also fought against changes to art schools which would make it more difficult for female students to attend.[38] They lobbied for exhibition fees and resale rights (whereby the artist receives a percentage of the price when the work is sold on), which was strongly opposed by commercial galleries.[39] This was not actually put into effect until much later, with the EU directive on *droit de suite* (implemented in member states, including the UK in 2006).[40]

Members of the AU became involved in local government, such as the Greater London Council, the Greater London Arts Association, and the Tower Hamlets Arts Committee. As Atkinson described, it was at this level that many of the recommendations of the AU were actually put into practice. He said that at the GLC, the decisions on whether or not to award funding were made in the open, so that artists affected could sit in the audience and even intervene on the decision-making process. He mentioned a children's dance company from East London which had not received a grant. Following this, the company staged a protest in which the children actually came in and danced on the table. Atkinson commented

---

[34] Saltsman, "What was the Artists Union?"

[35] Artists' 1976 newsletter, cited in ibid.

[36] Artists Union, *National Membership Campaign,* 1972.

[37] Walker, *Left Shift: Radical Art in 1970s Britain,* 85.

[38] Harrison, "Notes on Feminist Art in Britain 1970–77," 215.

[39] Saltsman, "What was the Artists Union?".

[40] See "Artists' Resale Right," *Artquest,* http://www.artquest.org.uk/artlaw/artists-resale-right.htm.

that it was like the French Revolution.[41]   It is hard to imagine this happening now, within the current managerial climate of arts funding.

The AU also undertook considerable research. Avis Saltsman was the AU's librarian from almost since the beginning, and kept an archive of many of the documents. In an internationalist spirit, Saltsman also collected information on artists' organisations in other countries, as well as pieces of legislation pertaining to artists' conditions, so that they could serve as models when it came to lobbying organisations such as ACGB.[42]

The AU was involved in many activities and campaigns, but I will concentrate on three, because they draw out some of the tensions inherent to the definitions of both art and union organising. Two of these activities involved the Hayward Gallery in London, as the "public face" of the ACGB. The AU's 1972 newsletter describes how the AU set up an information and recruiting table outside an exhibition at the Hayward Gallery called *The New Art*. They were told to leave by the ACGB staff, who saw their stall as a form of self-promotion not connected to the exhibition. Nonetheless, the AU continued to set up their table and recruited over a hundred members.[43] If we consider this activity from the perspective of union organising, how different is it from leafleting at the factory gates? However, the ACGB's response reveals certain assumptions inherent to the art discipline: that art is not political, and that artists do not really engage in political activity, as all they really want is to get their work seen and further their careers. From this perspective, how else could the recruitment table be interpreted as anything but a publicity stunt?

Atkinson described another important activity at the Hayward Gallery, focused on an exhibition called Modern British Sculpture, which involved 101 artists and only two women. The Women's Workshop staged an intervention where they proposed a woman artist who worked in a similar way for each male artist. For example, if it was a man working with welded steel, they would propose a woman working with welded steel. This was to counter the inevitable arguments from the curators that "we would have chosen a woman, but we couldn't find one."[44] This could be seen as a precursor to the Guerilla Girls in the US, who drew attention to the lack of women in major museum exhibitions, as well as unacknowledged patriarchy of concepts of "artistic quality".

Another campaign took place towards the end of the AU's activities. Loraine Leeson described a boycott of the 1983 exhibition at the

---

[41] Atkinson interview.
[42] Interview with Avis Saltsman, June 2008.
[43] Artist Union, *Artist Union Newsletter,*1972.
[44] Atkinson interview.

Whitechapel Art Gallery in East London. According to Leeson, the gallery was mainly focused on raising its international profile, under the directorship of Nick Serota, who would move on to the Tate. One vestige of its original centrality to the area was an exhibition called *The Open*, in which any artist in the East End could participate. In 1983, the exhibition was being sponsored by Barclays Bank, which at the time participated in the apartheid regime in South Africa. The AU members all refused to participate in the show, and circulated a letter calling on artists to withdraw; over twenty artists withdrew their work, and held an alternative exhibition next door in the Whitechapel Public Library.[45] The boycott of *The Open* involved drawing connections between the institutions that supported art, and the corporations that funded them and their political interests (in this case, Barclays Bank and the Apartheid regime). This action can be seen as an example of the tendencies described earlier; questioning the conditions within which art is presented and creating an alternative context. This makes a statement of cultural democracy which involved literally rejecting the Gallery for the Public Library next door.

The end of the Artists' Union and thoughts on the future

The AU came to an end in 1983, within a wider climate of trade union defeat. As part of the interviews, I asked the four members of the AU about their thoughts on the AU's demise. All agreed that Thatcher made it difficult for all trade unions, let alone an organisation as small as the AU. Saltsman said that if artists withdraw their labour, nobody would really notice.[46] Leeson said that the late 1980s saw a backlash against the politicisation of the arts in the 1970s and early 1980s which has since continued: that it was an era of individualism and get-rich-quick schemes, values exemplified by Young British Art (YBA).[47] Atkinson said that people simply ran out of energy, but also that he himself had shifted his focus to organisations like the GLC where concrete change could be made.[48] Dunn had a more specific response. He said the resale rights campaign, if it had succeeded, would have changed the art world. However, he argued, that it also led to the AU becoming drawn into a protracted bureaucratic struggle that sapped all its time and energy. This was at a time when the government was unsupportive, and was being

---

[45] Interview with Loraine Leeson, June 2008.
[46] Saltsman interview.
[47] Leeson interview.
[48] Atkinson interview.

lobbied by the Bond Street commercial galleries: in a wider sense it was battling practically the entire labour movement, in a climate of near collapse, economically speaking.[49] Drawing on the earlier discussion, I would also add that there has been a shift in the focus and definition of culture since the 1970s: the creativity of the artist has been transposed onto the dynamism of the manager (celebrated by a decade of new management literature about "thinking outside the box").[50] This is generally associated with the flamboyance of celebrity culture and big money. Whether or not the current recession will see another shift in values is difficult to say.

I will conclude by asking what can we learn from the AU? Does a trade union for artists remain a viable model for England?[51] To an extent, Artists' Interaction and Representation currently serves a representative function and has a much larger membership (12, 000 members) than the AU ever did.[52] Although without legal power, many of its recommendations (such as the suggested pay rates for artists) remain at the level of guidance.[53] In interview, Atkinson said that the disappointment of the labour movement in the 1970s was that it did not react to new forms and did not really engage with culture. He said that, for example, the TUC did not replace their education officer, David Logan. Logan was central to the collaboration between the Labour Party Working Group on Culture, and the TUC Working Group on Cultural Policy, giving artists a voice within the labour movement. However, the Right did in fact engage with culture, such as Alistair McAlpine and Charles Saatchi, both involved with the Conservative party, who went on to dominate the visual arts.[54] They were instrumental in redefining culture in terms of the glamour of big money. The 1970s, then, were a missed opportunity for the labour movement, with disturbing consequences.

The changes affecting society in general have also affected the arts; the inequalities that existed in the 1970s have if anything been exacerbated. The expansion of the art market over the past 20 years, the rise of the star curator and dealer, and the increasing role of art schools as a launch pad

---

[49] Dunn interview.

[50] See Tom Peters, *Liberation Management* (1992), *Crazy Times for Crazy Organisations* (1993) and *The Circle of Innovation* (2003).

[51] However, in Scotland, the Scottish Artists' Union (SAU) has existed since 2001. See "Scottish Artists' Union," http://www.sau.org.uk/index.php.

[52] See "A-N The Artists Information Company," http://www.a-n.co.uk/about_an/article/473466.

[53] Susan Baines and Jane Wheelock, "Fees And Payments for Artists," http://www.a-n.co.uk/publications/article/193995

[54] Atkinson interview.

for an art market hungry for fresh young talent also cannot be underestimated. Several theorists, notably Andrew Ross and Pierre-Michel Menger, have observed that the typical conditions of the cultural sector, including hyperexploitation, casualisation and extreme competition, have become generalised to other sectors of the workplace.[55]

One of the questions I asked the former AU members was what today's version of the AU might look like. Avis Saltsman suggested lobbying on an international level such as the European Union, and making use of the Internet to share information internationally. She said the reason for keeping an archive of the AU at the Tate was to inspire future action.[56] Peter Dunn said that artists could only have leverage though a larger organisation representing the cultural industries, as visual artists as a group were too small and marginal.[57] For me, the AU serves as a reminder in reactionary times that artists can think and act collectively. Remembering these possibilities is crucial if we are to imagine a viable future.

---

[55] Pierre-Michel Menger, *Profession Artiste* (Paris: Editions Textuel, 2005); Andrew Ross, *No Collar: The Humane Workplace and its Hidden Costs* (Philadelphia: Temple University Press, 2004).
[56] Saltsman interview.
[57] Dunn interview.

PRESSING DEMANDS:
LABOUR ATTITUDES
TO NEWSPAPER OWNERSHIP

SEAN TUNNEY

By the late 1960s, the political and economic settlement upon which the West had based its development after World War II was under threat. The social consensus initiated by the 1945 Labour government had survived periods of Conservative rule; indeed welfare coverage had extended. But, by the late sixties, this settlement, based economically on the Keynesian policy of demand management, upon which Labour had increasingly relied,[1] faced ideological challenges from the Right and Left. Edward Heath's election in 1970 seemed likely to presage a break with the consensus from the Right, but the Conservatives retreated from this course in the face of a huge strike wave by a movement allied to the Left: the resurgent unions. As unemployment and inflation rose to new peaks, and states of emergency were proclaimed under the Tories, the increasing sense of destabilisation was heightened when the government lost its majority in February 1974 after calling an election on the highly indicative issue of "who governs?" The Right's reaction was to blame the perceived failure of the previous "social democratic settlement" on an excess of democracy. Minority pressure groups, most prominently the unions, had been able to bring to bear inordinate force in order to increase welfare provision and state spending, leading to the alleged crisis of governability.[2]

From the Left, the post-war settlement had also been subject to a radical critique. An innovative agenda emerged which was ascribed to the "new social movements". In addition, there was the development from the late 1950s onwards of a "New Left", which was influenced by a more heterodox and creative form of Marxism than that of the ossified

---

[1] Mark Wickham-Jones, *Economic Strategy and the Labour Party* (New York: St. Martin's Press, 1996), 34–38.
[2] John Callaghan, *The Retreat of Social Democracy* (Manchester: Manchester University Press, 2000), 39–45.

leadership of the Communist parties. While the movements challenging the arms race and more latterly, sexual inequality, Western dominance, and the Vietnam war were not necessarily linked, they all helped invigorate the Left, and were united with the New Left demands for greater democratic involvement in challenging the prevailing assumptions of the social democratic consensus. Moreover, in direct contrast to the Right, some New Left thinkers sought to explain the fading of Keynesianism's powers by highlighting its inability to control increasingly oligopolistic multinational business, said to be evading democratic governmental direction.[3]

This chapter will explore this dimension of the challenge to the consensus, and particularly the lesser-known impact of this New Left in the Labour Party in the early 1970s and its influence on political policy in one specific area of British culture: its media and, specifically, its press. The nature of the role that newspapers played in British culture, for instance in the maintenance of an imagined national community,[4] obviously of particular note in the fractured seventies, is outside the scope of this short chapter, as are the concurrent Labour debates on democratic control of the press.[5] Instead, it will focus on is the way in which debates on cultural policy concerning the press reflected the political fracturing. We will consider how the particular circumstances of the early 1970s meant that the New Left came to have a significant voice in policy development, leading to the Labour Party's first ever report on newspapers and the media, entitled *The People and the Media*. From that, we will consider press ownership policy creation and debate within Labour during the 1974-9 government. The chapter will explore the distancing between the government and the party on the question of media ownership, as evidenced by the different attitudes of each to the Royal Commission on the Press. It will also consider other influences on party policy, including the pressure for Labour representation, before touching on the contemporary relevance of these debates.

---

[3] Ibid., 54–69.
[4] Martin Conboy, *Tabloid Britain* (London: Routledge, 2006).
[5] Sean Tunney, *Labour and the Press* (Brighton: Sussex Academic Press, 2007), 29–32, 45–52.

The role of New Left and the Communications Study Group

Raymond Williams was not only widely influential in laying the foundation for Cultural Studies, but he was also at the forefront of the New Left. Under his influence, it had been concerned with issues regarding democracy and the press and media. The New Left's ruthless criticism of "labourism" saw many refuse to become involved with Labour. Yet others, particularly a number of prominent New Left economists, sought to open up a mainstream space for the expression of these ideas by joining the party, alongside a new wave of community activists. Most prominently, as early as 1970 Tony Benn had announced his conversion to the "New Politics", subsequently becoming a figurehead for this movement; particularly championing New Left themes of participative democracy and concern about the power of the oligopolies.[6]

Meanwhile, the party's leadership was on the back foot after leaving office, and faced widespread disaffection concerning a relatively unsuccessful period in government. Moreover, its most gifted thinker, Anthony Crosland, refused to accept the extent to which the Keynesian edifice was under siege and insisted that the multinational corporations' rise had peaked.[7] There was thus a political and economic policy vacuum, which this New Left current helped to fill, while, organisationally, control by old-style cliques collapsed and a more left-wing trade union leadership helped weaken Labour leadership control.[8]

The New Left helped revitalise and reorganise the party's policy development around a series of 80-plus "study groups". Outside co-optees, including academics, had equal status with MPs and trade unionist representatives on these in-house committees, performing the sort of work that would later be pursued by think-tanks. Through this, the then young New Left academic, James Curran, who would become such a prolific and important figure in British media and journalism studies, had a crucial influence on press policy throughout the 1970s by means of the Communications Study Group.

---

[6] Leo Panitch and Colin Leys, *The End of Parliamentary Socialism: From New Left to New Labour* (London: Verso, 1997), 49–51; Callaghan, *Social Democracy*, 61.

[7] Callaghan, *Social Democracy*, 44–45, 58.

[8] Panitch and Leys, *Parliamentary Socialism*, 21–26, 56–59; Noel Thompson, *Political Economy and the Labour Party* (London: UCL Press, 1996), 209–12; Callaghan, *Social Democracy*, 54–61.

Within this body (which involved the mainstream of the party as well as its left), as well as more widely among Labour opinion-formers, there were a set of seemingly similar concerns. The first may well be surprisingly familiar to those aware of post-1970s debates regarding the media and democracy. Some considered that democracy did not have the press that it needed to function adequately. This was because press ownership concentration had risen, thus reflecting broader concerns over oligopolisation. By 1967, at its low point, only three companies accounted for 85% of national newspaper circulation.[9] Those involved thought that as fewer media companies dominated, the risks extended, whether or not it could be proved in all instances that they wanted some types of output to prevail. Attempts to resist this ownership concentration have been associated with what James Curran has termed the "social market model". Other examples of this form of interventionism have been successfully applied in various European, and particularly Scandinavian, countries; some schemes originating in the early 1970s.[10]

But some in Labour and trade union circles there were also concerns about the seemingly related issue of political balance in the press. This can be easily dismissed as politicians merely seeking to control the media: a battle which has a long history. Labour's concern with political communications dates back to the introduction of universal suffrage, but the 1970 election failure prompted a reaction against such methods.[11] Some instead considered whether there was a need for market intervention to allocate newspaper resources roughly similar to the distribution of opinions in society. There was a perception that there was a democratic deficit. Newspapers' support for parties, and particularly Labour, was seen to be at odds with the sympathies of the electorate.

The 1960s had seen Harold Wilson's honeymoon with the press end, with even Labour's erstwhile ally, the *Daily Mirror*, demanding the leader's resignation, as part of a sustained campaign. Labour's concerns over press representation were again fuelled by the bitter February 1974 election.[12] While not as partial in its coverage as it was to become, the

---

[9] Colin Seymour-Ure, *The British Press and Broadcasting since 1945* (Oxford: Blackwell, 1996), 42, 44.

[10] James Curran, *Policy for the Press* (London: IPPR, 1995), 13–14; Alfonso Sanchez-Tabernero and Alison Denton, *Media Concentration in Europe* (Manchester: European Institute for the Media, 1993).

[11] Dominic Wring, "Political Marketing and the Labour Party" (PhD thesis, University of Cambridge, 1997).

[12] James Thomas, *Popular Newspapers, the Labour Party and British Politics* (Abingdon: Routledge, 2005), 62–67.

"full-blooded campaigning partisanship in the press" saw 68% of titles support the Conservatives.[13] In the febrile atmosphere, stories baldly stated that "under a docile prime minister" dominated by "reds", Labour would put "£4,000 Million on Taxes".[14] Despite the past clashes, it was only the *Mirror*, in the words of one MP, which "reflected the aspirations of the people" who elected Labour.[15] Partly in response to this coverage against it and the unions, it was felt by some Labour protagonists that parties, and particularly Labour, should have press outlets where their ideas were not always vilified, but explored, and even represented. Some became fixated on launching a Labour movement paper.

These views were often linked to a radical version of what has been described as a public service model, applying a broadcast model to newspaper ownership, where the emphasis is on political balance.[16] The relationship between providing an informed public sphere and provision of specific political positions is complex.[17] Representing political balance by controlling newspaper ownership is problematic in terms of how opinion distribution would be gauged, who would impose this, and how the press would operate independently from political and state control.

Another important feature of the newspaper market, in relation to questions of political democracy and Labour representation, was the effect of advertising. The impact of advertising on press support or bias against Labour may not seem immediately obvious. There was little support for the view that individual firms directed their advertising budgets to pursue ideological aims. Instead, the concern within Labour ranks was that advertisers' influence on the national press market was more indirect, but still powerful. Advertising, it was felt, led to an important division in the national newspaper market. The "quality" titles, aimed at the wealthier, gained a much larger percentage of their income from advertising. The mass-circulation press, by contrast, raised a great deal of its revenue simply from its cover price. One consequence of this "bifurcation" has

[13] Martin Harrop, "The Press and Post-War Elections," in *Political Communications: The General Election of 1983*, eds. Ivor Crewe and Martin Harrop, 138, 141 (Cambridge: Cambridge University Press, 1983).
[14] Thomas, *Popular Newspapers*, 68.
[15] Ioan Evans, HOC (House of Commons), 21 March 1974, vol. 870, cols. 1320–21; Harrop, "Press and Post-War Elections," 139.
[16] James Curran, "Different Approaches to Media Reform," in *Bending Reality*, ed. James Curran, 99 (London: Pluto, 1986).
[17] John Street, *Mass Media, Politics, and Democracy* (Basingstoke: Palgrave, 2001), 258–59.

been that it is possible for upmarket titles to be competitive with a much lower circulation than the "populars".

Thus there was less diversity in one market sector, as less wealthy readers have been excluded from having the same range of press aimed at them as their richer counterparts.[18] But in addition, it was argued, this would also bias the press against Labour representation. As it was the poorer readers who tended to vote Labour, and to be union members, so it was the Labour movement as a whole that was less well served by a press dominated by advertising. Indeed, it was emphasised that a notable victim of this advertising effect was the last title with direct connections with the Labour movement, the *Daily Herald*, which had folded in the 1960s to be relaunched as *The Sun*.[19]

Reflecting these two different concerns, there was a covert contest regarding the study group. Its composition encompassed different wings of the Party. Nevertheless, the contest was between those led by the New Left, on the one hand, and some of the traditional Left, particularly those in the trade unions, on the other, who thought that encouraging diversity in the newspaper market was more a matter of providing a voice for the Labour movement, rather than of encouraging a potentially dangerous politically diverse press. There was a tension between the seemingly related conceptions of ownership diversity and the representation of Labour.

For those most focused on the latter aim, diversifying ownership among non-Labour newspapers was, at best, a diversion. So, one prominent study group member argued that to maintain and broaden this press by means of providing a universal subsidy would be "feeding the mouth that bites you".[20] While outside of the group, the small-scale party newspaper, *Labour Weekly*, was, perhaps not surprisingly, running parallel to this discussion a campaign called "The Case for a Labour Press".[21] However, the focus of the study group, championed most notably by James Curran, was on what the future Arts Minister, Hugh Jenkins, argued should be the general approach to the press and media. This was to put

---

[18] Labour Party, *The People and the Media* (London: Labour Party, 1974), 20, 27–28; Colin Sparks, "Concentration in the UK National Press," *European Journal of Communication* 10 (1995), 195–27.

[19] See, for instance, Labour Party, *Media*, 20; Huw Richards, *The Bloody Circus* (London: Pluto, 1997), 27–28, 169–70, 181–82.

[20] Martin Linton, "Policies for the Press," Labour Party Archive, RD (Research Department) 536, January 1973, 2.

[21] *Labour Weekly* (London), June 30, 1972.

diversity uppermost, not aiming to "encourage socialist media but to create a framework within which such media can and will emerge."[22]

This tension between the different viewpoints was reflected in the eventual production in 1974 of the study group's report, *The People and the Media*. This document was soon to form the basis of Labour Party policy, if not that of the incoming government. The report argued there was press bias, reflecting concerns for Labour representation. Nevertheless, the emphasis was that this bias was heightened by ownership concentration. Some rhetoric was in favour of a public service model. But the focus was on a social market model and extending plurality of ownership, with an Advertising Revenue Board, as argued for by Curran. This borrowed ideas from the Scandinavian systems, but also reflected the New Left enthusiasm to go beyond Keynesianism to utilise direct controls.

The policies advocated would aim at dealing with bifurcation, which would have aided Labour representation, but not exclusively so. This centralised Board would collect all revenue for press publications directly from advertisers, and could also fix advertising rates. It would redistribute funds directly back to publishers on the basis of reader numbers, not, as with advertisers, on the composition of the readership. Thus this would undermine bias against lower-income readership publications.[23]

But it was also aimed directly at increasing general diversity of ownership and publications. The Board would keep a proportion of funds both to subsidise newsprint costs and to provide a launch fund for new publications. A newsprint subsidy would offset the problem of the broadsheets' profitability being threatened, because of the end of the effective subsidy that bifurcation provided. Advertisers would still be free to choose which press to advertise in, and newspapers could still take as much of whatever advertising they wanted.[24]

The tension between concerns to promote Labour on the one hand, and increase press ownership diversity on the other, should not be overstated. Those involved were not necessarily even aware of it at this stage. Yet it continued with the Royal Commission on the Press, instituted after Labour entered government in 1974. This saw a four-way split, in effect.

---

[22] Hugh Jenkins, "A Framework for a Communications Policy," RD 597, February 1973, 1.

[23] Labour Party, *Media*; Curran, "Different Approaches," 112.

[24] Labour Party, *Media*, 26–29, 31–32; Curran, "Different Approaches," 112–13.

The Royal Commission on the Press

Firstly, the Labour Party proposed to the Commission what was contained in *The People and the Media,* involving diversity. Secondly, nevertheless, the party officials reporting to the Royal Commission made those proposals to focus on creating a Labour press, reflecting the tension.[25] However, a problem with advancing the proposals to argue for this was that it appeared self serving, which did not help the representatives' case on the Commission. But also, if they had been enacted, the proposals' effect would not have been as predictable as the officials seemed to believe. Precisely because the plans were also developed to provide diversity, they would not have guaranteed anything like political parity in terms of press coverage.

Thirdly, after initially hesitantly supporting the use of legislation to change the press market, the Labour leadership pulled back from reform. The concern for Labour representation had been taken up by Harold Wilson. He had come to share the wider Labour antipathy towards the press, following the eclipse of his personal honeymoon mentioned earlier. Wilson was, by 1974, at least prepared to consider structural change as one possible remedy. There was a tension here with policies to diversify ownership, but there was also a further strain within the interest in press representation. The leader faced a dilemma. How could any structural change be achieved to improve Labour's representation in the long run without further alienating the existing press from a Labour government in the short term? While traditional Labour marketing techniques were out of vogue, the leadership was primarily concerned to increase Labour's support in the newspapers by courting press owners and this strategy eventually ruled out structural reform.

At first Wilson displayed an ambivalence on setting up the Royal Commission, which reflected the pressures he faced. He took advice from James Curran on the terms of the inquiry and appointments to the Commission.[26] Wilson also expressed some interest in "economic intervention that would encourage the founding of new papers".[27] But he told Conservatives that he shared their worries over subsidies.[28] And he was under pressure from press owners and editors' representatives who

---

[25] Labour Party, Oral Evidence to the Royal Commission on the Press, 11 March 1976, 7–10.

[26] Interview with James Curran, May 2001; Interview with Martin Linton, July 2001.

[27] See Tom Baistow, *Fourth-Rate Estate* (London: Comedia, 1985), 60.

[28] HOC, 2 May 1974, vol. 872, cols. 1330–31.

closed ranks in response to the Labour Party's proposals for an Advertising Board on the Royal Commission.

The role of a board in fixing advertising rates, the publishers and editors suggested to the Commission would hinder competition and "subsidise inefficiency".[29] The publishers argued that advertising redistribution would not help economic viability, since it did not deal with the problem of overstaffing, which could be solved with new technology.[30] The press businesses also rejected a key assumption of bifurcation behind the Advertising Board. They argued that a disproportionate amount of advertising was not spent on attracting those with high income. They noted, for instance, that the broadsheets had lower social class readers.[31] However, the charge of inefficiency is similar to one that had been levelled against other subsidy systems, for instance in Norway, and which had been found to be largely unproven there.[32] The claim that staffing levels provided the primary obstacle to diversity was not borne out by the subsequent failure of new technology to extensively broaden the range of British national newspaper titles. Further, it is not surprising that the upmarket titles had some C/D/E social class readers. The more important question is whether these papers attract a larger percentage of A/B/C1 readers, which has been the case.[33]

Nevertheless, such a redistributive board was complicated and intrusive. In contrast, the TUC supported simply levying a tax on media companies' advertising to subsidise a broader range of publications and also tackle bifurcation. These proposals had wide support across the Labour Party.[34]

However, fourthly, it wasn't either of these proposals that Labour ministers had the opportunity to consider. Following submissions, the Royal Commission on the Press was divided. The majority rejected the Labour and the TUC proposals. However, two of the commissioners

---

[29] Newspaper Publishers Association, "Evidence to the Royal Commission on the Press," 46; Newspaper Editors' Guild, "Evidence to the Royal Commission on the Press," 17.

[30] Newspaper Publishers Association, "Evidence," 6, 44; Newspaper Editors' Guild, "Oral Evidence to the Royal Commission on the Press," 17.

[31] Newspaper Publishers Association, "Evidence," 42–44.

[32] Helge Østbye, "Norway," in *The Media in Western Europe*, ed. Stubbe Ostergaard Bernt, 174 (London: Sage. 1997); Sigurd Høst, "The Norwegian Newspaper System: Structure and Development," in *Media and Communication*, eds. Helge Ronning and Knut Lundby, 295 (Oslo: Norwegian University Press, 1991).

[33] Jeremy Tunstall, *Newspaper Power* (Oxford: Oxford University Press, 1995), 8–9.

[34] Interview with James Curran, May 2001.

produced a Minority Report, which the Labour Party latterly promoted after their plans had been rejected.[35] Although they were concerned about the concentration of ownership, the focus of both the Labour government adviser and *Daily Mirror* political editor Geoffrey Goodman and the union leader David Basnett was again on press bias against the Labour movement.

The Minority Report reintroduced a call for another proposal, a National Printing Corporation, which had been dismissed earlier by the study group, as members felt there wasn't a press print capacity shortage. This was a hybrid solution. The use of a commercially viable print works could be seen as part of a social market proposal. And a launch fund, which was part of the package, had the potential to increase diversity. Yet the authors explicitly saw the printing corporation as in the public service tradition with the aim, in part, of creating an official Labour movement press.[36] In addition, rather than the money coming from media advertising, Goodman and Basnett felt that launch funding should be provided out of general taxes. However, the bitter experience of the failure of the *Scottish Daily News*, a new newspaper launched in 1975 and financed by a loan worth more than £1 million from the public purse, but with too small a potential circulation base, had undermined such calls.[37]

By 1977, when the Royal Commission and its minority reported their findings, James Callaghan had succeeded Wilson as Prime Minister. It is now clear that members of the Cabinet held secret meetings with the authors of the Minority Report. Those ministers involved—from the Right Roy Hattersley, the Centre-Left Peter Shore and Left Michael Meacher—were prepared to set up a ministerial committee to discuss the report.[38]

However, with the Left in the Cabinet marginalised by this time, politicians were also concerned about Labour representation in the existing press. As Labour's majority now hung by a thread, "a huge outcry from the Conservative press" was the last thing they and the Labour leader wanted.[39] Before he died, Lord Callaghan cast doubt over whether any scheme that involved either giving financial assistance to the press or redistributing advertising revenue would have "ever [been] a runner"

---

[35] Geoffrey Goodman and David Basnett, *Royal Commission on the Press: Minority Report* (London: Labour Party, 1997).
[36] Interview with Geoffrey Goodman, July 2001. See also Royal Commission on the Press, *Final Report* (London: HMSO, 1977), 10, 11.
[37] For a full account, see Ron McKay and Brian Barr, *The Story of the Scottish Daily News* (Edinburgh: Canongate, 1976).
[38] Interview with Geoffrey Goodman.
[39] Ibid.

facing such hostility, including from the Royal Commission.[40] As such, the proposals were quietly kicked into the long grass. There was no mention of government intervention in the press in the 1979 Labour manifesto, the drafting of which Callaghan dominated.[41]

Epilogue

So what, if anything, can be said about these 1970s Labour debates subsequently? That such solutions to the problems of the press became the position of a mainstream political party reflects the radical ferment of the period. The legacy of that radicalism survived in the Labour Party into the 1980s.

Nevertheless, although it appeared to those involved that the demand for Labour to be promoted in the press was synonymous with the demand for diversity of ownership, subsequent events showed this was not the case. This inherent tension came to a breaking point from the mid 1980s onwards, when the party strategy for Labour to have its voice heard in the press started to switch from campaigning for structural change towards an evolving political marketing strategy, which reached its apogee under Tony Blair and has been pursued less successfully by Gordon Brown. To advance that strategy, it was a positive hindrance to tackle concentration of ownership, which faded from the political agenda.

Such a possibility was not at all apparent to those during the 1970s seeking to promote Labour in the press through structural change, some of whom also wanted to broaden diversity of ownership. Yet it can be argued that one key division in this important party cultural policy could be seen in terms of the underlying tension between these two seemingly similar demands; for press ownership to be diverse, and for Labour to be represented.

---

[40] James Callaghan, private correspondence.
[41] Geoff Bish, "The Manifesto," in *What Went Wrong*, ed. Michael Barratt Brown and Ken Coates, 187–95 (Nottingham: Spokesman, 1979); Kenneth Morgan, *Callaghan: A Life* (Oxford: Oxford University Press, 1997), 687.

PART II:

THE MEDIA AND SOCIAL CHANGE

1970S CURRENT AFFAIRS – A GOLDEN AGE?

DAVID MCQUEEN

The 1970s has been described as a "golden era" or "classic period" of current affairs broadcasting in Britain both by long-serving journalists, such as Peter Taylor, and academics in recent studies of the form.[1] This reputation is built on the success of programmes such as Granada's *World in Action* (1963-1998) and Thames Television's *This Week* (1956-1992) at ITV and *Panorama* (1953-) at the BBC. At a time of social, political and economic upheaval these programmes explored controversial issues, exposed hidden scandals and often challenged powerful vested interest. Conflicts at home (in the political sphere and on the economic front) and abroad (especially America, South-East Asia and Southern Africa) were explored with a new-found candour and willingness to defy established viewpoints. This confident, challenging turn in investigative television journalism drew audiences of many millions, at a time when current affairs programmes were guaranteed a prime time slot on ITV by a mandate from the Independent Television Authority (ITA) and by the BBC's Charter requirements.

Nevertheless, an examination of programmes from the decade reveals that the quality of current affairs was far from consistently high. Different series had distinct, competing identities and Independent Television (ITV) often appeared to dominate the form in terms of creativity, ratings and critical reputation. And whilst there were many outstanding investigations on both the BBC and ITV, there were also many examples of unchallenging, mediocre and lacklustre work. If the era does in fact produce gold, it is gold mixed with a good deal of grit.

Where distinctive qualities are found in current affairs coverage of the 1970s, they reflect the particular tensions, conflicts and social changes

[1] Particularly Peter Goddard, John Corner and Kay Richardson, "The Formation of *World in Action:* A Case Study in the History of Current Affairs Journalism," *Journalism* 2, no.1 (2001) and Patricia Holland, *The Angry Buzz* (London: I.B.Taurus, 2006), both of which are drawn on extensively in this essay. Many thanks to Peter Goddard and Pat Holland for their excellent feedback on an early version of this article.

documented by the form. The "Troubles" in Northern Ireland, the oil crisis, a severe economic recession, race riots, industrial unrest, feminist activism, political protest and cultural ferment, all mark a decade of challenge to the British post-war liberal-corporatist consensus.[2] This challenge was sometimes mirrored in tensions and disagreements around definitions of impartiality and balance in the relationship between broadcasters, the government and the regulatory authority overseeing commercial broadcasting, the ITA. This became the Independent Broadcast Authority (IBA) from 1972. Concerns over "slanted" or "authored" viewpoints are repeated through the decade on a number of topics including investigations into the tobacco, asbestos and pharmaceutical industries, poverty in Britain, the war in Vietnam, injustice in apartheid South Africa and sectarian conflict in Northern Ireland.

This account draws on recently published material and archive research at Bournemouth University's Centre for Broadcasting History, to gain a sense of the state of current affairs in this turbulent decade. By examining major, parallel developments in four well known series: *Panorama, This Week, World in Action* and LWT's *Weekend World* (1972-88), I will indicate why the 1970s was, indeed, a significant and broadly successful decade for the current affairs form, a success that is unlikely to be repeated given the dramatically different broadcasting conditions of the 21st century.

Panorama

Panorama, which had, to some extent, set the pace for current affairs in the 1950s and early 1960s entered the 1970s somewhat in the doldrums, with far lower audience ratings and a lukewarm critical reception.[3] The programme was extended to one primetime hour (8-9pm) from September 1970, making more use of the debate-type programme after success with this format earlier in the year, on the South African cricket tour and hanging, with Robin Day as main presenter chairing live discussions. *Panorama* also now devoted more time than its ITV rivals (with the exception of LWT's analytical *Weekend World*) to political interviews regarded as Robin Day's forte. In 1970, for example, he interviewed two

---

[2] See James Curran and Colin Leys, "Media and the Decline of Liberal Corporatism in Britain," in *De-Westernizing Media Studies,* ed. James Curran and Myung-Jin Park (London: Routledge, 2000).
[3] See Richard Lindley, *Panorama: Fifty Years of Pride and Paranoia* (London: Politicos Publishing, 2002).

Prime Ministers: Harold Wilson on Biafra and the Common Market (tx: 12.1.1970), and Edward Heath on rioting in Belfast (tx: 31.7.1972).

While there were some single-subject programmes, most *Panorama* episodes continued to have two or three segments. The *Panorama* of 21 December 1970, for instance, was made up of a 17 minute report on the rural poor in Devon, a 15-minute live studio discussion on "the situation in Poland", and 24 minutes of filmed interviews by Robin Day from Vietnam with the country's Ministers, the President Nguyen Van Thieu and the US Ambassador. It also included film of the Saigon slums, workers in fields and villages, and US soldiers on patrol on the river and in the jungle.[4] *Panorama* at this time aimed to produce authoritative, reflective, analytical and "professional" reports, rather than the independent-minded exposés and challenges to the status quo more frequently found on *This Week* and *World in Action*.

Julian Pettifer, who joined the programme in 1969 as a reporter, typified the new emphasis on cool, detached professionalism over the "chummy" camaraderie of *Panorama's* stars of the 1950s and 60s. Pettifer's reports exemplified some of the strengths and weaknesses of *Panorama* in the 1970s. Despite his widely admired intelligence and professionalism, critics took note of his detached manner and notices were not always glowing. His *Panorama* report from Chile following the overthrow of President Allende was compared unfavourably with that of ITV rival *World in Action*. *Panorama* had interviewed the Generals and their supporters who had taken over the country, while *World in Action* concentrated on their victims. Stuart Hood, former Controller of BBC Television, writing in *The Listener* in 1973 was critical of *Panorama's* "coolness", anticipating in his argument some of the debates that would surface two decades later in Bosnia over "journalism of attachment":

> It is clear that the *World in Action* team, which brought back from Chile interviews with the victims of the men whom *Panorama* questioned with its usual polite aloofness, feel that neutrality is not possible in every situation [...] this is one of the reasons why *World in Action* is more interesting and successful than *Panorama*.[5]

As other current affairs programmes had developed in the 1960s and early 1970s, such as the BBC's *Tonight* (1957-65), *24 Hours* (1965-72) and *Nationwide* (1969-83*)*, they had begun to take the wind out of

---

[4] Bournemouth University, "Panorama Project," http://panorama.bufvc.ac.uk/.
[5] Stuart Hood, cited by Lindley, *Panorama: Fifty Years of Pride and Paranoia*, 114.

Panorama's sails, and according to Lindley, the programme had grown rather slow, old-fashioned, predictable and "self-important".

Criticism grew of *Panorama's* lack of attention to "ordinary people", particularly as *Tonight* had shown in the 1960s that a popular, incisive current affairs programme was possible that, in Bernard Levin's words, was "sceptical towards received opinion and indeed authority."[6] Cultural critic Raymond Williams criticised *Panorama's* attention to "superficial high politics" and its habit of bringing to the screen "men whom we know, because we have heard them so often" who "say nothing but say it purposively and with an official presence."[7]

Regarded in this way as somewhat remote and elitist, *Panorama* also appeared lacking in direction at a time of political and cultural upheaval. It may be partly in response to this perception that David Dimbleby was appointed *Panorama* presenter in 1974 a position he held until 1977 and to which he would return in the 1980s. David Dimbleby was a freelance reporter for *Panorama* in 1967 and was first offered "Robin Day's vacated chair" in 1972. David had gained notoriety from *Yesterday's Men* in 1971, a BBC documentary which both mocked and enraged former Prime Minister Harold Wilson. Unlike "Garrick Club" anchor Robin Day, the young Dimbleby could not easily be caricatured as "establishment friendly" despite inheriting the role from his father, Richard, who had been "virtually a living embodiment of the programme".[8] In fact, although an effective presenter, David Dimbleby's interviews were less adversarial than those conducted by self-styled "Grand Inquisitor" Robin Day and *Panorama* still lacked energy and "bite" until the arrival of Peter Pagnamenta who became Editor in 1976.[9]

With regard to the "Troubles" in Ireland, as former Editor Robert Rowland admitted, until the outbreak of violence: "we failed considerably to report the festering difficulties of Northern Ireland."[10] *Panorama* did report extensively from Ireland in the 1970s, but from 1971 a system of reference upwards operated in relation to interviews with the IRA. As Anthony Smith explains, permission had always to be sought and therefore

---

[6] Watkins, Gordon, ed. *BFI Dossier 15: Tonight.* London: BFI, 1982, 66.
[7] Raymond Williams in *Raymond Williams on Television: Selected Writings*, ed. Alan O'Connor, 43 (London: Routledge, 1968).
[8] *The Times,* February 9, 1972, 12.
[9] See Lindley, *Panorama: Fifty Years of Pride and Paranoia.*
[10] Robert Rowland, "Panorama in the Sixties," in *Window on the Sixties: Exploring Key Texts of Media and Culture,* ed. Anthony Aldgate, James Chapman and Arthur Marwick, 177 (London: I.B.Tauris, 2000).

was requested less and less often, and when requested it was more and more frequently refused.[11]

Nevertheless, the BBC's current affairs coverage of "the Troubles" led to a number of clashes with Labour and Conservative governments when the Corporation's "self-imposed restraint" was not exercised sufficiently in the view of some MPs or Ministers. By 1977 this had culminated in Northern Ireland Secretary Roy Mason's explicit threat to the BBC's Charter and income, as well as the Prime Minister Jim Callaghan's White Paper for appointed "Service Management Boards" to secure greater government control.[12] The pattern of intimidation that had characterised government reactions to the BBC's coverage of conflicts stretching back to Suez certainly continued, and some critics argue, intensified following Margaret Thatcher's election victory in 1979.[13] For if the supposedly "establishment friendly" *Panorama* had entered the 1970s in a somewhat becalmed manner, it would leave the decade in a storm of protest over events in Northern Ireland.

Panorama's reputation improved in the second half of the 1970s after Peter Pagnamenta reduced the role of "star" reporters and injected more pace into the programme whilst moving towards more single subject programmes. The appointment of Roger Bolton as Editor in 1979 ensured that a bold, agenda-setting, investigative focus on domestic issues would keep *Panorama* in the headlines, perhaps more than it might have wished. Bolton, in his own words, set out "to lead the public debate as opposed to reflecting it." He was a graduate from Liverpool University, unlike many staff and reporters who were "Oxbridge" educated, and he appeared more willing to challenge the status quo at a time when, as he saw it, "consensus had broken down." Bolton had already experienced controversy as Editor of *Tonight* which concluded its twenty-two year run by broadcasting an interview with the INLA, an organisation responsible for killing Thatcher's close friend and adviser Airey Neave that year.[14] Reflecting later on Thatcher's furious reaction to *Panorama's* reporting from Northern Ireland, Bolton observed: "My job was to push the questions. And I think

---

[11] Anthony Smith, "Television Coverage of Northern Ireland," in *War and Words: a Northern Ireland Reader*, ed. Bill Rolston and David Miller, 22–37 (Belfast: Beyond the Pale Publications, 1996).

[12] Robin Day, *Grand Inquisitor* (London: Pan Books, 1990), 279, 305.

[13] See Peter Walters, "The Crisis of 'Responsible' Broadcasting: Mrs Thatcher and the BBC," *Parliamentary Affairs*, 42, no. 3 (1989); Tom O'Malley, *Closedown? The BBC and Government Broadcasting Policy, 1979–92 (London: Pluto, 1994).*

[14] See Roger Bolton, *Death on the Rock and Other Stories* (London: WH Allen, 1990); Lindley, *Panorama: Fifty Years of Pride and Paranoia.*

that confrontation was probably inevitable with any government, but the Thatcher factor was very important. This was very personal for her."[15]

By the end of the 1970s it was extremely difficult to report the views and activities of militant Republicans and Nationalists, despite sizeable support in the north of Ireland. On the rare occasions such sectarian and paramilitary perspectives were aired, even in a "hostile" interview context, they usually prompted intervention by senior management at the BBC, or by the regulatory authority at ITV, and/or confrontation with the government. Reporting of serious and well-founded allegations against the police or the army also came in for sustained "flak", or was effectively censored.

Current affairs coverage of the apparently insoluble conflict proved to be so fraught that *Panorama* Editor Roger Bolton would lose his job for the untransmitted footage of an IRA roadblock his staff had filmed at the village of Carrickmore, despite attempting to follow BBC procedures and gaining approval in general terms for the programme being made.[16] Bolton was sacked following an inquiry by the acting Director General Gerard Mansell for not ensuring that the BBC Controller Northern Ireland had been informed by Head of News Belfast about the incident. Bolton's dismissal as *Panorama* Editor caused real anger at the BBC and threats of industrial action eventually led to his reinstatement. On resuming his position he was advised by Gerard Mansell to "raise his sights when dealing with such problems and to remember the wider interests of the BBC."[17]

Current Affairs at ITV

The strong, distinctive character of current affairs on the commercial network in the seventies may be partly traced back to recommendations by the Pilkington Report of 1962 and subsequent legislative and regulatory changes that placed new public service obligations on the private sector and encouraged intelligent, innovative and educational programming. The Television Act of 1964 empowered the ITA to exercise considerable control over ITV's television output and "mandate" certain serious kinds

---

[15] Interview with Roger Bolton, October 23, 2008.

[16] See Richard Clutterbuck, *The Media and Political Violence* (London: Macmillan, 1981); Bolton, *Death on the Rock and Other Stories;* Susan Carruthers, "Reporting Terrorism: the British State and the Media, 1919–1994," in *War, Culture and the Media: Representations of the Military in 20th Century Britain,* ed. Susan Carruthers and Ian Stewart (Trowbridge: Flicks, 1996).

[17] Lindley, *Panorama: Fifty Years of Pride and Paranoia,* 233.

of programmes, including two weekly current affairs programmes at peak viewing hours.[18] The ITA's more proactive role can be seen in the Authority's dramatic decision not to renew Rediffusion's licence to broadcast in 1967 for scheduling, despite warnings, too many "insubstantial" quiz shows. As Holland notes, the 1964 Act also gave ITA the power to interfere in news and current affairs to ensure "balance and impartiality".[19] This new interpretative role, as we shall see, soon brought the ITA into conflict with television producers and executives.

The second significant change was the government's move in 1971 from taxing ITV's advertising revenue to taxing profits. This resulted in companies investing heavily in programme making, including prestigious projects such as Jeremy Isaacs' hugely expensive 26-part *World at War* (Thames Television 1973-74). Encouraged to produce high quality, challenging material, ITV soon dominated current affairs production with popular, high impact and often controversial series such as *This Week, World in Action* (at Granada) and later *First Tuesday* (1983-93) at Yorkshire TV.

World in Action

During its thirty-five years on screen, Granada's *World in Action* was Britain's highest rating and, arguably, most influential and ground-breaking current affairs series. First launched in 1963, it quickly developed a reputation for hard-hitting investigations, tough, opinionated journalism and an appetite for trouble-making that often upset the targets of its inquiries, as well as the ITA in its role as television regulator. *World in Action's* apparent relish for controversy and distinct anti-establishment sensibility was encouraged by the senior management of the Manchester-based Granada Television, a company which already had a maverick reputation by the 1970s. This is evident in a 1977 interview with Denis Forman—then Granada's Chairman and a key figure in the development of serious programming—who was asked about *World in Action's* identity:

> One of the important things in television is to be able to make programmes about things that people don't want you to make programmes about. And unless you do that fairly frequently and with a good deal of vigour, you'll find that you're penned in and penned back. I mean you're either being

---

[18] Andrew Crisell, *An Introductory History of Broadcasting* (London: Routledge, 1997), 113.
[19] Holland, *The Angry Buzz,* 37.

pushed back or you're pushing against, there's no standing still on this. All the forces of Government and the Establishment want you to make the programmes that are helpful to Government and this is not at all our job. Often it is our job to make programmes the Government will not like one little bit.[20]

As Forman observes in the same interview, most journalists who worked on *World in Action* were newspaper-trained and had to learn how to tell their stories in the language of television. *World in Action* was the first current affairs shot entirely on 16mm film, and the gritty "anti-aesthetic" style[21] matched the tabloid TV techniques that Executive Producer Tim Hewat had first developed on Granada's *Searchlight* (1959-1960) and which he continued to use in *World in Action* until 1965. Goddard *et al.* show how the pioneering Hewat drew on his training and experience at *The Daily Express,* adapting that paper's tradition of "strong headlines" and "breezy, campaigning style" and applying it to his presentation of current affairs. *World in Action's* concise delivery and refusal to pull punches contrasted sharply with the "waffle and non conclusion" that Hewat believed to be the guiding principles of *Panorama* and *This Week.*[22] Consequently, *World in Action* did not shy away from "editorialising" or making judgements based on the facts assembled, which would remain a source of grievance for the IBA through the 1970s in its attempt to enforce what it regarded as "due impartiality".

Hewat's strategy of visually "grabbing the audience by the lapels" complimented the "declamatory and aggressive, inquiring and insubordinate" character of Granada's popular current affairs series.[23] David Plowright, who took over the series from Hewat in 1966 refined this style somewhat but it remained a distinctly tabloid format with broadsheet concerns that appealed to a broad audience. Both *World in Action* and *This Week* were regularly in the top twenty programmes with ten million viewers.[24] By contrast, the BBC's current affairs output seemed more cautious, reverential

---

[20] Eva Orbanz and Klaus Wildenhahn, "Journey to a Legend and Back: The British Realistic Film," in *Granada: The First Twenty-Five Years,* 100 (London: BFI, 1981).

[21] "Anti-aesthetic" was a term used by Brian Winston in an interview with Goddard in Goddard, Corner, Richardson, *Public Issue Television,* 87.

[22] Ibid.,12, 20–21.

[23] Tim Hewat quoted in N. Chanan's unpublished manuscript *Granada: The Early Years,* cited in ibid., 25.

[24] Ibid., 59; Holland, *The Angry Buzz,* 103.

and "establishment friendly" with audience figures around half those of *World in Action*.[25]

Innovation was particularly evident at *World in Action* in the 1970s where David Plowright's early decision to set up separate teams for producing reportage, inquiry and observational films had paid dividends. According to Goddard *et al.* "reportage" comprised the largest output with the quickest turnaround, responding to "the arguments and controversies of the moment", in a selective and innovative manner where possible. "Inquiry" required a slower turnaround, greater financial commitment and meticulous research for its "well researched exposés". "Observation", or the "implicit" rather than "explicit" mode of enquiry included gentler, more impressionistic films about personal lives which raised provocative social questions. These included the films of Denis Mitchell, often using the recorded speech of the interviewees as the only voiceover, such as "Quentin Crisp", "Bannside" (on Ian Paisley), "St Mungo's People" (homelessness), "Pigs" (the police in Cincinnati) and "American Radio" (all 1970-71).[26] Sexton also shows how the use of lightweight, 16mm cameras and the adaptation of "direct cinema" techniques, first introduced in the mid-sixties at *World in Action,* was highly influential on other documentary, current affairs and even drama productions of the era.[27]

By 1970 most, but not all, *World in Action* and current affairs films were in colour despite fears initially expressed by some broadcasters about the effect on audiences of gruesome colour coverage from the Vietnam War, Northern Ireland and other conflicts.[28] Technical and stylistic innovations at *World in Action* were accompanied by experimentation with "formats", or novel ways of exploring themes. Some of these formats would become strands or series in their own rights, whilst others would provide early templates for hybrid factual forms that would later be known as "Reality TV".[29] Early reality TV techniques can be found in such programmes as the challenge to a Staffordshire village to give up smoking

---

[25] Lindley, *Panorama: Fifty Years of Pride and Paranoia,* 361.

[26] See Goddard, Corner, Richardson, *Public Issue Television.*

[27] In discussing *Up the Junction* Ken Loach has described how "we tried to copy [*World in Action's*] techniques and cut with a rough, raw, edgy quality, which enabled us to deal with issues head on." Ken Loach cited in Jamie Sexton, "Televérité Hits Britain: Documentary, Drama and the Growth of 16mm Filmmaking in British Television," *Screen,* 44, no. 4 (2003): 443.

[28] The switch to colour which followed the introduction of 625-line TV sets began on BBC 2 on 1 July 1967 and on BBC 1 and ITV on 15 November 1969, but was not commonly adopted in current affairs until 1970.

[29] See Glen Creeber, *The Television Genre Book* (London: BFI, 2001).

in "The Village that Quit" (tx: 25.1.1971) and "The Luddenden Experiment" (tx: 20.10.1975) where another village gave up meat and "For the Benefit of Mr Parris" (tx: 23.1.1984) where a Conservative MP tried, and failed, to live on £26 unemployment benefit for a week. In the early 1970s *World in Action* expanded into longer specials and dramatisations, often in ITV's Tuesday documentary slot. These include *World in Action* strands such as *Seven Plus Seven* (developed from 1964's *7 Up* charting the hopes and experiences of a group of seven-year-olds drawn from different class backgrounds), the wildlife series *Disappearing World* (1970-93) and various drama documentaries developed by a dedicated unit first established for the making of "The Man Who Wouldn't Keep Quiet" (tx: 24.11.1970) about the trial of Soviet dissident Pyotr Grigorenko.

In the 1970s, "alternative", "counter-cultural" and "oppositional" perspectives and filmmaking practice both influenced and competed with the more traditional "committed" television journalism.[30] *World in Action* and *This Week*'s more probing investigations challenged both presented to entrenched business interests and establishment perspectives on political affairs, and these led to frequent and increasingly aggressive intervention by the ITA/IBA. This occurred over investigations into the tobacco, asbestos and pharmaceutical industries; the effects of the drug Thalidomide; corruption in Westminster up to ministerial level; and reporting from South Africa, Uganda, Vietnam and Northern Ireland.

In some respects the work of Jonathan Dimbleby at *This Week* and John Pilger at *World in Action* exemplified the "oppositional" tradition which particularly rankled with the IBA and elements of the mainstream press. The refusal to accept the definition of problems advanced by mainstream politicians and establishment figures on various topics led to their films being branded as "slanted" or "campaigning". At best this resulted in a voice-over distancing of the programme from the views expressed such as, "Tonight a personal report by the Daily Mirror's special correspondent John Pilger" on "The Quiet Mutiny" (tx: 28.9.1970). This

---

[30] See Philip Schlesinger's definitions of "alternative" and "oppositional" perspectives in relation to images and narratives of terrorism cited in Holland, *The Angry Buzz*, 114. More broadly Kristin Thompson and David Bordwell describe "a cinema of social engagement, addressing itself to concrete social problems and arguing for radical social change" emerging in the 1960s and early 1970s. Kristin Thompson and David Bordwell, *Film History: An Introduction* (London: McGraw-Hill, 1994), 642.

was after numerous changes imposed to the original cut of the film about US soldiers refusing to fight in Vietnam, according to Pilger.[31]

While *World in Action* had developed something of a "left-wing" or "radical" reputation, this is often overstated. Pilger made just three programmes for the series in 1970-71 but "lost confidence in senior Granada personnel, who he felt were conniving in 'inserting lies' into his films in response to ITA pressure."[32] Pilger's work stands out from the body of *World in Action* films as boldly dissenting. "The Quiet Mutiny", his first documentary, opens with rapid-fire intercutting between a cheerful American Forces Vietnam Network DJ calling out the "Dawn Buster" sign-on slogan, "Goooooood morning Vietnam" and depressed-looking soldiers washing amidst the barbed wire of a makeshift 1st Air Cavalry Division fort close to the Cambodian border. Against images of the slum-like, frontline camp where soldiers trudge through mud and are surrounded by a desolate landscape of felled trees, Anne Murray's wistful "Snowbird" plays on the radio with dissonant effect. Pilger's voice-over sets the scene:

> I hadn't been to Vietnam for three years. The war after all is a bore so why go back? What is there left to say? Surely we've seen it all on telly? But our boredom has not made the war go away so I've come back for the final act. No blood, no atrocities just the rejection of the war by those sent here to fight it. Just the quiet mutiny of the greatest army in history.[33]

Pilger's film is strikingly critical—siding openly with the young draftees against the "lifers" who "command from the rear" and the system that has sent them to fight the war:

> They are the eighteen year old drafted kids, the national service men on whom the entire army depends. They are the ones for whom the buck has finally passed from the President and Pentagon and the career men who catch colds in their air-conditioned command posts.[34]

Pilger explains that of 400,000 soldiers in Vietnam only 80,000 fight, and almost all of them are so-called "grunts" the "graduates of an American rebellion" who are "unravelling the very fabric of the army"

---

[31] To author in Q&A at the *Investigative Journalism Goes Global Conference*, University of Westminster, June 13, 2008.
[32] Cited by Goddard, Corner, Richardson, *Public Issue Television,* 130.
[33] John Pilger, dir., "The Quiet Mutiny," in *World in Action* [Television Broadcast] (London: ITV, 2001), first transmission September 28, 1970.
[34] Ibid.

many of whom are "growing their hair, wearing love beads, smoking pot, flourishing the V sign of peace. And some are refusing to fight." Interviews with these young soldiers show at best, low morale: "I don't know why I am shooting these people"; at worst, mutinous attitudes: "The unpopular officers, from what I heard, if they mess with a grunt too much they get shot at." For Pilger, the politics in America has little to do with the war's end and he states bluntly to camera: "The war is ending because the grunt is taking no more bullshit."

It is hard to imagine a current affairs programme today coming anywhere near such an openly critical tone, or as Yarrow points out, of catching the American army so "off-guard".[35] Pilger's cool, sometimes sarcastic defiance and the framing of the episode as an "authored piece" sets it apart from the usual "urgent, heavily narrated" form favoured by *World in Action*.[36] The ITA labelled Pilger's film as a "one-sided viewpoint" and its Director-General Sir Robert Fraser regarded it as "outrageous, left-wing propaganda".[37]

While Pilger was regarded as too opinionated for Granada's tastes, it is also clear why he was drawn to the series in the first place. For Goddard *et al.* the company's reputation for challenging authority and upsetting the status quo "came from the top" and the high morale at the programme was partly attributed to the management board backing *World in Action* "to the hilt" against legal and regulatory attacks. The fact that *World in Action* had the biggest complaint file with IBA was seen as "a compliment" by Sidney Bernstein; and Denis Forman attributed the success of the programme to the determination of management to resist "the moral blackmail through which the British Establishment seeks to smother any story that could cause them embarrassment."[38]

For current affairs producers at ITV the greatest source of conflict with the IBA was Northern Ireland. Many of the programmes made about "the Troubles" in the 1970s were censured, censored or, in two cases, not shown at all. *World in Action's* "South of the Border" (1971) about the effect of "the Troubles" in the Irish Republic was banned unseen and without explanation. Featuring interviews with senior politicians as well as IRA members the IBA eventually defended its decision to ban, without viewing, the programme in terms of the Television Act's prohibition on

---

[35] See Megan Yarrow, "Gimme Some Truth: The Documentary Films of John Pilger," *Screen Education*, 44 (2005).
[36] See John Corner, *Popular Television in Britain: Studies in Cultural History* (London: Macmillan, 1981).
[37] Cited by Goddard, Corner, Richardson, *Public Issue Television*, 195.
[38] Ibid., 151.

broadcasts "likely to lead to disorder".[39] The second, at Thames's *This Week*, was a discussion of an Amnesty International report into torture by Northern Ireland's security services in 1978 which led to black screens after unions refused to transmit the comedy that had been scheduled in its place.[40] The IBA, frustrated by aspects of Peter Taylor's persistent and controversial investigations in Ulster, advised Thames to "lay off Northern Ireland" and to "use another reporter".[41] Many more programmes were to be banned, censored or delayed on both BBC and ITV in the 1980s and 1990s.[42]

This Week

This Week was launched by Associated-Rediffusion in 1956 as ITV's answer to *Panorama*, and was even billed as "A window on the world behind the headlines" shamelessly plagiarising its heavyweight rival's tagline. The series was continued by Thames Television from 1968 when Rediffusion lost the franchise and between 1978 and 1986 was rebranded as *TV Eye* before returning to its original title until its demise in 1992.

By 1970 the counter-culture was making its mark on television and Holland (2006) notes the influence of independent filmmaking on current affairs practice of the time. On issues such as Northern Ireland and South Africa, "alternative" filmmakers rejected the role of the journalist as a "dispassionate observer" as well as the well-established program formats and distant professionalism of television structures, "all of which seemed rooted in establishment values."[43]   Jo Menell's brief stint as *This Week* Producer in 1970 brought current affairs close to the underground culture of the times with marginal and "morally suspect" topics such as group marriage, cannabis and hippie politics in the USA. Similar topics were the focus of *World in Action* from 1967 with programmes on drugs, the American civil rights movement, student militancy and the hippie movement helping to test the contemporary limits of "objectivity".

"Oppositional" perspectives are evident in some of Jonathan Dimbleby's reports at *This Week*. "A Lady Wrote to Me" (tx: 20.1.1977) about "benefit scroungers" in Salford concluded by reminding viewers of the far greater sums of money lost to the state in tax evasion:

---

[39] Ibid., 202–203.
[40] Holland, *The Angry Buzz*.
[41] Liz Curtis, *Ireland: the Propaganda War* (London: Pluto, 1984), 59.
[42] See Liz Curtis, "A catalogue of censorship 1959–1993," in eds. Rolston and Miller, *War and Words*.
[43] Holland, *The Angry Buzz*, 75.

Social security is not a fringe benefit. It was established out of common humanity to protect the deprived. The poor can't fight back. Can't remind us that their scroungers cost the state only 0.16% of the Supplementary Benefit budget. Cannot remind us of the millions they don't claim, theirs by right. Cannot remind us either of another world, a world where money is manipulated, tax evaded and avoided, where expense accounts are indulged on friends and family, but charged to the company. Where there are bosses who pay their workers below the rates set by law. A world where many more millions of pounds are stolen from the state, but a world without rhetoric or slogans or scroungers. No wonder New Year's Eve is bleak in Salford.[44]

Dimbleby's conclusion was judged to be "totally unacceptable" in an IBA review following a complaint from Conservative MP Ian Sproat.

Holland's study of *This Week/TV Eye* reveals how journalists in the 1970s, including Peter Taylor and Jonathan Dimbleby, were given the freedom to pursue their interests and develop their styles. It also emphasises the pivotal role Jeremy Isaacs played, particularly after becoming Director of Programmes in 1974. The dramatically different priorities of the period for commercial television are made clear in Isaacs' instructions to Peter Taylor: "The ratings are not your problem. They're my problem. You must do what you feel you ought to be doing and do it the way you feel you ought to do it."[45] This concern to maintain programme quality and investigative rigour, even at the expense of ratings, was not unique to Thames Television. At Granada and LWT there was a similar attitude to protecting current affairs from ratings pressures that can, at least in part, be attributed to the testing public service obligations imposed by the IBA and the need to win that regulatory body's support for future franchise bids. As Tracey (1983) notes in relation to LWT's *Weekend World's* notoriously low ratings (1% in 1972), praise from the IBA for the programme "was worth many points in the audience ratings" and so "the size of the audience never really mattered."[46]

Weekend World

In fact developments at *Weekend World* signalled an important shift in current affairs coverage during the decade. Tracey argues that the nature of

---

[44] Cited in ibid., 106.
[45] Ibid., 62.
[46] Michael Tracey, *In the Culture of the Eye: Ten Years of Weekend World* (London: Hutchinson, 1983), 51, 52.

some of the issues emerging in the 1970s resisted explanation simply through illustration by example, because the state of domestic and world politics had become more complex and interconnected:

> The sixties had been an age of apparent affluence, the emergence of détente, the further growth of a fascination and concern with the life of the individual expressed in an emphasis on interpersonal relationships, sexual problems, poverty and homelessness as discrete experiences rather than social forms. Current affairs television therefore tended not to address the abstract dimensions to political and social life. Suddenly the landscape was dotted with issues that could not, with any integrity and accuracy, be dealt with only in their human dimension.[47]

These issues included Watergate, the energy crisis, a global recession, the fall of the Heath government and the Yom Kippur War. As Executive Producer of *Weekend World* from 1972, John Birt felt that the key for exploring these crises and making the important connections between events was by giving primacy to the written word. This involved an early focus on a heavily researched and carefully written script around which a film might later be constructed, if required at all. As Tracey notes, this "essay" form relied predominantly on studio presenters and interviews with, at most, some "illustrative" film employing images or heavily prompted testimony to support the spoken script. This inverted the traditional investigative and exploratory mode of making current affairs that had been established at *Panorama, This Week* and *World in Action* in which a detailed script was usually only written after material was filmed and evidence gathered "in the field". *Weekend World's* meticulous attention to pre-filming research and script was rewarded in its coverage of the Watergate Affair in the summer of 1973, in which *Weekend World's* coherent account was thought to have clearly outperformed its rivals.[48]

Concerns about the ability of film or "image-led" documentary programmes to deal with complex issues were publicly expressed by John Birt and *Weekend World* presenter Peter Jay in a series of influential articles in *The Times* in 1975 attacking current affairs' "bias against understanding" and failure, in their view, to look beyond symptoms to the wider and more complex causes of particular events. Birt and Jay's thesis was an influential one and was eventually put into practice, first at *Weekend World*—denounced by some politicians as a platform for Peter

---

[47] Ibid., 68.
[48] Ibid., 67.

Jay's neo-liberal economic views—and later at the BBC as a "mission to explain". This led to an overhaul of production practices, a suspicion of more radical analysis, or what Jay dismissed as "bleeding heart journalism",[49] and a certain disengagement or distance at the investigative level. From the middle of the decade, particularly after the reversion to tax on revenue rather than profits, there was also evidence of current affairs on ITV being affected by "creeping commercialisation": a tendency which was to become more marked in the 1980s and which accelerated dramatically in the 1990s and beyond.

This Week was an early casualty of these market forces when Thames came under a new managing director Bryan Cowgill in 1977 who puts greater stress on entertainment and "building the audience". *This Week* was relaunched as *TV Eye* in a move supported by the new Head of Current Affairs, Peter Pagnamenta, against the wishes of former Editor David Elstein. This name change signalled a different organisational style and approach to its audience. The new Editor Mike Townson, poached by Pagnamenta from the BBC, shifted the emphasis away from long-running, slowly developing investigations to more immediate concerns of the moment and human interest stories. Alongside this Townson made a conscious move to avoid the politicised context that caused so much trouble for *This Week*. The new direction taken by *TV Eye* was received with dismay by many of the existing team.

While *This Week* returned nearly a decade later under Roger Bolton to cause further government outrage with "Death on the Rock" (tx: 28.4.1988), in retrospect it is clear that *TV Eye* marked the beginning of the end for the so-called "golden age" of current affairs. The particular conjunction of institutional, economic and political circumstances that marked out the first seven years of the decade could not be repeated and British current affairs would never be simultaneously quite as bold, innovative, challenging and popular as it had been, at its best, in the 1970s.

Conclusion

There is a body of current affairs programmes produced in the 1970s that allows us to view the decade in its rapidly changing complexity and gain some insight into its transitional and sometimes violent character. These programmes could probe behind sensational headlines, investigate social ills, explore complex foreign and domestic affairs and, on occasion, question, defy or embarrass elite power and entrenched interests.

---

[49] Cited in Tracey, *In the Culture of the Eye: Ten Years of Weekend World*, 64.

However, there were limits to this challenge, as seen in the handling of John Pilger's brief work at *World in Action*, or Roger Bolton's editorship of *Panorama*. Television in the 1970s, as Curran observes, had a Janus-faced relationship to the liberal-corporatist system of power: "progressive in supporting a modestly redistributive social system, but conservative in that it tended to exclude radical voices outside corporatist networks of influence."[50]

Nevertheless, with a degree of protection from ratings and other commercial pressures, programme makers could rework current affairs conventions and push at the restrictive boundaries of a highly regulated and heavily monitored broadcasting industry to produce challenging and innovative work that gave some voice to dissenting opinion. This occurred less often at a post Hugh-Greene BBC, with self-policing mechanisms usually preventing more controversial material from being aired, but more often at ITV where Thames and especially Granada actively encouraged "testing the limits" for a time at *This Week* and *World in Action*. LWT's *Weekend World* saw the emergence of a different, less socially engaged tradition which privileged analysis, elite opinion and the centrally-controlled crafting of an explanatory script, often around post-Keynesian, neo-liberal assumptions. This tradition would grow in importance, especially for BBC current affairs in the 1980s under John Birt's control.[51] Commercial pressures would also begin to blunt the edge of current affairs on ITV as the decade progressed, especially at *This Week/TV Eye* under Thames Television's new management.

Despite these setbacks, the 1970s are likely to be remembered as something of a high point for British current affairs. It was a decade when highly constraining, not to say misleading, notions of "balance" and "objectivity" were challenged, despite persistent and often unreasonable opposition from broadcasting regulators. This challenge came in its sharpest form from producers and journalists confronting vested interest in their reporting of crises, conflicts and injustice. More importantly, this challenge was only possible with the assertive support of television producers and executives who did not readily compromise when it came to commissioning and defending well-researched and incisive factual programmes and investigative reports that were inconvenient or threatening to the established order. It is these programme makers that we remember and their body of work is evidence of a hard-won "golden era".

---

[50] James Curran, *Media and Power* (London: Routledge, 2002), 49.
[51] See Lindley *Panorama: Fifty Years of Pride and Paranoia*; Georgina Born, *Uncertain Vision: Birt, Dyke and the Reinvention of the BBC* (London: Vintage, 2004).

PRINTING LIBERATION:
THE WOMEN'S MOVEMENT
AND MAGAZINES IN THE 1970S

LAUREL FORSTER

The interventions of magazines into their surrounding cultures are both intriguing and elusive. Recent print culture studies have raised significant questions about the position a magazine holds in its circle, about the influence a periodical may have over its readership, and about the range of potential meanings of a magazine.[1] My essay discusses the relationship of an emergent and radical movement in Britain in the 1970s, the Women's Liberation Movement (WLM), with its surrounding print culture. In looking at the way in which women's magazines responded to the feminism of the decade, I want to raise questions about the ways in which events, ideas, and convictions of a newly-empowered movement, sometimes making national news via small pockets of activism but mostly involving a minority of women, were mediated through wide-circulation magazines so that they might be nationally understood by a much wider audience. The three magazines of particular interest here, *Spare Rib*, *Cosmopolitan* and *Woman's Own* offer a range of perspectives between counter-cultural, politicised argument and indulgence in the "cult of femininity". However, all three also, at some level, engage with the momentum of women's liberation in Britain in the early 1970s.

As the late 1960s gave way to the early 1970s, so concepts of youth, music and free love were replaced with anxieties, especially for women, surrounding work, home and identity. The WLM emerged as a complex set of challenges to the political establishment. It both demanded that society and institutions at large think about the role and rights of women; and concomitantly it challenged women to individually and collectively

---

[1] See Ann Ardis, "Staging the Public Sphere: Magazine Dialogism and the Prosthetics of Authorship at the Turn of the Twentieth Century," in *Transatlantic Print Culture 1880-1940: Emerging Media, Emerging Modernisms*, eds. Ann Ardis and Patrick Collier, 31 (Basingstoke: Palgrave Macmillan, 2008).

reflect upon, and become articulate about, their own lives. What emerged through both avenues were groups of women motivated by very diverse interests: some academics were debating arising and existing issues, some women were seeking their first access to further education. Some working women were demanding equality at work, some housewives were envisaging changes to their domestic setup; some women were hoping for improved legal status in their personal circumstances, whilst others were demanding better conditions for all. The 1970s in Britain was a decade where a range of social and cultural circumstances were being challenged and through a variety of means, including the written word, there was a sense of impending change.

Feminist momentum of this period can be partially understood as building on a number of counter-cultural, radical and already existing movements. It had origins in student and women's socialist groups as well as ongoing and sometimes uneasy relationships with hippie movements and alternative cultures, trade unions and academics. Some women continued campaigns which had started as early as the 1950s, for equal pay, state nurseries, proper obstetrics care for working-class women, and support for one-parent families.[2] Others took up new challenges to the establishment. Any actual summarising of feminist expression in the 1970s is a difficult task. Sheila Rowbotham describes early 1970s feminism as having a strong Utopian impulse, where women's self-expression and creativity "sprang from a desire for personal transformation which went deeper than any ideology."[3] However, some early guiding principles were set at an early women's conference held at Ruskin College, Oxford in February 1970, where a heady mixture of women, feminist consciousness and desire for political activism resulted in the official founding of the WLM, now known as second-wave feminism.[4] At this conference four "demands" were formulated concerning equal pay; improved education; twenty-four hour nurseries; free contraception; and abortion on demand. These demands acted as a blueprint for much feminist action and intent, particularly on a local level,[5] within an umbrella

---

[2] Elizabeth Wilson, *Only Halfway to Paradise: Women in Postwar Britian, 1945-1968* (London: Tavistock Publications, 1980), 180–84.
[3] Sheila Rowbotham, *A Century of Women: The History of Women in Britain and the United States* (London: Penguin, 1999), 398.
[4] Michelene Wandor, *Once a Feminist: Stories of a Generation* (London: Virago, 1990), 1–5.
[5] Sheila Rowbotham, "The Beginnings of Women's Liberation in Britain," in *The Body Politic: Women's Liberation in Britain, 1969-72*, ed. Michelene Wandor, 23 (London: Stage 1, 1972).

of a national declaration. The desire for change became evident in diverse ways, for example: media-savvy organised feminist activism through protest marches, sit-ins and the disruption to the Miss World contest of 1970; individual consciousness-raising through local groups often held in women's homes; and local community and household changes such as nurseries and childcare to enable women to do more with their lives. Thus feminism in the early 1970s both looked back to previous decades, often regenerating socialism,[6] and moved forwards with current concerns.

Feminist ideas in print had a number of earlier sources too. Resistant writing of the early twentieth century "first-wave" feminists is evident in tracts, speeches, literary works, and many specialist magazines such as *The Suffragette*.[7] Early second-wave texts such as *The Second Sex* by de Beauvoir (trans. 1953) and *The Feminine Mystique* by Freidan (1963) had considerable impact. Women novelists of the sixties were calling conventionality into question,[8] and some magazines such as *Honey* (1960-1986) and *Nova* (1965-1975) were breaking the mould of women's magazines. Discussion of the situation of the housewife and married woman in the *Observer* and *Guardian* newspapers was prompted by the National Housewives Register (1962).[9] And whilst these broadsheets encouraged debate and engaged with feminist issues, other newspapers ridiculed feminists as one-dimensional angry women, humourless and man-hating. Some feminist writers emerged from the sub- and counter-cultural magazine scene (such as *Black Dwarf*, *Frendz* and *Oz*) so had a background of suggesting alternative cultural formations. They moved towards feminism after experiencing blatant sexism in the underground presses.[10] One commentator even suggested that "What finally knackered the underground was its complete inability to deal with women's liberation."[11]

Providing at least one point of opposition for feminist writings of the early 1970s were mainstream magazines for women. Described as "trade papers" or domestic "handbooks," these are advice manuals for the

---

[6] Wilson, *Only Halfway to Paradise*, 196.
[7] Barbara Green has helpfully discussed how suffrage periodicals were linked to the complexities of modernity in Barbara Green, "Feminist Things," in Ardis and Collier, eds., *Transatlantic Print Culture 1880-1940*, 66–82.
[8] Wilson, *Only Halfway to Paradise*, 154–61.
[9] Ibid., 183.
[10] Dominic Sandbrook, *White Heat: A History of Britain in the Swinging Sixties* (London: Little, Brown, 2006), 663.
[11] David Widgery, "What Went Wrong?," *Oz*, 1973, cited in Dave Haslam, *Not Abba: The Real Story of the 1970s* (London: Fourth Estate, 2005), 66–67.

housewife.[12] Conventional femininity was presented in this important sector of the women's press as a totalising version of womanhood, where interests, sexuality and creativity are confined to home, family, and the production of one's personal appearance. For feminists, this monolithic magazine-driven notion of womanhood as a solely domestic entity was seen both as an inadequate proposition for half the human race and a sinister and ubiquitous cover-up of women's inferior social and legal status.

Feminist print media of the 1970s then, had a variety of antecedents, and as more formalised feminism emerged in the 1970s, so a specific print culture accompanied that developing movement. A close relationship between magazines and their readership is apparent in the array of newsletters and small magazines emanating from early activist and consciousness-raising groups. It is estimated there were about seventy such groups by 1969.[13] Many of them produced a regular newsletter, transcribing their feminism into print, revealing the potential of a printed response to a movement. These publications ranged in format from broadsheet newspapers to mini-magazines of little more than a few sheets, with a mixture of type and handwriting, reproduced and assembled at minimal cost in a very home-made way. However, the content of these newsletters, some quite hard-hitting in their debates, others containing much personal testimony, provides a fascinating insight into the development of a movement. The deliberate combination of political debate, personal stories, humour, sardonic commentary, amateur illustrations, local contacts and information, bears witness to the complexities of women's lives, the diverse interests of the readership group, and the grass-roots attempts to improve women's levels of consciousness about their own situations and feminist ideals. At such a local level the relationship between women's liberation and print media is immediate. In these newsletters, women interested in liberation are talking to each other, sometimes in a straightforward way using everyday language and an informative tone when sharing information about a group or a meeting or local work for the cause, and sometimes in an ironic or creative way through poetry, fiction or illustration about deeply-felt issues and concerns. For these self-published, home-produced small feminist magazines could respond to members' concerns and/or national issues as they chose, as well as provide an outlet for personal expression.

---

[12] Cynthia White, *Women's Magazines 1693-1968* (London: Michael Joseph, 1970), 298; Ros Ballaster and others, *Women's Worlds: Ideology, Femininity and the Woman's Magazine* (Basingstoke: Macmillan, 1991), 145.
[13] Sandbrook, *White Heat*, 663.

In addition to individual group newsletters created by and for small groups, some feminist magazines were produced for a slightly wider audience. *Shrew*, for instance, was initially published collectively across five women's liberation groups in Greater London, on a rotating basis, as the journal of the Women's Liberation Workshop. *Red Rag: a magazine of women's liberation* was produced by a Marxist collective. The sharp political content of such magazines reveals socialist /feminist sources as well as a palpable commitment to the women's liberation movement and the raising of women's feminist consciousness. These early feminist magazines were not standardised; indeed individual groups had to produce consecutive issues of *Shrew*. However, they did start to borrow from at least the format if not the content of more mainstream women's magazines. These new publications blended counter-cultural alternative production ideas with some aspects of regular women's magazine format, whilst maintaining strong allegiances to a range of egalitarian political notions, and providing an opportunity for women to talk about their lives. For instance one article discusses a woman's journey to a liberated consciousness, taking her reader through her two pregnancies and post-natal depression, her membership of the Tufnell park group, her sense of isolation from her friends, and her growing political consciousness:

> Where I am is nowhere. I'm not living a radical life and there are no socialist solutions in Britain for my problems. What has also been brought home is that W.L. as it exists now offers few solutions. [...] Somehow we've got to do something about our lives ... make possible some sort of change in the fucked up way we, as well as everyone else, are forced to live under capitalism.[14]

She goes on to talk about the prospect of collective childcare brought up in the last group meeting. This outpouring, which looks as though it is typed on a home typewriter, with inconsistent spacing and unevenness of ink quality, has the authenticity of personal testimony. It presents an abridged life story, and reflects upon it politically, taking into account the interventions of female friendships and the writer's local women's liberation group. Herein lies its power: not just in outlining a life of home and children, but in striving to make sense of this life in terms of women's liberation and seeking change, this article surely spoke to many.

The early 1970s was a moment when the traditional magazine-led "cult of femininity" was under threat, as women were publicly permitted to be

---

[14] Susan Cowley, "Rambling Notes," *Shrew*, May 1990, n. p.

tired of such instruction. Unsurprisingly, in 1972, early on in the second wave feminist movement, when different interpretations of feminism could exist side by side, when the official feminist demands were still in mind, and before divisions and factions became too prominent, two important magazines were launched for women: *Cosmopolitan* in March and *Spare Rib* in July. In their different ways, both publications brought something new to the world of women's magazines in Britain, and potential revolution to women's lives: *Cosmopolitan* with its emphasis on the sexual revolution for women; and *Spare Rib* with a mission to persuade women to feminism. The third magazine of interest here, *Woman's Own*, was forty years old in 1972. It had been innovative in style and format at the time of its launch in 1932, and continued to approach women from the domestic front but nonetheless responded to the 1970s with an interest in the feminist developments of the decade, albeit from a mainstream point of view.

When Rosie Boycott, one of the initial editors of *Spare Rib*, called a meeting of other women currently working on the underground presses to put forward the idea of a woman's magazine, she was conscious she was suggesting a cross-over product from the underground to regular publishing and national distribution.[15] A problem for *Spare Rib* was to secure the relationship of a movement, based in consciousness-raising and activism, to print media. Its editors wanted to reflect emergent ideas—from discussions in conference situations, in small local groups, and in media representations—through the printed word and format requirements of a magazine. Members of the WLM were initially suspicious,[16] and the opening editorial demonstrated awareness of the difficulty in bringing a political movement to bear in the printed form:

> We are not attempting the impossible. To try to explain Women's Liberation in one quick, easy lesson would be both ludicrous and wrong. Its basis is small group meetings and a magazine cannot achieve that necessary communication. What we can do is reflect the questions, ideas and hope that is growing out of our awareness of ourselves, not as a "bunch of women" but as individuals in our own right.[17]

The desire to communicate women's liberation is clearly stated, but equally understood is that by transforming the format of communication

---

[15] Rosie Boycott, *Sex, Shopping and Sisterhood: Politics in Women's Magazine*. Lecture given at The Women's Library, London, April 30, 2009.
[16] Janice Winship, *Inside Women's Magazines* (London and New York: Pandora, 1987), 132.
[17] *Spare Rib*, July 1972.

from small group meetings to a national magazine some sense of the personal is lost.

The sense of excitement surrounding this new development in publishing for women can be explained by the energised combination of written input from editors and contributors from the underground presses.[18] What contributed to its success was a sense of building on the work of earlier smaller-scale feminist magazines, and an astute editorial team who understood the popular appeal of more conventional print media forms, such as women's domestic magazines and newspapers.

Spare Rib is well-remembered for its explicit intention of educating women away from a narrow domestic servitude. The opening few issues indicate the breadth of engagement with serious, often taboo subjects concerning women: women's bodies, prostitution, trade unions, drugs and childcare are all tackled in the early issues. Romantic novels, marriage, the fashion industry and advertising are all critiqued from a feminist, socialist or counter-cultural angle. The range of issues soon extended to include discussions of women's sexuality, marginalised groups of women, and the family. Yet such a summary only partially explains the magazine, as every issue had a host of regular features, just like other women's magazines, and it is in these where we start to see cross-over between *Spare Rib* and more mainstream magazines. So that beauty, cookery, short stories and even knitting patterns formed regular aspects of *Spare Rib*, as did reviews of films and books. One intriguing article called "Munchy Business" borrows a standard Summer feature on picnics from the world of women's magazines.[19] The tone is alternative, as are the psychedelic photographs, harking back to 1960s counter-cultural phenomena such as health foods, the return to the rural, the rock scene and hippy (drug) culture, but the recipes for "Doreen's Kipper Paté" (sic) and "Hill House Oat Crunchies" echo women's domestic work. Like other articles, this spans multiple ideologies, and offers a not-too-strident, inclusive feminism which tries to make all women feel that this would be desirable and moreover, achievable. By combining the daily round with broader movements, a more accessible face of feminism is offered than in other more challenging articles.

Spare Rib also echoes a different mainstream print media through its regular "News" pages, in a pastel colour occupying the middle section of the magazine. These contain a variety of articles in subject and length, arranged in newspaper jigsaw style, which provide reportage on feminist

---

[18] Marsha Rowe, ed., *Spare Rib Reader* (Harmondsworth: Penguin, 1982), 13–17.

[19] Fran Fogarty, "Munchy Business," *Spare Rib*, Sept 1972, 31–33. Photographs by Sue Wilkes.

activism, liberation groups, and mainstream news items of interest to
women from home and abroad. An article "The First Cow on Chiswick
High Road" covers direct action by one group: their supermarket survey
following decimalisation; a march (led by a cow) after the notorious
School Milk Bill; and the setting up of a centre to house destitute
women.[20] This does work for women's liberation in a number of ways: it
keeps the national readership of *Spare Rib* very much in touch with local
activism; it brings items of national interest to the attention of readers,
helping them to make the links between the cause of feminism and the
wider world; and it offers a feminist spin to general news items. In many
ways these "News" sections of *Spare Rib* help to keep women's liberation
of the 1970s grounded in the wider world.

Furthermore, humour provides perspective manifestly and latently
through the much-enjoyed regular "Spare Parts" DIY column enabling
women to make home improvements with shelving (July 72), or learning
how to change fuses (October 72). There is much to be said about these
articles in the way they offer empowerment through self-sufficiency to
women regarding gender-stereotyped chores (especially tasks like
mending a toilet) around the home. Cleverly and knowingly, by
demystifying masculinised domestic tasks, these articles challenge the
status quo and reflect wider debates about domesticity, gender roles and
work. At the very least they help to facilitate alignment with the debates
and activism of more strident feminists.

The variation in tone added to the appeal of *Spare Rib*. Overtly
political articles were written with the authority of professional journalists
or academics; cross-over articles appealed to those women still committed
to some form of domestic femininity; news sections maintained grass-
roots connections; and other content was written and illustrated with a
combination of experimentation and "can-do" attitude, often with a good
dose of humour.

Rather than assuming an already feminist readership (such as of the
official WLM paper *Wires*), with an understanding of the politics of that
choice,[21] I suggest that *Spare Rib* felt the need to persuade women to the
cause and so used an appealing combination of varied layout, tone and
types of feminism to that end. It did this in various ways: materially by
melding the print media forms of political pamphlet, local newsletter,
newspaper and women's glossy; and intellectually through history, current
news, women's debates and issues. *Spare Rib* tried to reflect women's

---

[20] Caroline Charlton, "The First Cow on Chiswick High Road," *Spare Rib*, July
1972, 24–25.
[21] Winship, *Inside Women's Magazines*, 129.

lives in a much fuller sense than previously in regular women's magazines, offering feminist perspectives on ordinary aspects of the magazine format, even advertising. Through this diversity, *Spare Rib* successfully managed to negotiate the dilemma of wanting on the one hand separateness and on the other hand, access to the mainstream.

A different response to the feminism of the decade can be seen in *Cosmopolitan*, which aimed for both glossiness and a mainstream audience of young, sexually liberated females. This was an import of an American magazine that had been in existence since the 1920s in various incarnations as a family and then a woman's domestic magazine. Helen Gurley Brown, author of the revolutionary *Sex and the Single Girl* (1962) took over the US editorship in 1965 and changed the direction of the magazine. The much-heralded British launch ensured that the first edition of 300,000 sold out in a single day. The front cover of the first issue directs the tone: the provocative, décolleté model in an alluring red dress and the sub titles about lovers, sex and scandal invite us to enter the world of this new magazine.

The readership for *Cosmopolitan* in the U.K. was outlined in the first editorial by Joyce Hopkirk:

> you just have to think about yourself. You are that *Cosmopolitan* girl, aren't you? You're very interested in men, naturally, but you think too much of yourself to live your life entirely through *him*. That means you're going to make the most of yourself—your body, your face, your clothes, your hair, your job and your mind. How can you fail to be more interesting than that?[22]

The priorities of the magazine can be distilled from this list, but this is not a female version of *Playboy* as the editorial continues: "*Playboy* preaches a doctrine in which all their men are fantastic looking, rich, exciting and successful. I don't think *you* are so sure of yourself." A remark quite at odds, perhaps with the way the reader of *Cosmopolitan* in the 1970s is imagined. The sexual confidence of the 1970s cosmo-girl could be acquired, of course, through guidance from the magazine.

Cosmopolitan then, was a magazine borne out of a movement prior to second wave feminism: the sexual revolution of the 1960s. With accusations of recycling from its American counterpart, British *Cosmopolitan* focussed on sex and the female self. However this was not without contradictions: for every article which emphasises sexual freedom, there is another which focusses on marriage such as "How to Catch and

---

[22] Joyce Hopkirk, "Our Cosmo World," *Cosmopolitan*, March 1972, 10.

Keep a Lord".[23] Even those articles which on the surface seem to be celebrating sexual freedom are not all they seem: "I was a Sleep-Around Girl" is really a tender personal testimonial to the loneliness of mediocre relationships.[24] Articles with provocative titles such as "Why Men Like Sluts" is a strange plea for women to be less glamorous, less like *Cosmopolitan* cover girls perhaps?[25] Mundane regulars, the general stuff of women's magazines, are even given a sexual spin: travel articles become "A Lover's Guide to Paris" and "Sexy Cities."[26] Consequently *Cosmopolitan* echoes other women's magazines, but filters its content through a sexual template.

Yet despite this strong basis in the sexual revolution, *Cosmopolitan* does engage with feminism in some quite specific ways. When *Cosmopolitan* hit the shelves in 1972, it benefited from the combined impetus of the sexual revolution and second-wave feminism. Feminist demands for free contraception, abortion on demand, and improved education, led to much feminist discussion about contraception, sexuality and the body and sought to highlight women's enjoyment of sexual intercourse without the threat of unwanted pregnancy. Many articles in *Cosmopolitan* overlap with this discussion and so could be argued, at some level, to be involved with the demands of the WLM. Furthermore, the editors of *Cosmopolitan* understood that underlying sexual liberation was a need for improved education, often belying a level of ignorance or uncertainty in women about their bodies and their sexuality. So sexual freedom, enjoyment, and health became one of the significant traits within feminism, and this particular set of ideas also formed the underlying idea behind the new *Cosmopolitan*.

Cosmopolitan at this time carried a range of articles on contraception. One quite long article entitled "Why the Abortion Law Doesn't Work" quotes a number of well-known actresses such as Shirley Ann Field and Glenda Jackson who either have had abortions or who had strong views on the subject, and then goes on to discuss the difficulties faced by women

---

[23] Lucy Mockler, "How to Catch and Keep a Lord," *Cosmopolitan*, November 1972, 63.
[24] Bill Manville, "I was a Sleep-Around Girl," *Cosmopolitan*, March 1972, 72–75, 104, 108.
[25] Meg Rowland-Williams, "Talkabout: Why Men Like Sluts," *Cosmopolitan*, May 1972, 50, 52.
[26] Willa Beattie, "Travel Bug: A Lover's Guide to Paris," *Cosmopolitan*, April 1972, 23; Hazel Meyrick, "Travel Bug: Sexy Cities," *Cosmopolitan*, May 1972, 23.

who have to endure opposition from their Gps and the NHS system.[27] A range of factors, such as the increased costs for late terminations, pregnancy testing as well as the personal price girls will pay, are all discussed in an informative and balanced way. And although *Cosmopolitan* is a magazine full of contradictory messages about love, sex and marriage, with a confused and sometimes openly hostile regard for "women's lib ladies,"[28] this particular article, and others like it, are informative, even educational, and unafraid to tackle a sensitive subject in a way worthy of the cause of women's liberation!

Spare Rib, and to some extent *Cosmopolitan*, then, were tentatively demonstrating how the printed form of the woman's magazine could respond to a movement, reflecting in print a mood of enquiry and information dissemination, intentionally re-establishing women's participation in the wider world. A complete study of how the dominant form of women's magazines—the domestic "trade journal"—responded to this new mode of representing women's liberation in print is beyond the scope of this essay. However, there are interesting observations to be made about some articles in *Woman's Own*, a woman's magazine originating from a quite different set of ideas, and a different era in women's history.

Woman's Own was launched in 1932 and marked a significant departure in British women's weekly magazines as it focussed on housewifery as a profession, a "service", and defined its target readership as "the up-to-date wife and wife-to-be".[29] Because of its innovative stance in approaching domesticity pseudo-scientifically, its classless tone and its reflection of economic changes, it started a new genre with a format later emulated by rival magazines.[30] It is a mainstream magazine, targeted at youngish married women, who have not lost touch with the outside world, but are also heavily involved in the domestic. Discussing *Woman's Own*, Winship argues that by the mid-1970s, the magazine "emerged with vigour to voice ideas about women's secondary place" describing how it "trod a careful line, encouraging women to take on a world beyond home

---

[27] Alice Lynn Booth and Romany Bain, "Why the Abortion Law Doesn't Work," *Cosmopolitan*, May 1972, 31–33, 118–20.

[28] Hopkirk, "Our Cosmo World," 10.

[29] Jill Greenfield and Chris Reid, *Women's Magazines and the Commercial Orchestration of Femininity in the 1930's: Evidence from Woman's Own.* Discussion Paper (Portsmouth: University of Portsmouth, Department of Economics, 1996), 5.

[30] Ibid., 5–7.

and hearth, but without undermining their commitment to marriage and family."[31]

Woman's Own is interesting to the present study insomuch as it simultaneously represents the mainstream and attempts to engage with social changes. Alongside well-worn women's magazine fodder, in the 1970s it started to produce material which, although not explicitly feminist, was representative of a broader range of issues for women. For instance, there was recognition of the imperfections of women's lives in "Can this Marriage be Saved?"[32] There was also a GP's discussion of depression in women.[33] There was increasing reference to women's life outside the home and in the world of work. In 1972 an article entitled "Your First Job" advises how to secure that first post, including (quite predictably) what to wear and how to do your make-up, but also extending to writing the application letter, preparing for interview questions, filling out a form and advice on general behaviour.[34] A collage of type-set and hand-written text, photographs and inserts, this perhaps has a double agenda: to make the idea of work seem possible and to appeal to a younger audience. The model illustrating a suitable interview outfit is very young looking, and the sample interviews are mostly with young women who have secured various junior posts in what remain fairly conventional careers for women. In other contexts work is acknowledged through recipes and food advertisements which purport to save time, and specifically through the magazine's "Working Woman's Cookbook", which is heralded with the question "How can you cope with cooking as well as a full-time job?"[35] Whilst all of these articles reflect the greater proportion of women in paid work during the 1970s, they offer authoritative advice regarding ways of coping with change rather than the intimacy of a direct call to radical action.

However, there were features in *Woman's Own* which did point to successful outcomes of women's action. Interestingly for a magazine with national circulation, some articles were particularly focussed on local issues. One such discusses how housewives in Sunderland, with no social life to speak of, converted the local working-man's club on a council

---

[31] Winship, *Inside Women's Magazines*, 83.

[32] Wendy Greengross, "Can this marriage be saved?," *Woman's Own*, May 11, 1974, 35–39, 41.

[33] Roderick Wimpole, "The Revolution in my Waiting Room," *Woman's Own*, July 8, 1972, 30–31.

[34] "Your First Job," *Woman's Own*, July 8, 1972, 24–27.

[35] "Next Week," *Woman's Own*, April 5, 1975, 27.

estate into a social club for all.[36] The author acknowledges that the housewives "were pretty downtrodden", but that "Now all that has completely changed, and it is entirely owing to the women themselves." The messages of self-empowerment and even activism are strong in these articles. There is acknowledgement that the lot of a housewife and mother can be grim and there is admiration for those women who have effected change. Here then, *Woman's Own* offers a more pragmatic variety of feminism, urging women to take responsibility for their own social milieu and to collectively improve their lot.

Articles in this magazine in the 1970s also looked outward to the wider world too. Jane Reed, editor of *Woman's Own* for much of the decade, argued that although they had to wrap topics up in familiar ways such as "mince and knitting", by the end of the 1970s they had covered all manner of women-centred and contentious issues ranging from women in work (a result of one of their many surveys) to rape, incest and paedophilia.[37] Women's Liberation may not be manifest, but politics of the family and domestic sphere as well as broader issues akin to activism and women's rights appear latently. In a number of ways we can see this mainstream magazine wanting to retain its market share and target readership and also wanting in some way to acknowledge the changes to women's lives in evidence in this decade.

The collective work of the WLM did much to bring the oppressive nature of consumer-driven domestically-bound femininity to public attention, and as we have seen magazines shifted from a totalising focus on domesticity to accommodate some sense of the changing landscape for women. Any quantitative measurement of the support for women's liberation is impossible, but it would be fair to conclude that magazines were no longer able to polarise women into feminists or traditional homemakers. This was a complex decade when a woman's magazine-led interests may very well have extended from recession-driven make-do-and-mend home crafts to Marxist-feminist debates about wages for housework. I suggest a conundrum appeared for women's magazines in Britain at this time. Feminist magazines had to reflect WLM activism and debates, but retain a sufficiently broad readership. And mainstream magazines needed to demonstrate contemporariness with feminism, yet not lose the mainstay of their publication direction.

---

[36] Max Caulfield, "A Night Out in the North," January 31, 1970, 10–13, 16–17.
[37] Jane Reed, *Sex, Shopping and Sisterhood: Politics in Women's Magazine*. Lecture given at The Women's Library, London, April 30, 2009.

However, to draw any conclusions about the relationship between print media forms of the 1970s and the central tenets, belief systems and activism of the WLM, we must consider the proximity or distance between two different types of political engagement: activism and the written word. I have looked at this relationship in two ways: firstly how activism of the WLM related to and had an impact on print culture; and secondly how mainstream, commercial women's magazines responded, or "talked back" to the WLM. Understanding the relationship of women's liberation in the early 1970s (a movement based in activism and small local groups) to a national magazine readership (with a much wider less politically motivated audience) can only help us to further understand a national sense of female liberation in that decade.

RACE ON THE TELEVISION:
THE WRITING OF JOHNNY SPEIGHT IN THE 1970S

GAVIN SCHAFFER

Johnny Speight began writing comedy for radio and television in 1955, and became famous as the screen writer of the Arthur Haynes show, which was broadcast on ATV between 1957 and 1966.[1] He is now best remembered as the writer and creator of *Till Death Us Do Part*, one of Britain's best-loved but most controversial situation comedies. *Till Death* was first broadcast on the BBC between 1965 and 1968, reappearing for a further three series between 1972 and 1975. The comedy centred around a working class London family, the Garnetts, specifically on the father of the house, Alf, played by Warren Mitchell. Speight wrote two feature films based on the show, and resurrected Alf again in an unsuccessful 1981 ITV spin off and another successful BBC series, *In Sickness and in Health* (1985, 1992).[2] This chapter will consider *Till Death* alongside two of Speight's other creations, the 1969 situation comedy *Curry and Chips* and the television play *If There Weren't Any Blacks You'd Have to Invent Them*, which was broadcast on British television by LWT in 1968. Working in the 1960s and 1970s, Speight was in many ways marking out a new terrain in British comedy writing. Writing his scripts for *Till Death* and *Curry and Chips* in working-class dialect, Speight consciously attempted to focus television comedy onto ordinary British people, "the dockers and neighbours around 111, Dale Road, Canning Town, where he

---

[1] See Johnny Speight, *For Richer, For Poorer: A Kind of Autobiography* (London: BBC, 1991), 125–34.
[2] See *Till Death Us Do Part* [Television Series] (London: Associated London Films, 1969) and Bob Kellett, dir., *The Alf Garnett Saga* [Motion Picture] (Columbia Pictures, 1972). The 1981 spin off *Till Death...* was produced by ATV and saw Alf move to Eastbourne. See *Till Death...*[Television Series] (London: Associated Television ATV, 1981).

lived as a child."[3] More broadly, Speight was determined to portray working-class attitudes and thinking in his comedy writing, specifically regarding the issue of black and Asian immigration to Britain.

In this period, broadcasters were still unsure about how to present immigrants and address the issue of racial conflict in British society. These issues had been thrust into the media spotlight in the wake of accelerated post-war Commonwealth immigration to Britain after the arrival of the Empire Windrush in 1948.[4] The arrival of greater numbers of black and Asian people (mainly from the Caribbean, India and Pakistan) had been controversial and was often perceived as unwelcome, especially in the wake of rioting in Notting Hill and Nottingham in 1958.[5] In an attempt to play a role in easing racial tensions, Hugh Greene, Director General of the BBC, hosted two conferences in 1965. One focused on immigrants from the Caribbean, the other on immigrants from India and Pakistan, in order to consider the role of broadcasters in the presentation of Commonwealth immigrants on British television and to discuss whether specific programmes should be made to help the integration of the immigrant population.[6] At the second of these conferences, to which the BBC invited representatives of Caribbean immigrants to discuss these issues, delegates urged Greene to ensure a natural infusion of blackness into British television. One delegate commented in this context: "I have often thought that one way in which the BBC could help the situation to a very great extent would be to use more and more West Indian or African or any other people on their programmes simply as people in their own right."[7] The idea here was that blackness on the British screen would educate the nation on race relations and undermine hostility, which was rooted in ignorance. R. E. K. Phillips, Chief Welfare Officer of the Jamaican High Commission told Greene at the conference:

---

[3] *News of the World*, January 15, 1967.

[4] Fryer rightly reminds us that Black immigration by no means began in this period. See Peter Fryer, *Staying Power: The History of Black People in Britain* (London: Pluto, 1984).

[5] See Edward Pilkington, "The West Indian Community and the Notting Hill Riots of 1958," in *Racial Violence in Britain in the Nineteenth and Twentieth Centuries,* ed. Panikos Panayi, 171–84 (London, New York: Leicester University Press, 1993) and John Solomos, *Race and Racism in Britain* (Basingstoke: Palgrave, 1989), 51–54.

[6] See BBC Written Archive Centre (WAC), Caversham Park, Reading, File R31/105/3 for details of these conferences.

[7] WAC, Comments of Mrs. P. Crabbe, "Second Conference on Immigrants," File R78/1/816/1, July 13, 1965.

It is not going to be so much a matter of…radio or television education for
the West Indian as it is, perhaps, education of the British public into
acceptance, into recognizing that the differences which they might claim
on the basis of stereotype do not really exist.[8]

While Greene may have accepted this strategy it is clear that the
presentation of racial conflict on British screens was to be a more complex
matter. Other speakers at Greene's conferences on immigrants told the
BBC that it would be misguided, even dangerous, to lecture the public
about what their attitude should be towards black newcomers. Philip
Mason, Director of the Institute of Race Relations, argued in this context:
"There is great danger in having too much of a message, because people
see through it so very quickly."[9] The BBC and the ITA, an independent
broadcasting company also represented at the conference, seem to have
heeded this advice and beaten out something of a middle path between
these opinions. Certainly, in the sixties and seventies, both the public and
independent networks repeatedly worked to support the integration of
immigrants through tailored broadcasting on radio and television.[10]
However, these same broadcasters also periodically left writers space to
engage in more complex and controversial presentation of immigration
and the idea of immigrant difference, and repeatedly allowed comedy to be
focused onto these issues.[11] Johnny Speight felt that this kind of comedy
was indeed important precisely because it had the power to make light of
potentially inflammatory issues. He explained the aims of his writing in a
retrospective interview with the *Evening Standard* in 1996: "You don't
cure a problem by sweeping it under the carpet. You have to talk about
it."[12]

Although there was some support for his approach, Speight's work was
perceived as controversial by both the BBC and the ITA. Speight had
considerable difficulty persuading either network to broadcast *If There*

---

[8] WAC, Comments of REK Phillips, "Second Conference on Immigrants," File
R78/1/816/1, July 13, 1965.
[9] WAC, Comments of Philip Mason, "Second Conference on Immigrants," File
R78/1/816/1, July 13, 1965.
[10] See WAC, R165/54/1, J. Cook and J. Robottom, "A report on the contribution
made by broadcasting to meeting the educational needs of immigrant workers and
their families in Great Britain," 1977.
[11] Alongside the work of Speight, other programmes focused on the issue of racial
conflict in Britain such as Thames Television's comedy *Love Thy Neighbour*.
Other programmes, such as the BBC's *It Ain't Half Hot Mum*, engaged these issues
in the context of the British Empire.
[12] *Evening Standard*, May 20, 1996.

Weren't Any Blacks You'd Have to Invent Them, which was only belatedly
shown by LWT in 1968, having initially been rejected by both the BBC
and Rediffusion in 1966. Similarly, *Curry and Chips* also ran into trouble
over its racial content. This sitcom revolved around the experiences of an
Irish-Pakistani immigrant named Kevin O'Grady (played by Spike
Milligan) who had come to live and work in Britain. Speight felt that the
show was unfairly discontinued after one series because television
executives were put off by its content. In the wake of the series he told one
journalist: "It got very high ratings, but Rupert Murdoch wouldn't do a
follow-on because he said the ITA objected to my laughing at colour
prejudice."[13] Speight believed that his difficulty in getting *If There
Weren't Any Blacks You'd Have to Invent Them* onto British television,
and the decommissioning of *Till Death* in 1975, was similarly rooted in
the refusal of Britain's broadcasters to allow his honest, uncensored
reading of racial interactions in British society.[14] In one of his final
interviews he complained to one journalist about the reluctance of
television producers to allow him to depict "real" opinions on race: "They
want fiction, real fiction, now rather than face up to unpleasant facts.
Cardboard characters and banality seem to be the in thing."[15]

Despite Speight's claim that his work helped race relations by bringing
tensions "to the top" of society, most analysts have subsequently presented
his race writing in critical terms, and dismissed the idea that the work
played any kind of positive role in helping immigrant integration in
Britain.[16] Angela Barry recollected that she had "shed a few silent tears"
when she first saw *Till Death* and argued that the programme gave racist
views "a real legitimacy."[17] More recently, Medhurst has labelled the
programme "that ambivalently monstrous Enoch Powell of the sitcom."[18]
The ambivalence that Medhurst ascribes to *Till Death* existed in the
potential for the audience to read the show as racist or anti-racist. It is

---

[13] *The Guardian*, May 31, 1971.
[14] Both the BBC and Rediffusion bought the play before deciding that it was "too
controversial". See *The Observer*, July 17, 1966.
[15] *Daily Express*, May 7, 1995.
[16] *Evening Standard*, January 22, 1974. Speight argued: "Alf cannot create race
relations problems, but can only bring them to the top."
[17] Angela Barry, "Black Mythologies: The Representation of Black People on
British Television," in *The Black and White Media Book: Handbook for the Study
of Racism and Television,* ed. John Twitchin, 89–94 (Stoke on Trent: Trentham,
1988. Also see Stephen Bourne, *Black in the British Frame: The Black Experience
in British Film and Television* (London and New York: Continuum, 2001), 243.
[18] Andy Medhurst, *A National Joke: Popular Comedies and English Cultural
Identities* (London and New York: Routledge, 2007), 38.

indeed this freedom to negotiate the message in Speight's work that other analysts have found problematic. Regarding *If There Weren't Any Blacks You'd Have to Invent Them*, Barry concluded: "In structuring a play around an overt bigot, the player offered the viewer the choice—of dismissing the bigoted view as nonsense or of agreeing with them."[19] Malik has criticised *Till Death* in similar terms, arguing that Speight's writing "lay itself open to extreme and disparate readings because of the space it left [for audience interpretation]."[20]

These concerns over the impact of Speight's writing were not lost on broadcasters. As has already been noted, LWT took the decision to withdraw *Curry and Chips* after the first series, and it took Speight two years to bring *If There Weren't Any Blacks You'd Have to Invent Them* into British living rooms because of its racial content. Whilst it is arguable that the longevity of *Till Death* and Alf Garnett points to a different conclusion, there is evidence that, by the 1970s, this show was kept on television in spite of, not because of, its racial content. The BBC had been concerned about the influence of *Till Death* from the start, but seem to have been reassured in the 1960s that its intentions and impacts were generally positive.[21] However, by the time of the programme's 1972 return, the BBC was well aware that its impact was more complicated.[22] In this year, an audience survey report, focused entirely on *Till Death*, was commissioned.[23] It found that far from combating prejudice, *Till Death* tended to make viewers less tolerant of immigrants.

The report was based on nearly 800 responses to questionnaires that were given out in UK "urban centres". It showed that viewers of the

---

[19] Barry, "Black Mythologies," 94.

[20] See Sarita Malik, "Representing Black Britain: Black Images on British Television from 1936 to the Present Day," (PhD Thesis, Open University/British Film Institute, 1998), 236–37. Also see Stuart Hall, "The Whites of their Eyes: Racist Ideologies and the Media," in *Silver Linings: Some Strategies for the Eighties,* eds. George Bridges and Rosalind Brunt, 43 (London: Lawrence and Wishart, 1981).

[21] Hugh Greene corresponded with leading race relations experts, including Jim Rose, who reassured him that *Till Death* was generally securing positive responses. WAC, File R78/2350/1, Rose to Greene, January 15, 1968.

[22] The departure of the famously liberal Greene as Director General in 1969, and the replacement of Lord Normanbrook with Lord Hill as Chairman of the Board of Governors in 1967, was almost certainly significant in toughening the BBC's stance towards *Till Death.*

[23] This report is retained in full in the BBC Archive. WAC, File R9/757/1, Viewing Report (VR 73-175): "An Audience Research Report: 'Till Death Us Do Part' as anti-Prejudice Propaganda," 1973.

programme were often supportive of Alf's opinions. For example, when
asked whether Garnett was "right more often that he's wrong" the
audience was completely divided, 45% agreeing with the statement, 46%
disagreeing.[24] More alarmingly, viewers of the programme were almost
twice as likely to believe that "coloured people" were inferior to white
people.[25] The conclusion that the BBC chose to draw from this survey was
that Speight's comedy did not have a major impact on popular thinking on
race. The report outlined "that Till Death is no more than a minor
influence in determining present attitudes, but that is all."[26] That the
organisation opted for such a conclusion seems anomalous given the
decision to withdraw Speight's other race writing in this period, and can
only be explained in terms of Till Death's enormous popularity. Speight
certainly felt that it was the programme's success which enabled it to
survive criticism about its racial content. He told The People in 1968 that
the BBC "don't seem to care so long as we keep the big audience."[27]

Whatever the sagacity of Speight's approach to challenging racism, it
is arguable that his characters and plot situations have the potential to
unlock dominant attitudes and issues regarding immigration and race
relations in the 1970s. These issues were certainly a major matter of public
and political concern in this period. After Peter Griffith's notorious 1964
election victory at Smethwick, and in the wake of Powellism, both
politicians and the media were well aware that race and immigration issues
had the power to ignite and retain public interest.[28] Political strategies for
dealing with these incendiary issues were fairly consistent, evolving in the
wake of watershed 1960s legislation, specifically the Commonwealth
Immigrants Act of 1962 and the Race Relations Act of 1965. On one
hand, the Commonwealth Immigrants Act marked the start of post-war
restrictive immigration legislation. The Act (and subsequent legislation in
1968 and 1971) reconfigured the legal notion of Britishness, a transition

---

[24] WAC, File R9/757/1, "An Audience Research Report," 8.
[25] Ibid., 22.
[26] Ibid., 19.
[27] The People, January 21, 1968.
[28] See Solomos, Race and Racism in Britain ; Paul Gilroy, There Ain't No Black in
the Union Jack: The Cultural Politics of Race and Nation (London: Unwin
Hyman, 1987); Kathleen Paul, Whitewashing Britain: Race and Citizenship in the
Postwar Era (Ithaca, London: Cornell University Press, 1997); Randall Hansen,
Citizenship and Immigration: The Institutional Origins of a Multi-Racial Nation
(Oxford: Oxford University Press, 2000); Ian R.G. Spencer, British Immigration
Policy Since 1939: The Making of Multi-Racial Britain (London: Routledge,
1997).

that Hampshire has described as a journey "from citizenship to belonging".[29] In this process, the legal concept of Britishness was racialised, as legislation began to use personal ancestry (and not Empire and Commonwealth residence) as the key barometer of rights to UK residency. These measures have universally been read by historians as barely covert attempts to limit black and Asian immigration and settlement.[30] But another side of government policy on race is also evident in this period. In 1965 and 1968, iconic race relations legislation was enacted to protect black and Asian people from discrimination. Although these measures were rather limited in scope, they reveal a counter-pressure in political approaches to race and immigration.[31] Put simply, by the 1970s there was a degree of political consensus that both black and Asian immigration, as well as racism, needed to be contained. Speight's writing on race reveals much about these currents of thinking on race relations in the 1970s, about questions of who did (and who did not) belong in Britain, and about the tensions which surrounded government attempts to curtail racism through legislation.

At the heart of Speight's writing was a fundamental ambivalence about race, Britishness and belonging. His narratives frequently questioned the construction of colour difference and racial categories, unpicking the idea that there was anything certain or static about these concepts. In *If There Weren't Any Blacks You'd Have to Invent Them*, Speight narrates an encounter between a Young Man and two older men, one of whom is "Blind", the other "Backwards".[32] As the Backwards Man refuses to use his eyes, he and the Blind Man insist on constructing the Young Man as "black" even though he is not. Other characters attempt to assure the Blind Man that the Young Man is white. However, he will not have his mind changed. The Backwards Man is left to explain his friend's position: "He's a free thinker. He thinks exactly what he wants to think. If he thinks you're black then to him you're black … and that's all there is to it."[33] The Blind Man tells another character that blackness transcends what you can see, and that the actual colour of the Young Man is irrelevant: "So he's white

---

[29] James Hampshire, *Citizenship and Belonging: Immigration and the Politics of Demographic Governance in Post-War Britain* (Basingstoke: Palgrave, 2005).
[30] See Solomos, *Race and Racism*, 57–58.
[31] See Shamit Saggar, *Race and Politics in Britain* (London: Harvester Wheatsheaf, 1992).
[32] One critic described the plot as "a rather wooden allegory reminiscent of the art theatre of the thirties." See *The Daily Telegraph*, August 5, 1968.
[33] Johnny Speight, "If There Weren't Any Blacks You'd Have to Invent Them," in Johnny Speight, *Three Plays* (London: Oberon, 1998), 47.

... a white black."[34] Eventually, the other characters decide to execute the Young Man (who they have covered in boot polish) because of his blackness. Here again, his actual colour is dismissed in favour of a use of blackness as an agreed social label. Prior to his execution he is told: "What's the difference between pigmentation and boot polish? They've chosen you to play the coon."[35] In what was clearly intended to be a moral tale, Speight used the narrative to explain the political and psychological roots of colour prejudice as he saw it. The Blind Man explains: "We must have something to hate apart from ourselves. Something to blame our failure on to."[36]

In his other writing in this period Speight repeatedly played with the idea and meaning of colour. In *Curry and Chips*, the central character is a Pakistani Irishman (Kevin O'Grady) played by the "blacked-up" Spike Milligan. Jokes about colour lie at the centre of this situation comedy which focusses on O'Grady's attempts to work in a British toy factory. The audience laughs at O'Grady's repeated protests that he is white Irish and not Pakistani, while also laughing at the underlying white Irishness of Milligan playing a Pakistani. The black actor Kenny Lynch plays a black British factory worker who is racist towards O'Grady.[37] Lynch's character tells the factory foreman, Arthur (played by Eric Sykes), "I wouldn't fancy a bloody wog staying with me."[38] When the white shop steward, Norman, threatens to strike over the employment of O'Grady, Arthur defends his decision to employ him by questioning Norman's colour. He tells him: "How do we know what you are? You could be coloured."[39] Here, and throughout, we see the same idea that infuses *If There Weren't Any Blacks You'd Have to Invent Them*, namely that colour, and the way it is employed as a category, is highly subjective. In *Till Death Us Do Part*, when Alf Garnett is confronted by a black doctor (an encounter which challenges his belief that black people are uneducated) his response is to

---

[34] Ibid., 51.

[35] Ibid., 60.

[36] Ibid., 57.

[37] Speight used Lynch's blackness to defend his script. In the *Guardian* he commented: 'I personally just don't believe in colour at all. Kenny Lynch is one of my greatest mates, and what's his colour mean? I mean he's cockney, just a cockney'. *The Guardian*, February 10, 1969.

[38] *Curry and Chips* [Television Series] (London: London Weekend Television LWT, 1969), November 21, 1969.

[39] Ibid.

question the blackness of the individual in question. He tells Mike: "He's not a proper black, so I mean he don't apply, do he?"[40]

Speight's thinking on race relations was aligned to his broader Marxist world view. Despite the fact that he was one of Britain's best paid writers by the 1970s, Speight still identified with his working-class roots and Marxist politics. He was a man who proudly identified Stalin as one of his heroes, and who claimed that he understood colour prejudice as a tactic of class conflict.[41] Speight, like many Marxist social theorists of his generation, saw racial prejudice as a mechanism for exploitation.[42] Thus it did not matter, as is illustrated through the murder of the Young Man in Speight's play, whether you were black or not. Someone in society (sometimes immigrants, sometimes the working classes) had to "play the coon".

Whilst Speight's writing on the ascription and meaning of colour can be seen as posing a challenge to racist thinking in the 1970s, at the same time the ideas within his comedies reveal a more complex authorial engagement with the meaning of race. Speight's jokes may offer the historian some access into the ideas of the writer and his audience. However, as we have seen, reading agenda into Speight's (or any) comedy is not easy because of the complexity of clarifying the space between comedic intention and impact.[43] Nonetheless, Stuart Hall's idea that the lightness of comedy offers protection, a channel for views that are otherwise difficult to express, is worthy of attention.[44] Through comedy, it seems that Speight could raise concerns about race and difference that were hard to raise elsewhere. In this way, *Till Death Us Do Part* and *Curry and Chips* serve as valuable sources of prevailing social attitudes, in-keeping with Medhurst's assertion that: "If you want to understand the preconceptions and power structures of a society or social group, there are few better ways than by studying what it laughs at."[45]

---

[40] "Intolerance," *Till Death Us Do Part*, June 7, 1966.

[41] Speight identified Stalin as his hero in an interview in *The Guardian* in 1971 and again in an interview in *The Sun* in 1975. See *The Guardian*, May 31, 1971, and John Dodd on Speight in *The Sun*, January 18, 1975.

[42] For a Marxist analysis of race in post-war Britain in the immediate wake of this period see Ambalavaner Sivanandan, *Different Hunger: Writings on Black Resistance* (London: Pluto, 1982).

[43] See Jerry Palmer, *Taking Humour Seriously* (London, New York: Routledge, 1994), 166, and Michael Billig, *Laughter and Ridicule: Towards a Social Critique of Humour* (London: Sage, 2005), 175–99.

[44] Hall, "The Whites of their Eyes," 43.

[45] See Andy Medhurst, "Introduction: Situation Comedies," in *Black Images in British Television: The Colour Black,* eds. Therese Daniel and Jane Gerson, 15

The overwhelming message on racial difference in Speight's work contrasts sharply with his aforementioned critiques of the meaning of colour. On balance, in *Till Death Us Do Part* and *Curry and Chips*, the idea that black and Asian immigrants are totally and irreconcilably different to white Britons comes through strongly. It is however arguable that this message emanates from characters with whom we (as an audience) are not supposed to identify, namely Alf Garnett and Norman, the shop steward. Both of these characters express repeated hostility towards black and Asian immigration and support for Enoch Powell's stance on repatriation. Journalists had little trouble in aligning Powell's success with the popularity of *Till Death's* supposed anti-hero. John Heilpern, in the *Observer*, thus noted:

> In the past two weeks, Enoch Powell and several hundred dockers have proved something that everyone was surprised to know, but nobody wanted to admit: Alf Garnett, the know-all embodiment of every conceivable form of bigotry and ignorance, actually exists.[46]

Norman, in *Curry and Chips*, overtly stated his approval for Powell, despite his general support for Labour. Responding to Arthur's challenge that socialists should not be opposed to immigration, he replied: "When it comes to coons, I'm with Enoch."[47] At the core of Garnett's and Norman's hostility towards black and Asian immigrants was the idea of black primitivism and inferiority. Repeatedly in *Till Death*, Alf dismissed immigrants as little more than animals. In an early episode from 1966, Alf reminisced about a past where the government knew that immigrants were primitive and could not be part of Britain. He comments that Churchill would not have welcomed these immigrants but instead would have told them: "Get back to the jungle .... Get your bloody drums out."[48] This kind of slur was a repeated theme in Garnett's constructions of immigrant difference, in which he alleged that black people were not created by God, that famine in Africa had been caused by the decline of cannibalism, and that white British patients now avoided the NHS for fear that black staff

---

(London: British Film Institute, 1989). Also see Mahadevhi Apte, *Humour and Laughter: An Anthropological Approach* (Cornell University Press: Ithaca, London, 1985), 121.

[46] *The Observer*, May 5, 1968.

[47] *Curry and Chips*, November 21, 1969.

[48] "Peace and Goodwill," *Till Death Us Do Part*, December 26, 1966.

would eat them.[49] Similarly, Norman, in *Curry and Chips*, was equally convinced of black inferiority. When he is told that Kevin O'Grady will not eat pork because he is a Moslem, he retorts: "A few years ago they were eating each other, now they won't eat pig."[50]

It would be inaccurate to conclude that Speight stood in simple opposition to his bigoted characters. In particular, his relationship with his longest-standing creation, Alf Garnett, was extremely complex. Speight seemed to believe that Alf served a valuable social function, rescuing the immigration debate from middle-class liberals. He told the *Daily Mail* in 1974: "he has performed a service. He has infuriated the lily white liberals, exposed them for the hypocrites that they are, and that is a good thing."[51] At the core of Speight's thinking was a belief that an immigration debate was necessary, and that working-class people had every right to be concerned.

This does not of course mean that Speight agreed with the bigotry of Garnett or Norman in any obvious sense. It does however indicate that he believed that the kind of working-class disaffection which was represented by these characters was far from groundless. Speight felt that the British middle classes were reaping the benefits of immigration policy while the working classes were paying the social cost. Furthermore, Speight believed that these same middle classes were stifling debate about immigration (and his writing on the subject) by making allegations of racism. As he put it: "so-called liberals who hate Garnett pretend the world is different. Maybe it is for them. But what would be the story if a coloured moved in on their street or wanted to marry their daughter?"[52] Here, Garnett and Norman stepped into the breach as working-class representatives, challenging the hypocritical liberal silencing of immigration concerns in Britain. Looking back on *Till Death*, Speight argued: "I don't think the public was ever shocked by Alf. Coloured people loved it, they were glad everything was put in the open at last."[53]

At the core of Speight's concerns about the liberal stifling of discussion concerning the impacts of immigration was his hostility towards the Race Relations Acts of 1965 and 1968. He feared these would outlaw open debate about immigration and perhaps his own comedy.

---

[49] Garnett argued that God did not create black people in *Till Death Us Do Part*, February 20, 1974, that cannibalism has caused famine in episode January 22, 1975, and that patients were fearful of black workers in the NHS, January 2, 1974.
[50] *Curry and Chips*, November 21, 1969.
[51] *The Daily Mail*, December 3, 1974.
[52] Ibid.
[53] *The Evening Standard*, August 30, 1985.

Indeed, in the wake of the 1968 legislation, some parliamentarians and trade unionists (as well as the *National Viewers and Listeners Association*) did attempt to question the legality of both *Till Death Us Do Part* and *Curry and Chips*, if to no avail.[54]

Ultimately, in the volatile race relations climate of the 1970s, Speight saw a value in his racist characters which transcended his oft-stated agenda of deflating racial prejudice by laughing at bigots. In all of his race writing in this period Speight had a more complicated agenda, hoping to invigorate frank discussion of racial difference and challenge what he perceived as a liberal silencing of legitimate working-class disaffection about immigration. What the popularity of Speight's work tells us about British thinking on race in the 1970s remains somewhat unclear, lost between the stated intention of the writer and what is known about the reception of his writing. However, the popularity of other programmes which had racial themes at their centre, particularly Thames Television's *Love Thy Neighbour*, suggests that racial comedy played an important role in shaping as well as reflecting social thinking on race in 1970s Britain.[55] In this process, for good or ill, no writer was more influential than Johnny Speight.

---

[54] For example, AW Pickering, Chairman of the *National Viewers and Listeners Association*, wrote to the Attorney General in 1968 to ask whether *Till Death* breached the new race relations legislation. PRO, LO 2/460, BBC Programmes – "Till Death Us Do Part," Pickering to Jones, January 13, 1968.

[55] *Love Thy Neighbour* was a sitcom starring Jack Smethurst and Rudolph Walker about racial conflict between Black and White next door neighbours. It ran on ITV between 1972 and 1976. *Love Thy Neighbour* [Television Series] (London: Thames Television, 1972–76).

"YOU ARE AWFUL ... BUT I LIKE YOU!": THE POLITICS OF CAMP IN 1970S TELEVISION

PERI BRADLEY

The Politics of Camp

Ronald Bryden defined the term "camp" on *Woman's Hour* (BBC Radio 4) in 1966 stating that: "Under an affectation of bored fashion, it conceals a sharp sexual hostility, a repudiation of sexual roles ... [and] it covers itself with protective humour; it is a joke, a tease, it didn't really mean it. Or did it?"[1] Although this was by no means the first definition of camp, Bryden's perspective both condensed, and extrapolated from earlier discussions and considerations of the expression, and revealed a more serious impulse behind the façade of excess and exaggeration. This definition demonstrates an awareness of the potential significance of camp and most certainly announces its arrival on the contemporary media scene. Bryden identifies camp as possessing a "protective humour", necessary at a time when homosexuality was still illegal. Camp was a "safe" way to express an unsafe sexuality in an era when the establishment was still frantically defending normality and the status quo. At the time camp had various methods and means at its disposal including the excess and exaggeration of the drag queen and the sexual ambiguity of the dandy. Both questioned sexual roles by way of alternative representations of masculinity that confused gender boundaries. However these were rendered palatable to the constrained audiences of the 1960s through their humorous presentation. Camp performance presented homosexuality as something to be laughed at and consequently was non-threatening. Therefore under the guise of humour, outrageous statements that challenged accepted wisdom could be articulated without consequence, leaving us to wonder whether, as Bryden enquired, "it didn't really mean it. Or did it?"

---

[1] Keith Howes, *Broadcasting It: An Encyclopaedia of Homosexuality on Film, Radio and TV in the UK 1923–1993* (London: Cassell, 1993), 101.

This essay will analyse the aesthetics and function of camp as a political force that enabled two of the marginalised groups of the 1970s— women and gay men—to instigate a gradual and covert revolution that acted as a liberating force in the sexual politics of the time. At the heart of this camp revolution are very politically-*in*correct figures such as Dick Emery (*The Dick Emery Show*, BBC1, 1963-1981) and John Inman as Mr Humphries, (*Are You Being Served?* BBC1, 1972-1985), two iconic stars of camp in the 1970s. *Are You Being Served?* takes place in an old-fashioned department store that is struggling to survive in the youthful and experimental period of the 1970s. It is a sit-com that questions aspects of gender, class and sexuality through the proximity of its characters and the rather claustrophobic workplace in which they find themselves. The members of staff represent various facets of 1970s society: Mr Grace and Mr Rumbold as the upper echelons of management who could be seen as the redundant symbols of authority; Captain Peacock and Mrs Slocombe as the older generation still desperately adhering to a rapidly disappearing class-system; Mr Lucas and Miss Brahms as the younger generation with a distinct lack of respect for both authority and class; and finally Mr Humphries, neither young nor old, masculine nor feminine and so apparently classless and as such, on the periphery of society.

In comparison, the *Dick Emery Show* displayed the talents of Dick Emery in quick-fire sketches that feature a range of characters all played by himself. The most important of these are his camp characters: Clarence the effeminate gay man, and Mandy the glamorous blonde who excel at innuendo. *The Dick Emery Show* and his characterisations of camp are of particular relevance as the first and most influential of camp representations in the 1970s. Significant for this analysis is that Emery's camp characters brought attention to the group that they represented, previously disregarded within society.

"Camp" has always been a contested term, but Bryden's definition retains relevance within contemporary culture, and is particularly useful when analysing the troublesome, tasteless and exploitative texts of the 1970s. However, various academic writings further illuminate the significance and purpose of camp, and need to be addressed. The definition of camp has changed over time and from its initial recognition as an unstable concept in the 1950s, to our present appreciation of its significance, there are subtle shifts in the way it has been deployed. As one of the first engagements with the idea of camp, Susan Sontag's seminal 1964 essay *Notes on Camp* produced a list that attempted to define it as a "sensibility".[2] This "stream of consciousness" list presents each new definition as it reveals itself to the author, emphasising the difficulties in defining the term. Out of 58 points, Sontag only addresses camp's close relationship with homosexuality at point 51. She spends 3 points covering it, and argues that:

> While it's not true that Camp taste *is* homosexual taste, there is no doubt a peculiar affinity and overlap ... homosexuals, by and large, constitute the vanguard—and most articulate audience—of Camp. The two pioneering forces of modern sensibility are Jewish moral seriousness and homosexual aestheticism and irony .... Homosexuals have pinned their integration into society on promoting the aesthetic sense. Camp is a solvent of morality. It neutralizes moral indignation, sponsors playfulness .... Nevertheless, even though homosexuals have been its vanguard, Camp taste is much more than homosexual taste.[3]

Despite the acknowledgement of the genesis of camp within the queer community, Sontag denies that camp remains exclusively defined as homosexual, thus freeing the concept for the explanation of a range of other cultural manifestations. This broadening has been identified by Fabio Cleto and others as recreating camp as "Pop-camp," thereby heterosexualising and neutralising it. Moe Meyer accuses Sontag of "detaching the signifying codes from their queer signified."[4] He recognises her interpretation as being directly responsible for the initiation of Pop-camp, which "un-queers" it, thus removing it from the realm of political representation and radicalism. In an attempt to reclaim camp as queer and activist he states that:

> Thus there are not different types of Camp. There is only one. And it is queer. It can be engaged directly by the queer to produce social visibility in the praxis of everyday life, or it can be manifested as the camp trace by the un-queer in order, as I will argue, to provide queer access to the apparatus of representation.[5]

Consequently Meyer firmly re-establishes camp as a homosexual practice that can, however, be appropriated by non-homosexuals to

[2] Susan Sontag, "Notes On Camp," *Partisan Review* 31, no. 4 (1964): 515–30.
[3] Susan Sontag, "Notes On 'Camp'," in *Camp: Queer Aesthetics and The Performing Subject. A Reader,* ed. Fabio Cleto, 65 (Edinburgh: Edinburgh University Press, 1999.
[4] Moe Meyer, *The Politics and Poetics of Camp* (London: Routledge, 1994), 5.
[5] Ibid.

challenge dominant ideology. This practice then identifies camp as a weapon rather than a tool that can be both political and radical in nature.

With thirty years between Sontag's and Meyer's texts, a process obviously occurred which de-politicised but not necessarily disempowered camp. Somewhere between 1964 and 1994 there appeared a perception that camp was both trivial and meaningless. In part this can be attributed to the rapid onset of postmodernism in the 60s and 70s. As Cleto identifies:

> While the relationship between camp and the postmodern has not yet been fully addressed in all its complexity, the striking convergence of the two notions has produced a constant, if unsystematic, referral to both camp as a feature of the postmodern, and to postmodernism as camp—most notably by Frederic Jameson.[6]

The postmodern and its ability to evacuate meaning from culture and its artefacts have a direct correlation with camp and its consequences. Although Christopher Isherwood defined High-Camp and Low-Camp in *The World in the Evening* as early as 1954, recognition of its characteristics was slow to develop. Retrospectively camp can be identified in numerous media texts, like film and television, in the 1950s and 60s and earlier. However, camp did not truly come into its own until the 1970s, renowned as the time that taste forgot. Its excesses in fashion, music, food and sexual ambiguity are all closely aligned with Pop-camp. As observed earlier Pop-camp is un-queer and non-political and Meyer seems to believe that Pop-camp existed at the expense of a radical and political camp. However I would argue that running parallel with this strand of Pop-camp at the time there was the corresponding element of radical-camp. This camp *was* queer and political and worked quietly on behalf of both homosexuals and women.

Camp Television

In the 1960s there was a deficiency of camp in comedy and satirical programming in series such as: *That Was The Week That Was* (1962); *Do Not Adjust Your Set* (1968); *Steptoe and Son* (1962); *The Liver Birds* (1969); and *Monty Python's Flying Circus* (1969). Formats and television aesthetics were developing in the 1960s and comedies began to work subversively and challenged dominant ideology by exploring the darker

---

[6] Fabio Cleto, in "Pop Camp, Surplus Counter-Value, or the Camp of Cultural Economy. Introduction," in *Camp: Queer Aesthetics and The Performing Subject. A Reader,* ed. Fabio Cleto, 305 (Edinburgh: Edinburgh University Press, 1999).

side of life. However, although this subversiveness may have examined issues that affected the lives of ordinary people in a realistic manner, those on the margins of society were still unable to find themselves represented anywhere on television. The 1970s offered radical-camp representations in many cultural artefacts, but it is camp television that offers the most significant examples. In the 1970s, television as a medium was rising rapidly in popularity and at a time when British cinema was struggling to survive, British television went from strength to strength. Competition between ITV and BBC motivated the production of a variety of programmes that entertained more than they educated. This included comedies, dramas and soap operas.

Humour in comedy programming in the 1970s penetrated the furthest reaches of sub-cultures in the quest for innovation. The sketch show format which had been initiated in the 1960s became more prevalent, and sitcoms moved away from purely family situations to alternative circumstances aimed at a younger audience. Comedies in the 1970s included sketch shows, sitcoms, and satires such as: *Dave Allen at Large* (BBC 1971-9); *The Two Ronnies* (BBC1 1971-87); *Love Thy Neighbour* (ITV 1972-6); *Fawlty Towers* (BBC2 1975, 1979); *The Fall and Rise of Reginald Perrin* (BBC 1976-9); and *Not the Nine O'clock News* (BBC2 1979-82). These examples include a mixture of high culture and low culture. Much has been written about the more respectable *Fawlty Towers* and *Perrin* as intellectual comedy that is knowing and intelligent. *Love Thy Neighbour*, which represents ethnic minorities in a questionable and sometimes embarrassing manner is, in my opinion, an example of low culture. The discussion of high culture versus low culture is much the same as high-camp versus low camp. As Isherwood's character Charles explains in *The World in the Evening*:

> You see true High Camp always has an underlying seriousness. You can't camp about something that you don't take seriously. You're not making fun of it; you're making fun out of it. You're expressing what's basically serious to you in terms of fun, artifice and elegance .... You have to meditate on it and feel it intuitively.[7]

In contrast his explanation of low camp involves:

[7] Christopher Isherwood, "The World in the Evening," in *Camp: Queer Aesthetics and the Performing Subject*, ed. Fabio Cleto, 51 (Edinburgh: Edinburgh University Press, 1999).

a swishy little boy with peroxided hair, dressed in a picture hat and a
feather boa, pretending to be Marlene Dietrich? Yes in queer circles, they
call that camping. It's all very well in its place, but it's an utterly debased
form.[8]

As with the friction between high culture and low culture, this appears
to be a discrepancy based on class. High camp is associated with the
upper and middle classes, and low camp with the lower classes and
vulgarity; it is a matter of taste and discretion. Cleto identifies this as
providing the act of gay drag with a philosophical dimension that moves
camp into an elitist and critical space. As Philip Core recognises, camp,
whether high or low, is the "heroism of people not called upon to be
heroes."[9] He reveals that camp bravely reacts with and against public taste,
constantly and restlessly entertaining whilst simultaneously challenging
cultural and political boundaries. At the heart of camp lies the fundamental
sensibility of resistance and revolution. Its excesses and exaggeration
continually question and oppose authority and the establishment. In this
way it is an ideal weapon for the oppressed and repressed that do not have
recourse to the usual channels of protest. Therefore, the most extreme
form of camp is the most effective. The physical performance of low camp
is actually more successful in altering perceptions and changing cultural
conditions than the philosophical and elite construction of high camp. In
light of this I would argue that the meaning of high camp has changed over
time, coming to mean the most camp, the epitome of camp rather than an
intellectually superior form of camp. Therefore high-camp has become
low-camp taken to its extreme. This reveals all camp, whether identified as
high or low, as capable of possessing an underlying seriousness and
political impetus.

Dick Emery

I now want to consider Dick Emery as a case study television camp
comedy, in order to comprehend how camp could operate as a political
and liberating force that resonated with the spirit of the 1970s. His work
encouraged the acceptance of alternative modes of male and female
sexuality and power relations. The *Dick Emery Show* began in 1963 on the
BBC. Having spent his childhood travelling round the country on the

---

[8] Ibid.
[9] Philip Core, "From Camp: The Lie That Tells The Truth," in *Camp: Queer
Aesthetics and the Performing Subject. A Reader*, ed. Fabio Cleto, 86 (Edinburgh:
Edinburgh University Press, 1999).

music hall circuit with his parents, who were a double act, Emery received
no formal education and was brought up in the theatre. When he was nine
years old his parents divorced and he lived with his mother, whom he both
adored and feared. During the Second World War he entertained the troops
with Ralph Reader's Gang Show but after the war found work on the stage
hard to come by. Eventually in 1948 he secured a position at the Windmill
Theatre alongside other newcomers like Tony Hancock. By the 1950s
Emery was working for BBC Radio and was already developing the
characters that would form his repertoire for television. Working with Jon
Pertwee he appeared regularly on both radio and television from 1952
onwards. He was offered a show of his own in 1963 that was scripted by
Mel Brooks and Mel Tolkin, and ran until 1981.[10]

A particular feature of the *Dick Emery Show* was the fake vox-pop
interviews with a "vivid cast of comic grotesques."[11] One of the most
memorable of Emery's "grotesques" is Mandy, the sex-obsessed blonde,
who managed to find sexual innuendo in almost any phrase. Mandy is
Emery in drag and as Caryl Flinn states:

> comedy is often generated from a sense of the "incoherence" of a
> performer's body .... The disunified body, the funny body that doesn't
> quite fit with itself, is, of course, the body of camp, as any drag queen will
> attest. It is also, through its failure to maintain boundaries—or its refusal of
> them—the body of grotesque realism .... Like the disunified grotesque,
> camp also works to violate the standards of "good taste", allying itself with
> filth, the profane, and an overall sense of disreputability.[12]

In the 1970s Emery and Danny La Rue were called "female
impersonators" in an attempt to remove them from the openly gay, and
disreputable, connotations of the drag-queen. However both La Rue's and
Emery's female characters as drag-queens of a sort, engage with Judith
Butler's notion of performativity. They perform femininity and female
sexuality thereby forcing us to question the concept of gender as being
natural. By donning all the paraphernalia that created a female identity in
the 1970s—heavy make-up, false eyelashes, blonde coiffured hair, short
skirt, tights and high heels—Emery "performs" Mandy and by doing so

---

[10] "The Dick Emery Show," http://www.televisionheaven.co.uk/emery.html.
[11] "The Dick Emery Show,"
http://www.bbc.co.uk/comedy/dickemeryshow/index.shtml.
[12] Caryl Flinn, "The Deaths of Camp," in *Camp: Queer Aesthetics and the
Performing Subject. A Reader*, ed. Fabio Cleto, 447 (Edinburgh: Edinburgh
University Press, 1999).

undermines models of both femininity and masculinity. As David Bergman writes:

> For Judith Butler, however, camp is at the heart of a radical program for transforming consciousness. Because of its capacity to stand received ideas on their head, by inverting notions, and by emphasizing the "unnaturalness" of what the dominant society believes to be "natural," camp has a central part to play in sexual politics.[13]

This identifies camp as capable of initiating fundamental change. The 1970s was a particularly fertile environment, both receptive and responsive to the idea of political and sexual revolution. Although feminists of the time would never have regarded camp as working on their behalf, and often saw the figure of the drag-queen as a misogynist expression of homosexuality, their high profile and popularity proved capable of changing the ways in which women and the gay community were perceived. Emery's camp characters, including Mandy, although designed to merely entertain, actually comprised representations that instigated Butler's "transformation of consciousness" that was to alter social acceptance of both "queerness" and feminism.

Emery's character Mandy is both camp and grotesque but also strangely alluring. She is actually a "drag-queen" personality who takes on a life separately from Emery and who expresses all the camp aspects of a character named after Mandy Rice-Davies, the infamous "mistress" revealed in the Profumo affair. Just like Rice-Davies, Emery's Mandy is an overtly sexual woman, representing a burgeoning feminist freedom that characterised 1970s feminist culture. An example of Mandy's camp subversiveness is evident in the sketch quoted below, where she arrives on the scene dressed in a blue silk maxi dress with matching short fur jacket, silver platform shoes and a small contrasting pink handbag. Mandy's posture is poised with hands together over her handbag, her head held slightly to one side with eyes demurely lowered. Her tone is soft and gentle as she answers the interviewer:

Vox-pop interviewer:	Excuse me Miss.
Mandy:	Well hello!
Vox-pop interviewer:	Hello! Here's a charming young lady!
Mandy:	Oh. Thank you.
Vox-pop interviewer:	Tell me, do you plan to do anything special on the next Bank Holiday?

---

[13] David Bergman, "The Political Ramifications of Camp," www.glbtq.com/literature/camp,5.html.

Mandy:	Oh yes. My boyfriend and I go pot-holing together every chance we get!
Vox-pop interviewer:	You mean exploring underground caves?
Mandy:	Oh yes.
Vox-pop interviewer:	So you actually enjoy groping about together in all the mud?
Mandy:	Pardon?
Vox-pop interviewer:	Well it looks like you and your boyfriend are in for a really dirty weekend!
Mandy:	Ooh! You are awwwful. But I like you![14]

The scene ends with Mandy slapping the interviewer on the shoulder so hard she knocks him over. She then walks away at some speed in silver platforms, which she contrives to trip over for comic effect. Emery's masculine strength and feigned inability to master high heels, calls attention to the random nature of socio-sexual symbolism questioned so prominently in 1970s culture. A large element of the comedy in Emery's sketches is derived from the performative style rather than the dialogue. His camp characters are the most mannered and visually flamboyant of his portfolio, which certainly corresponds with the criteria of excess and exaggeration that defines camp. Emery's careful choice of dress for his camp characters demonstrates their special qualities, setting them apart from other characters. Clarence, his outrageously camp, gay character, and Mandy are never seen in the same costume twice and each set of clothing is carefully orchestrated for characterisation and fashion. Their accessories are meticulously chosen, and Clarence always wears a large, ostentatious hat. The colours are vivid and vibrant; reds, greens, blues and yellows, which are especially combined to produce a visual "movement" or vibration that emphasises their excessive personalities. Mandy's surfeit of sexuality is expressed through her attire and her body language. Her wide-eyed innocence is belied by the infamous catch-phrase: "You are awful ... but I like you!" With her flirtatious approach, Mandy betrays underlying liberal attitudes beneath an exterior of assumed modesty. Ultimately the character is significant for her ability to alter perceptions of femininity and feminine sexuality. The tension between the performance of Mandy's femininity and Emery's essential masculinity confuses the boundaries between the sexes, and this allows Mandy to emerge as an active, sexual woman, thereby granting permission to the 1970s female population to follow suit. The dialogue is loaded with sexual innuendo and indicates an

---

[14] "Dick Emery Bank Holiday,"
http://www.youtube.com/watch?v=qVpS4kJ8ZOg&feature=related.

unsophisticated humour based on bodily functions (such as sex) rather than intellect. This is low-class, vulgar humour that is attached to the common people, which reflects a fundamental reality and truth and so counteracts the artifice of camp. It is this sensibility that is so effective in appealing to, and consequently changing, the audience's beliefs and perceptions.

Emery's other camp character was Clarence, who had been part of Emery's act for some years before his television show and had undergone the biggest transformation. When Clarence was first created, homosexuality was only hinted at in the vaguest terms and was more acceptable in the context of cabaret rather than television. Emery stated of Clarence that "adopting a camp attitude was a useful ploy when faced with an unresponsive audience"[15] and that he found it puzzling that audiences found homosexuality funny. However he declared that "perhaps our laughter is a defence, a reaction against hidden fears about our innermost tendencies."[16] This is a revealing statement that is indicative of the cultural environment of the 1960s and 1970s. The general radicalism of the 1960s had begun to erode numerous culturally constructed boundaries, and the 1970s saw this liberalisation of attitudes increase, resulting in the ultimate rejection of many outmoded restrictions. This resulted in an acceptable gay representation on television:

> By the 1970s gay characters appeared more openly although they were farcical and camp and created purely for comic relief. At the same time as Clarence became a staple of Emery's repertoire, John Inman was starring on television as Grace Brothers' decidedly effeminate (but undeclared homosexual) menswear salesman Mr Humphries in *Are You Being Served?* And Larry Grayson was making a name for himself camping it up as the comedian with a decidedly gay persona, which actually formed the mainstay of his act.[17]

Prior to the 1970s Clarence's look was easy for Emery to assemble in order to represent a gay character. However as men's fashions began to become more flamboyant, he had to become decidedly more exaggerated and excessive to express Clarence's homosexuality in terms of camp performance. *The Persuaders* (1971-72) and Jason King as the eponymous hero of his own series (1972-73) are prime examples of men's fashion

---

[15] Laurence Marcus, "Clever Dick. Dick Emery's Comedy Characters Part Two," http://www.teletronic.co.uk/dickemery2.htm.
[16] Ibid.
[17] Ibid.

being foregrounded in the 1970s. These programmes displayed their protagonists as objects of desire for women and as role models for men. However their appearance and performance which was happily accepted as masculine in the 1970s, is evidently camp to contemporary audiences as this quote from Leon Hunt's *British Low Culture, from Safari Suits to Sexploitation* demonstrates:

> When they showed the pilot episode [of *The Persuaders*] as a part of "TV Heaven", someone walked into my lounge and accused me of watching some ancient gay-porn film, such was the puffed up body-language and dramatic glances.[18]

The television exposure of Clarence, Mr Humphries and Larry Grayson helped to normalise camp masculinity to a point where it was not only acceptable but almost desirable as an element of any genre rather than just comedy. As a result "dandyism" returned in the 1970s, modifying masculinity and allowing *all* men the freedom to express their identity through their appearance. However as a *political* impetus, camp acted on behalf of the gay community to raise their profile and create a space where they could legitimately exist as part of a spectrum of sexuality. As can be seen in Clarence's sketches he openly expresses his queerness through his appearance and overtly declares his sexuality through the dialogue. In this scene Clarence is mincing down the street in a large yellow and red checked tam o'shanter and matching tight-fitting trousers and waistcoat when a policeman runs into him;

Clarence: Hello honky-tonk. You're in a hurry!
Policeman: I'm looking for a man!
Clarence: Join the club!
Policeman: I'm chasing a fella who has just robbed a bank!
Clarence: What's he look like?
Policeman: Big, dark, broad, well-muscled.
Clarence: (Gasp) Ooh I say!
Policeman: Have you seen him sir?
Clarence: No—but I've dreamt about him![19]

---

[18] Laura Lee Davies, *Time Out* (1993) quoted in Leon Hunt, *British Low Culture: From Safari Suits to Sexploitation* (London: Routledge, 1998), 66.
[19] "Hello Honky Tonks,"
http://www.youtube.com/watch?v=GkHYApbbdL0&feature=related.

With this parting line Clarence flounces away and as the camera follows him he performs a very theatrical ascent of the stairs, accompanied by a small kick and flick of the head. This scene is relevant for its visual flamboyance that announces Clarence as an openly gay man and also for its dialogue that clearly declares his sexual orientation. Such a scene would have been impossible in the 1960s, as homosexuality was illegal until 1967. Representations like Emery's, which may have been stereotyped and humorous but openly displayed homosexuality, encouraged its acceptance in the 1970s. These camp bodies changed perceptions and were part of the impetus behind the liberalisation of women and gay men that is specific to the 1970s. By disturbing the concept of what constitutes femininity and masculinity, camp managed to accomplish a revolution not only in what we wore and how we looked, but also in how we were allowed to express our sexuality as part of our identity. For all its playful irony and excess, the camp body acted as a powerful and effective weapon in the struggle against repressive and oppressive ideological mechanisms.

THE SELF-SUFFICIENCY MOVEMENT AND THE APOCALYPTIC IMAGE IN 1970S BRITISH CULTURE

GWILYM THEAR

In his 1980 book *The Seventies*, Christopher Booker ventures the influential argument that the decade can be read as "a kind of prolonged 'morning after' to the euphoria and excesses of the Sixties", an image that has repeatedly been used to sum up the disillusionment and gloom many present as the defining qualities of 1970s British society.[1] The heart of the 1970s was of course a time of global economic hardship, of domestic political instability and a retreat from the utopian dreams of the 1960s towards a more insular, less spectacular cultural expression. However, the rest of Booker's argument has received far less exposure: that it is these qualities that help define the 1970s as "the most important decade of the twentieth century", defined by a loss of faith in "the belief in human progress" and a recourse to "re-create the simplicities of the past".[2] This paper does not engage with Booker's wider arguments, nor does it necessarily agree with his judgement on the pre-eminence of the decade. It does however examine one important sub-cultural movement that challenged notions of temporal progress and whose ideas found an influential place in mainstream mid-1970s culture. The essay will examine post-apocalyptic drama, an important and flourishing genre in 1970s television, and in particular the series *Survivors* (1975-1977) in the light of what came to be called the self-sufficiency movement: a back-to-the-land philosophy of self-reliance and organic sustainable production which had much in common with the burgeoning ecological and environmental movements developing at this time.

Survivors was a BBC television drama that ran for three series between 1975 and 1977 and which focused upon the attempts of a tiny number of

---

[1] Christopher Booker, *The Seventies: Portrait of a Decade* (London: Allen Lane, 1980), 7.
[2] Ibid., 5–6.

survivors of a global pandemic to subsist and rebuild some form of community. Achieving both a measure of contemporary critical acclaim and strong audience figures, the three series have retained over the years a strong fan base which helped lead to the successful release of DVD box sets in 2003. This renewed interest in the series led to the BBC remaking *Survivors* in autumn 2008, and at the time of writing a second series has already been confirmed for 2009. Academic interest has also grown over recent years alongside a high level of activity from the large and vigorous fan community. Indeed *Survivors* may be the only television series to have had an entire website dedicated to just one episode.[3] The interest in apocalyptic scenarios, of course, remains as strong as it has always been but there is perhaps even more interest in the scenario posed by *Survivors* today than thirty years ago; then, the apocalyptic pandemic was widely seen as a metaphor for nuclear war which was, at the time, a taboo subject for television drama in the UK. Following the effective banning of Peter Watkins' docudrama *The War Game* by the BBC in 1965, the subject of war was to remain almost entirely undiscussed on television screens until the showing of Mick Jackson's *Threads* in 1984. Today the threat of nuclear catastrophe has receded considerably in the public consciousness along with the cold war, but the menace of a global pandemic is much more widely discussed given recent concerns over SARS, Avian Influenza H5N1 and most recently Swine Influenza H1N1.

In one sense it is easy to see how *Survivors* fits into a specific genre of post-apocalyptic science fiction that developed from an initial flourishing in the immediate post-war era. This was a period that saw a range of texts on apocalyptic themes as diverse as Tolkien's *The Lord of the Rings* (1954-55), John Christopher's *The Death of Grass* (1956), Ray Bradbury's *The Martian Chronicles* (1950) and Neville Shute's *On the Beach* (1957). Arguably the most influential apocalyptic novel of this period however was John Wyndham's *The Day of the Triffids* (1951) which, through its much-imitated scenario of a tiny group of survivors being forced to cooperate and rebuild civilization, established itself as the founding text of what Brian Aldiss categorised as the "cosy catastrophe" genre.[4] Aldiss' term signifies how limited and parochial he considered the form (he famously described *The Day of the Triffids* as "utterly devoid of ideas")[5] nonetheless it has found a widespread currency in defining a certain kind

---

[3] Rich Cross, "Survivors: Mad Dog," http://www.survivors-mad-dog.org.uk/.
[4] Brian Aldiss and David Wingrove, *Trillion Year Spree: The History of Science Fiction* (Thirsk: House of Stratus, 2001), 279.
[5] Ibid.

of (post-) apocalyptic narrative. There is no build-up towards a disaster, no prefiguring of doom, no attempts to hold it off. Indeed, the first stage of the complex apocalypse Wyndham depicts is already complete by the time the novel opens. The main character William Masen, having been fortunate to miss the blinding cosmic light show, is only witness to the aftermath, as first disease and starvation and then the predation and scavenging of the triffids take their toll on the blinded citizens. *The Day of the Triffids* remains the most well-known example of the genre and has led to a number of adaptations in the UK alone: several radio serials, one film, but most significantly a major BBC series which developed out of the 1970s boom in apocalyptic television drama and was transmitted in 1981. It is now being remade by the BBC to be shown in 2009.

Survivors fitted this post-apocalyptic mould perfectly. Its initial scenario of a pandemic that kills virtually the entire population of the world leaving only a tiny number of the eponymous survivors to struggle to stay alive was straight from the Wyndham model. The playing out of the narrative beyond the opening apocalypse proved to be rather different however: although *Survivors* with its deserted cities, its hostile local chieftains and its return-to-nature imperative clearly owed a great debt to the *The Day of the Triffids*, in its focus on communal living rather than the nuclear family, its lack of an enemy force other than hunger and hostile communities, and the open-ended television format that enabled it to explore a much wider area of experience. *Survivors* transcended many of the limitations of the genre, even as it remained in thrall to others. For in many ways it is undoubtedly a very cosy catastrophe. The genre has been criticised for being very much a polite, English, middle class vision of the apocalypse where, despite the breakdown of society, the economy and law and order, middle class mores survive when all else fails. This is, I feel, rather an unfair dismissal of what has proven to be a remarkably influential vision of what may be to come, yet it is undeniable that British apocalyptic visions from Wyndham through to *Survivors* and beyond have featured a central cast of middle class protagonists who show an unerring belief that an inherent decency and recourse to traditional morality will be enough to survive in the post-apocalyptic world. It is an oft-made but well-made point how middle-class the survivors were; those with accents deriving not from the home counties are either lazy and/or troublesome labourers or jumped-up hostile chieftains. As one television critic noted at the time: "it's the poor what gets the plague".[6]

---

[6] Rich Cross, *Survivors: Viewing Notes*. DVD Booklet (London: BBC Worldwide, 2003), 9.

Undoubtedly, an important part of the thematic divergence *Survivors* demonstrates is due to its form: as an open-ended television drama, *Survivors* is inevitably obliged to depart from the structure of much previous apocalyptic narrative due to its inherent seriality. In the bounded forms of post-apocalyptic novels and their adaptations, the narrative most commonly takes the form of a quest to a place of safety where the process of survival and later renewal are implied but beyond the temporal limits of the diegesis. This can be clearly seen in works like *The Day of The Triffids* or *The Death of Grass*. It is possible to view the overarching narrative arc of *Survivors* comprising three distinct phases, with the first half of the first series largely following these familiar post-apocalyptic generic conventions. In the latter half of the series and throughout the second series, by contrast, the survivors have achieved the goal of their quest and must settle down and engage with community building and day-to-day living in their new world. The third series moves into new narrative ground as the characters leave their settlement and try to build and renew intra-community links, transport, government and, finally, an electricity supply. There is a great deal of interest to consider in this third phase, but this study is concerned with the second and, I argue, most radical section: it is in the survivors' establishment of settlement and their engagement with agricultural production, communal living and self-regulation that the contemporary interest in self-sufficiency begins to shows its real influence.

The self-sufficiency movement in Britain was a loosely defined set of groups with different backgrounds and different philosophies of life that were nonetheless united around a common interest in ideas such as growing your own fruit and vegetables, raising livestock and living a more organic, sustainable life. People were drawn to it from many areas: some came from the ecology movement and brought with them in particular ideas about the dangers of pesticides and additives; others came out of the hippy movements of the 1960s and brought ideals of communal and co-operative living; some were middle-class dropouts from the rat-race who wanted to live a simpler, more home-oriented and fulfilling lifestyle and some were political activists who wished to create a new society. Indeed, there was a rich mix of other motives and philosophies, as an examination of the contemporary literature demonstrates.

The important thing about these various groups is that they began to coalesce to the point that in 1975 the self-sufficiency movement was well-enough established for several things to happen: as we have already seen, *Survivors* started on television but it was not alone in the BBC spring schedules. Also making its debut at the same time was the classic sitcom *The Good Life* (BBC 1975-8) about a suburban couple who attempt to become self-sufficient in their back garden to the horror of their straight-laced and snobbish neighbours. In the same year the Centre for Alternative Technology opened in Machynlleth as a visitor attraction and educational centre—which it remains to this day—and *Practical Self-Sufficiency* magazine appeared, demonstrating that there was enough of a movement to sustain a regular publication (it continues today under the name *Country Smallholding*). The opening editorial of issue one sets the tone for what the magazine, and the movement it represented, believed:

> This magazine has come into being because there is a need for it.
> The country faces grave economic difficulties and the likelihood of severe shortages. Rapid inflation, unemployment, soaring food prices, chemically adulterated foods and the increasing dehumanising of our Society, have all contributed to a growing awareness of the need to be more self-reliant—to grow more of our own food—to make less demands on a welfare state which can no longer cope with the needs of its citizens...The need is for direct experience of the whole and natural life, irrespective of the situation in which we find ourselves—whether it be in the centre of a city or in a commune in Wales. This is of paramount importance, not only for us, but for our children—for knowledge and experience gained in childhood are never lost.[7]

The economic situation of the early seventies had certainly done a lot to contribute to a widening interest in the ideas of self-sufficiency. The 1973 oil crisis, the miners' strike in 1974, rampant domestic inflation and the introduction of the three day week in the UK, leading to widespread and long-lasting power cuts around the country, meant that alternative ideas about energy production and living more independently of central services found a wide audience. In addition, they made the post-apocalyptic world of the *Survivors* with its candlelight, oil lamps and enforced separation from modern infrastructure perhaps a little more familiar to its contemporary audience in the mid-1970s than it would be today. A crucial element of the philosophy of the self-sufficiency movement is the importance placed upon the knowledge of traditional skills. From the same editorial it is claimed that:

> this is primarily a practical magazine where we shall seek to rediscover and pass on knowledge of traditional skills and practices of good husbandry and craftsmanship. Much of this "small-scale" knowledge is in danger of dying out—so accustomed have we become to having everything "laid on"

---

[7] Editorial, *Practical Self-Sufficiency*, November/December 1975, 3.

for us. In order to do this we need your help in the form of letters, suggestions, advice and contributions from your experience.

We must, of course, be cautious in reading texts like *Survivors* as being clear expressions of contemporary cultural notions, yet it would seem that the growing discourse of self-sufficiency did have an influence on the shaping of the series. Indeed, according to the programme's creator Terry Nation, it was his main interest and drive in creating the series. The central character Abby in Episode Two says: "our civilisation had the technology to land a man on the moon but as individuals we don't even have the technology to make an iron spearhead—we are less practical than iron-age man." This also echoed a favourite point of argument made by John Seymour, one of the most important and influential figures in the self-sufficiency movement. He liked to challenge people to work out the multi-layered processes of manufacture that led to the creation of even the most basic items. The building-up of an "archive" of traditional skills—from woodworking to animal husbandry to growing wheat to making soap—was a central preoccupation of the self-sufficiency movement, and one that came to shape the narrative of *Survivors* to a powerful degree. We follow the characters in the community as they try to remember what they knew about gardening, as they research veterinary skills from any books they can find, as they experiment and make mistakes and as new people arrive broadening the success of the community with their previous experience and skills. It is in many ways not unlike a dramatised version of *Practical Self Sufficiency*'s "Getting it Together" pages, whereby several pages were set aside in every issue for short items sent in by readers sharing experiences, offering surplus for barter, asking for advice and swapping tips on such subjects as making butter, using paraffin lamps, finding cheap working clothes and preparing herbal remedies.

What, it seems to me, was so radical about the self-sufficiency movement is that in both re-evaluating the past and proposing a fundamentally different view of what the future might look like, it was also challenging some basic tenets of historical temporality. Apocalyptic texts throughout the twentieth century have proposed that the effect of some global disaster would be to compel the survivors into returning to a kind of autarkic squalor; the nightmarish visions of post-apocalyptic landscapes have been in a large part defined not by what they contain but by what they have lost. The familiar visual grammar of the post-apocalyptic—the ruins, the deserted city streets, the empty houses and abandoned cars and the declining roads—offer eloquent testimony to everything that will be forcibly abandoned after the apocalypse. Being

compelled to return to the land and eke out a basic sustenance while
having to make do without all the comforts and facilities remembered
from the pre-apocalypse world has long been an accepted narrative trope
in conceptualising these futures. Such tropes also provide the reader of
these texts with the reflexive frisson offered by reading a speculative
future nightmare from the comforts of the modern world. These attitudes
were particularly sharpened in the 1970s when the discourse of being
forcibly medievalised was surrounding events in South East Asia. While
the American army seemed intent on carrying out the notorious threat of
General Le May to "bomb [the Vietnamese] back into the stone age",[8] at
the same time the domestic revolutionary movements they were combating
seemed intent on a similar mission themselves. This keystone year of 1975
also saw a far more sinister version of middle classes abandoning urban
life and moving to agricultural communes when the Khmer Rouge took
control of Phnom Penh and ended the long civil war in Cambodia. They
launched the most radical revolutionary plan ever witnessed: the cities
were emptied and former urban dwellers reassigned to live in farming co-
operatives. All "former people" were now declared "peasants" and Year
Zero was proclaimed in what seemed far closer to medieval serfdom than
anything else. Yet the revolutionary authorities of Democratic Kampuchea,
far from considering their actions backward-looking, saw the purging of
"old" (modern, capitalist) Cambodia as wiping the slate clean and
allowing the foundation of a new, peasant society. They referred to
themselves as the most advanced country in the world.[9] Khmer self-
sufficiency was their goal, just as *juche*—"self-reliance"—had replaced
Marxism-Leninism as the official state ideology of North Korea in 1971.
Of course, the western reaction to the Khmer Rouge revolution was to
denounce it in horrified terms and view it, in the words of Elizabeth
Becker, as "a deliberate step backwards—away from modernity…
shunning the advances of the industrial revolution in its effort to become a
self-sufficient agricultural nation."[10] And yet for the British economist
Malcolm Caldwell who visited Democratic Kampuchea in 1978 this
wasn't necessarily a bad thing: "I have seen the past and it works" he

---

[8] Curtis E. LeMay, *Mission with LeMay: My Story* (Garden City, N.Y.:
Doubleday), 565.
[9] David P. Chandler, *Brother Number One: A Political Biography of Pol Pot*,
revised ed., (Boulder, Col. & Oxford: Westview Press, 1999); Ben Kiernan, *The
Pol Pot Regime: Race, Power, and Genocide in Cambodia under the Khmer Rouge
1975–1979* (New Haven, London: Yale University Press, 1996).
[10] Elizabeth Becker, "A Journey Into the New Cambodia," *The Washington Post*,
First Section, December 26, 1978.

reflected, ironically reflecting Lincoln Steffens' famous 1921 comment on the Soviet Union "I have been to the future and it works."[11] Marxism, that philosophy of progress and modernity, seemed to have been radically reconfigured in Cambodia.

It was a long way from the people's communes of Democratic Kampuchea to the smallholding co-operatives of Britain (although Allaby and Bunyard, two of the leading theorists of the self-sufficiency movement, wrote approvingly of Maoist communes as a model for the self-sufficient society).[12] Yet a certain kind of shared apocalyptic discourse ties them distantly together: a retreat from modernity, a neo-medievalism, a confusion of traits associated with the present and the past. This mixing of codes is one that I argue is a central defining characteristic of apocalyptic narrative, which typically sees its characters forced to adopt a medieval agrarian lifestyle among the ruins of cities, airports and shopping centres. In a gentle way, it seems to me also to be the tension which underpins much of the comedy of *The Good Life*. For Margo, the fact that her neighbours keep goats, chickens and pigs isn't in itself too much of a problem. Indeed, at times she enjoys displaying the Goodes' garden to her guests in the manner of an exhibit. What seems to upset her most is the apparently unexplainable fact that her neighbours seem *happy* to have their electricity and gas and telephone cut off, to live without dishwashers, hairdryers and colour televisions, to patch their worn clothes and fashion garments out of old bits of material, to make do and mend. To a wealthy middle-class woman of the 1970s like Margo, these activities would seem like memories of the enforced self-reliance of her parents' generation during the war—the very thing that post-war consumerism was supposed to have served to banish. And this is the real radicalism of the self-sufficiency movement—it proposes that our future may look something like our past but, unlike the apocalyptic texts of Wyndham and others, it views this as something to be celebrated rather than dreaded. The *Ecologist* magazine, an important influence upon the self-sufficiency movement, described itself proudly in its advertising in this period as the "journal of the post industrial age". Again, a challenge to temporal progress ("post industrial"), is at once futuristic and suggestive of neo-medievalism. This strange tension was pivotal also in another piece of BBC television drama from

---

[11] Kiernan, *The Pol Pot Regime*, 445; Martin Malia, *Russia Under Western Eyes: From the Bronze Horseman to the Lenin Mausoleum* (Cambridge, Mass., London: The Belknap Press, 1999), 340.
[12] Michael Allaby and Peter Bunyard, *The Politics of Self-Sufficiency* (Oxford: Oxford University Press, 1980), 229–31.

1975—the curious children's series *The Changes*, in which the adult population suddenly reject all forms of technology and return to pre-industrial ways of life—a stone age society within the diegesis of 1970s Britain. One fan website describes the show's resolution, where *The Changes* are reversed and the world returns to modernity, as a "shame".[13]

It is in *Survivors* though that we see this radicalism at its keenest. The first series began, in its initial episodes, by inhabiting a well-trodden post-apocalyptic diegesis of brutal, lawless settlements, people afflicted with disease and starvation and nomadic searches for safety and shelter. Tensions between series creator Terry Nation and producer Terence Dudley were mirrored in a narrative tension between nomadism and settlement that led, by the second half of the first series and the whole of the second series, into a quite different drama: one no longer about men in Land Rovers with guns, but about long-term planning, food production, craft development, community building and all the other concerns of the self-sufficiency movement.[14] Here was a post-apocalyptic drama where people enjoyed themselves, where life was purposeful and fulfilling, where celebration and play were featured, where, it seemed, the sun shone more. The *Survivors* still have to scratch an unstable life from the soil, they still contend with disease and the weather and hostile neighbours, they still inhabit essentially the same diegesis as post-apocalyptic survivors in many other texts, and yet the discourse of the self-sufficiency movement has transformed this from a nightmarish future to something rather more novel: a positive post-apocalyptic survival. At a time when we are being forced to consider a coming world without cheap oil, transport, power and the advantages of our recent decades, the influence of *Survivors* and the self-sufficiency movement should remind us not only that the future could potentially be rather less progressive than we tend to assume, but that if a return to a more traditional, agricultural way of life is forced upon us, it may not be entirely the nightmare that we might fear.

---

[13] Tony Gosling, "The Changes," http://www.bilderberg.org/changes.htm.
[14] Jonathan Bignell and Andrew O'Day, *Terry Nation* (Manchester , New York: Manchester University Press, 2004); Rich Cross and Andy Priestner, *The End of the World? The Unofficial and Unauthorised Guide to Survivors* (Tolworth: Telos, 2005).

PART III:

YOUTH CULTURES

CULTURAL ADVENTURERS

DAVE ALLEN

"Authentic subcultures were produced by subcultural theories, not the other way round"[1]

In 2007, Jon Savage opened his comprehensive history of young people by reminding us that when the Americans began using the term "teenager" regularly from 1944 it was "from the very start, a marketing term."[2] It soon crossed the Atlantic, and in addition to its links to advertising and sales, it was explored by the mass media and social scientists in respect of behaviour and lifestyles. This was especially the case regarding what was deemed to be anti-social behaviour, which manifested particularly around identified "subcultural" groups like Teddy Boys, Rockers and Mods. By the 1970s, subcultures had also become the focus of academic research, not least in Britain, and they were represented in fictional tales of recent popular cultural history.

This chapter will focus on one of those representations, the 1979 film *Quadrophenia* (dir. Franc Roddam), located in the mid-1960s London Mod scene. The film depicts many typical aspects of this working-class urban culture. We see the Mods on scooters, refining their appearance, dancing in clubs to British rhythm & blues groups, scoring and consuming drugs and invading Brighton for confrontations with their deadly rivals the Rockers. In addition, there are two familiar adolescent themes running through the film, which are not unique to the Mods—generational conflict and teenage sexuality—focussing on the character of Jimmy (Phil Daniels) and his relationship with his parents, employers and girlfriend Steph (Leslie Ash).

My main purpose in focusing on *Quadrophenia* is to ask how and to what extent the film might contribute to our understanding of Mod subcultures. This in turn invites broader questions about cinematic

---

[1] Steve Redhead, cited in David Muggleton, *Inside Subculture: The Postmodern Meaning of Style* (Oxford: Berg, 2000), 163.
[2] Jon Savage, *Teenage: The Creation of Youth 1875-1945* (London: Chatto & Windus, 2007), xiii.

representations, subcultural theories and cultural history. Can fiction ever contribute to our sense of how things were? Mainstream cinematic fictions often imply a certain "realism", but even then they must depend to some degree on narrative conventions and recognisable stereotypes, which perhaps led *Quadrophenia* to offer a limited representation of Mods. *Quadrophenia* was not alone in this, and I will examine other representations of the Mod movement to suggest two consequences. Firstly, they identified visual styles and behavioural characteristics derived partly from historical events like the seaside riots of 1964, while omitting the subtleties and shifts of subcultural life. Secondly, this relatively fixed representation of typical Mod styles and behaviour was highly influential on various Mod revivals in the decades following the release of the film.

In academic studies, Mods are always identified as one of the key British subcultural groups, normally preceded by Teddy Boys and contemporaneous with their antithesis the Rockers. In 1979—the same year as the release of *Quadrophenia*—Hebdige published the best-known work from the first phase of these studies, *Subculture: the Meaning of Style.*[3] It emanated from the highly influential Birmingham Centre for Contemporary Cultural Study (CCCS) and was important in establishing subcultural studies within the British academy. Nonetheless it has attracted a number of critiques, partly for its focus on subcultures as centres of working-class resistance, and its methodological emphasis on semiotic analysis and visual signifiers.

In 2000, Muggleton published *Inside Subculture: the Postmodern Meaning of Style,* a title clearly referring to Hebdige's seminal work.[4] Muggleton shared some of the critiques of the CCCS approach and placed greater emphasis on empirical work, proposing that claims to "'proper' or 'genuine' membership" of any subcultural group "can only be properly addressed by having recourse to the views of individual members themselves." He added, "the categories and definitions of sociologists must be derived from, rather than imposed upon, the sensibilities of the people under study."[5] By, contrast, CCCS preferred the alternative of *a priori* criteria established as a measure of legitimacy. Muggleton was nonetheless respectful of Hebdige and his colleagues, while offering a less "fixed" account of subcultures based not least on his own experiences as a punk in the 1970s. In his consideration of dominant subcultural theories he wrote, "I completely fail to recognise my own past...in these

---

[3] Dick Hebdige, *Subculture: The Meaning of Style* (London: Routledge, 1979).
[4] Muggleton, *Inside Subculture.*
[5] Ibid., 59.

interpretations."[6]   This was unusual. It is increasingly apparent that academics who study popular music and youth subcultures bring to those studies some of the experiences of being fans of the music and participants in popular culture. However the more focused studies of subcultural groups have been conducted through theoretical approaches, with little indication from the researchers and writers that they were ever members of those groups. Frith summarised this methodological problem, asking: "All researchers have been teenagers and none of them are when they do their research. Where should their own experience come in?"[7]   The phrase "their own," implies *ownership* in that second word. To what extent can we as academics incorporate the lived experiences that we own and draw them into our professional work? Frith suggests that few of us do but Muggleton argues differently. For him, personal experience seems an important stimulus and starting point since it presented a disjunction between what he remembered and what he was being told.

The question of memory is important. Participant observation is now a well-established methodological choice within social studies for subcultural groups, but it is complicated by the fact that participants of current groups are unlikely to be the principle researchers. In addition, the study of earlier teenage groups can no longer adopt participant observation approach for the obvious reason that the time has passed: such studies are now cultural *history*.

I am interested in Muggleton's response because it accords for the same experiential reasons with many of my doubts about theoretical and historical accounts of youth culture the 1960s and more specifically the Mod subculture. It may be that, like Muggleton, but unlike most of my academic peers, I was "subcultural" before I was "academic" and so I am interested in examining *Quadrophenia* partly in terms of my memories of that period without assuming any objective truth. Unlike Muggleton, I find something that I can recognise in theoretical accounts and popular representations of Mods but almost always the stories seem too fixed to represent the subtlety of the reality. Moreover, some accounts seem to be simply inaccurate.

If we take *Quadrophenia* as one of those popular representations, we might begin by asking how many Mods there were in Britain in the early and mid-1960s. There are popular histories (most notably Hewitt) that

[6] Ibid., 166.
[7] Simon Frith, "Afterword," in *After Subculture: Critical Studies in Contemporary Youth Culture,* eds. Andy Bennett and Keith Kahn-Harris, 176 (Basingstoke: Palgrave, 2004).

suggest there were only a dozen in north London in the very early 1960s.[8] I will address that limited, rather elitist view later but follow for the moment alternative accounts of Mods which take us into the mid-1960s and outside London across south-east England, the Home Counties, parts of the Midlands and one or two major northern cities.[9] There were thousands of young people who thought of themselves and their peers as Mods and by comparison the numbers at any of the seaside riots—including those depicted in the film *Quadrophenia*—were tiny. In popular folk "devil" memory, Mods are always associated with fights with Rockers on Brighton, Hastings or Clacton seafronts. But the majority of Mods and Rockers did not participate in those media-hyped events and on a day-to-day basis, Mods paid relatively little attention to Rockers (and *vice versa*).

My strongest memories of being a Mod in the period around 1964-1966 are of the music, the clubs, the clothes and the groups of like-minded individuals, a few of whom have become life-long friends. In terms of *Quadrophenia's* representations, these memories are triggered mostly by the smaller details such as being measured for a bespoke suit, having just the right haircut, gate-crashing parties and listening to rhythm & blues groups (British) and records (American) in the clubs. I can still name the local style icons ("Faces") who were older than me and earning enough money to stay ahead in terms of appearances and while my home-life was far less confrontational than Jimmy's, there was never any sense that my parents understood my obsession with the music on *Ready Steady Go!* or the need to walk around wearing wet Levis. My Mum particularly approved of the short haircuts, suits and ties, without recognising their symbolic function among my peers.

However, in 1964 I was just too young to own a scooter, never wore a Parka, never went to Brighton on a Bank Holiday, did not lose my virginity to a young Mod girl, did not take pills and unlike Jimmy, never suffered an identity crisis. In some respects that last point is crucial. Some of the aspects of *Quadrophenia* that are most important to the narrative are those that are most easily interchangeable with other social contexts: young man, unsure of his identity, falls in with bad lot, has complex adolescent relationships, is charged with a crime and confronts a personal crisis. There is nothing new there, but the cult status of the film lies not in

[8] Paolo Hewitt, ed., *The Sharper Word: A Mod Anthology* (London: Helter Skelter Books, 1999); Paolo Hewitt, *The Soul Stylists: Forty Years of Modernism* (Edinburgh: Mainstream, 2000).
[9] Nik Cohn, "England after the Beatles: Mod," in Nik Cohn, *Awopbopaloobop Alopbamboom: Pop from the Beginning,* 194–210 (London: Pimlico, 1969).

those general points, but in its representation of a very precise moment in British subcultural history. This has powerful meanings for all of us who participated in that moment, and for all those who have chosen to re-work it for themselves and their peers since 1979.

So the point of my memories, and the memories of all the other 1960s Mods, is that they help to examine the extent to which *Quadrophenia* represents a certain truth about its time and the extent to which it is limited, stereotypical and influential on subsequent cultural revivals. It is a representation that at least in those details identified above seems to accord with my memories. But an important methodological question here is whether my memory is reliable? Perhaps it is a memory constructed by *Quadrophenia* and other popular representations? Perhaps I choose to remember those details in an attempt to authenticate my own past, to tell tales not so much about Mods but about "me"?

I have two answers to that. One is to integrate what I remember with others' memories and accounts, building a complex picture of the period. The second is to set aside questions of reliability and truth, and ask instead whether my recollections are plausible in terms of published accounts. This too requires that they be woven into other accounts and representations, until a multi-layered or multi-dimensional account emerges. In many respects the key point in this essay is not whether I went, like many other Mods, to a local bespoke tailor for suit fittings (I did) since those memories do no more than confirm a cliché about Mods. Similarly, the fact that I identify my lack of a scooter as noteworthy seems to confirm the importance of scooters in Mod subcultures.

However, I wish to claim a particular significance for my memories of that period where there is a disjunction between what I remember and stereotypical accounts. I wish to explore the extent to which those disjunctions are the key to a more sophisticated understanding of historical subcultures. Having raised certain questions about familiar accounts, I will attempt to set these accounts against others and this will necessitate some rethinking of historic subcultures in general and Mods in particular. In taking this approach I am very definitely engaged in a cultural "history" project, including a consideration of the extent to which *Quadrophenia*— and similar artefacts—can ever contribute to historical understanding.

In this process there are three key ideas that inform my approach. Firstly I wish to question the assumption that British subcultures, especially Mods, could ever be classified simply by class. I am content to align myself with Muggleton's view that "youths from different class backgrounds can hold similar values that find their expression in shared membership of a particular subculture."[10] The second key idea from which my title is derived originates with Frith and is developed by Muggleton who suggests that the (interviewed) subjects of his book are "the culturally adventurous of all classes" providing "the continuity of bohemian concern that runs from the beats to the punks." That is a generic definition, not one that is tied to any single subcultural group.[11]

I will return to these two issues, but I now wish to consider the third idea. Sweetman observed that contemporary youth groups have become "increasingly heterogeneous and fluid" so that by comparison with certain subcultural groups in the 1960s, they "no longer exhibit the same degree of internal cohesion and commitment."[12] This sense of "fluidity" is useful in making sense of contemporary groups but Muggleton draws on a number of commentators to suggest that while postmodernism allows a new reading of subcultures, the earlier subcultural groups were not as fixed as we tend to believe. For example, he cites Kotarba and Wells who discovered "a surprising amount of sub-cultural mobility."[13] In addition he cites Osgerby's observation that:

Many accounts of post-war youth subcultures ... overlooked the dynamic quality to their styles. All too frequently, subcultural forms are discussed as though they were immutably fixed phenomena...[but] constant change and flux have been endemic to the universe of youth subcultures."[14]

Osgerby added "subcultures have always been fluid and fragmented 'hybrids'".[15] Other popular and academic historians seem determined to produce limited accounts of what it was to be a Mod. To some degree I am suggesting that this fixed view is confirmed by many of the representations in *Quadrophenia*; popular fictional cinema must deal to some extent in stereotypes and will produce representations which become fixed in popular consciousness.

A number of "popular" yet fairly extensive accounts of 1960s Mods have been published: some written by former Mods such as Barnes or

---

[10] Muggleton, *Inside Subculture,* 31.
[11] Ibid.
[12] Paul Sweetman, "Tourists and Travellers? 'Subcultures', Reflexive Identities and Neo-Tribal Sociality," in *After Subculture: Critical Studies in Contemporary Youth Culture,* eds. Andy Bennett and Keith Kahn-Harris, 79 (Basingstoke: Palgrave, 2004).
[13] J.A. Kotarba and L. Wells, cited in Muggleton, *Inside Subculture,* 128.
[14] B. Osgerby, cited in Muggleton, *Inside Subculture,* 50.
[15] B. Osgerby, cited in ibid., 164.

Rawlings,[16] and others collecting oral accounts of participants' memories such as Hewitt.[17] It has to be emphasised that none of these accounts concern themselves with methodological reflexivity: they simply present the spoken memories of Mods about music, fashion, clubs, transport, inspirations and Rockers.

Claiming that I was a Mod of course begs questions of definition and verification. Paolo Hewitt is at least one popular chronicler of the Mod movement who might dispute my claim, and I shall attempt to address those possible objections. Elsewhere Dominic Sandbrook has recently published comprehensive surveys of Britain in the 1960s which pay very little attention to subcultural groups but offer an account of Mods which if accurate excludes my experiences and those of most of my peers and friends.[18] In the case of some of Hewitt's work and the brief account of Sandbrook, I do not recognise myself in the accounts offered.

During a lecture given to our 1970s project at the University of Portsmouth, Sandbrook insisted on a clear distinction between Mods and Rockers in terms of class, since Rockers were working class and Mods middle class. He repeats this view in his justifiably respected work on Britain in the "Sixties". The broad scope of his work affords little detailed enquiry into subcultures and here certainly, Sandbrook's understanding contradicts mine. Firstly, he is content to draw upon the best known "popular" writing about the period including George Melly's 1970 publication on the pop arts.[19] Sandbrook uses this to justify his claim that "Modernist fans or Mods" enjoyed "markedly middle-class" experiences.[20] However, Melly's point is actually about Modern Jazz not Mods, and appears in a section subtitled "*before* Tommy Steele" [my emphasis] and almost wholly about the musicians who emerged "immediately after the war", not as part of the Mod subculture that emerged more than a decade later. Melly says that the Modernists: "understood not only the musical complexity of bop but the spirit that created it and within that emotional means *they tried to play*" [my emphasis].[21]

There is a common view of early English Mods of the late 1950s onwards, which identifies their fondness for modern jazz although this is

[16] Richard Barnes, *Mods!* (London: Eel Pie Publishing, 1979); Terry Rawlings, *Mod: A Very British Phenomenon* (London, Omnibus, 2000).
[17] Hewitt, *The Soul Stylists.*
[18] Dominic Sandbrook, *White Heat: A History of Britain in the Swinging Sixties* (London: Little Brown, 2006).
[19] George Melly, *Revolt into Style: The Pop Arts* (London: Penguin Books, 1970).
[20] Sandbrook, *White Heat,* 196.
[21] Melly, *Revolt into Style,* 22–24.

generally thought to be the later, "cooler" work of Miles Davis. But very few accounts of Mods describe them as musicians, for they are far more often consumers than producers of culture. Sandbrook's conclusions about Mods and class derived from Melly's writing are therefore inaccurate.

Sandbrook's other source, Cohn, wrote contemporary magazine articles about Mods, and in a famous piece he does describe the "roots" of Mods in "a few dozen" London-based, middle-class "sons of clerks and small businessmen" who were "purists". That is a common version of events and not one from which I dissent, but roots are not the only determinant, and a few dozen middle-class teenagers did not, as Cohn confirms, attract any media attention or popular representations, because "their influence was only local."[22] If we are still able to talk about Mods as a subcultural group and a part of English social history, it is not because of a few dozen highly stylish young men in London, but because the movement spread widely and quickly and was disseminated through the mass media.

If *Quadrophenia* offers us any kind of accurate representation of Mods it is at odds with Sandbrook's view, for this is no small group of middle-class youths. A key characteristic of the film is that the protagonists are clearly working-class, especially Jimmy who we see at home and work, as well as in the clubs and other favourite Mod locations including hairdressers and tailors shops. We also see them gate-crashing a suburban middle-class teenage party in which the social differences between the hosts and the unwelcome guests is very clear. Where does the truth lie?

The growth of the Mod subculture, linked inevitably and increasingly to marketing and commodification is an important issue for one of the major popular chroniclers of the Mods: the journalist Paolo Hewitt. For some, 1964 and 1965 are the "Mod Summers" but Hewitt claims Mod had actually died by the time of the seaside riots in 1964.[23] He notes regretfully that ITV's *Ready Steady Go!* "nationalised mod" and suggests that "sods not mods fought on the beaches in 1964." He is dismissive of these "sods" implying that they were not authentic and argues that by mid-1964, the leading stylists had packed their bags as their "elite movement ... died." He goes on to suggest that it "quickly resurfaced ... in other ways, other guises".

Elsewhere, however, Hewitt tells a different tale. His book *Soul Stylists* claims to be about "forty years of Modernism" and while this perpetuates the idea that publicity "diluted the essence of the scene" it also

---

[22] Nik Cohn, cited in Sandbrook, *White Heat,* 139.
[23] Paolo Hewitt, *The In Crowd.* Sleevenotes to the CD Collection with the same title (Dearm, 2001), 2–4.

describes a chronologically "extended family" which covered early modernists, Mods, skinheads, northern soulers, soulboys and casuals. For Hewitt "the most enduring and fertile relationship" for these subcultures "is the one that links British working-class fashion to contemporary American black music."[24] This might be construed as Hewitt's definition of "authenticity" among the young: that it is working-class, fashion conscious and in love with the music of another culture.

Soul Stylists is presented through a fascinating collage of memories of various participants in these movements. In his introduction Hewitt quotes Eddie Harvey "a modernist who was there" saying ("with a wink") "forget about the '60s. Soho in the '50s – that's where it was at."[25] Harvey's attitude is consistent with the dismissal of later participants as "sods" and with the constant tendency within subcultures to claim authenticity as brief and chronological. It signals two key criteria for popular depictions of subcultures. The first is that virtually *all* participants will claim that their experience of it was the most authentic one. The second is that the subculture can only be authentic as long as it is underground or invisible to the mass of the population, including the mass media. *Quadrophenia* worked against those views because, like *Ready Steady Go!* it helped to popularise the movement.

However, my experience and perhaps more importantly, my reflections on the Mod experience, contest those views which oversimplify a more complex reality. What interests me is the lived experience of the sod's generation (my peers) who thought they were Mods and have discovered in later life that they are excluded from Hewitt's "extended family". Hewitt's idea of re-surfacing is a crucial one and it may be helpful to re-name the first generation of Mods as "stylists". This is partly to indicate their obsession with style over other elements and partly to allow us to be more generous to the "nationalised" young people who are represented as Mods (*not* sods) in *Quadrophenia.* Such renaming also invites us to consider more thoroughly the label "modernist" as an all-embracing concept for subcultures, which appeared just as modernism in its broader sense was apparently losing its cultural impact. What we understand of the modernists suggests that they were so called because of their celebration of "modern" fashion, music and drugs. But of course that was only possible as certain elements of cultural modernism became more available economically and in the breadth of its representation. Previous generations of ordinary young people enjoyed little exposure to the experimental

[24] Hewitt, *The Soul Stylists,* 16.
[25] Eddie Harvey, cited in ibid.

culture of the international avant-garde, and even when they did, they were offered little help in understanding it. In this sense, popular modernism was never quite as underground as it may have seemed, although there was always the question of how hard one might work to uncover it.

Hewitt has made a significant contribution to the chronicling of the Mod phenomenon despite being too young to have experienced it first-hand in the 1960s. Nonetheless, he seems determined to pursue an argument for the authenticity of the "original" Mods, the early demise of the movement and by implication, the importance of its elitism. However, there is a contradiction at the heart of these arguments, for he acknowledges that the extension of post-war democracy and increased affluence for ordinary young people were key factors in the increasing independence of teenagers. It makes little sense to celebrate relative political and economic freedom by proclaiming the importance of self-defined elites. We might add to this that the tendency to see 1960s Mods as a predominantly male subculture, which is in itself problematic, has to take some account of the fact that they were the first generation for twenty years to escape conscription or national service. It is perhaps significant that when Jimmy meets his mate Kevin the Rocker in *Quadrophenia,* the latter has been in the army.

Hewitt's *a posteriori* rationalisations of authenticity are undermined by some of his accounts of the experience of being a Mod in the 1960s. One of these accounts by Ian Hebditch was published by Hewitt. This calls into question Hewitt's assertion that the Mod scene was over by 1964 because in his introduction he describes Hebditch as an "original Mod".[26] Hebditch's account describes the Portsmouth Mod scene that I participated in between 1964-1966.[27] In fact we can date it more precisely from Spring 1965-1966 because of the references to a specific club, The Birdcage, then at the heart of the Portsmouth Mod scene.

Hebditch's chapter was written in the late 1960s as a student project, and accords with many of my memories of the Portsmouth Mod scene. My own detailed recollections are assisted by a number of scrapbooks of press articles I collected in the 1960s. I also kept a daily diary in 1966, which refers frequently to aspects of that Mod experience. At a distance of more than forty years, I would suggest it is an historical document that can now be approached with a degree of objectivity. It lists many visits to clubs to see popular groups, purchases of records and clothes and visits to London, Brighton and elsewhere. Through such particular histories, a more

---

[26] Ibid.
[27] Ian Hebditch, "Weekend," in *The Sharper World, The Sharper Word: A Mod Anthology,* ed. Paolo Hewitt, 132 (London: Helter Skelter Books, 1999).

sophisticated account of Mod cultures can be written, and in the light of this, *Quadrophenia* becomes only one of those contributory texts to be interrogated and compared with all the other accounts: useful in places, irrelevant or inaccurate elsewhere.

Fig. 11.1.   Although this looks like a shot from *Quadrophenia*, it is actually Portsmouth Mods outside their Birdcage Club in the mid-1960s.
Photograph by the author.

I knew most of the Mods named in Hebditch's account and some are still friends who I see quite regularly. I shared teenage experiences with them and one key point I would make is that we became Mods having previously explored the largely American fashions and music of the early 1960s. We were not born Mods, and at a key moment we moved from mohair jumpers, ice-blue jeans and pointed shoes to the cooler Mod look. From 1964-1966 there was a thriving Mod scene in Portsmouth for which considerable documentary evidence remains and yet, as my diary records, by late 1966 suits, pills and soul music were giving way to more colourful fashions, longer hair, cannabis and experimental rock music. Cream played at The Birdcage in December 1966 and Pink Floyd, with lights, the month after. That world changed fairly rapidly and many of us changed with it, confirming the key ideas stated above that we were "the culturally adventurous of all classes" participating in a world that was "increasingly heterogeneous and fluid."

By the end of 1967 we had become what Ted Brooks, one of those participants, called "Heads": the stylish forerunners of hippies, discovering the creative counter-culture, psychedelic music and drugs. The change was documented by Nik Cohn in one of the new Sunday colour supplements in August 1967 when, at the height of the Summer of Love his article "Ready Steady Gone" was introduced with the view that:

> The Mod movement grew into the biggest teenage cult this country has ever known. It produced Carnaby Street, "Ready, Steady Go!" and the purple heart…. But now the cool cult is freezing to death. In Britain's new Hippieland, ten thousand flower-children bloom.[28]

It is important to recognise that many of the flower-children bloomed not just from new seeds but from the Mods themselves. In cinematic representations, that transition can be seen most clearly by comparing the Mods in *Quadrophenia* with the audience at the Yardbirds' gig which is recreated in the "Ricky Tick Club" in Antonioni's *Blow Up* (1966). The extras who made up that audience were almost certainly "authentic" and they are a clear representation of the shift towards more exotic, cosmopolitan fashions. Yet critic Andrew Sarris described the film as a "mod masterpiece."[29] Hewitt would certainly disagree, and I would suggest it is more representative of the Swinging Sixties, but when I saw it on release it pointed towards another cultural adventure.

Inevitably, some of the Mods regretted those changes and some shifted towards the very different skinhead subcultures. But those of us who were cultural adventurers were excited by new possibilities and moved on in an essentially optimistic transition typically of the fluidity of our lives. *Quadrophenia* showed nothing of that, since the only transitional moment of note in the film is Jimmy's breakdown. I like to think he might have turned his back on Brighton and London, made his way along the coast to Portsmouth and joined a new, creative adventure.

---

[28] Nik Cohn, "Ready, Steady, Gone," *Observer Magazine,* August 27, 1967.
[29] Andrew Sarris, "No Antoniennui," *Blowup,* http:en.wikipedia.org/wiki/Blowup.

"UNDERGROUND, OVERGROUND": REMEMBERING THE WOMBLES

KEITH M. JOHNSTON

The Wombles was one of the most popular and pervasive children's entertainment formats in 1970s Britain. The stories of furry animals who tidy up after litter-happy humans first started in books and then became a BBC animated television series (1973, 1975). These spawned an array of merchandise, and launched a 'live action' pop group and film adaptation. Through these various media incarnations, the narrative set-up remained the same. Three elder Wombles (Great Uncle Bulgaria, Madame Cholet, and Tobermory) and four young Wombles (Wellington, Tomsk, Bungo and Orinoco) live together in a burrow under Wimbledon Common. As the television series' title song says, the Wombles' life is based around litter collecting and recycling, making "good use of the things that they find, things that the everyday folk leave behind." *The Wombles'* characters are a self-sufficient and tight knit community that exists slightly outside the bounds of normal (human) society. Tidying up litter is the singular, worthy, purpose in their lives and they work at it steadfastly, with little complaint. They are a largely fraternal society, with the only sign of femininity a mostly kitchen-bound French cook-maid, Madame Cholet.

Because of *The Wombles'* immersion within 1970s British culture, it is impossible to ignore suggestive links between the programme and major social and cultural aspects of the decade. The most obvious is the link to the Keep Britain Tidy campaign: in early episodes "A Sticky End" and "Peep-Peep-Peep", the Wombles pick up litter and recycle it, using leftover toffee wrappers and tin cans to mend a leaking ceiling and create a telephone system. Yet other cultural links are equally strong. The episode "Time and Slow Motion" illustrates the characters' ethos of hard work in an era of unemployment and strikes, while also mocking the trend for time and motion studies of those still in work. When they grow their own food in "Marrow Pie" and "The Picnic," the programmes mirror the concurrent societal trend towards being self-sufficient. "Madame Cholet Returns" and "Madame Cholet and the Blackberries" focus on the continental French

Womble—and her place within the 'British' Womble burrow—as Britain voted to join the European Economic Community (EEC). Even the introduction of a Scottish character, Cairngorm MacWomble the Terrible, across six episodes in the second season, can be seen in relation to both the rise in prominence of the Scottish National Party, and equally, given the Wombles' move into pop music, the popularity of the tartan-clad Bay City Rollers.

Yet despite containing these potent links, *The Wombles* is a piece of youth culture that resists simple definitions. It can be seen as politically both right and left wing. Great Uncle Bulgaria does sit, like a good aristocrat, reading *The Times*, while his workers forage for raw materials, and a female cook slaves over a hot stove making Bramble Pie. Yet the Wombles equally function as a collective body, working together to achieve their goals, and sharing the dividends among the group. Any microcosm of Britain that could be drawn from the stories appears to be more in line with traditional views of British society of the 1940s, not the 1970s. There are echoes of earlier British cultural themes: the message of hard work, environmentalism and rural community versus a faceless conglomerate (of human litterbugs) suggests the comic tradition of the post-war Ealing Studios films *Passport to Pimlico* (1948) or *The Titfield Thunderbolt* (1953). Equally, the show's narrative structure—and the recurring spatial and temporal location of Wimbledon Common—links it to British television situation comedies such as *Dad's Army* (1968-77) which also hark back to an imagined past.

This article is, therefore, interested in identifying and exploring the range of cultural influences that are present in *The Wombles*, particularly what the disparate narrative and aesthetic approaches of the various Wombles incarnations might reveal about the series, the characters, and 1970s British culture. As the decade progressed, and *The Wombles* moved towards a global marketplace, changes to the Wombles' universe challenged these traditional ideas of "Britishness." Exploring this move from local to global, from small-scale book success to big screen stardom, reveals that the shifting identity of *The Wombles* is intrinsically tied to the media and culture within which it was created.

"The Wombles of Wimbledon Common are we"

If *The Wombles* represents a traditional, and potentially outdated, view of Britain, the source of that idea is writer-creator Elisabeth Beresford, who used traits from her own largely upper middle class family to create the personalities of the furry characters. Great Uncle Bulgaria was her father-in-law, Madame Cholet her own 94-year old French mother, Tobermory her 50-year old brother, with the younger Womble personality traits drawn from herself, her husband and her children.[1] This cultural and historical background offers some clue as to why her book *The Wombles* (1968) had only occasional connection to contemporary events, revolutionary youth movements or political upheaval. However, Beresford's apparent interest in an earlier British identity also coincided with a larger cultural phenomenon that Barbara Klinger describes as having "a strongly nostalgic component ... bygone eras constituted a substantial percentage of media productions."[2] While Klinger's examples are from American popular culture, this nostalgia is mirrored in British film and television of the late 1960s-early 1970s: *The Prime of Miss Jean Brodie* (1968) and *Doctor in Trouble* (1970) look back to the 1930s and 1950s for models of British society, while television serial *Adam Adamant Lives!* (1966-67) finds conventional British character in an out-of-time Edwardian mode.

The traditional view of Britain in *The Wombles* books continued when they were adapted for television. The BBC first broadcast Beresford's stories in a 1970 series of *Jackanory* episodes, but by 1971 was in negotiations with Beresford and animation company, Film Fair, to produce a fully animated version. Although she would be employed as the main scriptwriter, Beresford was not the sole author of this television success. Ivor Wood's visual design work gave each character distinctive visual identities—Orinoco's red scarf and floppy hat, Wellington's blue and black-striped cap, Great Uncle Bulgaria's tartan hat and cloak—while his direction and animation expertise gave them physical life and movement. Equally, the characterisation of all seven Wombles (and the omniscient narrator) was not complete without the dry and comic tones of Bernard Cribbins. Elisabeth Beresford may have created the Wombles, but Wood and Cribbins gave them animated life, comic timing and personality.

The first thirty episodes of *The Wombles*, produced during 1972, were an immediate hit when they were broadcast in February 1973. Beresford's characters now reached a wider audience than they ever had in print, and the television success led to the release of a range of Womble products. Merchandising of TV shows was still a relatively small business in the early 1970s. ITV had made some inroads with shows like *Thunderbirds* (1965-66), and the BBC had set up BBC Enterprises in 1960 to expand its programmes beyond the screen. After limited success with licensing book

---

[1] Anna Pavora, "Wombles must not take their heads off in public," *The Observer Magazine* (London), October 13, 1974.
[2] Barbara Klinger, *Melodrama and Meaning: History, Culture and the Films of Douglas Sirk* (Bloomington: Indiana University Press, 1994), 88–89.

tie-ins for titles like *Doctor Who* (1963-) and *Blue Peter* (1958-), BBC Enterprises wanted to become the central agent for merchandising based around their programmes. In the case of *The Wombles*, Film Fair owned the visual copyright on the shows, while Elisabeth Beresford had formed Wombles Incorporated with her husband and her literary agent. In a move that signalled its commitment to the show, and the revenue it expected to gain from merchandise rights, the BBC started negotiations with both companies in 1971, before the programme was even broadcast, becoming the Wombles' official merchandising agent in 1972. Within three years Wombles products were worth over 17 million pounds a year, of which the BBC took between thirty and forty percent in royalties.[3]

By 1975, audiences could buy Wombles products for the bathroom (toothpaste, bubble bath), the bedroom (duvet covers, lampshades), and the kitchen (placemats, cutlery). Children could wear a Wombles T-shirt and slippers, eat Wombles sweets, and bounce around on a Wombles space hopper. Adults could keep track of the week on a Wombles calendar, use Wombles giftwrap for presents, and have a cup of Wombles coffee in their own Wombles mug. In all, there were over 150 separate Wombles items licensed, produced and sold throughout Britain: and that list does not include the singles and albums that were released. The commercialisation of *The Wombles* in this period fits within the consumerism that flourished in the 1970s, despite uncertain economic conditions. These products are all largely disposable gift items aimed at a youth audience, commodities whose purpose is the continuation of a brand identity that began in an act of single authorship, expanded into a successful television show, and then spawned this army of kitsch, mass-produced "trashy objects."

The popular success of *The Wombles* meant the BBC wanted a second series. Yet letters to the Corporation had raised a specific concern: how did Wombles reproduce? In particular, did Great Uncle Bulgaria and Madame Cholet ever have a bit of a Womble under the covers? This debate cropped up in messages to the BBC from parents and children, asking where they could buy a real Womble, whether Wombles came in eggs, and whether there would be any Womble babies in the next series. Discussed in at least one pre-production meeting for series two between the BBC, Film Fair and Elisabeth Beresford and her husband, the eventual decision, in an age of pre-marital sex, the pill, and feminism, was to add a

---

[3] Palmer, "The Amazing Wombles Inc.," *The Sun* (London), August 7, 1975; Tony Slaughter, "Wombling away to a fortune," *Sunday Telegraph* (London), December 15, 1974.

men's dormitory and show that Bulgaria and Cholet had separate rooms.[4] Yet what goes unsaid in the debate over Womble sex is the fact that Cholet is not British. Britain may have become a full member of the EEC in 1973, but the French Womble, on the fringes of the television burrow, featured in less than a third of the episodes. However, while Madame Cholet's French status was not referenced in the BBC correspondence, her nationality and sexuality became prominent aspects of the television show's most successful offshoot: the Wombles pop group.

"The Wombling Song"

During production of the first television series, composer Mike Batt created a piece of music called "Underground, Overground" that was played over the show's opening and closing credits. As the success of *The Wombles* grew, Batt expanded this song for release as a single, then followed it up with a series of single and album releases between 1973 and 1977. Although never achieving the number one spot—*Wombling Merry Christmas* made it to number two in December 1974—the Wombles "band" had eight top thirty hits in two years, and the best-selling album *Remember You're A Womble* spent over thirty weeks in the UK album charts. The Wombles band was named "Singles Group of the Year" by *Music Week* in 1974 for selling more singles than any other group.

Batt's music took *The Wombles* away from Elisabeth Beresford's direct control and redefined (and in some cases, sidelined) its British heritage, aiming instead at a wider cultural target. As the B-side of the first single makes clear, Batt was looking beyond the confines of Wimbledon Common. "Wombles Everywhere" is a song about the different Womble nationalities, and it positions the Wombles as a global phenomenon. It was more than a lyrical device. Batt's music took on the characteristics of different international musical genres: "The Womble Square Dance" and "Nashville Womble" borrowed from country and western music; "Wombling White Tie and Tails" referenced classical Hollywood musicals; "Minuetto Allegreto" is based on Mozart's Jupiter Suite; "Banana Rock" and "Let's Womble To the Party Tonight" used styles similar to the Beach Boys and the Beatles; "The Empty Tidy Bag Blues" referenced American blues legends; while "The Myths and Legends of King Merton Womble and his Journey to the Centre of the Earth" offered a pastiche of 1970s progressive rock concept albums (particularly those of Rick Wakeman).

---

[4] Cynthia Felgate, Letter to Head of Children's Programmes, BBC Written Archives Centre, Caversham, WAC T2/292/1 14 January 1974.

By playing with these disparate musical styles, Batt moved the Wombles from a traditional British base to one that could be influenced and guided by cultural forces beyond Britain's shores. There were songs about a Womble James Bond, a superhero Womble, Wombles in Space, and a Womble cowboy (The Orinoco Kid). With a suggestion of individual desires rather than community values, these pop songs were a departure from the existing narratives of *The Wombles*, and they revised what *The Wombles* was capable of as a global youth brand. At the same time, they represent an awareness that Britain was looking outwards for inspiration, particularly towards the USA (think of the musical genres listed above: country-and-western, Hollywood musicals, blues, the Beach Boys). Although the myths of "Swinging London" and "Beatlemania" had been potent in the mid to late-1960s, fewer British cultural products dominated international music and fashion in the 1970s. Britain may still have produced popular music by artists as diverse as Led Zeppelin, T Rex and Elton John, but the Wombles (like other pop groups of the time, such as the Bay City Rollers) increasingly looked to America for popular (and commercial) musical influences.

The move into pop music also affected the legacy of the Wombles because it expanded their image beyond Wimbledon Common, away from a nostalgic Britain, and on to staples of 1970s youth television: *Blue Peter*, *Crackerjack* (1955-84) and, perhaps most importantly, *Top of the Pops* (1964-2008). The expansion of *The Wombles* universe through Batt's musical borrowings had a lasting impact on public perception of how the Wombles sounded and appeared. The "overground" success of the live action Wombles band—6-foot tall abominable furry monsters rather than small, cute animals in a tiny burrow—grew from regular appearances on *Top of the Pops* to being the interval act during the 1974 Eurovision Song Contest. By 1976, band member Uncle Bulgaria was being photographed next to Miss America (issues around Bulgaria and sexuality had apparently been resolved). This musical popularity expanded aspects of the main Womble characters. Orinoco may still think with his stomach, but the songs paint a picture of his dream life as a western hero or a space adventurer; Wellington may still be a shy wannabe inventor, but he is the only Womble to release a solo record; and while Great Uncle Bulgaria may sit behind *The Times*, as a young Womble he hung around with Mozart.

The most successful character revision came with Batt's treatment of Madame Cholet. The female Womble is recreated in a variety of different guises, from a Womble Ginger Rogers to the bass player in the Wombles band. This re-imagining of Cholet's character may have been a belated (if limited) acknowledgement of the feminism movement in Britain, but it showed that a female Womble had more to offer than maternal cooking skills. Cholet now had equal prominence as a band member, and she featured in songs that suggested she was in control of her own sexuality (at one point borrowing Mae West's line, "Come up and see me sometime"). Cholet's expanded role was not simply a musical note: it also featured in the next development of the growing Wombles universe. In 1976, despite the Wombles' slipping popularity in the pop charts, no new TV shows, and a decline in the merchandising boom, the Rank Organisation announced the production of a Wombles film.

Wombling Free

Rank, once a powerhouse of British film production, was a shadow of its former self in the mid-1970s. The company's investment in British filmmaking had declined since the heyday of the 1940s and 50s, and by the mid 1970s, it was mainly distributing films. Those few films it did fund, stuck to tried and true genres. Rank did however back a proposal for a Wombles film called *Wombling Free* (1977). Filmed during 1977, for a Christmas release, *Wombling Free*'s producer Ian Shand noted that as "the first film project that Rank has invested in 100 per cent in a long time" it was "very important" that it should do well.[5] With Rank using the film to judge whether British cinema was a wise investment, one trade press article summarised the mood of the time: "After they cleaned up on Wimbledon Common... can The Wombles do the same for the British film industry?"[6]

Ultimately, the answer was no. Many critics saw the film as being too little, too late, released almost two years after the main flurry of Wombles-mania had died down. But the lacklustre commercial success of the film does not prevent it being an interesting endnote to the Wombles 1970s adventure, most notably because of the way it attempts to balance the television and pop music incarnations, treading a path between British tradition and the international focus of Batt's Wombling songs. Opening with a voiceover that describes how Wombles have been clearing up after humans since Adam & Eve first discarded an apple core in the Garden of Eden, the film cuts to baseball cap-clad American Wombles at a New

---

[5] Iain M. McAsh, "After they cleaned up on Wimbledon Common... Can the Wombles Do The Same For The British Film Industry?," *Films Illustrated* 7, no. 73 (1977): 31.

[6] Ibid., 30.

York ticker tape parade; Russian Wombles in thick (red) woollen hats wombling through the snow; and Indian Wombles dredging the ornamental pool in front of the Taj Mahal. Even after settling down in Wimbledon Common, the film seems dissatisfied with the drab opportunities offered by this British location, shifting to other fantasy or nostalgic dream spaces. One musical sequence sees the Wombles turning their British burrow into Café Cholet, a French pavement café with tables, umbrellas and a paper Eiffel Tower; and another creates a fantasy world based on Hollywood musicals.

This latter sequence, halfway through the movie, shows the Wombles in a dilapidated cinema. Ruefully, Great Uncle Bulgaria surveys the ripped seats, paper-strewn floor, and half-dismantled screen, telling the younger Wombles about the days when such places were dream palaces. Sighing, he suggests they tidy up and give the place some dignity. As Orinoco unfolds a Fred Astaire poster, the film dissolves to a faux-Busby Berkeley routine set to the tune of Mike Batt's "Wombling White Tie and Tails." As tuxedo-wearing Wombles tap dance and swing their canes, the film directly references famous scenes from *Singin' in the Rain* (1952), *On the Town* (1949) and *The Sound of Music* (1965), while also showing Madame Cholet as Ginger Rogers, Mae West and Julie Andrews. Reaching a crescendo, the film returns to the day-dreaming Orinoco, as the Wombles leave the cinema and head back to the burrow.

The cinema scene is important for a number of reasons. It starts in a British location, but continues the Batt tradition of commenting on larger cultural forces: in this case, the power of Hollywood film production over British, and the cinema's decline in 1970s Britain. Despite being British Wombles, Orinoco's matinée idols are Fred Astaire and Ginger Rogers, not Michael Wilding and Anna Neagle. The film sequences being parodied come from big MGM Gene Kelly musicals like *Singin' in the Rain* or *On the Town*, not British musicals starring George Formby or Gracie Fields. While the British film musical may have been less well known, the inclusion of this sequence does talk to the way that, by the 1970s, British culture had become permeated with American film and television product rather than homegrown. The scene also continues Batt's development of Madame Cholet. Earlier in *Wombling Free*, during the song "Cholet," she is a mysterious female figure around whom the male Wombles flock; in the Hollywood parody, she is Rogers, West and Andrews. Yet while these may open up the figure of Cholet beyond the maternal cook, it still roots her in a nostalgic past: Rogers and West were not sexual or romantic icons in 1977, replaced by the contemporary female figures of Jane Fonda or Julie Christie. The music and film versions of the Wombles may give

Cholet more to do, and present her as more than a maternal cook, but they still restrict how audiences saw the only female Womble in town.

This cinema sequence also reflects the narrative structure of the film. Built around short, five-to seven-minute sketches, the film recalls both the original short stories and the five-minute animations that launched *The Wombles* to a wider audience four years earlier. Any attempt at an overarching narrative is disrupted by other plot distractions: a visit from MacWomble, Bungo digging a burrow in Buckingham Palace gardens, or Tobermory inventing a new machine. Although loosely related to the film's environmental message, there is little to link together these disparate references to alternative energy sources, dwindling fossil fuel supplies, air pollution, and recycling. Unlike earlier iterations, Great Uncle Bulgaria baldly states the problem has become too big for these furry litter activists to make a difference. In an echo of their 1970s role as youth ambassadors for Keep Britain Tidy, the Wombles conclude that Earth's future is in the hands of human children. Unfortunately, given the lack of any strong or useful child characters in the film (Bonnie Langford's Kim Frogmorton has little purpose in the narrative), the film actually suggests that Earth needs *The Wombles* more than ever.

"Remember You're A Womble"

Wombling Free may have been a coda to the 1970s success of the Wombles, but the film's failure has not stopped the Wombles from retaining a degree of cultural visibility into the 21st century. The original sixty animated shows have been repeated on the BBC, ITV, and satellite channel Nick Jr.; new Wombles episodes were made in the late 1990s; Wombles books have been continually published; the Wombles pop group released a new Christmas single and several compilation albums; and a Wombles band marched during a parade for the Queen Mother in 2000. Then, in 2008, PACT (Producers Alliance for Cinema and Television) launched an Internet campaign to raise awareness of how few British voices there were on children's television, hoping to convince the government to offer more protection for British children's programming. Their main public campaign came in the form of an Internet video, which re-edited original footage into an Americanised and fake episode of *The Wombles*. Entitled "Bad Ass Wombles of Central Park," the video contains a canned American laugh track alongside references to American language such as "fanny pack", "awesome", "sunny side up", and cultural totems for example calling 911, and referring to NYPD. At the end of the video, Great Uncle Bulgaria, voiced by Bernard Cribbins, notes "Tell those

Wombles in government we need to start making British programmes for British kids again...before it's too late." Echoing the American dominance of British culture seen in the cinema sequence of *Wombling Free*, the PACT video suggests that *The Wombles* programme might be as relevant now as it was in 1973.

The Wombles was an intrinsic part of 1970s British culture, one that was forged through the interaction of novel, TV, music and film. As demonstrated here, the Wombles were, at once, conservative and liberal, stuck in the past and forward thinking, based in ideas about a nostalgic Britain but also suggesting a more global outlook akin to the 1960s or 70s. Ultimately, their legacy remains one of family and community: these threads run from the books to the film, and they continue to inform the way in which *The Wombles* are perceived, talked about, and portrayed, to this day. Aesthetically, the Wombles went from foot-high puppets to six-foot-tall furry costumes, but Orinoco retained his red scarf and hat, and Great Uncle Bulgaria still wore a tartan hat and shawl. These recurring motifs have helped *The Wombles* of the 1970s remain visually identifiable, alongside the narrative and thematic focus on family, community and cooperation. The recent video from PACT (although itself nostalgic for an earlier era) acknowledges this legacy by its subversion of a very recognisable British family. Its call for communal protest, of people working together for a common cause, stands firmly in the themes and traditions of *The Wombles*, and its impact on popular youth culture of 1970s Britain.

"AND FINALLY ... NEWS FOR CHILDREN": AN INSIGHT INTO THE INSTITUTIONAL DEVELOPMENT OF THE BBC CHILDREN'S NEWS PROGRAMME, *JOHN CRAVEN'S NEWSROUND*

JULIAN MATTHEWS

Introduction

This paper discusses an important innovation in children's television programmes of the 1970s: the development and production of the first news programme for children: *John Craven's Newsround*. It reflects critically on the description of news production offered by ethnographic news studies of the time, and in contrast to descriptions of standardised news product generated by routinised news production processes, introduces a unique news form. This developed according to ideas about the interests and sensibilities of children, and the expected qualities of a public service BBC news programme, within unique institutional arrangements. As such, this paper offers a detailed account of the historical development of a news programme and a moment when news broadcasting for children begins.

The historical shaping of form

Despite selected attempts to piece together the historical development of news as a unique form,[1] as well as a series of sub-genres more recently,[2]

---

[1] Paddy Scannell and David Cardiff, *A Social History of British Broadcasting, 1922-1939* (Oxford: Blackwell, 1991); Kevin Barnhurst and John Nerone, *The Form of News: A History* (London: The Guildford Press, 2001); Stuart Allan, *News Culture* (Buckingham: Open University Press, 2005).

[2] Jackie Harrison, *Terrestrial TV News in Britain: The Culture of Production* (Manchester: Manchester University Press, 1999).

the established expositions of news programmes have taken the standardised nature of programmes as a given, in an effort to examine the context of their production. The groundbreaking ethnographic accounts in the 1970s, for instance, focused attention on the production operations of major news outlets, producing a coherent and functional working model of the news production process. Designed purposefully to supersede previous professionally-held explanations of journalists as autonomous and critical, or the academically prevalent views of them as subaltern to paymasters and ideological convictions,[3] or simply as individual decision makers and gatekeepers,[4] these placed them as part of a highly organised and bureaucratic production process. They described their actions as determined by a mediated economic logic,[5] news policies,[6] and the control of the editor.[7] Notions of autonomy were challenged further as part of their accounts of a routinised production process with the segregation of journalists into news beats[8] and strict newsroom roles amidst a rigid newsroom hierarchy; stories sourced and planned in advance as part of news diaries,[9] and with standardised professional ideologies,[10] news values,[11] and inferential frameworks,[12] informing the selection of news material and news access opportunities.[13] Viewed in context, it is without doubt that these accounts provide a strong sense of the culture and

---

[3] Graham Murdock and Peter Golding, "For a Political Economy of Mass Communications, " in *The Socialist Register 1973*, eds. Ralph Milliband and John Saville, 205–33 (London: Merlin, 1974).
[4] David M. White, "The Gatekeeper: A Case Study in the Selection of News," *Journalism Quarterly* 27 (1950): 383–94.
[5] Edward Epstein, *News from Nowhere: Television and the News* (New York: Random House, 1973); David L. Altheide, *Creating Reality: How TV News Distorts Events* (Beverly Hills: Sage, 1976).
[6] Warren Breed, "Social Control in the Newsroom: A Functional Analysis," *Social Forces* 33 (1955): 326–55.
[7] Leon V. Sigel, *Reporters and Officials: The Organization and Politics of Newsmaking* (Massachusetts: Health and Company, 1973).
[8] Mark Fishman, *Manufacturing the News* (Austin: University of Texas Press, 1980).
[9] Phillip Schlesinger, *Putting Reality Together* (London: Methuen, 1978).
[10] Peter Golding and Peter Elliott, *Making the News* (London: Longman, 1979).
[11] Gay Tuchman, *Making News: A Study in the Construction of Reality* (New York: The Free Press, 1978).
[12] James Halloran, Philip Elliott and Graham Murdock, *Demonstrations and Communications: A Case Study* (London: Penguin, 1970).
[13] Herbert Gans, *Deciding What's News: A Study of CBS Evening News, NBC Nightly News, Newsweek and Time* (New York: Random House, 1979).

institutions of news making within the 1970s. But the subject of their observations, the major news outlets situated at a particular time, does delimit the explanatory potential of their insights particularly in terms of accounting for the differentiation among news programmes and the historical context that has informed their development. This is the starting point for our discussion of the character and institutional development of *John Craven's Newsround.*

John Craven's Newsround was a BBC programme developed in the early 1970s that sought to provide a bulletin of news stories for children.[14] For our proposes, it provides an example of a news programme that is unique by design and one which contrasts sharply with the focus adopted within other children's programmes in the 1970s. Indeed, the BBC appears to have deliberately challenged their established understandings of appropriate programming for children when producing this programme. As Stephen Wagg and others have documented, BBC programmes although having moved forward in design terms from the first Director General's view of producing for children "wholesome programmes that could take them away from the squalor of the streets", these still retained a strong sense of paternalism and protectionism in the 1970s.[15] In light of this, the intention followed by *John Craven's Newsround* to comment on adult world affairs for children appears to question notions of the preferred media childhood that underpinned such broadcasting. A closer examination of the events leading up to the programme's production, however, shows that an intention to develop a radical and challenging media form did not inspire its creation. This is made clear in the writing of Anna Home, a former Head of the Children's Programmes Department, who describes how *John Craven's Newsround* was produced in response to a dilemma present within the department's activities.[16] Hence, now we shall look more closely at this and the general institutional context that informed its production.

The children's department, as part of an effort to develop a rounded schedule of programmes, had begun to include imported material from American broadcasters in the 1970s. In doing so, it had difficulty maintaining the appropriate timings in its schedule in the early part of the

---

[14] The programme's name was changed to *Newsround* in 1989 when John Craven left the show.

[15] Stephen Wagg, "'One I made earlier': Media, Popular Culture and the Politics of Childhood," in *Come on Down: Popular Media Culture in Postwar Britain*, eds. Dominic Strinarti and Stephen Wagg, 150–78 (London: Routledge, 1992).

[16] Anna Home, *Into the Box of Delights: A History of Children's Television* (London: BBC Books, 1993).

decade. The advertisement breaks in the American programmes produced an annoying ten-minute gap in the overall programme timings that required urgent attention. Faced with this predicament, the department decided that the best strategy was to devise a new programme to fill this gap and asked those involved in production to think hard about potential ideas. Among those that offered suggestions, Edward Barns, the then Assistant Head of Children's Programmes, recommended that the department produce a small and compact news bulletin for children. This suggestion was gratefully received and later given the go-ahead on account of the difficulties inherent in the other proposed solutions.

After this point, Barns worked on some early ideas with the help of another individual who was to become involved with the programme, John Craven. Craven up until this time had been working as a BBC regional employee in the West Country and, unbeknown to him, was acquiring the appropriate credentials for a producer and presenter of a children's news programme. He was approached by Barns as a replacement for the first choice of presenter, Jonathon Dimbleby, on the basis of his experience in reporting hard news when working as a journalist as well as in factual children's programmes when fronting a current affairs programme produced for children called *Search*. After accepting the proposal, Craven then helped Barns to explore various ideas and suggested along the way the name "*Newsround*" for the programme, to which Barns, then wishing to place Craven in the role of presenter, added the personalising touch of "*John Craven's Newsround*".

The BBC institutional context was important in providing the appropriate conditions for the programme to emerge, and also in encouraging the idea of a news programme for children to germinate—albeit in a rather unorthodox way. Thus, it is important to return to the department's initial problem for a moment and explain the two immediate issues that it faced with the task of developing such a programme. The first was that the department lacked significant funds to create a sustainable and robust solution to fill the time-gap in the schedules in the first place. A second and related concern was that it was deficient in the know-how and particularised resources to produce a news programme, because its expertise and resources lay within the production of children's genres. Barnes, already convinced of the importance of the programme, now responded to these emerging problems by cajoling his friend and colleague, Derek Amoore, the then Chief Editor of BBC news, to help to rescue the project. Amoore obliged, and sometime later supplied a range of newsgathering resources and technical facilities. He also secured space in a corner of the newsroom (of *Foreign News*) to allow for the programme to be produced. As a consequence of this intervention, the programme was developed and then broadcast initially for two days, Tuesdays and Wednesdays, on a six-week trial that began in April 1972 (4/4/72 - 10/5/72). Received favourably by children who were reported to describe the programme fondly as "our news" within BBC audience research,[17] the programme returned for a six-month run in September of that year, and this pattern was continued through 1973 and 1974 with the number of shows increased to four in the latter part of 1974 and all year broadcasting following in 1979.

The BBC institutional context also contributed significantly to the particularised way that the programme was developed. The programme's character was shaped as part of its unique position within the institution. As many have remarked, *John Craven's Newsround* significantly benefited from being part of the BBC. Those working on the programme in the 1970s whom I interviewed, described in particular how its distinctiveness grew from the institutional situation that allowed these significant advances to be made. At this time, for instance, the programme was allowed to operate with relatively few constraints from the departments that subsidised its existence (The News Department and The Children's Department). The original three staff worked with a desk and two typewriters in the corner of the foreign news studio and were free to attend regular news meetings and to learn techniques and skills without contributing to the running of adult news programmes and to use the resources designated for these programmes, with some negotiation, without answering for what would be produced. In short, the news department was used as a resource without having to account for what was appropriated and why. This privilege contributed directly to the identity of the programme:

> One of its great strengths actually was that it wasn't anywhere. The News Department whenever it tried to do anything was stamped on because it [*John Craven's Newsround*] wasn't part of the News Directorate, and Children's [programme department] didn't really understand it and so they left it alone. So it just went off and did its own thing really.[18]

However, this comment slightly misrepresents the reasons behind the programme's new-found position. To explain this point further we need to consider the children's programme department's role in the programme's

---

[17] BBC Internal Memo, 1973. Newsround Archive, BBC Television Centre, London.
[18] Interview with Ex-Newsround reporter (anonymised), September 21, 1999.

development. My research has revealed that rather than granting such autonomy on the basis of simply lacking an understanding of the programme as is suggested above, the children's department did so on purpose. This arrangement followed an original policy to staff the programme with experienced journalists who would bring the understandings and skills which were lacking and thus required in the department. The programme's news team was also to be given control to define the programme's news agenda and identity as they were judged to be the best qualified to manage these particular aspects of the programme. Such decisions created a sanctioned distance between the programme and the department that allowed the team to go forward and develop a unique news form.

The BBC children's news form

As discussed above, the ideas for the children's news programme came first from discussions between Edward Barns and John Craven. However, shortly after this time Jill Roach, another journalist and specialised employee in the department, joined them (as well as the two other members of the team) in an effort to develop these ideas further. As a news team of BBC employees, all were aware of the need to produce a news service for children that reflected the wider ethos of BBC broadcasting or in other words, as Craven later outlined in interview, "to explain the most important items, or news of the day."[19] Further, it was believed that children required such a service, as they were increasingly experiencing such issues within their everyday encounters with adult media in the home. Nevertheless within these discussions the team were also mindful of how recent research had provided worrying findings about children's dislike of news programmes which made the task of manufacturing a news programme for children more difficult. Craven summarises these in the following:

> British children had an antipathy to the news...they were tired of being told to "be quiet" by their parents because the news was on the radio or the television. Quite simply, children thought news was boring.[20]

---

[19] "How John Craven see his Newsround Role," *Evening Standard,* September 6, 1980.
[20] John Craven, "Newsround," (paper presented at the EBU News Working Group Discussion on News and Children, Athens, September 7, 1978), 4.

On this basis, it was decided that the BBC news programme for children had to include some substantial changes to the adult news form to counter this general disapproval of news programmes. As a consequence, several key ideas were produced that later formed a blueprint for the programme. They agreed firstly, that the programme should not include stories that the audience would find hard to understand, and secondly, that it should avoid the wallpaper film that was often used in adult news as it was believed that this would distract from, rather than add to, the audience's comprehension of the news item. Thirdly, they were clear that the programme would not include a presentational style that would talk down to children. Finally, and most importantly, it was heartily acknowledged that they did not want to produce a programme that would make the audience want to switch off.

With these planks in place, the team moved to then develop a specific news presentation to be implemented throughout the elements of the programme. This introduced a youthful news presentation to counteract the formal conventions of the adult news programme and children's experience of teaching and teachers within schools at the time. However, an agreement was reached on the basis of early discussions that *John Craven's Newsround* would not feature children reading the news for the reasons that became clear from later examples of American children's news programmes, as Craven outlines in a newspaper article: "I've seen one show from America, a 10 year old Anna Ford reading the news, terribly coy. I just think that children are too bright to imagine that other children had much to do with putting the programme together."[21]

Instead, the presenter delivered the news with a different dress style, demeanour and body position to accompany news stories that were simplified and personalised, in order to enthuse, but not patronise, this new news constituency. Indeed, the overall upbeat presentation, including the unique introduction and conclusion to the programme, was manufactured to address poignant concerns with children's limited attention spans when watching factual material.

They also forged a different agenda around a perception of their audience as is outlined in the comment here:

> We did not have a great consultation panel or anything like that when the programme was set up. Instead, we covered what instinctively we thought the audience would want. Edward (Barns) was a great one for instinctively knowing the audience. His background was *Blue Peter* and things like that.

---

[21] "How John Craven See his Newsround Role," *Evening Standard,* September 6, 1980.

I knew roughly that children would be interested in wildlife, adventure, sport and space and all of those sorts of key areas. So, we built the bulletin around the things that we thought the audience would be interested in. We put in what might be the most significant [adult] news stories of the day but not necessarily as the lead on Newsround rather as half way through the bulletin or as not at all.[22]

As is made clear above, the programme's developing agenda included the various story types of: relevant adult news stories; news stories that would interest children; those that feature children; and stories that would entertain. Appearing as part of the programme's public service commitment, the first category of stories reproduces those "relevant" aspects of the adult news world within the programme and justifies these selections in terms of the impact of media saturation on children as was outlined above and is further articulated here by Craven:

A five year old can read newspaper headlines—even the sexiest ones; an eight year old listening to pop music on radio will suddenly hear the latest news, delivered in a strident styles. They may not understand the news but they can't escape from it.[23]

As a consequence, *John Craven's Newsround* was envisaged to "tell the stories in a way that they [children] will understand."[24] But, as the producer Jill Roach outlined in a newspaper article later in the decade, the selection of political stories are generally eschewed as on one level "the complications of an industrial dispute are difficult for anyone to comprehend, let alone a ten year old."[25] Despite this and in the first year of broadcast, the programme covered various topics: the Vietnam War, including troop movements and bombing raids; a report from a Vietnam village produced by Martin Bell; the storming of the Olympic village and subsequent deaths of the hostages; and accounts of "the troubles" in Northern Ireland. Similarly, these early bulletins in 1972 were filled with stories about the environment, adventure, sport and space that were considered to be of interest to children. These included the first news of the panda breeding programme in Japanese zoos; the first expedition to Everest without oxygen; Mark Spitz's seven gold medal haul in the Olympics; the first bedside interview with the England goalkeeper Gordon Banks; and the various Apollo space missions.

---

[22] Interview with John Craven, December 17, 1999.
[23] Craven, *Newsround*, 3.
[24] Ibid.
[25] "Newsround Gets a Big Brother," *Daily Mail,* May 28, 1977.

Additionally, a unique feature of these bulletins was the presence of news stories that featured children and those that were included to entertain them. Craven explained that the programme was the first to tap this source of "alternative news that you won't find anywhere else."[26] In placing a focus on the lives of children in 1972, it included stories on a special school for gypsy children in Wandsworth; school children's expedition to the cross the Sahara desert; an interview with children who met the Queen; and those experiencing "the troubles" in Northern Ireland. Equally, within the first year of broadcast, the programme also included many stories that would entertain children prefacing these with the now famous "and finally..." introduction and placing them as the last news item. Craven and Rowan, when reflecting on their presence sometime later, explained that the selection of such stories came from an early decision made to "report good news as well as bad and to look out for the off-beat, but still newsworthy happenings."[27] So in addition to stories on the Sports Personality of the Year, the arrival of pop stars to Britain such as Donny Osmond, and the opening of new shows such as *Jesus Christ Superstar* in London, there were the more off-beat ones such as Bagpipes being taught as an "O" level subject in Scotland, and the abandonment of a protest about a popular cartoon that was introduced in the following way: "Hello, and there's good news tonight for Tom and Jerry fans. An MP has called off his campaign to get it banned—the reason, a huge protest from children."[28]

Also, news stories were presented to the audience with a new particularised news stance which offered personalised entry points so as to make news events appear relevant for them. In line with this, the serious subjects included in particular were reported as early press release explains with a "news peg to help the audience identify" such as "the danger of using toy guns in Belfast"[29] in context of news of "the troubles" in Northern Ireland. Similarly, while personalising news content, the team also recognised a need to be mindful of the "fragile sensibility" of its audience and in doing so developed strategies to address sensitive topics with the self-censoring of news pictures—including those of death, crying adults and misery—and language.

---

[26] Ibid.

[27] John Craven and Eric Rowan, *And Finally: Funny Stories from John Craven's Newsround* (London: BBC/ Knight, 1983), 7.

[28] *Newsround*, December 7, 1972.

[29] BBC, *Newsround,* Press Release, Internal Memo, 1973. Newsround archive, BBC Television Centre, London.

In sum, it was hoped that the effort to fill the programme with watchable and well-illustrated stories would produce an audience of eight year olds with a taste for news. BBC audience research from 1973 seemed to support this proposition when offering figures that explained how watching was rising to 43 % of five to seven year olds; 43 % of eight to eleven year olds; and 41.4 % of twelve to fourteen year olds.[30] Such success reassured the team as to the appropriateness of their news form.

Conclusion

At the beginning of this paper, I suggested how exploring a case study of the development of *John Craven's Newsround* would offer evidence of the institutional factors that shaped its development, in contrast to a view of standardised programmes and production processes offered in previous news based research. This is certainly the case in terms of how the programme was made and introduced to the BBC children's schedules. But, more specifically the particularised discourses of "BBC public service news provision" and the "child news consumer" that emerge here have played a considerable part in programme formation. Seeking to encourage its audience to engage with serious news events, *John Craven's Newsround* reflected an ingrained sense of "public service broadcasting." As I have suggested elsewhere, this is less the case with the modern programme where production is now informed by perceptions of a competitive broadcasting environment and uninterested news consumers.[31] Similarly, we have seen how a view of children operated as a "check and balance" on the production of the programme's bulletin in the 1970s with views on their cognition, sensibilities and interests shaping story selection, the news frames used, as well as the character of the material represented. On reflection then, this paper has described the process of negotiating a news childhood for children in the 1970s, in addition to providing unique

---

[30] BBC, *Newsround,* Press Release, Internal Memo, 1973. Newsround archive, BBC Television Centre, London.
[31] Julian Matthews, "Cultures of Production: The Making of Children's News," in *Media Organization and Production,* ed. Simon Cottle, 131–45 (London: Sage, 2003); Julian Matthews, "A Missing Link? The Imagined Audience, News Practices and the Production of Children's News," *Journalism Practice* 2, no. 2 (2008): 265–80; Julian Matthews, "Negotiating News Childhoods: News Producers, Visualized Audiences and the Production of the Children's News Agenda," *Journal of Children and Media* 3, no. 1 (2009): 3–18.

insights into the development and operation of one of the more unusual news forms.

LOST IN THE SEVENTIES: *SMASH HITS* AND THE TELEVISUAL AESTHETICS OF BRITISH POP

STEPHEN HILL

Introduction

Smash Hits, the British music magazine launched by EMAP in 1978, is synonymous with the 1980s. And it is easy to see why. Though the magazine continued until 2006, the apex of its success coincides with Margaret Thatcher's second term in office and the rise of what is often labelled "new pop" in the 1980s.[1] Less widely considered, however, is the period in which *Smash Hits* was edited by Nick Logan and Ian Cranna (1978 to 1981) and the magazine's footprint in the 1970s. That this period has been passed over is remarkable, given the longevity of music from that era and the widespread recognition of Nick Logan's work on both *New Musical Express* (*NME*) and *The Face*. In a broader sense, *Smash Hits* reflects the rise of consumer lifestyle in the 1970s. More specifically, the space the magazine occupies is the no-man's-land between punk and the new romantic era: what is often defined as post-punk. However, as Dave Hepworth has suggested, that term is problematic:

> I have a great problem with "post-punk". The fact that there is the expression "post-punk" indicates punk's major problem, which is that it had a massively over-inflated sense of its own importance. Punk rock was just one of the things that was going on at the time. You might as well say the post-disco mainstream, because actually if you're looking for a real commercial phenomenon in the mid-1970s, it was disco music.[2]

---

[1] Dave Rimmer, *Like Punk Never Happened: Culture Club and New Pop* (London: Faber and Faber, 1985), 5.
[2] Interview with Dave Hepworth, 27 January 2009.

That said, disco itself is a contested term: embodying a complex history in terms of both racial and gender politics (Dyer, 1979 and Braunstein, 1999). However, as Barker and Taylor (2007) suggest, the invocation of disco is useful because of the way in which it embraced commercial culture and challenged traditional modes of authenticity. That is not to say *Smash Hits* was a disco magazine (though it did feature the disco charts). Rather it embodied a disco sensibility and positioned disco stars on the same footing as their rock-orientated contemporaries. In this sense, the success of *Smash Hits* reflected the diversity of the mainstream at the end of the 1970s. And, indeed, the speed with which it overtook its competitors suggests the magazine was perhaps more in tune with audience taste than *NME, Melody Maker* or *Sounds*. However, *Smash Hits* shaped, as well as reflected, the popular music scene at the time.

When it was launched in 1978, *Smash Hits* framed popular music in a way that was very different to the music press that preceded it. Firstly, it disrupted what Keir Keightley defines as "romantic" and "modernist" notions of musical legitimacy in its preference for pop product.[3] The rejection of commoditised cultural forms had been central to rock ideology since the 1960s: a Baudrillardian "deterrence" mechanism used to distract us from popular music's intrinsically capitalist sensibility.[4] Secondly, *Smash Hits* challenged what Eamonn Forde defines as the polyglottic style of the music press in the 1970s. Typified by the *NME,* the polemical style of Tony Parsons and Julie Burchill drew upon New Journalism modes of reporting popularised by US essayists like Tom Wolfe. Thirdly, *Smash Hits* paved the way for a more fluid conception of musical authenticity, sensitive to British pop's more "carnivalesque" sensibility. In this sense, *Smash Hits* embodied a reflexive celebration of artifice that underpins much of British pop culture from Cliff Richard through to Lily Allen. This strand has of course been recouped elsewhere within narratives of Britain's art-school aesthetic, and the politics of camp is well documented. For example, Jon Savage looks at the stylised parodic quality endemic to British pop and what he calls "the sign of gayness".[5] However, it is the role played by the music press as both "gatekeepers" and "cultural intermediaries" that is central to this chapter and the re-evaluation of the written and visual culture of *Smash Hits*. In this direction I will conclude

---

[3] Keir Keightley, "Reconsidering Rock," in *The Cambridge Companion to Rock and Pop,* ed. Simon Frith, 136 (Cambridge: Cambridge University Press, 2001).
[4] Jean Baudrillard, "Simulations," in *Continental Philosophy,* ed. Richard Kearney, 428 (London: Blackwell, 1981).
[5] J. Savage, "Tainted Love" in *Consumption, Identity and Style,* ed. Allan Tomlinson (London: Routledge, 1991), 158.

by suggesting that *Smash Hits* reacquainted the music press in the UK with what Simon Frith has defined as pop's "televisual aesthetic".[6] In this sense the 1970s can be viewed as period in which popular culture embraced—as opposed to simply embodied—post-modern cultural forms and thereby anticipated the more explicit commoditisation of lifestyle in the 1980s. In particular, *Smash Hits* sowed the seeds for Logan's next venture, *The Face*, which, as both Frank Mort (1996) and Sean Nixon (1997) have observed, pre-empted a revolution in men's lifestyle publishing.

The late 1970s: 7-inch Singles and Music Videos

The trajectory of the mainstream pop scene in the UK during the 1970s is dominated by two major epochs: the glam rock and punk era. Though musically adventurous, within the Academy these moments are typically recouped within narratives of sub-cultural identity and style. Less widely considered is the period at the end of the 1970s. And yet this represents a period of unprecedented diversity and sales. For example, 86 million singles sales were sold in 1979, the highest yearly sales figures for singles in the UK to date.[7] Genres enjoying success during the period 1978 to 1980 included rock'n'roll, easy listening, euro-pop, punk/new wave, electronica, singer-songwriter, Reggae and country and western. For Gary Mulholland this diversity within the mainstream of pop is something unique to the end of the 1970s:

> 1979 was in pop music terms at least, gloriously nuts. Punk and disco had taken the music industry by surprise and, as they struggled to understand what kind of strange noise and voices pop fans wanted, they allowed artists a degree of freedom and adventure that echoed the joy and tumult of the mid-60s. 1979 saw the peak and end of that process.[8]

Of particular significance was the influence of European disco on some very mainstream rock acts such as Rod Stewart, The Rolling Stones and Pink Floyd. In many ways the collision of rock and disco set the template for the modern pop song: most significantly in their use of synthesisers

---

[6] Simon Frith, "Look! Hear! The Uneasy Relationship of Music and Television," *Popular Music* 21, no. 3 (2002): 284.
[7] D. Roberts, *The Guiness Book of Hit Singles and Albums* (London: Guiness Publishing, 2006), 8.
[8] Gary Mulholland, *This is Uncool: The 500 Greatest Singles Since Punk and Disco* (London: Cassel, 2002), 76.

and their appropriation of reggae rhythms. For example, the hits of post-punk stars borrowed heavily from Caribbean music: most notably Blondie's "Heart of Glass", (a reggae song set to a Moroder beat), and The Police's "Message in a Bottle" (reggae meets new wave). It was, in short, a period in which every flavour was on the menu and no style seemed to clash. And yet, within the Academy the period has almost been written out of pop history.

Another aspect of 1970s popular music culture that is often forgotten and yet is highly significant to the success of *Smash Hits* is the proliferation of music video. There is a common perception that music video was not a significant medium until the 1980s, subsequent to the launch of *MTV* in America in 1981. This is, however, inexact: music television shows like *Top of the Pops* in the UK (BBC, 1964-2006) and *American Bandstand* in the US (ABC, 1952-89) defined the conventions of the "pop promo" from the 1960s onwards. Likewise, British bands had been experimenting with music video since the 1960s. The centrality of this visual culture is well documented in Popular Music Studies. As Lawrence Grossberg points out: "when you heard rock, you saw it as well, whether live or in films or on television or on the record sleeves."[9] And, it is this sensibility in *Smash Hits*, which Simon Frith defines as pop's very "televisual aesthetic"[10] to which I will return in my conclusion.

However, what perhaps marked out the latter half of the 1970s from the glam era or indeed punk was the proliferation of satellite television in America which was so pivotal in shifting audience tastes in the UK. The American communications company Time Warner had been experimenting with playing music videos on their cable network in the US as far back as 1975. The launch of *Pop Clips*, a show that ran from early 1979 up until the launch of MTV two years later, enforced the importance of the new medium. Major budget productions by British artists during the period include Rod Stewart's "Do Ya Think I'm Sexy?" (1978), Roxy Music's "Angel Eyes" (1979), The Rolling Stones' "Miss You" (1978) and Paul McCartney's "Wonderful Christmastime" (1979). That these songs were also hits in the UK meant that audiences were exposed to more sophisticated forms of music video, not only on shows like *Top of the Pops* but also on regional magazine shows and those aimed at children like *Tiswas* (ITV, 1974-82) and *Multi-Coloured Swap Shop* (BBC1, 1976-82). In short then, long before "new pop", the forms and conventions of music

---

[9] Lawrence Grossberg, "The Media Economy of Rock Culture–Cinema, Postmodernity and Authenticity," in *Sound and Vision: The Music Video Reader,* ed. Simon Frith, 188 (London: Routledge, 1993).
[10] Simon Frith, "Look! Hear!", 284.

television and film were determining the way in which audiences thought about popular music.

The Language and Visual Style of *Smash Hits*

In the various populist accounts of the magazine's history, like the Chris Fouracre's documentary *25 Years of Smash Hits*[11] and Frith's book *The Best of Smash Hits*, much is made of the magazine's visual style. The general consensus seems to be that the magazine changed the way music magazines looked: its visual style, A4 format and use of colour were very different to the magazines that preceded it. Moreover, *Smash Hits* presented pop culture in a way that was very different: the design and layout was influenced by fashion photography, and the copy deployed stylistic conventions of consumer journalism, evaluating pop music as a product. The magazine embodied a whole new sensibility for thinking about pop music: a more post-modern aesthetic in which the consumption of pop music was viewed as a part of the reflexive construction of self. Yet, when academic writers consider *Smash Hits*, there is a tendency to neglect this innovation. Typical of those approaches to *Smash Hits* that overlook the importance of the magazine is Gustur Gudmundsson, who mentions the title only briefly in his history of the British music press, suggesting that the title re-invoked "the teen mag idea of 'pop as magic'".[12] Likewise, Eamonn Forde (2001) focuses on the "monoglottic" corporate register of the magazine:

> The *Smash Hits* aesthetic and explicit mainstream orientations were forged within the central notion that the era of the personality writer had run its natural course and readers were no longer interested in convoluted and protracted theorization or partially autobiographical NJ. [sic][13]

What these accounts, and those of Shukar and Gorman, ignore is the ground-breaking way in which the magazine combined text and image in ways that both reflected and shaped the way audiences thought about pop

---

[11] Chris Fouracre, dir., *25 Years of Smash Hits*. [Television Documentary] (London; Channel 4, 2003).
[12] Gunter Gudmundsson and others, "Brit Crit: Turning Points in British Rock Criticism 1960-1990," in *Pop Music and the Press,* ed. Steve Jones, 56 (Philadelphia: Temple University Press, 2002).
[13] Eamonn Forde, "From Polyglottism to Branding. On the Decline of Personality Journalism in the British Press," in *Journalism* 2, no. 1 (2001): 28.

at the end of the 1970s.[14] In part this can be attributed to methodological issues: Forde is interested in the media economy and Gudmundsson in the history. Likewise, Gorman's account is essentially oral history, while Shukar's commentary is restricted to a chapter on the music press as whole. My research aligns with Frith (1984) in that it is the ideological structure underpinning the consumption of pop product that I wish to examine. And in this respect, Kembrew McLeod's analysis of the semantic dimensions of the music press in which he identifies ideological discourse markers is most useful.[15]

From a detailed examination of the way in which ten lead articles communicate in words and pictures, focusing on the cover shot as well as the layout and positioning of the article, a number of key findings emerge. Firstly, there is no genre bias: disco, punk, ska and Reggae are all covered. In part this can be attributed to the reconstructive sensibility of popular music in the 1970s, after punk and the proliferation of electronic dance music. However, the melting pot of musical styles was also a function of successive waves of immigration to the UK from the 1950s onwards. Moreover, music was arguably more international in the 1970s: it cohered around Afro-American musical hegemony from the mid-60s onwards. Though the artists featured are predominantly white, this reflects the demographic of the singles chart rather than a separate ideological agenda. For the purposes of the investigation, issues featuring both Bob Marley and Donna Summer were selected. Though race is not foregrounded in interviews with either star, the feature article on Bob Marley is elaborate in its exposition of the cultural context of Rastafarian religion, denoted by the singer's crocheted hat and dreadlocks on the front cover. And, indeed, the solemnity of the shot selected of Marley for the cover betrays an overt reverence for the reggae star, which counterpoises the more objectifying gaze characteristic of other cover shots.

The second remarkable feature of early *Smash Hits* is the sophistication of the art direction and photography. It is without question that the house style was much more seductive than *NME* or *Melody Maker.* In part this can be attributed to the luscious colour and quality of the paper. And, indeed the addition of poster supplements and pictures to stick on bedroom walls was key to the magazine's teen appeal. The magazine reflects the

---

[14] Roy Shuker, *Understanding Popular Music* (London: Routledge, 2001), 96; Paul Gorman, *In Their Own Words*: *Adventures in the Music Press* (London: Sanctuary Publishing, 2001).
[15] Kembrew McLeod, "Abandoning the Absolute: Transcendence and Gender in Popular Music Discourse," in *Pop Music and the Press,* ed. Steve Jones, 93 (Philadelphia: Temple University Press, 2002).

rise of music video production during the 1970s and an increasingly visual portmanteau of stars from the glam rock era onwards. This increased reliance upon the visual is also reflected in the occlusion of straplines to identify the cover star. Recognition of a band or performer is based upon their appearance rather than name. This very visual sensibility is reflected also in the colour palette used for fonts and text boxes: the use of garish pinks and yellows alludes to the visual codes of punk and the Pop Art sensibility of Warhol. Indeed, it is this presentation of stars as consumer objects that is perhaps the key to the magazine's appeal.

The third key trend emerging from analysis of *Smash Hits* is that typically musicians are not depicted in naturalistic poses. Instead, the visual style favours hyper-real Technicolor, foregrounding either a pin-up status or cartoon-like quality. In this sense *Smash Hits* re-invoked a very 1950s pop aesthetic: reacquainting pop music culture with a more European carnivalesque sensibility. Likewise, it reflected the proliferation of colour television and pop music video. In the case of a band like The Police this works very well: the rugged good looks, tanned complexion, and tousled blond hair lend the mid shot of this robust threesome from the cover of *Smash Hits* in August 1979 a naturally iconic quality. While *Smash Hits* addressed a less singular demographic in the 1970s than its core readership of teenage girls in the 1980s, early editions are remarkable for the way in which some quite improbable male subjects are reconstructed as pin-ups: an unlikely "boy band", the homo-social bonding depicted on The Clash's front cover from December 1979 renders the quintet impassive and objectified. Likewise, the stylised studio shot of The Jam positions Paul Weller in the role of teen idol. By contrast the portrait of Ian Dury from the same month plays up the eccentric qualities of the Blockhead's front man: the singer's optician-style glasses serving as a visual motif for Dury's musical idiosyncrasy. The shot purposefully eschews depiction of Dury's impaired gait (incurred through a bout of polio in childhood) and focuses instead upon his glasses which serve to reconstruct Dury as a more cartoon-like figure: a less defective caricature, more easily assimilated into the mainstream. And, indeed, *Smash Hits* does not subvert the hegemony: solo female stars like Donna Summer and Kate Bush are presented in ways that festishize their sexuality. An anomaly in this sense is the image of Deborah Harry on the cover of *Smash Hits* from December 1979, in which the singer appears androgynous, positioned amongst her male band mates, dressed down in casual jeans and a jacket. As in its depiction of genre, it would seem that *Smash Hits* is remarkable for the parity in its depiction of gender: a level playing field in which the subject may be sexualised and objectified regardless of sex, race or musical style. However, perhaps where the magazine most challenges received thinking is in the sophistication of its written style.

In part, the preoccupation with the visual culture of *Smash Hits* can be attributed to a higher ratio of image to text than the music press that preceded it. Yet, the articles themselves are in-depth, assuming high levels of discursive ability on the part of the reader in terms of both vocabulary and grammatical construction:

> MADNESS' ALBUM presents a fifty/fifty split between ska-inspired dance numbers and their own earthy tales of London low life. Lee Thompson's coarse sax is well to the fore as is Mike Barton's pumping keyboard technique. The band have chosen to label it the "nutty" sound, a term thought up by Thompson to describe the noise of fairground organs. It's a rough lively sound, jaunty and old fashioned. On stage Chas Smash does his strange ratchet dance to the real delight of packed houses. A few shortcomings in the vocal department and an over reliance on the same tempo apart, they're enormously enjoyable. Family fun.[16]

Here the mixture of assonance (ska-inspir*ed*, d*a*nce, numb*e*rs) and alliteration (London low life) creates a haughty timbre. Likewise the ambiguity of the adverbial phrase "well to the fore" leaves it up to the reader to decide whether that is a good or bad thing. As the section proceeds, Hepworth's affectation of conservative befuddlement is reinforced by the selection of certain outmoded words and phrases; "lively sound", "jaunty", "delight", "enormously enjoyable" and "family fun". These all sound like manners of speech from a previous era, to be enunciated in the clipped tones of Received Pronunciation. In *Smash Hits*, the subtle combination of words and phrases assumes high levels of both literacy and "cultural capital" on the part of the reader.[17] For example, the verb "don" is polysemic, meaning in this sense to put on a garment but also signalling to the noun that signifies a person of great importance. Likewise, "white coat" is a play upon "madness" as a clinical diagnosis and the garb common to medical practitioners in a sanatorium. Elsewhere metaphorical reference to the "sweetness" of chart success, idiomatic expressions such as "the ska 'gravy train'" and a theatrical allusion to "the boards" keeps things varied and makes the adolescent audience work hard. In this way, a subtle and secret code is embedded within the magazine,

---

[16] Dave Hepworth, "They Call It Madness," *Smash Hits*, November 29, 1979, 27.
[17] See Pierre Bourdieu, *Distinction: A Social Critique of the Judgment of Taste* (London: Routledge, 1979).

which includes the reader and purposefully subverts the more pompous impulses of the earlier music press.

It is perhaps the use of irony that most marks out the written style of *Smash Hits* from the "inkies". For example in the short editorial by Dave Hepworth to accompany a photomontage of Blondie on the set of the Alan Rudolph film *Roadie* (1980), the satire is affectionate rather than biting:

> EVERYBODY GOT popcorn? OK, it's Film Fun Time! So settle down in your seats and quit eyeing the person next to you for a minute while we fill you in on progress made so far on Blondie's World Domination-By-The-Eighties Plan (Silver Screen Division). The pix (below and over the page) were all snapped in Austin Texas, deep in the heart of cowboy country where men are men and mules are mules and never is heard a discouraging word. This is where the band have been filming "Roadie" with weightwatchers favourite rock and roll star, Meatloaf.[18]

Hepworth injects new life into worn-out stock phrases: intensifying tired idioms with an ironic tone and self-effacing mockery. While the use of rhetorical devices, punctuation for effect, hedges and causal connectives are all fairly standard, it is the invitation to inhabit a parallel fantasy world that is most compulsive: a landscape demarked by the hyper-real iconography of the populist imagination. From the cinematic optimism of the "Silver Screen" to the cold-war anxiety of "World Domination" Hepworth's imagery is painted in the heightened colours of a Warhol silk screen. In this sense the magazine paves the way for the polished journalism of *Q*. This is evidenced also by the retrospective sensibility when dealing with older recording artists. In a feature article on Roxy Music for example, Steve Taylor's prose assumes high levels of cultural capital on the part of the reader in her consideration of the "glitter era" and the band "post-re-union".[19] While defending *Smash Hits* against the accusation that it was mercantile flies in the face of its own Pop Art project, as Mark Ellen suggests, the assumption that the magazine was low-brow and charmless is historically inaccurate:

> Conventional wisdom decrees that *Smash Hits'* success was down to the "speaking to the kids in a vernacular they understood." This wasn't strictly true: the magazine and its readers had jointly cooked up a language of their own. It pitched way beyond their world and watched them rise delightedly to the challenge.[20]

---

[18] Dave Hepworth, "Presence Dear Blondie," *Smash Hits*, December 27, 1979, 15.

[19] Steve Taylor, "Roxy Music," *Smash Hits,* June 12, 1980, 6.

[20] Mark Ellen, "Amateur Hour," *The Word* 38 (2006): 85.

Conclusion: the Carnivalesque and the Televisual Aesthetic of *Smash Hits*

Clearly the visual culture of *Smash Hits* challenged the production of meaning in the music press that preceded it. It opposed the polemics of the personality writers and the primacy of the written word. However, from my own perspective, the real significance of *Smash Hits* at the end of the Seventies is the ideological shift it marked in the way in which audiences thought about popular music: challenging the primacy of authenticity as a barometer of culture taste. In part, this can be attributed to the playful and ironic tone of the editorial. And indeed, in this sense, the magazine opened up a space of the more sophisticated consumer journalism of *Q*. However, it is without doubt that the visual culture of *Smash Hits* is potentially most interesting: reacquainting popular music with its more performative dimension. In this sense, *Smash Hits* side-steps the tension between musicological approaches to popular music and those emanating from the social sciences, by celebrating the synthetic qualities of the surface culture. It also challenges received thinking about romantic and modernist conceptions of authenticity, which, as Keightley delineates so clearly, are inextricable from Afro-American rock ideology. Instead, *Smash Hits* re-inscribes an inherently "parodic" sensibility that is central to British pop mythology. This mimetic quality can be partially attributed to the subaltern position of British bands in relation to the American rock hegemony: success being contingent upon the representation of what Keightley describes as a lost musical heritage. Likewise, it can be viewed as an extension of the European tradition of the carnival in which "the world is turned upside down".[21] The "world" in this sense is the hegemony of Afro-American rock authenticity. This is something Diane Railton considers in her analysis of *Smash Hits* in the 1990s.[22] However, in the case of *Smash Hits* in the 1970s, it would seem that it is what Simon Frith has described as pop music's "televisual sensibility" that is central to understanding the magazine.

Focusing on popular music since the 1950s, Frith argues that rock stars not only have to be telegenic in order to succeed, but that the conventions of a good television performance have come to define what is understood by a good rock performance. In this sense the visual artifice of *Smash Hits*

---

[21] Mikhail Bakhtin, "Carnival and the Carnivalesque," in *Cultural Theory and Popular Culture,* ed. John Storey, 254 (London: Prentice Hall, 1998).
[22] Daine Railton, "The Gendered Carnival of Pop," *Popular Music* 20, no. 3 (2001).

is perhaps closer to the core aesthetics of British pop music than the superannuated postulations of the American commentators. As Frith suggests: "for all the ideological importance of its live performance, rock is the first popular musical form to be constructed in the studio."[23] Deposing genre distinction is the key to this sensibility, as is the levelling of cultural order imposed by the primacy of the visual in *Smash Hits*. The legacy of the magazine is that it exposes the ideological parameters within which popular music texts are deconstructed as contingent mythologies, to which the audience does or does not subscribe in their reading(s) of the text. In this sense pop, rock, punk and reggae are not discrete genres in *Smash Hits*, but shifting strategies. Such strategies are used by the audience to understand not only the popular music to which they listen, but also their own identity as audience members. The significance of the televisual aesthetic of *Smash Hits* then stretches beyond the moment of its inception at the end of the Seventies and the begetting of video pop in the 1980s, and offers instead a viable mode of deconstruction for all popular music culture formed in the image of the cathode ray.

---

[23] Frith, 2002, 286.

PART IV:

FILM PRODUCTION CONTEXTS

THE PRECARIOUSNESS OF PRODUCTION: MICHAEL KLINGER AND THE ROLE OF THE FILM PRODUCER IN THE BRITISH FILM INDUSTRY DURING THE 1970S

ANDREW SPICER

Introduction

Although Michael Klinger was the most successful independent producer in the 1970s, he has become one of the legions of the lost in British cinema. This occlusion is symptomatic of the neglect of the producer's role within British cinema studies, and within Film Studies in general.[1] This neglect is particularly deleterious in any attempt to understand the British film industry because of its chronic instability—nowhere better exemplified than during the 1970s—which led John Caughie to conclude: "The importance of the producer-artist seems to be a specific feature of British cinema, an effect of the need continually to start again in the organization of independence."[2] A "producer-artist", of course, is not the same entity as the *auteur* director whose artistry may be recognized through a signature visual style or consistent thematic preoccupations which can be elucidated through the detailed textual interpretation of his or her films. As with most producers, Klinger's *oeuvre* was diverse and heterogeneous and would elude such an analysis. On the contrary, understanding a producer's art, as Vincent Porter argues, lies in appreciating his or her ability to manipulate creatively the complex and interlocking relationship between four key factors: an understanding of public taste, and of what subjects and genres could attract a broad

---

[1] See Andrew Spicer, "The Production Line: Reflections on the Role of the Film Producer in British Cinema," *Journal of British Cinema and Television*, 1, no.1 (2004): 33–35.
[2] John Caughie, "Broadcasting and Cinema 1: Converging Histories," in *All Our Yesterdays: 90 Years of British Cinema*, ed. Charles Barr, 200 (London: BFI Publishing, 1986).

audience; the ability to obtain adequate production finance; the understanding of who to use in the key creative roles and on what terms; and the effectiveness of her or his overall control of the production process.[3]

Appreciating that ability is to understand the "art" of commercial feature film-making, an artistry all the more elusive because it is, for the most part, invisible. The critical challenge is to render that art visible by a detailed examination of the production process, understood as encompassing not only the shooting of the film, but also its genesis, distribution, marketing and exhibition. Documenting the production process is always a laborious and often frustrating endeavour, as key items may be unobtainable. However, in the case of Michael Klinger, the usual sources such as the trade press, reviews, newspaper articles and official papers can be supplemented by the Klinger Papers that have been deposited at the University of the West of England. These are an extensive source of information including scripts, production costs, film grosses, correspondence, financial agreements, promotion and publicity decisions. Drawing on this material facilitates an understanding of Klinger's "artistry", but also, because the producer is involved with the film industry on several levels, opens a wide window onto the 1970s. Because a comprehensive account of Klinger's output in the 1970s is beyond the scope of this chapter, the focus here will be on the internationalist action-adventure films, chosen because the rise and fall of the British action-adventure film—critically derided but continuously popular—is an unwritten history and I wish to contribute a little to its documentation.[4]

Klinger and British film production in the 1970s

Rotund, cigar-chomping and ebullient—Sheridan Morley described him as resembling "nothing so much as a flamboyant character actor doing impressions of Louis B. Meyer"[5]—Michael Klinger might seem a caricature of the producer, but this image belied a quicksilver intelligence, photographic memory and a cultivated mind. Born in 1920, the son of Polish Jewish immigrants who had settled in London's East End, Klinger

[3] Vincent Porter, "The Context of Creativity: Ealing Studios and Hammer Films," in *British Cinema History*, ed. James Curran and Vincent Porter, 179–180 (London: Weidenfeld and Nicholson, 1983).
[4] See James Chapman, "Action, Spectacle and the *Boy's Own* Tradition in British Cinema," in *The British Cinema Book*, ed. Robert Murphy, 217–225 (London: BFI Publishing, 2001).
[5] "Klinger the Independent," *The Times*, December 20, 1975.

had had a mercurial career in the 1960s film industry.[6] In partnership with Tony Tenser, Klinger set up a production-distribution company, Compton-Tekli, making a series of low-budget "sexploitation" films, horror and sci-fi pictures and two "shockumentaries"—*London in the Raw* (1964) and *Primitive London* (1965). Keen to take creative risks—he produced Roman Polanski's first two British films *Repulsion* (1965) and *Cul-de-sac* (1966)—Klinger broke with the unadventurous Tenser and set up Avton Films in late 1966. Klinger's policy of promoting young, talented but unproven directors who were capable of making fresh and challenging features (Peter Collinson, Alastair Reid and Mike Hodges) was financially rewarded when Hodges' brutal crime thriller *Get Carter* (1971) became an international success, enabling Klinger to mount a more ambitious production programme in the 1970s.

Part of Klinger's success was his ability to tap into various markets. He continued to make low-budget sexploitation films with the *Confessions of...* series (*Window Cleaner/Pop Performer/Driving Instructor/Holiday Camp*, 1974-78) for which he acted as executive producer. Their modest costs could be recouped (in fact they made substantial profits) even from a rapidly shrinking domestic market: cinema admissions declined by 42 per cent during the decade and cinema visits became special occasions rather than a social habit.[7] Producing a series of films could partly compensate for an industry that now lacked a stable production base, was almost completely casualised, and where there was a chronic lack of continuous production.[8] Klinger continued to produce more recherché and challenging crime thrillers, including Reid's neglected *Something to Hide* (1972), Collinson's *Tomorrow Never Comes* (1978) and Claude Chabrol's *Les liens de sang* (*Blood Relatives*, 1978). These productions often required Klinger to engage in co-production deals (*Blood Relatives* was made in Canada) and niche marketing at home and abroad because the medium budget film, the traditional mainstay of the British film industry, was in sharp decline.[9] However, Klinger's main energies went into the production

---

[6] For details see John Hamilton, *Beasts in the Cellar: The Exploitation Career of Tony Tenser*, Chapters 1–4 (Surrey: FAB Press, 2005).

[7] Linda Wood, *British Films 1971–1981* (London: BFI Publishing, 1983), 3; Justin Smith, "Glam, Spam and Uncle Sam: Funding Diversity in 1970s British Film Production," in *Seventies British Cinema*, ed. Robert Shail, 67–69 (London: BFI/Palgrave Macmillan, 2008).

[8] See Andrew Higson, "A Diversity of Film Practices: Renewing British Cinema in the 1970s," in *The Arts in the 1970s: Cultural Closure?*, ed. Bart Moore-Gilbert, 219–221 (London: Routledge, 1994).

[9] Wood, *British Films*, 5.

of big-budget action-adventure films—*Gold* (1974) and *Shout at the Devil* (1976)—aimed at the international market.

Given the parlous state of the British film industry, such a strategy may seem odd or even reckless. However, the selection of the action-adventure film was based on Klinger's estimation of public taste— particularly the popularity of the Bond films—and his conviction, in the context of a declining domestic market, that international productions which could hope for worldwide sales were the route to survival for the British film industry. Indeed, he repeatedly attacked the insularity, parochialism and timorousness of the British film industry in the trade press.[10] Klinger also saw an opportunity, with the withdrawal of large companies (notably Rank) from production, for ambitious (and, one might add, courageous) independent producers to fill a production vacuum. His problem, documented below, was that he could no longer rely, as he had done for *Get Carter* and *Pulp* (1972), on American finance. As Alexander Walker has shown, it was largely American money that had sustained the British film industry in the 1960s, and the withdrawal of Hollywood studios from the industry in the 1970s was swift, unceremonious and catastrophic.[11] The production history of both Klinger's action-adventure films would reward extended analysis—*Shout* was "one of the biggest independently financed films in British cinema history"[12]—but for brevity's sake I will focus on *Gold*.

Gold: genesis and production context

Even with the action-adventure genre, Klinger was looking to produce a series of films all derived from the bestselling novels of Wilbur Smith. Klinger acquired the rights to *Shout at the Devil* (1968) and *Gold Mine* (1970), buying the latter even before publication, judging that Smith's brand of modern exotic action-adventure was ideal cinematic material.[13] In May 1970, while *Get Carter* was still in production, Klinger was in active

---

[10] "British Film Industry Missing Boat by Emphasizing Insular Pix: Klinger," *Variety*, May 17, 1972; "Int'l Mkt. Key To British Production's Recovery: Klinger," *Variety*, September 26, 1973.

[11] Alexander Walker, *Hollywood, England: The British Film Industry in the Sixties*, 2nd ed. (London: Harrap, 1986), 441–465; see also Smith, "Glam, Spam and Uncle Sam," 69–70.

[12] "Ex-Engineer Klinger Film Plans Run to 43 Mil. In Two Yrs.," *Variety*, November 5, 1975.

[13] Klinger also acquired the rights to *The Sunbird* (1972), *Eagle in the Sky* (1974) and *The Eye of the Tiger* (1975), but was not able to produce any of these.

Fig. 15.1.Michael Klinger as hands-on producer: on location with *Gold*; the man to his left is Peter Hunt, the director.
Photograph by kind permission of Tony Klinger.

discussion with Smith over a screenplay based on *Gold Mine*.[14] Klinger was anxious to build on the cordial relationship he had developed with *Get Carter*'s financiers, MGM-British, who had made the only Smith adaptation so far: *Dark of the Sun*, released in Britain as *The Mercenaries* in 1968. MGM-British bought out Klinger's option on *Gold Mine* (for £25,000) and engaged him as *Gold*'s producer on similar terms to those he had negotiated for *Get Carter*, thus affording him what he believed would be a free hand in scripting and casting.[15] However, although Klinger engaged Smith to complete the adaptation of his own novel, MGM-British played safe by bringing in an experienced scriptwriter, Stanley Price, to rewrite. A clearly exasperated Klinger complained that he had "no knowledge whatsoever of your deal with Stanley Price other than the overall figure I understand you have agreed to pay him is £5,000."[16]

---

[14] Letter to Michael Klinger from Wilbur Smith's solicitors, 13 May 1950; Klinger Papers (KP).
[15] Letter from Peter Stone at MGM-British to Klinger, 3 December 1970; KP.
[16] Letter from Klinger to Stone, 6 April 1971; KP.

However, as part of the sudden withdrawal of American finance noted above, MGM-British withdrew its interest in August 1973.[17] Klinger purchased the rights to the Price screenplay and, as an accomplished script editor, made some changes himself.[18]

However, while he might have been free of interference, with MGM's withdrawal Klinger lost his major source of production finance and also his distribution guarantees in the all-important American market. To overcome these problems took a huge effort, particularly as Klinger was unable to raise the necessary finance in Britain, where the dearth of production finance was officially acknowledged to be chronic.[19] Klinger himself had drawn attention to this on a number of occasions, lamenting: "I try—and fail—to get British money every time …. It is the hardest place in the world to raise money for films. As a result, we are letting ourselves be used as a workshop."[20] Emphasising that *Gold* would be shot entirely on location, Klinger turned to South African businessmen, who were not used to backing films but whom he persuaded would see a handsome return on their investment.[21] Although this deal ensured that *Gold* could be made (for around $2,000,000, a figure quoted in several reviews), it was always a precarious arrangement that generated considerable mutual mistrust. In particular, there was a protracted wrangle over who was responsible for paying the overages when the film went over budget, as the mine-disaster sequences proved to be more costly to shoot than was anticipated and involved an expensive studio recreation at Pinewood. Klinger's South African financiers expected to see a return on their investment based on the original estimates that they had agreed, and not the final costs.[22]

---

[17] See the letter from Klinger's solicitor Raffles Edelman to Klinger, 7 August 1973; KP.

[18] There is copy of a contract made with Chadwick Hall for "rewriting and polishing" the screenplay (17 September 1973; KP), but I have been unable to unearth any information about this writer.

[19] See Cmnd 6372 - *Future of the British Film Industry: Report of the Prime Minister's Working Party* [the Terry Report] (London: HMSO, 1976).

[20] Quoted in Garth Pearce, "Klinger's crusade – put Britain back into its own big picture", *Daily Express*, January 21, 1977.

[21] See the covering letter from Edelmann, 6 August 1974, and the three agreements with Tony Factor, Dennis Bieber (Soco Properties) and the Ellerine Brothers; KP. The agreements were made with Metropic, Klinger's holding company based, for tax reasons, in Vaduz, Liechtenstein.

[22] See the letter from London lawyers Fluxman and Partners acting on behalf of the South African financiers, 1 April 1977; KP. The matter dragged on and was the subject of legal proceedings, finally being referred to arbitration in 1981.

Because the scope and scale of *Gold* was extraordinarily ambitious for an independent British producer, its production required adroit budgeting, careful casting and strict overall control. Convinced that Roger Moore was ideal for the lead and could guarantee international sales, Klinger had negotiated with Moore even before he attained superstardom as Bond. As the lynchpin, Moore was offered a lucrative deal: a fee of $200,000 plus five per cent of *Gold*'s gross.[23] Although Klinger could use Moore's star power positively—to raise finance and persuade other star names (John Gielgud, Ray Milland and Susannah York), to take prominent parts—it could also work negatively. Klinger judged that the director of *Duel* (1971), Steven Spielberg, was ideal for an action picture, and another talented young film-maker whom he wanted to promote. However, Moore was unwilling to entrust the direction of a major film, at what he judged to be a critical point in his career, to someone aged only 27 and he vetoed Klinger's choice.[24] Klinger then decided to opt for the experienced Peter Hunt who had edited several Bond films before directing *On Her Majesty's Secret Service* (1969). Hunt was particularly appropriate for *Gold* because he had tried to shift the Bond series away from gadgetry in favour of a "marvellous adventure story", with Bond surviving "by his own physical skill and ingenuity".[25] Several other key creative personnel were Bond regulars: Maurice Binder, who designed the distinctive title sequence; production designer Syd Cain; art director Robert V. Laing; sound recordist John Mitchell; and editor John Glen. Glen had also worked previously for Klinger, as had art director Alex Vetchinsky and director of photography Ousama Rawi. Klinger also hired the highly experienced composer Elmer Bernstein to score the film and placed his own son Tony in charge of the second unit direction.

Thus although Klinger may have been frustrated by not getting Spielberg, he assembled a talented crew, experienced in action-adventure film-making, many of whom he knew well, and over whom he was able to exercise close supervision. Klinger was a "hands-on" producer, present throughout the shooting in South Africa as well as the restaging of some of the underground sequences at Pinewood. In particular, he arranged the viewing of the daily rushes to check for quality. His presence became very necessary because the craft union, the Association of Cinema and Television Technicians (ACTT), disapproved of its members working in the apartheid state of South Africa and threatened not to handle the film in

---

[23] Contract, dated 18 January 1974; KP.
[24] Information obtained from an interview with Tony Klinger, June 11, 2008.
[25] Quoted in Herb A. Lightman, "The 'Cinemagic' of 007," *American Cinematographer* 51, no. 3 (March 1970): 204–205.

post-production and discipline the crew. Klinger robustly defended his choice of location as the only appropriate one, and argued that he should be supported for creating work in a time of crisis within the industry.[26] He also appointed a QC to act for the technicians once they returned to England.[27] Reluctantly, under pressure from some of its own members, the union agreed not to hinder the production.

Gold as an international action-adventure film

Both *Gold* and *Shout at the Devil* made a significant contribution to the flourishing of the British action-adventure genre in the 1970s, which boasted 53 films.[28] The genre itself is a loose amalgam of various sub-types and *Gold* is primarily a disaster movie, beginning and ending with lengthy and spectacular sequences depicting underground flooding in a South African gold mine. As such, it is very characteristic of the development of the genre during this decade.[29] The first disaster is accidental, the second contrived by the mine's devious bisexual boss Manfred Steyner (Bradford Dillman), who is married to Terry (Susannah York), daughter of the mine owner Hurry Hirschfield (Ray Milland). Unbeknown to Hirschfield, Steyner works secretly for a shadowy international cartel led by Farrell (John Gielgud). Steyner uses the skill of the mine's General Manager Rod Slater (Roger Moore) to mastermind an operation to tunnel through to a supposed new vein of gold, but which Steyner knows will breach the sides of a vast underground lake. Slater is thus an unwitting pawn in the cartel's scheme to flood the whole of South Africa's central mining complex and thereby force up the price of gold.

In common with eleven other British action-adventure films in the 1970s, including *Shout*, *Gold* is set in Africa. This exotic location afforded the genre's typically expansive and spectacular visual style, emphasising panoramic vistas and elaborately choreographed action sequences. *Gold* emphasises its exotic African location by including aerial shots of big game, and its (rather perfunctory) depiction of black tribal dancing. But, as the dispute with the unions indicated, Africa was a key centre of political interest during the 1970s, the arena in which a number of ideological struggles were being fought. Inescapably, African action-adventure films contain the legacy of imperialism. When Slater returns in the nick of time

---

[26] Hugh Herbert, "Will *Gold* bite the dust?," *Guardian*, November 24, 1973.
[27] John Mitchell, *Flickering Shadows: A Lifetime in Films* (Malvern Wells, Worcestershire: Harold Martin & Redman, 1997), 215.
[28] My calculations, based on Gifford, *The British Film Catalogue,* Vol. 1.
[29] See Roddick, "Only the Stars Survive."

Fig. 15.2. On-screen rugged action: Big King (Simon Sabela) and Rod Slater (Roger Moore) try to save the mine from flooding.
Photograph by kind permission of Tony Klinger.

to save the mine, he is assisted by the strongest black miner, Big King (Simon Sabela) who sacrifices his life to save the mine from disaster. Critic Alexander Walker saw King, the noble savage, as a residual element of the pre-war Empire film, a latter-day Bosambo from *Sanders of the River* (1935).[30] *Gold* also emphasises the modernity of South Africa, with shots of the panoramic cityscape of Johannesburg as a cosmopolitan metropolis.

Characterisation in the action-adventure film tends to be straightforward, even two-dimensional. As *Gold*'s hero, Slater is a contemporary, classless, self-made man of action, whose virility derives from his dangerous, exacting work. We frequently see him engaged in activities (tunnelling, blasting, and fighting) that emphasise his muscularity, agility and courageous male prowess. But Slater shares with James Bond—particularly through the casting of Moore who had just had starred in *Live and Let Die* (1973)—a refined hedonism and compulsive womanising. He needs little enticement to begin an affair with Terry and much is made of their

[30] Alexander Walker, review, *Evening Standard*, September 5, 1974.

amorous weekend at Hirschfield's country retreat that takes him away
from the mine at a crucial moment.

Gold: distribution, publicity, exhibition and reception

In addition to struggling to raise production finance, Klinger had
immense difficulties as an independent in obtaining a distribution
agreement, crucial to *Gold*'s financial viability. He first approached
British Lion in November 1973 as UK distributors, describing *Gold* as a
"British Quota [that] has *Poseidon Adventure* possibilities", a reference to
the most successful of the early disaster movies.[31] British Lion's Chief
Executive Michael Deeley declined, arguing that the drastic reduction in
the British "cinema market" coupled with rising costs for releasing a
picture meant that "there is only a limited chance of making a profit out of
a straight UK deal".[32] Deeley's response reveals much about the domestic
market at this point. The Rank Organisation also declined, as did Nat
Cohen at Anglo-EMI, but a deal was struck with Hemdale, a relatively
new organisation, founded in 1968 by David Hemmings and John Daly.

Although Hemmings had left the company in 1970, Hemdale had
established itself as an up-and-coming production-distribution company
and it was ambitious to increase its share of the market. Knowing the
pressures on independent producers, Hemdale was able to drive a hard
bargain, offering Klinger a guarantee of only £100,000 from the UK
market, not the £200,000 he had been seeking. Eventually a figure of
£150,000 was agreed upon.[33] As was customary, the distributor recouped
its money first and there was considerable dispute about the Eady
revenues, a tax levied on cinema admissions, some of which could be
recouped by distributors and producers. Under pressure, Klinger had
concluded a deal with Hemdale whereby it received 50 per cent of the
Eady monies until the gross receipts reached £300,000, after which he
received them in full; but payments were withheld by Hemdale which then
disputed the wording of the contract.[34] There were further wrangles too
over promotion and publicity expenses which Klinger regarded as
excessive. In a letter in January 1975, James Robertson justified
Hemdale's expenses because although "generally speaking the film has
done well", Hemdale had had to "work very hard" as "the results have been

---

[31] Letter from Klinger to Michael Deeley at British Lion, 23 November 1973; KP.
[32] Letter from Deeley to Klinger, 3 December 1973; KP.
[33] Letter from John Hogarth at Hemdale to Klinger, 16 January 1974; KP.
[34] Letter from Hogarth to Klinger, 6 February 1974; formal agreement between
Hemdale and Avton Films dated 19 March 1973; KP.

Fig. 15.3. *Gold* and its makers – left to right: John Hogarth (executive for Hemdale, distributors); Paul Kijzer (sales agent for Avton Films); Michael Klinger (producer and head of Avton Films); Peter Hunt, standing (director); John Daly (co-founder of Hemdale and chief executive).
Photograph by kind permission of Tony Klinger.

really rather spotty and interestingly it is in the harder areas that the film does not seem to have had a great success, the north-east of England and the rougher areas of London and so on."[35] This affords many potential insights into audience taste, including, perhaps, the nature of Moore's appeal; was it predominantly middle-class? Notwithstanding the "spottiness", by May 1975 *Gold* had grossed a very respectable £454,538 in the UK market.[36]

Negotiating an American distribution deal was equally tortuous. Klinger hired Irvin Shapiro of Films Around the World Inc. in order to tout *Gold* around the Majors. However, it is indicative of Klinger's status in the USA that his film was considered seriously, even if no deal was struck. For instance, Paramount expressed an interest and its President, Frank Yablans, commented somewhat equivocally: "the characters tend to be two-dimensional and the story is not original" but "the mine sequences

---

[35] Letter from Robertson to Klinger, 15 January 1975; KP.
[36] Royalty statement from Hemdale, 31 May 1975; KP.

could work out to be very exciting visually."[37] In the end, Paramount passed on *Gold* and it was the lower-ranking Allied Artists (AA) that finally offered to finance the film. Klinger, disappointed by Shapiro's failure to conclude a deal, had negotiated the arrangement himself at Cannes. AA guaranteed to pay Klinger a minimum of $2,000,000, the first half on delivery of the film, the second half withheld until it had grossed $8,500,000 overall; AA also agreed to spend $750,000 on promoting *Gold*.[38] However, on its release in America during the run-up to Christmas, *Gold* was up against it, competing against *Earthquake, Airport, The Towering Inferno* and *The Godfather Part II*, which was surely unlucky! As a result, AA withdrew *Gold* from exhibition quite rapidly, intending to re-release in the quieter February/March period with a fresh campaign. In the event, this campaign hardly happened, probably, as Klinger's American lawyer noted, because the ailing AA judged that the only way for *Gold* to make even a modest profit was to demand a high price for network television based on its *lack* of exposure.[39] Although *Gold* had made only $1,055,376 by April 1976, Klinger did receive his second $1million because AA had to secure his agreement to auction the television rights.[40] In addition, Klinger had negotiated a separate deal with Columbia to distribute *Gold* in Europe and Australia and had followed his usual custom of pre-selling the film in other territories once the major financial package was in place. Klinger and his agent Paul Kijzer were acknowledged masters in what had become a standard industry practice. As a result, *Gold* eventually grossed £12,100,000 worldwide despite what Klinger acknowledged was a disappointing performance in America.[41]

Conclusion

More could be said about *Gold*—its uneven critical reception and its relationship with other British action-adventure films—but the focus here has been on what its production history demonstrates about the British film industry in the 1970s. Even though *Gold* had several elements that had proven box-office appeal, Klinger's acute problems in making this

---

[37] Letter from Yablans to Shapiro, 6 November 1973; KP.
[38] See the agreement concluded with Emanuel Wolf at Allied Artists at Cannes, 15 May 1974; the final contract was signed on 27 August 1974; KP.
[39] Paul Sawyer to Klinger, 24 July 1975; KP.
[40] Allied Artists Outside Producers Report no. 6, 2 April 1976; KP.
[41] Figure from Avton Communications Entertainment Booklet, n.d. (1989?), n.p.; KP. ACEB; comment on *Gold*'s performance in Addison Verrill, "Michael Klinger Also Assays British Film Chances Upcoming," *Variety*, February 12, 1975.

film reveal the extreme difficulties producers faced in this period in raising production finance, but even more in gaining distribution deals. As has been shown, it was a decade in which distributors ruled the roost and independent producers had to be nimble-footed even to survive, let alone prosper. These problems were particularly acute with an expensive production, aimed at an international market, and mounted by someone who guarded his independence fiercely: one who wished to control the major elements of the film—the budget, casting, scripting and choice of locations—without direct interference from the Hollywood Majors. Although Klinger's determination to make internationally-orientated films and his continual efforts to put together packages of films that might guarantee some continuity of production in a chronically fragmented industry did not endear him to the British critical establishment, it was a logical response to a shrinking domestic market if, as Klinger thought was imperative, the British film industry was to continue to make ambitious films capable of engaging a broad audience.

Had space permitted, I would have liked to examine Klinger's career in the 1970s in greater detail—his later career in the 1980s was lacklustre following the failure of *Riding High* (1981) and he produced little before his death in 1989—and to have contextualised it through comparison with other independent producers, for instance David Puttnam or Don Boyd, in order to establish his distinctiveness and his typicality. I am conscious that almost nothing has been said about his Jewishness, which his son Tony has suggested was the key to understanding his career and which led to the production of *Rachel's Man* (1974) a Biblical love story shot in Israel that Klinger knew was parlous box-office material but which he felt compelled to make. However, what I hope to have indicated in this brief assessment is his interest and importance as a "producer-artist". Although, as I have demonstrated, understanding that role requires considerable efforts of excavation as well as analysis, without that effort, and without appreciating the cultural and economic significance of the "producer-artist', we are not going to understand the 1970s, or the history of the British film industry in general.

MUSIC/ INDUSTRY/ POLITICS:
ALAN PRICE'S ROLES IN *O LUCKY MAN!*

JOHN IZOD, KARL MAGEE,
KATHRYN MACKENZIE
AND ISABELLE GOURDIN[1]

Let's begin at the end. In the final scene of Lindsay Anderson's 1973 film *O Lucky Man!*, the director steps out from behind the camera and places himself in the centre of the action. The film's young hero Mick Travis (Malcolm McDowell) has been engaged on a futile quest for wealth and success which has ended with him destitute, wandering the streets of London. A billboard catches his eye inviting passers-by to audition for a starring role. He drifts none-too-hopefully into the casting session, where Anderson plucks him from a large group of young men and photographs him in various poses. Instructed by the director to smile, however, Travis protests repeatedly "I can't smile without a reason. What's there to smile about?" Anderson hits him across the face with the script and (after a long pause during which a great deal of what he has lived through may well be going through his mind) Mick smiles. Alan Price and his band kick off what turn out to be the film's final celebrations with a reprise of the film's title tune bringing things full circle.

This moment has been described by, among others, Anderson's old friend Gavin Lambert as the character experiencing a Zen-like revelation.[2] Lambert's reading of the final scene picked up the association with Zen that Anderson had noted in his private journals in the hours after shooting it.[3] Not that Lambert would have needed access to Anderson's private writings to know of his interest in this worldview. In a 1957 review of

[1] The authors gratefully acknowledge the financial support of the Arts and Humanities Research Council for the project "The Cinema Authorship of Lindsay Anderson" of which this article is a product.
[2] Gavin Lambert, *Mainly About Lindsay Anderson* (London: Faber, 2000), 168.
[3] Diary, LA 6/1/64/160 (16 June 1972). Archived materials held by the University of Stirling are referenced by folder, document number and, where recorded, date.

Tokyo Story published in *Sight and Sound* (the journal Lambert had edited until 1955), Anderson wrote of the wisdom and acceptance of life that comes with practising the Zen philosophy.[4] Years later, when promoting *O Lucky Man!*, the director expounded this idea to journalists, reflecting on the way the final smile echoed the grin with which Mick had ingratiated himself as a salesman at the start of his epic journey: "I thought of it more as Zen master and pupil than as director and actor. It's where the film comes full circle, where the smile at the end echoes the smile at the beginning."[5] Anderson added, "it's not the facile smile of compromise" with which Mick Travis had tried to work his way into the favour of those who had in their gift the money, power and esteem he so greedily desired. Rather, this is "the hardened smile of acceptance."[6]

These references provide useful pointers toward one of the film's principal themes; however, they are all exterior to the text itself. Happily, *O Lucky Man!* has its own built-in reference system which buttresses Anderson's and Lambert's claims for Mick's undergoing a Zen-like experience. That back-up resides, as we shall see, in the music of Alan Price and his band.

Our essay begins with the commercial value of Price to the project. We give an account of the personal and professional relationship between him and the director during the making of the film, and touch on their different experiences of class and culture. Then we examine the process through which the lyrics evolved, and how Anderson came to recognise that Price's own qualities enriched the grand theme underlying the narrative's many twists and turns, such that he became a principal figure standing both in, and to the side of, the drama.

A Frustrated Beginning

Prior to directing *O Lucky Man!*, Anderson had actually been planning to shoot an on-the-road documentary about Price and his band. David Sherwin (Anderson's scriptwriter) kept a diary of production on *O Lucky Man!* and his account—corrected by Anderson at the other man's invitation—reads:

---

[4] Lindsay, Anderson, "Two Inches off the Ground," in *Never Apologise: The Collected Writings*, ed. Paul Ryan, 582–583 (London: Plexus, 2004).
[5] Mary Blume, "A Smile, an Echo, a Director," *International Herald Tribune*, October 27–28, 1973, 16.
Alexander Walker, "What Happened After *If...,*" *The Evening Standard,* May 3, 1973.
[6] Blume, "A Smile, an Echo".

Lindsay had been planning a film about Alan Price after Alan had written the music for *Home*. It was to be a documentary featuring gigs, travel, digs and one-night stands. Like the old actor-managers with their travelling fitups. But when Alan teamed up with Georgie Fame the project ran into difficulties chiefly on copyright for the material they were using (£1,000 a minute for a Ray Charles number).[7]

Music and Marketing

When the documentary project fell through, Anderson decided instead to use Price in the feature, which is now a neglected critique of British society in the early 1970s. This was a choice welcomed by the film's distributors. Warner Bros' senior executives and their publicity agents had, from the start, recognised the potential for marketing *O Lucky Man!* of three principal names attached to the film. Lindsay Anderson could be expected to draw audiences on both sides of the Atlantic for *If....* ; Malcolm McDowell likewise for his striking performances in the same film and more recently in Stanley Kubrick's 1971 *A Clockwork Orange*; and Alan Price for his hit singles and albums, his work with The Animals and with Georgie Fame.[8] Price had the additional attraction for Warners that his music could be sold in two markets.

In letters and telexes written while preparations for the North American release of *O Lucky Man!* were under way, the music features heavily, with the main emphasis on publicity and promotion. Warner Bros had not only financed the film, but (in the decade when cross-media deals were becoming common) had also contracted to purchase rights to the songs that Price was to write and perform. As part of the deal, the company was to release music from the soundtrack on their own record label. That Anderson attached great importance to the music is clear from his characteristically fierce communications with the studio. Heated disputes arose over, firstly, the want of timely confirmation of arrangements for the band's tour in the USA and, secondly, delays in the schedule for bringing the album to market, both events intended to anticipate the film's North American release and awaken interest in it.[9]

It should be said that, no less than Anderson, the studio's executives

---

[7] LA 1/7/1/8.
[8] See details of Warner Bros' promotion campaign at LA 1/7/3/5/34; and proposals for the UK campaign by Fred Hift Associates LA 1/7/3/8/1–10 (April 1973).
[9] Correspondence LA 1/7/3/6/6–9 (May 1973); LA 1/7/3/3/15 (2 August1973); LA 1/7/3/3/19 (15 August 1973).

expected the band's music to provide valuable publicity for the film.[10] As it turned out, both parties were correct. The tour did go ahead. And the album, whose release had been held back by manufacturing problems rather than the studio indifference that Anderson seemed to suspect, enjoyed favourable reviews and strong sales. This was particularly the case after June 1973 when it came out in the USA. Jon Landau wrote that Price "infuses clichéd topics with fresh spirit and discordant asides that generate a peculiar form of rock ambiguity ... Swinging, pounding and thoroughly professional, intelligent and blatant rock and roll—that is the secret to the title cut and this very unexpected and very much appreciated surprise album of the year."[11] Ultimately the music for *O Lucky Man!* was to earn Price a BAFTA award, an Oscar nomination, and his first US chart album.[12]

Anderson & Price—Price & Anderson

Even prior to the period of research for the documentary and pre-production for *O Lucky Man!*, observations of Price's personality and *modus operandi* dominate the entries relating to him in Anderson's private journals. They had already worked together when Price wrote music for Anderson's Royal Court production of David Storey's *Home*. He had attended rehearsals on two occasions in May 1970 recorded by the director:

> He is less insistently aggressive than when we met [previously] ... Alan is funny: there is a sort of *intellectual* rigidity, I don't know how much he takes in, some of his responses don't seem exactly bright ... but there is such brightness and emotional commitment in his response: his laughter and sudden bursts of attention.[13]

Ten days later, Anderson writes, "Alan has an urgent animation that I find immensely attractive"[14]

In February 1971 Anderson notes his observations that the younger man swings wildly between exaltation and depression; and although he admits that he cannot recall the medical term for the condition, Anderson

---

[10] Ibid.
[11] Jon Landau, "Loose Ends," *The Real Paper,* 27 June 1973, 15.
[12] "Alan Price Biography,"
http://alanprice.absoluteelsewhere.net/biography3.html.
[13] Diary, LA 6/1/58 (9 May 1970).
[14] Diary, LA 6/1/58 (20 May 1970).

plainly has manic depression or bipolarity in mind.[15] By July he is actually musing about casting Price rather than McDowell as lead in the new feature film: "It is an interesting phenomenon—the tough, sexy, sensitive rebel—can I do this for Malcolm in *O Lucky Man*? But really Alan is the character."[16] In the outturn, of course, both men were to have key roles.

Six months after that entry, in January 1972, Anderson confesses his personal fascination with Price, writing that notwithstanding the latter's ruthless dedication to his personal objectives, the singer has acquired, at the level of fantasy, a sudden, unexpected potency in his imagination.[17] We believe, judging by the recurring pattern of Anderson's feelings toward other tough men such as Richard Harris, that what Anderson perceived as Price's ruthlessness and remoteness actually augmented his attraction.[18] A homosexual whose celibacy was a consequence of physical fastidiousness rather than want of desire, Anderson had fallen for Harris during the making of *This Sporting Life* (1963). Almost a decade later his thoughts still returned to him from time to time in fantasies of the actor brutalising him sexually.[19] Indeed Anderson's journal entries (always unblinkingly frank) often return to his sexual fantasies and preference for men who manipulate and command him.[20] In the case of Price, however, Anderson's feelings modulated by degrees away from the hopeless passion he had felt for Harris and other men, and toward increasing professional respect and friendship.[21] It is pleasant to speculate that in working with and getting to know Price well, Anderson himself may have come to enjoy as close to a Zen-like relationship as he was to achieve with any of his collaborators.

Initially, when researching material for his documentary, the filmmaker had accompanied the band to a number of gigs where the disorganised pattern of work of both the musicians and their roadies drew his disapproving attention.[22] Doubtless this was in part because it differed so greatly from the firm control that he liked to exert when working with a film crew. Observing the want of a rigorous plan of action for the gigs, he more than once reflected on the weakness inherent in this informality.[23]

---

[15] Diary, LA 6/1/61/20 (February 1971).
[16] Diary, LA 6/1/61/29 (12 July 1971).
[17] Diary, LA 6/1/64/24 (22 January 1972).
[18] See, for example, diary, LA 6/1/64/50 (17 February 1972).
[19] Diary, LA 6/1/64/294 (19 May 1972).
[20] Diary, LA 6/1/64/265 (5 October 72).
[21] See, for example, diary, LA 6/1/64/104–5 (15 April 1972).
[22] Diary, LA 6/1/59 *passim* (1–9 October 1970).
[23] See, for example, diary LA 6/1/59/19 (October 1970).

The same concerns returned when he noted what he described as Price's nerves, tension and inability to provide leadership for his musicians as they recorded the tracks for *O Lucky Man!* in the studio.[24] For his part, Price admitted his nervousness, recalling why he had asked to write and record the songs before the film was shot. Having worked with Anderson previously, he valued the affinity in their thinking. His respect for the older man was such that he wanted to make his contribution and not be overawed by the standard set by Anderson and his co-writers, Sherwin and McDowell.[25] In actuality, Anderson's relationship with Price as a writer was based on mutual respect. This differed from his working pattern with Sherwin, whom Anderson dominated to make him write acceptable scenes.

After that first recording session, Anderson wrote a detailed account in his journal of those four tough days. He thought that progress had been made, but not before he had intervened asking for changes in the lyrics. Price had first resisted but eventually came round under pressure. With these sessions finished, Anderson thought the music good.[26] And relations between the two men improved during the forthcoming months of work on the film. Anderson noted, after another studio session in May 1972, that Price had been unusually open to suggestions.[27]

Class and Culture

Factors other than the different ways they organised concerts and recording sessions would have added to Anderson's sense of alienation from the band's working methods. He was to some degree distanced from the culture of young people through his class background. This may help explain his choice of Price who (to judge by music press reviews) was not seen as being as "cool" as some of his contemporaries. His work with Georgie Fame was described as "a smooth and polished cabaret act" by *NME*,[28] but Eric Burdon, fellow founding member of The Animals, is given more respect.[29] Consonant with this, the Preface to the script's first

---

[24] Diary, LA 6/1/64/65–68 (5–8 March 1972).
[25] Eric van Lustbader, "O Lucky Men, How Did Your Movie Grow?" *Zoo World*, 25 October 1973, 29.
[26] Diary, LA 6/1/64/65-68 (5–8 March 1972).
[27] Diary, LA 6/1/64/125 (6 May 1972).
[28] "Gig Guide," *NME*, 30 June 1973, 21.
[29] Keith Altham, "Interview with Eric Burdon," *NME*, 2 June 1973, 9.

draft describes Price as "a singer with a group—who are neither trendy or aggressively 'pop'."[30]

Anderson himself had been educated as a boarder at Cheltenham College and completed his studies in Classics and English (interrupted by wartime service in the Intelligence Corps) at Oxford University.[31] All these factors marked him out as a scion of the upper middle class, rooted (despite his early years in India) in the Home Counties. Meanwhile, British pop music of the 1960s and early 1970s found it useful to let its Northern, working-class roots show. Both, of course, were authentic ingredients of Price's life. That Northern aura amplified the ethos of youthful rebellion from the culture of the establishment, which remained centred on London and the South-East.

As mentioned, Anderson belonged to a different generation, and the crew marked his 49th birthday during the shoot. Although he may not have known that two days later Alan Price turned thirty, he could not have been unaware of the age gap between them. In fact, at a time of life when most people consider themselves middle-aged, Anderson consistently wrote of himself as being old, as plenty of entries in the diaries testify.[32]

However, his vibrant public voice must also be weighed in the balance, not least because he consistently projected a satirical, angry rebellion against his background. David Wilson helpfully summarises one of the thrusts in Anderson's 1957 essay "Get Out and Push!" Principally focussed on revitalising British cinema, the paper also castigated society's stultifying mediocrity, philistinism and the smug, directionless self-display of a Little England still intoxicated with the illusion of Great Britain.[33] Added to this were the cumulative effect of his equally strong writing in *Sequence* and *Sight and Sound*; his associations with the Angry Young Men through the plays he staged at the Royal Court Theatre; his portrait of greedy power mongering by the rich in *This Sporting Life*; and his satirical attacks on the upper middle class in *If...* .

Public statements such as these drew audiences who were disposed to seek out a theatre and a cinema more thoughtful or rebellious than mainstream Anglo-American fare was providing in the 1960s and 1970s. As Wilson also pointed out in reviewing *O Lucky Man!*, Anderson's

---

[30] David Sherwin, "O Lucky Man!" Preface to first draft screenplay, LA 1/7/1/5 (October 1971).

[31] Paul Ryan, "Introduction," in *Never Apologise,* 3.

[32] See, for example, diary LA 6/1/64/72 (12 March 1972); LA 6/1/64/112 (23 April 1972); LA 6/1/64/295-6 (19 May 1972); LA 6/1/64/144 (27 May 1972).

[33] David Wilson, "O Lucky Man," *Sight and Sound* 42, no. 3 (1973): 127.

diagnosis of British social malaise in 1957 remained valid in 1973.[34] And it is not hard to argue that the same themes (corruption and big business, torture, medical experiments on human guinea pigs, African dictators and the arms trade, exploitation of the developing world and poverty) remain relevant today.

Writing the Lyrics

When in 1971 Anderson had travelled with the band to research the proposed documentary, he recognised that Price's music raised fascinating questions about its sources; but he appears not to have explored them, noting instead that he intended to focus on the singer's work at its most pure, personal and passionately lyrical.[35] With these words Anderson echoed his own trumpet call twenty years earlier in *Sequence* for British films, as part of the rebellion he urged against Britain's ossified cinematic culture, to prioritise the personal and passionate. That call was to form one of the main elements giving loose coherence to the films by several directors (including himself) that had been released through the Free Cinema programmes of 1956-59. It also identified him as "a charter member of the [European] New Wave".[36] By the time he came to preparing *O Lucky Man!*, however, Anderson's approach had altered somewhat. It was not the sources but the philosophy of the songs to be written and recorded for the film that he discussed with the bandleader. For his part, Price remembered that the script interested him both because of its philosophy and the idea of a young man coming down from the North trying to make money and be successful, just as he had tried to do.[37] So whereas in the film Price is like the street singer in Brecht's *Threepenny Opera*, in the drawn-out process of making the film he became to Anderson what Kurt Weill was to Brecht: an essential musical partner.

Interviewed by David Robinson for *The Times* shortly before the film's release, Anderson described the method he and Price had adopted in collaborating. Early drafts of the script simply note the themes ("song of luck", "song of opportunity", "song of money", etc.) which Price was to write. In fact, for each point at which music was to be inserted, the director wrote a paragraph stating what he thought the song should be about. Price

[34] Ibid.
[35] Diary, LA 6/1/60/27 (January–March 1971).
[36] Elissa Durwood, "O Lucky Man!," *Crimmer's: Journal of the Narrative Arts* (Spring 1976): 11.
[37] van Lustbader, "O Lucky Men," 29.

took that and reinterpreted it in terms of his feelings and attitudes, which Anderson found sufficiently different from his own to provide creative tension, but also sufficiently the same for that tension to be productive.[38]

After a production meeting in the month before shooting commenced, Anderson mused in his diary: "In a sense the final zen-existential feeling of the film corresponds to [Alan's] own feeling about life: be what you are: you are what you are: decisions won't change anything. But of course this is mixed with an instinctive, romantic individualism."[39] Making this last remark, Anderson was reflecting his belief that words only mattered to Price when they came to him in a flash.[40] Anderson believed (and in our view the film justifies his assertion) that this mix of the political and the deeply personal characterised the songs when considered as the Chorus. He thought that they "express the ironic attitude of the film quite directly, [and] the persona that Alan presents takes on an air of *knowledgeableness*."[41] As Price himself said, "In some ways the presence of me and my music is to be sort of an opposite to Malcolm. You know, I'm the guy who's been there and can now adjust and reflect on it all."[42] For Anderson, Price remains slightly enigmatic as a character in the film, as if apart from the action. He has attained the attitude to life that it takes Mick the whole story to reach. In short, Price's character is a portrayal of someone who knows what life is about.[43]

Performance

Janet Maslin evaluated the impact of Price's performance, finding that his songs are:

> performed with such utter charm that their essential seriousness remains remarkably unobtrusive. And while Lindsay Anderson's film, which Price's appearances so delightfully punctuate, uses a series of bizarre but concrete episodes to suggest allegorical generalities, Price reverses that method – with sterling results. He may sing and write about the big issues, but his easygoing method reduces them to ironic everyday terms, making them all the more potent for their illusion of familiarity.

---

[38] David Robinson, "Stripping the veils away," *The Times,* April 21,1973, Review, 7.
[39] Diary, LA 6/1/64/41 (8 February 1972).
[40] Ibid.
[41] Robinson, "Stripping the veils away," 7.
[42] Alan Price interviewed by Knippenberg, in Jim Knippenberg, "The Price is All Right," *The Cincinatti Enquirer*, August 5, 1973, 16H.
[43] Robinson, "Stripping the veils away," 7.

[This rests upon] the basic contradiction of Price's style, with its abrasive energy camouflaged by disarming pleasantries. Price's vocals, loose but perfectly suited to his material, play upon that seeming same contradiction, as do his superb arrangements and keyboard work, and the end result is a full-blown irony that's more than merely verbal. It's not just the lyrics, but rather the whole production, that contrast the sinister with a mood of simulated naïveté.[44]

When one reads the lyrics on paper (for example, those accompanying the opening titles) they do indeed seem to give too much away. Heard in the cinema, they do not. In addition to the light touch described by Maslin, other factors contribute to this effect. The first is the placing of the opening titles. They follow a prologue that mimics a grotesquely over-acted, black and white silent film in the style of the century's first decade. After the card "Once Upon a Time", we are in a colonial coffee plantation: an impoverished labourer (McDowell) steals a handful of the beans he has harvested. A brutal white police officer observes the crime, and arraigns the unfortunate man before a slavering white judge who, with no evidence, pronounces him guilty. The police officer carries out the sentence with relish, chopping off the unlucky man's hands. Cut hard to Alan Price, titles, music and song:

If you have a friend on whom you think you can rely—
You are a lucky man!
If you've found a reason to live on and not to die—
You are a lucky man!

[...]

If you've found the meaning of the truth in this old world—
You are a lucky man!
If knowledge hangs around your neck like pearls instead of chains—
You are a lucky man!

Takers and fakers and talkers won't tell you,
Teachers and preachers will just buy and sell you,
When no one can tempt you with heaven or hell—
You'll be a lucky man!

You'll be better by far
To be just what you are—

---

[44] Janet Maslin, "Abrasive energy, disarming pleasantries," *Rolling Stone*, 2 August 1973, 41.

You can be what you want
If you are what you are—
And that's a lucky man!

The silent prologue amounts to a deliberately crude lampoon that produces shock. Then suddenly eyes, ears and mind are busied upon the hard cut to the present, which comes apparently out of nowhere at the very moment we expect the story proper to start. In addition to Price performing with his band, the director himself (in his famous leather jacket) wanders among the musicians to leave a sheet on Price's music stand. Meanwhile the main titles are superimposed on this scene.

Jim Knippenberg noticed a specific example of this method of juxtaposition of dramatic action and music referring to a moment when Mick has reached the summit of his ambitions as personal assistant to a rich city businessman, but Price suddenly appears and forewarns of disaster "look over your shoulder/ 'cos there's always someone coming after you." However, Price is grinning and playful, gently making sport of everything in sight. As a consequence, profound and weighty topics don't seem ponderous.[45]

Music and dramatic mode

While in marketing the film, the band were portrayed as working in the mainstream, but their dramatic function in *O Lucky Man!* ran counter to dominant culture. Anderson had been influenced by Brecht's principles and practice ever since *Mother Courage* had played in London in 1956. *O Lucky Man!* was constructed broadly in harmony with those principles and with the purpose of casting a new, hard-edged light on contemporary society. The band participate as characters in the narrative and also comment as if from outside it, operating, as we have seen, like an all-knowing Greek chorus. In that role they have two functions: firstly, strengthening the structure and secondly, providing the moral context that frames the protagonists' self-seeking behaviour.

Reviewing the film, George Melly wrote that although the Brechtian mode seldom works in cinema, it does so triumphantly in *O Lucky Man!* He identified several factors that bond it firmly. They included McDowell's Candide-like hero; excellent performances by several actors playing multiple roles; and Sherwin's screenplay. The music too helps avoid the looseness to which the episodic picaresque form is liable: the

---

[45] Knippenberg, "The Price is All Right," 16H.

wry edge of the songs links and illuminates the various episodes obliquely. Then too, Anderson's coherent view of how society works gives the narrative its scaffolding.

Concerning the moral and political contexts, Melly noted that all the incidents (such as police looting a crash site, the sale of arms to an African despot and scientific experimentation on human beings) can be paired with reality. He added, "in the week of the Watergate disclosures, the film's relevance needs no underlining."[46] The happy accident (which in its day *If...* too had enjoyed) of being released at a historical conjuncture that illuminated the film is one thing, although not the same as a political programme. Satirists generally agree with Matthew Hodgart, however, that the form is devoted to showing how things really are and demolishing existing follies rather than advocacy for a new dispensation:

> The satirist appears in his noblest role when he accepts the challenge of oblivion, by taking on an ephemeral and unpleasant topic ... [Politics] offers the greatest risk and the greatest rewards: politics is traditionally considered a dirty business, yet the satirist is most a hero when he enters the forum and joins in the world's debate ... What is essential is that he should commit himself boldly to his 'impure' subject, yet retain a purity of attitude, in his aesthetic disengagement from the vulgarities and stupidities of the struggle.[47]

As on-screen co-author of the satire, Alan Price retains the purity of attitude that Hodgart advocates. Yet he goes further, simultaneously playing the fulfilled existential, while indirectly serving the community through his music. Not a political programme as such, but a return to the basic starting point of so many renewed ventures—knowing oneself.

Having suffered Anderson's famous slap, Mick is given the part. Alan Price, his band and the entire cast celebrate the film's completion, singing and dancing exuberantly with the Brechtianly disassembled Mick Travis/ Malcolm McDowell grinning delightedly and cavorting among the other actors, some in, some out of character:

> Because on and on and on and on we go,
> And it's around the world in circles turning,
> Earning what we can
> While others dance away the chance to light your day.

---

[46] George Melly, "Mick grins and bears it," *The Observer*, May 6, 1973, 34.
[47] Matthew Hodgart, *Satire* (London: Weidenfeld and Nicolson, 1969), 31–2.

ANGLO ARGENTO:
A CRITICAL REASSESSMENT OF THE FILMS
OF NORMAN J. WARREN

ADAM LOCKS

Fig. 17.1. Norman J. Warren on set with Glynis Barber. *Terror* (1976).
Photograph by kind permission of Norman Warren.

When it comes to discussing British horror cinema in the 1970s, certain directors are usually cited, such as: Pete Walker, Roy Ward Baker, Freddie Francis, Anthony Balch, Alan Gibson, Peter Sykes, and Norman J. Warren. The latter's horror repertoire rests on four films: *Satan's Slave* (1976), *Prey* (1978), *Terror* (1979), and *Inseminoid* (1981). The 1970s are often viewed as the golden age of horror cinema. Nevertheless, it was during this decade when the two drivers of British horror—Hammer and Amicus studios—went into commercial decline. Both production companies had continued to produce Gothic horror that seemed maladroit and anachronistic when viewed against American imports. When Hammer did try to update its Dracula myth, the results were camp and disconnected from the youth market to which they had once appealed.[1]

Warren's three horrors from the 1970s reflect a period of permissiveness and playfulness that was far removed from most of Hammer's output. And whereas, for example, Pete Walker's movies had an obvious political subtext that explains the violence, Warren's pictures made no such excuses. This was horror that was designed to shock for shock's sake. Nonetheless, his films from this period are beautifully shot and richly atmospheric, and are the artistic equal of the work of Peter Sykes. Warren also managed to provide a much higher quality story than either his budget or the time limit should have allowed.

Throughout the 1970s, British cinema was unceremoniously propped up by not only horror, but also sexploitation. Both genres were critically perceived as crude and puerile.   British sex films, however, made considerable sums of money since they offered sexual images which were not permitted to be shown on television.   As David McGillivray, who wrote screenplays for numerous British sex comedies and also for two of Norman Warren's films, states: "You'd have to have been an imbecile not to make money from sex films in those days. You shot it, released it and started counting the profits immediately. It was so easy." [2] Warren established his name in British cinema by directing the first British sex film, the profitable *Her Private Hell* (1967). After directing another successful sexploitation movie entitled *Loving Feeling* (1968), he declined the offer to work on the follow-up, *Wife Swappers* (1970), deciding instead to make the switch to the horror genre.

This paper's genesis stems from a recent interview I conducted with Norman J. Warren.[3] He was one of the New Wave of British horror directors working in the 1970s, but he wouldn't see this label as a badge of serious artistry. In spite of this, I want to take Warren's films seriously. There is nothing new or startling about horror directors presenting a warped and surreal view of the world. Yet this stimulates interesting readings, because of the time in which these films were made and the cinematic history to which they belong.

---

[1] For a useful discussion upon the demise of Hammer, see Winston Wheeler Dixon, "The End of Hammer," in *Seventies British Cinema*, ed. Robert Shail, 14–24 (London: Palgrave Macmillan, 2008).
[2] Simon Sheridan, *Keeping The British End Up: Four Decades of Saucy Cinema* (Richmond: Reynolds & Hearn, 2001), 29.
[3] Interview by the author with Norman J. Warren, April 16, 2008.

The title of this paper points to the importance of Warren as a British director and the way that, like Dario Argento, he too used the language of cinema as an outlet for some distinctly British surrealism; in other words, Warren's films blend rational life with the unconscious. Argento was a key influence on Warren in the latter part of the 1970s, encouraging him to make anti-narrative horror that supports the analogy between cinema and dreams. A further influence on Warren's horror output is *The Avengers* (ATV, 1961-1969), a British TV show that revelled in the surreal. Although not mentioned explicitly as an influence by the director at interview, it provides some helpful comparisons. In particular, *The Avengers* continually contrasted "Old Englande" against the modern, a theme particularly evident in Warren's first three horrors.

Warren's films were made when Jim Callaghan's Labour Government presided over a country in economic melt-down. It is in such a socio-economic context that Warren's films operate. I would suggest that these movies work against Leon Hunt's comment that "there is a danger of over determining these films on the basis of setting."[4] I suggest that they offer up a psychogeography: a theoretical tool that has been used by various writers to make the modern world more interesting while simultaneously unmasking ideological deception. Warren uses bucolic imagery to combat the more unpalatable, dull and depressing aspects of 1970s Britain. It is widely agreed that psychogeography has become something of a buzzword in recent years, moving away from its origins in 1950s and 1960s Paris to—at worse—a vague label to do with walking in a city exemplified by Will Self's titular column, "PsychoGeography" in *The Independent*. Indeed, Ian Sinclair calls psychogeography "a new form of tourism" which exemplifies Self's questionable approach[5] Here, I echo Mervin Coverley's understanding of psychogeography as a way "to overcome the process of 'banalisation' by which the everyday experience of our surroundings becomes one of drab monotony."[6] Cinema is an obvious tool to help overcome this banality of the everyday. An example of this is the multi-storey car park in Gateshead, which made such an impact in the film *Get Carter* (Mike Hodges, 1972) that a concerted protest was made by fans in a vain attempt to halt its demolition. Although psychogeography is a term

---

[4] Leon Hunt, *British Low Culture: From Safari Suits to Sexploitation* (London: Routledge, 1998), 154.
[5] See Chapman's interview with Sinclair: Tim Chapman, "When in Doubt, Quote Ballard: An Interview with Ian Sinclair," *Ballardian*,
http://www.ballardian.com/iain-sinclair-when-in-doubt-quote-ballard.
[6] Merlin Coverley, *Psychogeography* (Harpenden: Pocket Essentials, 2006), 13.

used more often to map the urban environment, it is applied here to the pastoral.

Satan's Slave focuses on Catherine Yorke (Candace Glendenning). Near the beginning of the film, we see her and her parents drive out to her Uncle Alexander's house in the countryside. She has never met this mysterious uncle, and her father has not seen him since they were children. In an early sequence in the film, Catherine and her parents drive through suburbia; then the camera cuts to their passage through a village; then a country lane; and finally they drive off-road and are surrounded by forest.

This journey operates as a kind of re-programming for the audience with memories and associations disconnected from the modern and the urban. Even the family car, an old Rover, is decidedly antiquated. It is has a time-machine effect like the journey itself. In psychogeographical terms of the relationship between the individual and space, there is the clichéd yet interesting idea of the road leading to nowhere. Catherine's father gets temporarily lost, perhaps unsurprising as this is a generic feature of many horror films. Horror is invariably reduced to a set of geographical icons: the haunted house, the forest, the country lane and so on. Many of these icons are what could be termed "nowhere places". Horror is a genre that takes great pleasure in representing this sense of being lost, which often reflects the characters' mental state in the environment itself.

Arriving at the house, the father suddenly gets a pain in his head forcing him to lose control of the car which then crashes into a tree. Catherine gets out for help, but as she staggers away, it explodes with the parents still inside. The uncle, his psychotic son Steven (Martin Potter) and his secretary Frances (Barbara Kellerman) offer to look after Catherine. It is soon learnt that she is the direct descendant of an evil witch whom the uncle is attempting to reincarnate, and that only her blood, spilt on her 20th birthday, will suffice.[7]

---

[7] The common theme of Satanism and the Occult in horror cinema at this time is mentioned by Ian Conrich, "The Divergence and Mutation of British Cinema," in *Seventies British Cinema,* ed. Robert Shail, 33 (London: Palgrave Macmillan, 2008).

Fig. 17.2. Uncle Alexander (Michael Gough) and his secretary (Barbara Kelleran) comfort a shocked Catherine (Candace Glendenning). *Satan's Slave* (1976). Photograph by kind permission of Norman Warren.

Uncle Alexander, performed by horror stalwart Michael Gough, is the lynchpin of the film, a sartorially-immaculate gentleman who lives in a Tudor mansion full of antiques. Yet Catherine is told by his son, Stephen, that the family no longer have the money they once had; his father is helped by friends and other sources. His father's 1965 model Rolls-Royce and the historic property with its acres of woodland suggest former glories. Uncle Alexander is a nostalgically fossilised version of English masculinity. Before it is revealed that he is a sociopathic Satanist, he functions as an atavistic amalgamation of various icons of British gentlemen: particularly the eccentric British aristocrat, the kindly family doctor, and the chivalrous knight. To quote Ruth P. Rubinstein in her book *Dress Codes,* "The code of chivalry [...] included a pledge to protect women."[8] In *Satan's Slave* this code of chivalry is inverted by Alexander's need to sacrifice his niece; earlier in the film he is seen sacrificing his wife.

---

[8] Ruth Rubinstein, *Dress Codes: Meanings and Messages in American Culture* (Boulder, San Francisco, Oxford: Westview, 1995), 89.

In *Satan's Slave*—as with *Prey* and *Terror*—Warren's mise en scène has strong visual and narrative echoes of the sixties TV series *The Avengers* (a series that Gough was to star in three times). The world of *The Avengers* is set in a location referred to in fandom circles as "Avengerland".[9] This is an area that was within three miles of the series' production studios, the Associated British Elstree Studios in Borehamwood, Hertfordshire. But *The Avengers*' narrative took place within an iconic Olde Englande; a place which no longer existed and for the most part, never had.

The Avengers depicted England as a mythic space construed as a psychogeography. The producer, writer and main creative instigator behind the series in the mid-to-late 1960s was Brian Clemens, who commented that the ideology behind this imaginary England "was to set the stories against a tongue-in-cheek panorama of the picture postcard Britain illustrated in tourist brochures."[10] These two sides of British life, namely the modern (and hence industrial) and the rural (and hence utopian) provide the underlying, and conflicting, drivers of the programme. Nearly all the episodes take place in rural communities where the camera lingers over country houses, villages and village greens, pubs, red telephone boxes and meandering country lanes. Warren's films strongly echo this trait and, equally, follow certain patterns of Surrealist art in the way that outdoor locations are often empty. As with *The Avengers*, these locations are deserted—or at best populated by a handful of actors—and in terms of production, this was due to budgetary restraints.

Warren's films, like *The Avengers*, always demonstrate some underlying disquiet about their locations, and the familiarity of "Englishness" is transformed and warped. Behind the façade of mundane England, threatening figures or forces—be they crooks in *The Avengers*, or Satanists in *Satan's Slave*, or aliens in *Prey*—plan to disrupt the everyday world. Andrew Graham Dixon comments on the surreal qualities in British popular culture:

> Pop in [Richard] Hamilton's sense of the word, never truly came to pass in art, only in popular music. Certain forms of visual self-expression—convulsive, violent, hallucinogenic, and subversive—could not flourish in

---

[9] See "A Guide to Avengerland," *Geocities*,
http://www.geocities.com/Hollywood/Film/8165/index.html.
[10] *The Avengers: The Official Souvenir Magazine* (London: Titan, 1998), 35.

the world of fine art in Britain so they took the form of rock music instead. Britain did not produce Dadaism, but The Sex Pistols.[11]

One could add that Britain did not produce a Giorgio de Chirico, but it did produce a more popular visual equivalent with *The Avengers* and 70s horror, exemplified by Norman Warren's oeuvre. As with a film such as *Satan's Slave*, de Chirico's art was all about fragmenting space by presenting empty areas cut up and spliced by shadows and atypical angles. His vision of Italy transformed the subject matter into what Sarane Alexandrian calls "unknown worlds."[12]

The rural settings in Warren's films create an introverted view of England that is utopian, romantic and, most significantly, static in the sense of negating industrial changes brought about by modernity. And yet in accordance with the (un)reasoning of Surrealism, it is a deeply irrational view of England, preferring to depict the country as a kind of dreamscape imbuing everyday objects of Englishness—the pub, the telephone box, the bus, the village, even the local milkman—with the kind of mythicism perpetuated by the tourist brochures mentioned earlier by Brian Clemens. This procedure follows a similar pattern to de Chirico who would re-use again and again images of the tower, the arcade, the piazza, statues, mannequins and shadows, to bring about a new sense of awareness, but also, alienation from the modern environment.

In such a respect and for all their horror, Warren's films offer a deeply romantic view of England. The mise en scène of *Satan's Slave* alludes to that heritage England which subsequently was so strongly portrayed in popular television programmes such as *Brideshead Revisited* (ITV, 1981). Warren comments on the eerie location found by the film's production designer, Hayden Pearce:

> The house was near Guildford in Pirbright. It's now owned by a Dutch family. The Baron and Baroness who owned it when we used it were on hard times. That's why I think they were renting it out for films. They were a wonderful couple who were quite hard up. They'd moved over from France from a chateau and that was why the house was full of all these wonderful objects.[13]

---

[11] Andrew Graham-Dixon, *A History of British Art* (London: BBC Books, 1996), 226.
[12] Sarane Alexandrian, *Surrealist Art* (London: Thames and Hudson, 1996), 54.
[13] Interview with Norman J. Warren.

There is an earlier scene in *Satan's Slave* where the uncle answers the phone in the sitting room and, oddly, it's kept behind a large red curtain. As Warren comments: "It's always amazed me what you can get away with in films. For some unknown reason, Michael Gough's character keeps a telephone behind the red curtain. The whole reason for that was that we needed the bit where Catherine finds Stephen's body—that was the primary reason why the phone had to be kept behind the curtain."[14] Nevertheless, the curtain also functions as an irrational way of hiding and negating technology. The house has no visible popular appliances: we never see a television set or a radio or anything which suggests the modern world.

In *Prey*, the narrative focuses on two lesbians: Josephine (performed by a splendidly barmy Sally Faulker), and Jessica (Glory Annen). They live in a huge country house which has a surreal quality as Warren attests:

> We were given the free reign of the old house on the Shepperton Studios back-lot, and we were also told we could use any prop that was in the prop store at that time. Our designer, Hayden Pearce, had to work with whatever he could find. He really didn't have any choice. But somehow, with Hayden's own magic, he managed to give a strange mix to the sets which certainly helped create the right atmosphere. I'd also challenge anyone to make a floor plan of the house, because none of it really makes any sense, but then it does, if you see what I mean.[15]

As with *Satan's Slave,* there are similar echoes of a mythic English past. Apart from the radio in the kitchen, this film also plays down the impingement of technology. The interruption of their bucolic existence is caused by the arrival of a young man—Anderson—who is actually an alien called Kator who has come to test the suitability of humans as a source of food for his race.   The house is isolated like the female characters. They have been ostracised by the local community because of their sexual relationship. This is another locale that suggests a break-away from the modern industrial world. When Jessica expresses her desire to go away to the city, Josephine replies, "You'd get screwed up." The long camera pans of their walks through the garden and forest and the gentle love theme played on a piano suggest a disavowal of the modern.

This tranquillity is shattered by a very long scene where Anderson/Kator nearly drowns in a lake. Jo and Jessica go to his rescue and for a few minutes, we watch the three in slow motion as they writhe about in the

---

[14] Ibid.
[15] Ibid.

stagnant black water. Over this scene, the film's composer, Ivor Stanley, plays a brutal and fierce synthesiser line which is dark and brooding while the piano sounds stuttering and panicky. For all Kator's primitivism, he is also modern, after all, he arrived in a (unseen) spacecraft. It's a moment that reveals a deep anxiety over technological and economic expansion since the 1960s, and the scene operates as a hysterical reaction to the intrusiveness of modern cultural change.

Fig. 17.3. Josephine (Sally Faulker), Jessica (Glory Annen) and Anderson/Kator (Barry Stokes) in the lake. *Prey* (1978).
Photograph by kind permission of Norman Warren.

Prey and *Terror* also continue that surrealist tradition begun by Lewis Carroll in his *Alice's Adventures in Wonderland* (1865) and *Through the Looking Glass and What Alice Found There* (1871). In a discussion of *The Avengers'* relation to an especially English slant on Surrealism derived from Lewis Carroll, Grant Morrison writes:

> As is well documented, the original Surrealist Movement of the 1920s picked up and developed a number of ideas which emerged out of the work of the pre-war Futurists and Dadaists. One of the most important of these ideas involved the transformation of ordinary objects by placing them in extraordinary settings [...] What was more unusual and, indeed, more

radical was the fact that here was surrealism taken out of the galleries and placed in the living rooms of millions of television viewers.[16]

In this respect, Warren's films could also be interpreted as a part of the avant-garde tendency in British cinema best typified by Lindsey Anderson, whose films, such as *If...* (1968) and *O Lucky Man!* (1973), to quote Michael Bracewell, showed "England's traditions and institutions […] as delinquent, corrupt or mad, and the landscape surrounding them as Alice-like in its sudden shift of purpose."[17] This shows certain similarities to Warren's surrealist take on "reality."

Many horror films have a narrative logic which, examined even a little closely, falls apart very quickly. Certain directors have not bothered with narrative coherence; instead they have privileged the spectacle of violence and death. Argento is an obvious case in point. In *Terror*, the audience is presented with horror set pieces that pay homage to early Argento. Warren was heavily influenced by him, and saw him as separating the spectacle of killing from any meaningful narrative logic. As he states:

> Horror films up until that date took a more conventional approach, although horror films often don't have to make a great deal of sense, they still had some logic. Well, with *Suspiria,* that film doesn't make sense at all. Yet that didn't bother you. It was just so great to look at. It had lots of energy […] The lighting used wild colours. Normally in films you'd see where the light is coming from; therefore you justify what colour it is. So suddenly, to have green light coming through the window or red or blue, it was so unusual, but it just worked for me.[18]

In one sequence the character Ann (Carolyn Courage) travels on the underground. In the next scene, she is running through a wood towards the house. This jump from tube to forest is noticeably dreamlike, although the station from which she alights—Barnes tube station—really does lead straight out to Barnes Common which is close to the centre of London. But the speed of Warren's editing distorts this "fact", and makes the narrative proceed quickly and disjointedly, as in a dream. The tube station is like a small island of civilisation in the middle of untamed nature: the reverse of psychogeographer Ian Sinclair's description of London encased

---

[16] Grant Morrison, "A World of Miraculous Transformations," in *The Avengers Companion,* eds. Alain Carraze, Jean-Luc Putheaud and Alex J. Geairns, 21 (London: Titan Books, 1997).
[17] Michael Bracewell, *England is Mine: Pop Life in Albion from Wilde to Goldie* (London: Flamingo, 1997), 84.
[18] Interview with Norman J. Warren.

by the modernity of the M25 motorway.[19] *Terror's* locale makes a strong contrast to Argento's *Tenebrae* (1982). Here, the locations used in Rome are of highly modern buildings and spaces. There seems to be a fetishisation of technology and distancing techniques from notions of "Italian-ness" or, "Italianicity."[20] Icons of Italian culture are usurped by minimalist functionalism, exemplified by a sequence where John Saxon's character, Bullmer, sits in a piazza which almost resembles Harlow Town centre in Essex in its (un)aesthetic rush to modernity. Argento has often commented that, for the film, he dreamed of an "imaginary city".[21] In contrast, for Warren, it is an imaginary British *countryside* that intensifies "Englishness".

To conclude, Norman J. Warren made some of the most innovative and interesting British horror films of the 1970s. He shared with fellow director Pete Walker a fascination for making productions that were deeply pessimistic. Most of Warren's films end with the heroine or hero's demise and, as with Walker, he presents, to quote Steve Chibnall, "a world without reassurance."[22] If the 1970s is sometimes referred to as a "feel-bad decade," then the fact that most of Warren's horrors end with the death of the protagonist only helps to support this. And yet unlike Walker, Warren's movies also often have a strong supernatural element. Most significantly, as Walker used horror to critique the injustices of the English class system in films such as *House of Whipcord* (1974), so Warren celebrates and laments Old Englande and continues a tradition of the surreal and absurd and that would became better known through art house cinema.

Near the end of *Satan's Slave,* we are presented one of the biggest twists in British horror; Catherine, panic-stricken and stumbling through the forest while in pursuit by her uncle and his acolytes, bumps into her supposedly dead father. Discussing the scene, Warren observes: "I've always hated movies where you find out that it was all a dream—it's such a cop out. But our twist was that we actually cheated the audience at that time because it's not a bad dream; the big twist is that it's her father who is the real villain. Michael Gough is not the leader of the coven."[23]

---

[19] Chapman, "When in Doubt, Quote Ballard".

[20] Roland Barthes, *Image/Music/Text* (New York: Hill and Wang, 1977), 33–37.

[21] See for example Maitland McDonagh, *Broken Mirrors/Broken Minds: The Dark Dreams of Dario Argento* (London: Kensington Books, 1994).

[22] Steve Chibnall, *Making Mischief: The Cult Films of Pete Walker (*Guildford: FAB Press, 1998), 15.

[23] Interview with Norman J. Warren.

Here it could be argued that the film becomes a rather curious, yet pleasurable, mélange of images alluding to other fictions that play with notions of reality; for example: Luis Buñuel's love of the inexplicable in cinema; the artist Paul Nash's fusing of the uncanny with the English landscape; Lewis Carroll's kaleidoscopic play with the "real" and Argento's (con)fusion of reality with dreams. It's a scene that connects Warren to the surrealist tradition where the calamitous and mundane are transformed into the giddily wondrous, the extraordinary, and the very silly. As Warren comments on Catherine's father: "The jewellery he's seen wearing at the end of the film is actually a glass door knob."[24]

---

[24] Ibid.

THE BOY FRIEND:
KEN RUSSELL'S "ANTI-MUSICAL"

ADRIAN GARVEY

> Twelve reels are too long to tell such a slim tale, and Sandy Wilson's music, however tuneful, has diminishing returns .... Despite the big Busby Berkeley routines, the novelty value of the stage show, the great singing and dancing by the cast ... the film was a flop. The acting was too broad, the gags too laboured and the pacing too slow.[1]

This is Ken Russell's own harsh retrospective verdict on his 1972 musical, *The Boy Friend*, coloured perhaps by memories of a fraught production process and subsequent studio-imposed cuts. Although generally well received by critics at the time, the film performed poorly at the box office and has had little serious attention since. Overshadowed by his more controversial work, an apparent incongruity even amongst the output of such a maverick filmmaker, it has certainly been marginalised by many critics of the director's output. This neglect has been exacerbated by its non-availability for many years.

However, rather than a curiosity or folly, it now seems a significant film, an unexpectedly apt conjunction of *auteur* and genre. It demonstrates many of Russell's strengths and enduring preoccupations, touching as it does on issues of authorship and creativity, in its emphasis on performance and performing, and in its evocation of early 20th century modernist culture and style. Additionally, in genre terms, it is an authentically British musical, rooted in national cultural tropes, and also playing skilfully on the contrast between Hollywood gloss and British amateurism.

The film is based on Sandy Wilson's stage musical of the same name, a small-scale entertainment which became a surprise success in the West End in 1954 and then, the following year, on Broadway, where it introduced Julie Andrews to American audiences. Inspired by the musical comedies of the 1920s, the show concerns the romantic adventures of a

---

[1] Ken Russell, *Fire Over England: The British Cinema Comes Under Friendly Fire* (London: Hutchinson, 1993),134.

group of young English girls at a finishing school in the south of France, and is described by Wilson as "a loving salute to those far-off days of the cloche hat and the short skirt, a valentine from one post-war period to another".[2] The tone throughout is affectionately mocking, and the principal setting is "Madame Dubonnet's School for Young Ladies".

In the film, set around 1930, we see the show being performed by a provincial repertory company, with backstage antagonisms and rivalries sabotaging the production. The naïve assistant stage manager, Polly, played by the fashion model Twiggy, has to substitute for the injured leading lady, and further tension is created by the presence of Mr De Thrill (Vladek Sheybal), a visiting Hollywood director considering a film of the show, who watches from a theatre box while the cast compete for his attention and approval.[3] Adding to this show-within-a-show structure, further diegetic layers are opened up by spectacular fantasy versions of some of the musical numbers, as imagined by the characters.

The source of Russell's period film is itself a pastiche: a 1950s evocation of the 1920s, re-imagined by him in the 1970s. Nearly forty years later, the film can perhaps more easily be seen in relation both to its own period, and to contemporaneous ideas of the era it evokes. While challenging simplistic recreations of the past, it also is an index of a wider interest in 1920s culture in the 1970s.

Critical response in Britain and America was largely positive, with the exception of Alexander Walker and Pauline Kael, who shared a deep-seated antipathy to Russell's work. Twiggy, who was making a highly-publicised acting debut in the leading role, was generally highly praised. The film was also seen as an unexpectedly successful change of direction for Russell after his recent work, with George Melly in *The Observer* declaring that "the surprising thing is that on almost every level he has succeeded."[4] Gavin Millar in *The Listener*, noting the begrudging nature of some praise, hailed the film's reinvigoration of genre elements:

> what has been too little said is that—at moments—*The Boy Friend* does not merely imitate or affectionately parody so much as recapture the brilliance of the originals. There are two or three things here which rival in audacious bezazz the great moments in movie musical history.[5]

[2] Sandy Wilson, *The Boy Friend: A Play in Three Acts* [Play Script] (Penguin: London, 1959), 12.
[3] Sheybal had earlier played the director of the film-within-a-film in Ken Russell, dir., *The Debussy Film* [Television Broadcast] (London: BBC, 1966).
[4] George Melly, "Films," *Observer*, February 6, 1972.
[5] Gavin Millar, "Bezazz," *The Listener*, February 10, 1972.

Among the few real dissenters, Dilys Powell concluded her review with the phrase which would provide John Baxter with the title for his monograph on Russell: "the talent is there all right. But somehow it is an appalling talent."[6] Powell's verdict, though meant despairingly, was acute. Russell's contrary, perverse approach transformed the source material to produce a multi-layered narrative, rich in visual and musical conceits. This essay considers the film as an underexamined and undervalued work from the director's heyday, looking especially at the ways in which it both contributes to, and comments on, British and Hollywood musical genres, and considering how it reveals both the 1920s and the 1970s to us in striking ways.

The film was produced in the middle of Russell's most prolific and successful period as a filmmaker: he directed ten features in the decade between *Billion Dollar Brain* (1967) and *Valentino* (1977). He was also enjoying exceptional commercial standing at the time of its British release in February 1972, when it joined *The Music Lovers* (1970) and *The Devils* (1971) in West End cinemas. Additionally, the controversy surrounding his work was contributing to a high public profile rare among British filmmakers; he was, arguably, the best-known British director since Hitchcock at this time.

Russell had established his reputation as a director of television arts documentaries in the 1960s, principally for *Monitor* and *Omnibus,* and continued his iconoclastic approach to high culture in early film successes. The increasing license permissible in this medium at the time also encouraged his exploration of taboo sexual themes. Never a realist, his outlook shares some of the Romantic visionary excess of Powell and Pressburger, but demonstrates a harsher demotic humour. High and low cultural values jostle continuously in his work, with transcendent moments deliberately punctured by comic bathos. Along with contemporaries such as Nicolas Roeg, John Boorman, Lindsay Anderson and John Schlesinger (another *Monitor* graduate), Russell benefited from the decentred world of 1970s British film production, when, as Sue Harper has shown, "many films now relied on mixed funding, and one-picture companies were inaugurated (often by the director) as a means of choreographing their incomes. Directors had to be extremely pragmatic."[7] In the early years of the decade, this unstable environment could offer considerable creative autonomy, and a number of British (and British-based) *auteurs* found both

---

[6] Dilys Powell, "Films: Guying the Dolls," *Sunday Times*, February 6, 1972.
[7] Sue Harper, "History and Representation: The Case of 1970s British Cinema," in *The New Film History: Sources, Methods, Approaches*, ed. James Chapman, Mark Glancy and Sue Harper, 28 (Basingstoke: Palgrave Macmillan, 2007).

finance and audiences for challenging work, briefly fostering a surprisingly commercial art cinema aesthetic.

A film version of *The Boy Friend* had first been proposed by Joseph Janni, then a producer for the Rank Organisation, during its original West End run. However, after the transfer to New York, the rights were acquired by MGM in a deal with the show's producers Cy Feuer and Ernest Martin, and the studio then spent several years unsuccessfully developing treatments of the property. In the mid-1960s MGM refused to sell the rights to Universal producer Ross Hunter, who planned a version starring Julie Andrews, by then a major Hollywood star.[8] Russell's production seems to have been initiated by Twiggy and her manager, Justin de Villeneuve, after they attended a West End revival of the show directed by Wilson.

In 1970, MGM had closed its UK production operation at Borehamwood as part of the general retreat by Hollywood investment in the UK film industry. In March of the following year, the studio formed a partnership with EMI, EMI-MGM, with *The Boy Friend* listed in the initial production schedule. The film was budgeted at $1.7 million, and eventually made for under $2 million, at a time when major studio musicals cost between $15 and $20 million.

The film was conceived as a diversion after the tortuous production of *The Devils*. According to Russell "I thought I would try making a musical film just for fun. But *The Boy Friend* turned out to be the most complicated project that I had ever attempted."[9] The director retained much of his key creative team from *The Devils*; cinematographer David Watkin, composer Peter Maxwell Davies to arrange the score, and his wife Shirley Russell, costume designer for all his films of the period. Tony Walton, known for his work on Broadway musicals, was engaged as production designer. The cast includes many of the director's unofficial repertory of actors, including Murray Melvin, Max Adrian and Georgina Hale. After apparently considering Julie Andrews, Russell cast Glenda Jackson, his signature female star of the time, in the cameo role of Rita, the injured leading lady.

Twelve weeks were spent filming at the Theatre Royal Portsmouth, and a further six at Borehamwood Studios. The theatre, which was derelict

---

[8] Sandy Wilson, *I Could Be Happy* (London: Joseph, 1975), 263–265. Hunter went on to fashion an original, and extremely successful, 1920s-themed musical vehicle for Andrews in George Roy Hill, dir., *Thoroughly Modern Millie* [Motion Picture] (Hollywood: Universal Pictures,1967).
[9] Ken Russell, quoted in Gene D. Phillips, *Ken Russell* (Boston: Twayne, 1979), 152.

at the time, provided an atmospheric but challenging location, with rain and birds entering through a hole in the stage roof. Studio production was then hampered by technical limitations. Russell found the facilities inadequate for the ambitious and spectacular sequences filmed there "because I was shooting with a British crew who had never done this sort of thing. Everything was late in being built, didn't work, or fell over."[10] As production costs increased, there were continuing problems in renegotiating the budget. The climactic "Riviera" number was finally staged as if being filmed in a movie studio, when money for the planned set was refused.[11] On the film's completion, there were protracted arguments between director and studio over the final cut. Russell finally acquiesced to an American-release version of 109 minutes (the only cut in circulation for many years), which lost three musical sequences and jumbled some subplots, on the guarantee of a longer British cut at 123 minutes.

Although he has made only two real musicals, *The Boy Friend* and *Tommy* (1975), music has been central to Russell's work, both as subject and element. If Wilson's reference points were the 1920s theatrical musical comedy of Rodgers and Hart, Nöel Coward and their imitators, Russell's version of *The Boy Friend* is steeped in references to musical film history. In Barry Keith Grant's words, the film "employs camp as a double-edged sword that simultaneously mocks and celebrates the classic Hollywood musical."[12] The plot device of the understudy forced to replace an injured leading lady, and some lines of dialogue, as when the company director Max (Max Adrian) exhorts Polly, "You're going to go out there as a youngster, you've got to come back a star", are from *42nd Street* (Lloyd Bacon, 1933). Two added songs, "You Are My Lucky Star" and "All I Do Is Dream of You" are 1920s standards, which were later used in *Singin' in the Rain* (Stanley Donen and Gene Kelly, 1952).

The musical form is inherently self-reflexive, often emphasising performance and its construction—"putting on a show"—and the film repeatedly emphasises this quality. The action of the film takes place in real time, beginning at the theatre entrance just before a matinée performance starts, with a brief coda at the stage door after the curtain falls. The onstage and offstage worlds are skilfully balanced throughout

---

[10] Ibid., 156.
[11] Interview by the author with Murray Melvin, 30 June 2008. I am extremely grateful for the insights into the film and its production provided by Mr. Melvin.
[12] Barry Keith Grant, "The Body Politic: Ken Russell in the 1980s," in *Fires Were Started: British Cinema and Thatcherism*, 2nd ed., ed. Lester D. Friedman, 184 (London: Wallflower, 2006).

the film, with parallel stories of romantic longing and impersonation. De Thrill functions as Russell's stand-in, a director reshaping the performance before him, and also as an explicitly comic variation of the director's many tortured creative visionaries. He is complemented by Max, who is consumed with rewriting and redirecting the 'live' performance to accommodate his substitute star and impress his distinguished visitor.

Most of the fantasy numbers are staged and shot in the style of Busby Berkeley production numbers of the 1930s, and "The Riviera" recreates a celebrated biplane routine choreographed by Dave Gould for *Flying Down to Rio* (Thornton Freeland, 1933). In generic terms, the film broadly follows backstage musical conventions, though there are three "integrated" songs. However, the key theme of community is rejected. In the backstage musical, according to Thomas Schatz:

> the tensions between object and illusion, between social reality and utopia, are worked out on at least two distinct levels of action. The first is through the overall plot structure, when the various complications resolve themselves in the production of a flawless show. The second is at numerous points within the narrative itself when the characters transcend their interpersonal conflicts and express themselves in music and movement.[13]

In *The Boy Friend*, however, demonstrating Pauline Kael's designation of the film as an "anti-musical"[14], the onstage show never coheres. Animosity and personal ambition override any communal ethos, and the happy ending is only achieved by the central couple's rejection of the world of entertainment for "a room in Bloomsbury".

However, the film does also incorporate some of the traditional pleasures associated with the genre. Maxwell Davies' orchestration serves Wilson's score extremely well. It is expertly delivered in the 1920s idiom, and appropriately tinny where necessary for the stage accompaniments. The talents of some prodigious musical performers are also displayed. The dancing duel between Maisie (Antonia Ellis) and Tommy (Tommy Tune) in "Won't You Charleston with Me?", for example, as they compete for De Thrill's attention, demonstrates virtuosity as well as rivalry and spite.

Only the fantasy sequences though, really suggest some of the qualities of transcendence and abundance characteristic of the musical form, and

---

[13] Thomas Schatz, *Hollywood Genres: Formulas, Filmmaking, and the Studio System* (Boston: Mcgraw-Hill, 1981), 188.
[14] Pauline Kael, *5001 Nights at the Movies: Shorter Reviews from the Silents to the '90s* (London: Marion Boyars, 1993), 96.

the tone of these numbers is artfully poised between homage and parody. "I Could Be Happy with You" begins on a gleaming Art Deco set, and marks the first onstage meeting of Polly and Tony (Christopher Gable). As in Wilson's original, both characters are concealing their wealthy upper-class backgrounds, while the film's Polly is additionally a stand-in for Rita, and also in love with the "real" (offstage) Tony. Ideas of imitation and performance are underlined by the staging. The couple begins the song by exaggerated miming to a wind-up gramophone recording, then adjust to lighter, more naturalistic singing for the tap routine which follows. Then, abruptly, the record sticks. This jolt breaks the spell of seamless performance which is integral to the genre, and the performers are left revolving in awkward embarrassment. De Thrill, in his theatre box, is shown laughing derisively, then intrigued by the suspended action onstage. He leans forward intently and begins to rework the number in his imagination. His fantasy version begins with a transition to the same couple now dancing on a huge revolving record disc, the surreal dream state emphasised by the repeating and echoing song words from the gramophone and the enhanced costumes: Tony's bellboy outfit is now silver, Polly's evening pyjamas have become a diaphanous gown. The number incorporates the overhead kaleidoscopic shots and massed chorus girls associated with Berkeley, concluding with a restaging of the extended tracking shot through dancers' legs, from 42nd Street's "Young and Healthy", which ends on the smiling couple.

The film's heightened style is crucial in establishing a tone towards the material. Wilson's "loving salute", framed within this structure, is being critiqued as it is staged, and the gaps between text and performance qualify the easy nostalgia for a lost world of privilege. An arch acting style is adopted for the stage world, stressing both artifice and an aspiration to sophistication which is repeatedly undercut by moments of low comedy. The tone is set as the onstage performance begins, with Hortense (Barbara Windsor), the French maid, on the telephone. As Max, the director, hisses pronunciation advice from the wings, Windsor's cockney vowels quickly intrude and she leers in disgust at his guidance. The "young ladies" have over-enunciated, clipped deliveries or pronounced drawls, and their stage movements are studied and stiff, with much regrouping into mannered poses. Twiggy's awkward naturalism and lack of artifice highlight the general air of theatrical pretence. She also functions crucially as a stable centre in a frenetic film.

The film repeatedly underlines the gulf between stage reality and screen artifice, and between British mundanity and Hollywood sheen. The camera often observes the performance from the auditorium, emphasising distance, with the awkwardness of the stage action underlined by the clump of footsteps, or, in characteristic Russell framing, moves in close, with harsh underlighting enhancing the grotesquerie of the stage makeup. The cinematographer David Watkin, collaborating here for the second and final time with Russell, is a key figure in British film of the period, with his work on *The Charge of The Light Brigade* (Tony Richardson, 1968), *The Knack* (Richard Lester, 1965), and *The Devils* demonstrating remarkable facility and range. According to Richardson, "he had been able to acquire a knowledge of technical processes, a daringness of experiment, a freedom of thinking which had been bred out of even the most experienced feature cameramen."[15] The use of the Theatre Royal as a location exemplifies this approach, with the shabby milieu providing a vital realist base for the fantasia.

The evocation of this downmarket theatrical milieu draws on Russell's own early experiences as a dance student, and later as an actor, when he joined the No. 3 touring company of *Annie Get Your Gun* and supported Jack Buchanan in *When Knights Were Bold* at Newton Poppleford.[16] An avid filmgoer in his youth, born, he has said with a silver screen in his mouth,[17] Russell's reminiscences of the time express a devotion to Hollywood entertainment and a distaste for most British cinema, which he characterises as dull and bloodless. Just as *The Boy Friend* acknowledges the vigour and inventiveness of Warner Bros musicals of the 1930s, it may also be seen as a rebuke to the more staid milieu of *The Good Companions* (Victor Saville, 1932). The perfected world of the Hollywood musical hovers over every British attempt at the genre, and the comedy of the gulf between the two is adroitly built into this film.

The film's period setting is characteristic of Russell's work, he is drawing here on one of his favoured cultural reference points. However it offers a deliberately constructed and contradictory sense of the past. *The Boy Friend* had not, of course, been written at this time. In addition, while the presence of a director of film musicals, and the Berkeley references suggest the 1930s, costuming, design and other details (like a Valentino pin-up) also point to the earlier decade.

Shirley Russell's contribution to the film's sense of period, and to much of Ken Russell's work, is crucial in rejecting many conventions of retro 1920s styling. Certainly, the grubby realism of Russell's *mise en scène*, with its suggestions of *Neue Sachlichkeit* painting, owes much to

---

[15] Tony Richardson, *Long Distance Runner*, 171 (London: Faber and Faber, 1993).
[16] Russell, *Fire over England*, 35–39.
[17] Ken Russell, "I was Billy Elliot until I became a space cadet," *Times*, 10 April, 2008.

her distinctive use of costume. Sandy Wilson's sketches for the play text suggest the characteristic tone of airy femininity which is conveyed to some extent in Twiggy's styling for the film, but Shirley Russell's typical costuming, reliant on original clothing and deliberately aged designs, lends a weight and authenticity to the characters.

Tony Walton's production design is expressed as a witty play of references, quoting Art Nouveau, Art Deco, the work of Erté,[18] and Natacha Rambova, amongst others. While some critics questioned the lack of stylistic separation between the "real" and fantasy worlds of the film, these distinctions seem intentionally blurred, with multiple points-of-view contributing to the confection.

An interest in 1920s and 1930s styles was expressed in many cultural forms during this time. Film examples include Russell's own *Women in Love* (1969) and *Valentino* (1977), and another D. H. Lawrence adaptation, *The Virgin and the Gypsy* (Christopher Miles, 1970), as well as *The Prime of Miss Jean Brodie* (Ronald Neame, 1969) and *Murder on the Orient Express* (Sidney Lumet, 1974), and, from Hollywood, such high-profile films as *The Great Gatsby* (Jack Clayton, 1974), *Cabaret* (Bob Fosse, 1972) and *The Sting* (George Roy Hill, 1973). It is the period which Fredric Jameson, specifically citing *Chinatown* (Roman Polanski, 1974) and *The Conformist* (Bernardo Bertolucci, 1970) identifies with the "nostalgia film" cycle , which "approached the past through stylistic connotation conveying pastness by the glossy qualities of the image and '1930s-ness' or '1950s-ness' by the attributes of fashion."[19] Russell's more ambiguous approach, in this film and elsewhere, is to re-present the past in a complex way which both foregrounds its construction and ironises ideas of nostalgia and period styling.

Retro, Elizabeth E Guffy has argued, "is suffused with an ambivalent view of Modernity and challenges positivist views of technology, industry and, most of all, progress itself."[20] Also evident then, in some of the nostalgia expressed in this period, is a paradoxical desire to embrace the modernity of the past. Russell himself claims to have been formed as a director by repeated childhood viewings of Fritz Lang's silent films on a home movie projector. The future influence on his work of these exemplars of modernity, made years before he enjoyed them in wartime

---

[18] The 1920s designer and illustrator, whose work was widely revived during this period, had accompanied Twiggy to the stage production of *The Boy Friend*.
[19] Fredric Jameson, *Postmodernism, or, The Cultural Logic of Late Capitalism* (London: Verso, 1991), 19.
[20] Elizabeth E. Guffy, *Retro: The Culture of Revival* (London: Reaktion, 2006) , 13.

Southampton, demonstrates some of these contradictions.[21] The early 1970s was also the era of "retrochic", a term originating in France to describe film and fashion trends for romanticised evocations of the recent past. Certain design styles of the interwar period had become emblematic of ideas of modernity and progress. In Britain there had been a great revival of interest in Art Nouveau in the 1960s, fostered by hugely successful exhibitions at the Victoria and Albert Museum. The style was not only rehabilitated by cultural tastemakers, but also appropriated by the young, to be merged with the aesthetics of psychedelia by the end of the decade. By this time, a major revival of Art Deco was underway (the term itself was coined during this period). This fusion was perfectly encapsulated by Barbara Hulanicki's design emporium Biba, with which Twiggy was closely identified, a company whose ideology Phil Baker describes as "fraught with contradictions, making elitist tastes and reactionary escapism more democratically accessible than ever before."[22] Russell's work emerges from, and draws on, this pool of historical and cultural references, combining elements that traverse high art and popular culture.

Reviewing the film for the *New Statesman*, John Coleman suggested that "Ken Russell has found the perfect objective correlative for his extravagant turn of image."[23] The director's radical approach to adaptation certainly provided a framework for a kaleidoscopic rendering of the original material, which is also a complex example of genre cinema. Avoiding the consolations of simple nostalgia, the film's layering of history, memory and imagination also confronts and challenges the process of representing the past.

---

[21] See Russell, *Fire Over England*, 10–12, where he recalls showing Lang's *Die Nibelungen* (1924) to an appreciative Auxiliary Fire Service.
[22] Phil Baker, "Welcome to Big Biba", *The Art Book* 14, no. 4 (November 2007): 65.
[23] John Coleman, "Films: The Taste of Fear", *New Statesman*, February 4, 1972.

PART V:

SOCIAL SPACES

ALEXANDRA ROAD AND THE TRIUMPH OF ARCHITECTURAL MODERNISM[1]

TIM GOUGH

Over the course of the 1970s, architectural theory and practice in the UK and the United States incurred perhaps its most dramatic and rapid transformation ever. This was under circumstances where practice and theory played off each other equally rapidly and with unusual effectiveness. The beginning of the decade was characterised by a continuation of the concerns of modernism, carried through in various strands of architectural style from the 50s and 60s. However, the breaking down of emancipatory debates of the 1960s under the onslaught of economic crises, increased terrorism, inflation and the response of reactionary movements accompanied, or perhaps resulted in, an almost total *volte-face* in the field of architecture by the end of the decade. The clearest symptoms of this were the publication of Charles Jencks' *The Language of Post-Modern Architecture* in 1977,[2] and the fact that the first Venice Biennale of Architecture in 1980 was given the title "The Presence of the Past".[3] This was a theme unthinkable ten years before. Buildings representative of the concerns of the early 1970s include Denis Lasdun's National Theatre on the South Bank in London completed in 1973, and in the US Louis Kahn's Yale Centre for British Art completed in 1974. Both were resolutely in a modernist tradition of an abstract architectural language presented in fair-faced concrete. Piano and Roger's Centre Pompidou in Paris from the middle of the decade represented for Kenneth

---

[1] I would like to thank Neave Brown and Catherine Croft (Director of the 20th Century Society) for their comments during the initial preparation of this essay; and the constructive comments of Sue Harper and Laurel Forster as it developed. All photographs are the author's.
[2] Charles Jencks, *The Language of Post-Modern Architecture* (London: Academy Editions, 1977).
[3] See William JR Curtis, *Modern Architecture since 1900* (Oxford: Phaidon,1982), 380.

Frampton the point at which architecture stopped learning from Le Corbusier.[4] However, in the nascent "high tech" tradition (also represented by Norman Foster's Willis Faber Dumas building in Ipswich of 1974) one can still perceive the influence of functionalism and a progressive faith in an abstract symbolism of the use of technology. By contrast, the end of the decade gives us the *bricolage* of James Stirling's *Staatsgalarie* museum in Stuttgart, where neo-classical elements are juxtaposed with an evocation of early 20th century German architecture, and the Chippendale profile of the AT&T office building by Philip Johnson in New York. These two buildings indicate, if not the beginnings of architectural postmodernism, then at least its entry into the mainstream. The close interplay between theory and practice as a driver of postmodernist architecture was evinced by the rapid reissue of a revised and enlarged edition of Jencks' book only a year after its initial publication, so fast was the field moving.[5]

This rapid movement of architectural theory and practice was, as noted above, certainly a response to other currents within British politics and society. But as in any cultural field, there occurred a mutuality of influences within a whole environment such that matters architectural fed back onto politics and culture. It is the aim of this essay not only to explore the specific characteristics of an exemplary work of 1970s architecture, but also to show how this disjunctive relationship of community, that is, "a reciprocity between agent and patient",[6] between architecture and what might misleadingly be termed the "underlying" culture, plays out over time. Further, it will be shown that this disjunctive community relation speaks to the ontology of the architecture itself. The question will be addressed: what is the type of being that this specific work of architecture evinces?

---

[4] According to comments made by him at the *Le Corbusier at the AA Symposium*, held at the Architectural Association, London, November 28, 2008.

[5] Charles Jencks, *The Language of Post-Modern Architecture,* revised and enlarged edition (London: Academy Editions, 1978). The page count went up from 102 to 135, with a rewritten introduction and a much larger third part on Post-Modern Architecture.

[6] To use a term from Kant's table of categories. Of the three categories of relation, he distinguishes that of "community" from cause/effect and substance/accident, and associates it with the disjunctive form of judgement. Immanuel Kant, *Critique of Pure Reason*, trans. Norman Kemp Smith (London: MacMillan, 1985), 113–17.

Fig. 19.1. Alexandra Road: view of east end of main terrace.
Photograph by the author.

Designed by Neave Brown, working at the newly-formed London Borough of Camden's architect's department in the late 1960s, and constructed during most of the 1970s, Alexandra Road has been dubbed the UK's "last great social housing project."[7] Within a few years of its completion in 1978, the whole post-war project of social house building in the UK was virtually to cease under the 1980s politics of Margaret Thatcher. Culturally, the post-war project of architectural modernism, of which this project stands in a clear line running from the early 20th century modernists, through the work of Team 10 and in particular Alison and Peter Smithson—along with Neave Brown at the Architectural Association in the 1950s—was virtually to cease. It did so under the combined onslaught of political doubt about the status of professionals such as architects, and the rise of a conservative aesthetics theorised by such writers as David Watkin in his influential 1977 book *Morality and Architecture*. In this, he argues against the view that there was a necessary morality in adhering to a supposed progressive architectural modernist *Zeitgeist*. The rejection of architectural modernism was later cemented by

---

[7] See Andrew Freear, "Alexandra Road: The Last Great Social Housing Project," *AA Files* 30 (1995): 35–46.

the attacks by Prince Charles, most notably when he dammed it in the name of traditionalism during a speech given at Hampton Court:

> For far too long it seems to me, some planners and architects have consistently ignored the feelings and wishes of the mass of ordinary people in this country [...] To be concerned about the way people live, about the environment they inhabit and the kind of community that is created by that environment, should surely be one of the prime requirements of a really good architect.[8]

These political and cultural attacks against modernist architecture in the UK were in turn strengthened by a battle on the front of postmodernism. Really an entirely different animal from postmodernism in critical theory, philosophy or other areas of "cultural production", postmodernist architecture turned away from an avowed abstraction in architecture. It espoused a figurative and more particularly semiological approach to architectural design, whereby the building as *sign* became a key consideration. A building should be readable, the argument went—and in this way an appeal was made to the issue Prince Charles raised—namely the question of how buildings related to the so-called "mass of ordinary people". Together with Jencks, one of the key theorists of this movement were the husband and wife team of Venturi and Scott-Brown. Their books on architecture theory, in particular *Complexity and Contradiction in Architecture* and *Learning from Las Vegas*, critiqued what they saw as abstract architecture and put forward a clear theory of the way in which architecture should act as a sign or series of unambiguous or ambiguous signs.[9] That this theory should be termed "postmodernism" is somewhat odd, since in all other fields postmodernism refers precisely to a *questioning* of the unambiguous sign, the overcoming of semiotics as a science, at the very least the opening of ambiguity and multiple levels of meaning, if not the entire destruction of meaning. In this respect, as sometimes happens with architectural theory, we find at this juncture in the 1970s that it behaves as a rather autonomous discipline, separate from other mainstream intellectual concerns.

It can be argued that the triple onslaught of Thatcherism, Prince Charles and postmodernism fairly much made illegal, for a decade or so

---

[8] Speech given at the 150th anniversary celebrations of the Royal Institute of British Architects in 1984.

[9] See Robert Venturi, *Complexity and Contradiction in Architecture* (New York: Museum of Modern Art, 1966); Robert Venturi, Denise Scott Brown and Steven Izenour, *Learning from Las Vegas: The Forgotten Symbolism of Architectural Form* (Cambridge, MA: MIT Press, 1977).

after the 1970s, the formal and abstract architectural language that Neave Brown deployed at Alexandra Road, as at his two earlier housing schemes. In 1963, he had designed a small row of five houses in Winscombe Street, Archway, North London. These were realised in 1966 by means of a housing association. In the 1960s it was possible for an architect to find a site, design a development, act as developer and obtain public funds via a tiny housing association in order to create small pockets of social housing. These days, housing associations are all very large scale organisations, and the practice of their being set up by architects was ruled out in the 1970s.

His second housing scheme, for 71 units, was in Fleet Road, just near the Royal Free Hospital in Gospel Oak. It shares many features with Alexandra Road, namely the car parking located beneath, a variety of types of accommodation, a concern with a shared public realm raised above the car parks, a mixture of rendered façades, chunky black-stained timber windows, balcony fronts and external staircases, and of course in-situ reinforced concrete used in a sculptural and somewhat abstract fashion, as indeed we can clearly see in the Winscombe Street housing. This was public housing for Camden, for whom he was working by the mid 1960s.

Alexandra Road was on an entirely different scale from Neave Brown's previous projects: 520 units packed onto a very tight site. The scheme was extremely dense, partly in order to made it financially viable in line with the government's housing cost yardsticks, and partly because the concept of a low-rise but dense development was seen by Neave Brown as a positive thing. As he said in an essay from 1967 entitled "The Form of Housing", architects should: "build low, to fill the site, to geometrically define open space, to integrate. And to return to housing the traditional quality of continuous background stuff, anonymous, cellular, repetitive, that has always been its virtue."[10]

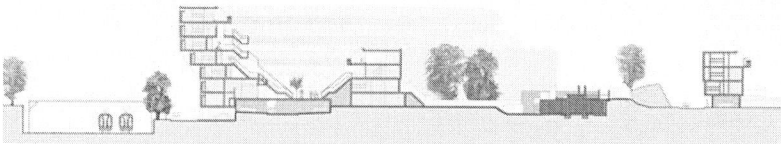

Fig. 19.2. Alexandra Road, cross-section through the site showing how the 7 storeys are arranged in a stepped section. To the left, the adjacent railway, the curve of which the main terrace followed. To the right, the existing social housing. Drawing by kind permission of James Woodward.

[10] Neave Brown, "The Form of Housing" in *Architectural Design* 37 (1967:433).

To a great extent, Alexandra Road does precisely what Neave Brown claimed it was his task to achieve. Compared to the high rise schemes prevalent in the 1960s (and encouraged by central government policies) it is of course very low-slung, being a maximum of 7 storeys but designed in such a way that it appears much lower than that. This perception is due to the raised walkways above the car parking, which nonetheless is not underground, but naturally lit and ventilated, which seemed to be at ground level. This is in contrast to some other "raised walkway" schemes such as those around the South Bank, where the experience of those on the walkways was always that there was a void beneath. Whilst the walkways are surrounded with penetrations to the car park below, these are arranged in such a way that you cannot actually see down into them. At each end of the site, the walkways connect with the local roads, thus reinforcing this impression of being at ground level, even though one is in effect one or one-and-a-half storeys about the ground. The other reason the architecture feels low is the stepped section itself, which opens up the perspective as one glances upwards. Where the section is not stepped, the buildings are generally kept lower relative to the walkways.

The distinctive stepped section of the scheme derives perhaps from Tony Garnier's *Une cité industrielle* of 1918 and some of Le Corbusier's architectural projects from the 1920s and 1930s, particularly those for Algiers from 1933, which has a very similar section with the housing raised on pilotis, balconies on one side and a racked back on the other. The device is familiar from Denis Lasdun's work, the National Theatre being the most famous, and from Patrick Hodgkinson's work at the Brunswick Centre. As Neave Brown has himself noted, this arrangement of a stepped section had by the 1960s become a common design strategy. It was a design philosophy concerned to counter the government-led, high-rise, design-and-build (that is, contractor-led rather than architect-led) high-rise system buildings which had come to dominate social housing at that time. Such schemes were also high density, but achieved that density by building upwards rather than continuing the low-rise high density of the existing fabric of cities and towns. The severe technical failings of many of the high-rise system-built schemes began to became evident with the disaster of Ronan Point in 1967, where a gas canister explosion blew out one panel of the building, leading to progressive collapse of the whole of one side of the 22-storey block of flats. Throughout the 1960s, progressive architectural design had already been arguing against the indiscriminate use of high-rise blocks of flats, because of the perceived social shortcomings. These arguments fell largely on deaf ears in central government. It could be therefore be suggested that if the abstract language of "heroic modernism"[11] at Alexandra Road became almost impossible to get through the UK planning system after the 1970s, the scheme itself was designed in the teeth of opposition from central government at the time.   In addition, local authorities were strongly encouraged to use high-rise system building by the government's housing cost yardsticks.   It was only the exceptionally large and powerful local authorities such as Camden which could resist this "guidance".

Returning to Neave Brown's stated intentions, Alexandra Road, it could be said, more than fills the site.   Not only is the housing itself at high density, but also car parking is provided in discreet fashion for the adjacent housing blocks, since they had been underprovided for originally. The density allows for precisely defined urban spaces, indeed "geometrically defined", as Brown says.   The whole ensemble is, one can argue, a masterpiece of integration, both within itself—for instance, the way in which the car parking, the urban park, the walkways and the housing units tie together in a seamless manner—and outside itself in the relation to the railway, the local streets and the local footpaths.

Fig. 19.3. Alexandra Road: a view showing what Neave Brown called "geometrically defined" spaces. Photograph by the author.

---

[11] To use Edward Jones' term in his article "Fleet Road: A Critique," *Architectural Design* 8–9 (1978): 526.

Architecture has an intrinsically dual and ambiguous structure, since it both responds to immediate and past concerns of the society for which it is created, and at the same time contributes to that society in a manner difficult to express because of the way in which it acts as an almost unseen backdrop to our everyday lives. It is questionable the extent to which architecture should be regarded as one of the visual arts, not because its pragmatic status undermines its artistic pretensions, but rather because outside the rare concerns of the critic or tourist gazing with conscious eye on significant buildings, it is doubtful whether architecture is in essence visible at all. What I wish to show in the following is how Alexandra Road is exemplary in respect of this dual aspect; it contributes and reflects *both* at the unconscious or subconscious micro level of its interventions in the lives of the people who live there, *and* at the macro level of the politics of architecture and the ethos of the nation within which it is constructed. Already a critical localised response to a top-down governmental decree, as a type of architecture, it is local, localised and anything but top-down in its form. However, this early reading of the work gets displaced within certain milieux. This is because project-specific technical and financial issues became matters of national concern and debate; a concern which was used for political ends to hasten changes in British politics and society at the end of the 1970s.[12]

Thus we find a complex matrix, varying over time, of the ways in which this particular project responds and contributes to broader cultural movements. This matrix has as a minimum the following axes: local/national; apparent or conscious/unnoticed or unconscious; intended/unintended. From the intended localisation of its response to a national political issue of the provision of mass housing, apparent and conscious in the writings of the architect and architectural journalists, and embodied in the built architecture in a manner no doubt unnoticed by the inhabitants—although all the more powerful in its real effects on their lives for that very reason—we move at the end of the 1970s to an unintended national-scale influence. This was driven by diametrically opposed political forces of conservatism which rightly, in their terms, saw this scheme and its ethos as one to be challenged both at the empirical and theoretical level. This task was undertaken on the one hand generally by journalists in the national press, and on the other by the architectural theorists already mentioned.

---

[12] The varied political and cultural readings to which architectural works are subject is the topic of the collection edited by Dana Arnold and Andrew Ballantyne, *Architecture as Experience – Radical Change in Spatial Practice* (London: Routledge, 2004), where a number examples of similar (mis)readings for political purposes are given.

That these architectural readings can change rapidly, or take a different trajectory through different parts of a heterogeneous body politic, is evidenced by the fact that the extraordinary quality of the architecture was reflected in the estate's listing, at level Grade II*, in 1995 by a conservative minister, Peter Brook. It is exceptional for a building to be listed prior to 30 years after its completion; in this case, the listing occurred after only 17 years, as a result of concerns that Camden, in carrying out repairs, were likely to damage the architectural integrity of the building.

As I have already intimated, the estate had become well known and well criticised for a number of pragmatic reasons. Firstly, the cost was huge, for many reasons including: the long period of gestation; the delay between design and construction; changes in the building industry over the period of design and construction; the lack of support for the project by some elements within Camden Council within the planning department; and the experimental nature of the scheme as a whole. Other problems were: bad management; changes in design and project scope as the scheme progressed on site; consequent late supply of design information to the contractors; and perhaps most importantly, labour shortages and a period of high inflation in the construction industry. There was a disaster on site halfway through: one of Bazalgette's brick-built Victorian sewers burst during heavy rain; this alone cost £1m to put right. It was estimated that it had taken 85 man-years of architects' time to design the scheme, due in part again to the long time-scales, and its complexity.

Secondly, the financial problems caused a national outcry, and the National Building Agency was commissioned to prepare a report to explain why this, and some other housing schemes in Camden, had been built at such huge cost. The scheme contributed to the idea that council housing under Labour councils was a profligate enterprise. This no doubt prepared the ground for the policies of the 1980s, which terminated virtually all public housing by local authorities. Cynicism, not only about the cultural and aesthetic qualities of such council housing, but also the very competence of non-market-driven agencies to commission housing set in, partly as a result of this scheme. We live with the results of this today, with the housing price boom and current "bust", combined with a critical shortage of housing. The private sector never managed to expand its house-building programme to make up for the loss of the construction of public sector housing, and as a result the UK has built too few houses for its need since the 1980s. Last year we were some 100,000 new houses short of a receding target.

Thirdly, there were technical problems with the scheme. For instance, the heating system was intended to act as background heating, and pipes were installed in the cross walls between flats, ostensibly to save money by feeding two flats at once. The system proved difficult to control, partly because it was upgraded to heat the flats fully, and partly because it was turned on before all the flats were complete, with the result that some flats were too cold and others too hot. As with any stepped section building with what are in effect complex roof gardens, the waterproofing was difficult to get right, particularly with 1960s technology, and it relied on an appropriate maintenance regime by the local authority in order to continue to function well. This maintenance, however, was not adequately funded, in common with many other social housing schemes.

Technical and cost issues of themselves do not relate directly to the judgements which must be made after the event about the architectural and cultural success of such a scheme, or the wide lessons which might be drawn from it. Rather, the question must be asked by both architect (before the event) and critic (after the event) about the way people live, about the environment they inhabit and the kind of community that is created by that environment. This should surely be one of the prime requirements of a really good architect and critic, even if there is no determined or determinable relationship between built form and the reality of the interplay between people and buildings. It is this *un*reduced interplay to which we must pay attention in attempting to address these questions, not to the reductive answers of aesthetic judgement, social determinism or political propaganda. In this sense, architecture of *all* types inevitably aligns with the minimalist, or "literalist", art which Michael Fried famously criticised in his 1967 essay *Art and Objecthood* as being too concerned with theatricality. He argues that this calls too readily for the involvement of the spectator—or, in the case of architecture, the inhabitant—and thus denies "aesthetic experience". Such a denial leaves the spectator within their own non-transcendent world; but it is perhaps the non-transcendent world of the city with which architecture at best engages.

Alexandra Road, in its apparently abstract architectural language, appears at first glance therefore to bear an analogy with the minimalism of the 1960s and 1970s, and we might point to the fact that in his work as an influential exhibition designer, Neave Brown created the spaces for the Tate's 1973 retrospective of Robyn Denny's abstract expressionist work, as he had for the *Léger and Purist Paris* exhibition there in 1970. However, Brown would draw sharp distinctions within this architectural language of brutalism between his concerns and that of, say, Paul Rudolph, whose work he regards as bombastic, confrontational and monumental, that is to say, non-theatrical in Fried's terms. For the stated and fulfilled aim of Alexandra Road was not to present a series of object-like entities of the monumental type, but rather to create an environment of sufficient density to lock into and become part of the existing cityscape. For this, both high density and low rise was necessary. Without high density, the scheme would have suburbanised the site and separated it out from the surrounding existing traditional streets and 1930s council blocks, in a manner perhaps similar to the strategies of the garden city approach. Without low rise, the buildings would have been expressed as a series of clearly defined objects within a landscape or, more likely, car parking and streets, in a manner derived from Le Corbusier's *Ville Radieuse*[13] and exemplified in London in the post war period by housing such as that at the Brandon Estate.

The architectural articulation of the scheme was carefully considered at various scales during the development of the design such that although cast in in-situ concrete (that is, poured on site within moulds), the individual elements such as balcony fronts, floors and cross walls are expressed by means of the horizontal and vertical joints between them. The concrete in places was expressed as being thicker than it technically needed to be, in order to ensure its visibility. Conversely, the use of horizontal lines of planters on the stepped balconies softened the effect of the floor levels. At a larger scale, this counter-play between the expressing of individual elements and their subsumption into a larger logic was played out by the repeated 2-1-2-1 rhythm of the cross-walls at lower level, the overriding upper storeys which proceed in continuous 1-1-1 rhythm down the blocks like a notional cornice as in the classical language of architecture.   At site-wide scale, the dramatic curve of the main pedestrian street ties the whole together and, in evoking the Regency or Georgian terraces of Bath or London, confirms that the realised intention was an architecture where individual elements were part of a considered city-scale composition of interrelated parts.

This strategy of interrelated elements, and the desire to avoid the architectural object, whether suburban or high rise, indeed speaks directly to and against Fried's point about minimalism, for these are not aesthetic or formal issues, neither in the mind of the architect nor in the existence of the architecture. Fried's criticism was that minimalism engaged the viewer inappropriately and theatrically, and ignored the question of art as object.

---

[13] As the Danish architect/planner Rasmussen had stated in the 1950s: the "Garden City and the Ville Radieuse represent the two great contemporary styles of modern architecture." Steen Eiler Rasmussen, *Towns and Buildings Described in Drawings and Words* (Cambridge, Mass: Harvard University Press, 1951), 52.

Alexandra Road posits on the contrary, that architecture (and, by implication we might guess, art) as object is bunk; that the ontology of architecture should *not* be aligned with the object but should rather wholeheartedly engage the inhabitant; and that it is possible to express the desire for this ontology within the architecture itself.

Thus Alexandra Road becomes part of the intense fabric of the existing city, intense not just because of the density of it, but also because of the range of "functions"—that is, means of engagement and encounter—for which it gave space. These included not only housing but a youth club, community centre, school for handicapped children, care home for children, home for handicapped adults, public open space, street, car parking for adjacent housing, integration of the existing housing adjacent to the site, a building department depot, and offices for council management. These are all "pieces of the city", intertwined and interdependent with that city fabric formally, but more importantly, experientially and in a manner that gave the chance for a wide range of encounters amongst those who lived and worked there. We can understand the way in which this piece of city allowed a rich life to be occasioned if we consider, for instance, children. Included in the ensemble are a series of places intended specifically for them, ranging from the educational and leisure facilities listed above, through to the park and playgrounds and, in the individual flats, bedrooms for young family members. The architecture does not let itself be determined, however, by function, which is a reductive characteristic always to be "wrapped" in a series of broader concerns or environments. In this case, the hierarchy of different scales, types, configurations and characteristics of spaces and architectural elements allows childhood to occur and be encountered in a potentially positive sense. Thus the steps to individual flats and gardens give place for play under the noses of the household. Beyond this, we will come across a group of relatively young children at play within the great curving "street", denuded as it is of cars and providing at once a grandeur implying a certain pride in and of place, and a spatial closure, through the effect of the curve in gently terminating a vista, which does not rely on a dead-end. This analysis of childhood *situations*[14] can be extended to the adjacent park and playground areas, more remote from the home and thus allowing a more adventurous activity appropriate to later years or the times when a parent accompanies. For this architecture, it is not a question of solving how defined functions associated with childhood are provided with buildings, but rather of considering how the life of a child as a whole

---

[14] Situation defined here by implication as the interplay of people and environment, inhabitant and building.

(considered synchronically and diachronically) is given various more or less open possibilities. The less open and more defined situations thus created, such as the school for handicapped children, we can reduce to the notion of "function"; but such reduction occurs in this case out of a more rich reality to which we should pay attention: as the original architects did.

Fig. 19.4. Alexandra Road, children in the main "street".
Photograph by the author.

Likewise, the life of adult employment occurs as much by means of the rather informal way that the offices and other workplaces are intertwined with the housing in unexpected locations, and the way the network of pedestrian alleyways ties in with the existing streets and shops at the east end of the site, as it does by the building functions *per se*. It is in this sense too that the scheme is a "piece of the city"; the city is the place, or rather event, of encounter, and Alexandra Road actively does this too.

Fig. 19.5. Alexandra Road, view of office building.
Photograph by the author.

In contrast therefore to the postmodernism of the following decade, Brown's concern was not at all for an architecture of the *sign*, which he associates with the theories of Venturi and Scott-Brown; we are in the best architecture of the 1970s very far from that ontology. The sign points to something outside of itself, we might say. Rather, the logic of Alexandra

Road is that of the *symbol*, that is, something which contains within itself its own meaning. Considered at the level of the architectural object (to permit ourselves this reduction for a moment), the logic of the symbol implies that the elements and forms making up the work will be perceived as abstract and self-contained, since they do not point beyond themselves in the manner of more figurative architectures such as postmodernism or the neo-vernacular of the 1980s. But at the level of an *un*reduced analysis which takes into account the interplay of people and place, a symbolic ontology of architecture reaffirms that interplay, by positing that the reality of architecture lies not in the built form but in that interplay. It therefore contains within its own concern the events and lives which occur within it, thus granting it an engaged and participatory meaning; and it operates at the level of that disjunctive relation of community—that Kantian reciprocity of agent and patient—to which I made reference to at the outset.

What therefore marks out Alexandra Road as exemplary of 1970s architecture is the way in which, at the tale-end of a political and "aesthetic" trajectory that extends from the foundations of architectural modernism in the post-first world war period, it affirms not so much a language of modernism, but rather its intrinsically societal concern. This would be very quickly eclipsed by an alternative (and, I would argue, impoverished) view of the nature of architectural reality in the 1980s. Alexandra Road might simply be thought to be a *socialist* architecture; indeed Brown was aiming directly in all his work to build places for an egalitarian society—how naïve will such aims appear in post 1979-Britain!—and it is no coincidence that he built nothing significant in the UK after this project.[15] It was, he says, intended to be normative housing for ordinary people, a scheme that did not *appear* to be "social housing". It rejected the *tabula rasa* of supposed conventional modernism, by staying with and respecting the life of the existing city and knitting in with its passages, its streets, its density and its engagement. It also rejected the political caricature of such modernism in the high-rise system building,

---

[15] It is telling that he worked later in the Netherlands, a society where the aims of social housing, together with the aims of modernism in general, were not simply disposed of in the 1980s. He also continued to design exhibitions, including the influential *Le Corbusier—Architect of the Century* show at the Hayward in 1987. Kenneth Frampton, speaks of this group of architects from the AA—of which he was one—as a "lost generation in many ways. There were and are peers of considerable talent, but they've had mixed careers. Neave Brown is surely one of them. He has had the long career as a housing architect, but it has not been easy for him." See "A Conversation with Kenneth Frampton," *October* 106 (2003): 35.

which claimed not a *normative* authority but the authority of a purely technical solution to the problem of housing shortage.

However, this is not merely a socialist architecture, admirable though it is in its moral and egalitarian concerns. Its societal concern lies wider than its socialism, beyond the question of Left/Right politics, and thus beyond the political divide that separates the late 1960s and the 1970s from the following decades. This concern and *care* not only for buildings and their design, but more fundamentally for society in its interplay with those buildings, transcends mere politics. This may in turn be the reason why Alexandra Road continues to present a valid exemplar for those willing to look beyond the question of style towards that of the timeless reality of architecture.

CONCRETE DREAMS: DRAMA AND SURVEILLANCE IN THE CITY

SUE EVANS

Introduction

Theatre in the 1970s crucially and diversely engaged with post-1968 political and artistic revolution. Early in the decade, it interrogated not only its subject, but mirrored contemporary disruption of social form by challenging dramatic form. Single plays could incorporate different styles and be performed at non-theatre sites, breaking with conventions of time and place.

The theme of urban engagement persistently captivates modern dramatists, but 1970s urban change initiated enduring cultural effects. I argue in this essay that these effects are manifested in texts which display a discernable *dis*engagement from urban life. These are subsequent to the post-war re-development which was, by the 1970s, revealing its actual and metaphorical fault lines. The redefinition of cities in this period was congruent with a desire for self-redefinition and liberation. Le Corbusier (Charles-Edouard Jeanneret: 1897-1965) had optimistically visualized cities as both functional and transcendental; performance spaces for our better selves. However, the fault lines of "brutalism" (derived from "béton brut" or raw concrete) paralleled the economic decline of the 1970s and its ensuing social disquiet. Some political drama of the period also alluded to the aspirations of modernism and its failure. This has long-term cultural consequences, with dislocation still reverberating, as some present day playwrights refer back to such debates in the 1970s.

Thirty years on, such issues were evoked for me by a play which addressed similar alienation, and indicated assimilation and internalization of the urban condition. *Catch*, by April de Angelis, Stella Feehily, Tanika Gupta, Chloe Moss and Laura Wade, premiered in December 2006 at the Royal Court Theatre.[1] Commissioned to mark the Court's 50th Anniversary,

---

[1] In the Jerwood Theatre Upstairs, Dir. Polly Teale.

Catch was an "indirect response" to a 1972 commission, *LayBy*, a collaborative play about pornography laws with characteristic early 1970s ideological debate and agit-prop stylistic disruption of naturalism.[2] *Catch*, showing gang violence and surveillance in contemporary London, was not only less overtly political, but also ostensibly naturalistic. However, *Catch* suggested a disturbing shift of boundaries within the urban environment, and evokes another 1975 work, *Hitting Town*, by Stephen Poliakoff, one of *LayBy's* writers.

Hitting Town is naturalistic in style and not explicitly political in tone; it responds to problems obliquely through characters' milieu rather than directly to topicality.[3] Its bleak precinct setting, its nascent awareness of surveillance, and its reference to the Birmingham IRA pub bombings, all recall a growing fear of both scrutiny and random violence in the intransigent concrete city. *Hitting Town* also recalls the sense of disempowerment evoked by 1970s environmental design and the placing on stage of objects from the period which had not yet gained the "kitsch" status granted by later nostalgia.

Catch hints at the outcomes of subsequent urban disengagement. In this play, surveillance is now commonplace, but its operation is tested with CCTV functioning as a mirror, as much as a judge. *Catch* underscores the current significance of the relativity of urban perspective and alienation suggested in *Hitting* Town. This essay examines the connections between the plays, and argues that this dislocated urban life has inspired redefinitions of realism and the imaginative in dramatization.

Urban Performance Space: the Dramatized City

Soft City, Jonathan Raban's 1974 account of cities as states of mind, refutes the usual conflation of modernism and the urban spirit; he describes the 1929 "Radiant City" manifesto of Le Corbusier as "repellent": "As happens so often in the manifestoes of modernism, what looks, at first sight, a brave and energetic release from slavery of old habits of thought, reveals itself to be in fact a shrilly puritanical backlash."[4]

---

[2] Howard Brenton and others, *Lay By* [Play Script] (London: Calder and Boyars, 1972). See introduction by Artistic Director Ian Rickson, 4.
[3] Stephen Poliakoff, *Hitting Town* and its companion piece, *City Sugar,* opened at The Bush Theatre, London, April and October 1975, respectively.
[4] Jonathan Raban, *Soft City –What Cities Do To Us and How They Change The Way We Live, Think and Feel* (London: Hamish Hamilton,1974), 17–18.

Raban protests that early aspirations to replace urban chaos with "vertical cities" made citizens fatally isolated in tower-blocks separated by forsaken greenery and flanked by service roads. For Raban, city life is anarchic by definition, inviting constant reinvention of self and re-imagination of place; the emergence of cities with, or as, designated "performance spaces" negating the true spirit of performance in the minds and daily lives of their inhabitants.

In *Cities and Urban Cultures,* Deborah Stevenson traces the links between urban culture and architecture from the impressive Le Corbusier idealism of "city as machine", to the 1960s' rise of "New Brutalist" ambition and ultimate failure to liberate the urban poor with a resultant decline of confidence in modernism.[5] Stevenson characterizes modernism as not just "bold affirmations of progress and scientific knowledge" but "potent symbols of the machine age, evidence of an historical rupture."[6] She echoes Raban's view that the modernist aesthetic influenced by Le Corbusier significantly effected this "historical rupture".[7] The transformation of the post-war cityscape into plate glass and open piazzas, whilst facilitating "performance", perhaps satisfies neither the traditional romantic desire for urban anonymity nor the glamour of personally inhabiting the historical, iconic cityscape.

The idealized city connected with widening perceptions of performance in the 1970s; the political gesture of taking theatre into the street. The act of creating an interface between theatre and reality, aside from dramatic content, itself constituted a performance. However, a "blank canvas" of created space, receptive to all social, political and entertainment values, can sacrifice specific, vital identity and spontaneous spirit of place against which any street performance should be tested. Stevenson, referring to the original practice of "reading" the authentic rhythms of the city, recalls Walter Benjamin's nineteenth century urban *flâneur,* following: "narrative maps which, although mythological, imaginary and partial, are central to the process of transforming cartographic space into places of meaning and memory."[8] Nonetheless, a utopian, benign city has, in Alison Oddey's words, "taken over from the garden, from the natural landscape, to become the new meditative and

---

[5] Deborah Stevenson, *Cities and Urban Cultures. Cultural and Media Studies* (Berkshire: Open University Press, 2003), 73–92.
[6] Ibid., 82–83.
[7] Ibid.
[8] Ibid., 55.

contemplative space."[9] Increased urbanization might create a more comprehensive desire for "greener" cities, but the "meditative" nature of such spaces here suggests privileges of time and freedom; a very different energy from the city life explored in *Hitting Town* and in *Catch* where "meaning and memory" take on another, darker, significance.

Urban-set drama traditionally emphasizes the city's rough authenticity as camouflage for dark, illicit acts; compensation for urban indifference. In *Cool Memories III* (1992-1995) Jean Baudrillard states that "what is sublime about cities is quite clearly their inhuman character."[10] Baudrillard is here referring to attempts to "humanize" city centres by pedestrianisation, a belief that is refuted in *Hitting Town,* where, paradoxically, such "humanized" space actually has the effect of *de*-humanizing.

In *Hitting Town,* the new precinct reflects both the "rupture" of historical familiarity and the characters' desired amnesia. Rebellion is futile when pre-empted by an establishment that has already obliterated history; the familiar, constraining gaze of the neighbour and the scrutiny of authority are both obfuscated. The concrete "blocking" frustrates and interiorizes violence, and the apparently free-flowing, egalitarian spaces paradoxically thwart progress with their maze-like design. Youth literally and metaphorically hits a concrete wall for which graffiti is the only response; *Hitting Town* portrays a half-hearted, middle-class, rebellion compounded by unease at the undefined gaze of surveillance.

Surveillance

Cities have long been sites of both unofficial and official surveillance. A primary reference, Michel Foucault's "eye of power", from the "panopticon" of Jeremy Bentham's eighteenth century work on prison design, is centred upon the possibility, rather than certainty, of surveillance as a behavioural curtailment.[11] Furthermore, Foucault's assertion that

---

[9] Alison Oddey, "Different Directions: The Potentials of Autobiographical Space," in *The Potentials of Spaces – The Theory and Practice of Scenography and Performance*, ed. Alison Oddey and Christine White, 44 (Bristol: Intellect, 2006). See also Alison Oddey, *Re-framing The Theatrical – Interdisciplinary Landscapes for Performance* (Basingstoke: Palgrave Macmillan, 2007), 133.

[10] Jean Baudrillard, "Cool Memories III (1992–1995)," in *Mass, Identity, Architecture*, 63.

[11] Michel Foucault, *Power/Knowledge. Selected Interviews and Other Writings 1972–77,* ed. and trans. Colin Gordon (Brighton: Harvester, 1980), 147–165; Michel Foucault, *Essential Works 1954–84*, ed. James D. Faubion, trans. Robert Hurley and others, Vol. 3 (London: Penguin, 2002), 349–364.

freedom is a condition of mind rather than of politics and environment recalls how, in the breach created by increasingly indistinct boundaries between the public and private, we constantly shift our perceptions of self-determination in the public space (and cyberspace) between extremes: paranoia and complacency.[12] Freedom as a state of mind thus cuts both ways, particularly when the "politics" are non-specific. This defensive ambivalence emerges in *Hitting Town,* where perception of surveillance shifts between significance and non-significance.

In *Loving Big Brother,* John McGrath posits a theory of ambivalence in spectatorship based upon his theatrical experiments with surveillance technology. McGrath concludes that surveillance is not all bad, opening up options rather than merely constraining its subjects with its gaze. He also dismisses the "easy and lazy cliché [...] that surveillance is turning the whole of life into a public performance."[13] He argues that:

> it was the non-equivalence of surveillance and theatrical systems which had opened the theatre space to new possibilities, and disrupted the sense of total representational control. Equivalently, the elements of performance which can no doubt be introduced to surveillance systems do not so much theatricalize our lived experience under surveillance as open our understanding of surveillance to encompass a recognition of its productive omissions and contradictions. A sense of this interesting gap, this productive tension between theatre and surveillance made me cautious of any attempts to explain surveillance simply in terms of the way in which it puts life on show—in terms of specularization.[14]

Just as performance can illustrate the "omissions and contradictions" of surveillance, so the increased absorption of surveillance into cultural experience raises the argument that these "contradictions", "interesting gap[s]" and "tensions" also inform the dramatization of realism.

McGrath also introduces the concept of "uptake" in surveillance, a space for decision between an event or invitation and the appropriate reaction, citing Timothy Gould's "The Happy Performative" he states:

> "Uptake" involves the recognition by the auditor that a speech act has occurred. So, for example, it means that in hearing someone say to me, "I

---

[12] See Foucault, *Essential Works*, 355.

[13] John McGrath, *Loving Big Brother: Performance, Privacy and Surveillance Space* (London: Routledge, 2004), 5.

[14] Ibid.

dare you to kick that policeman", I understand that a challenge has been issued—even if it is a challenge that I choose to ignore.[15]

"Uptake" here refers to levels of comprehension in viewing the pictures on a CCTV camera; suggesting that the viewer's reception is not entirely literal. "Uptake" might also apply to staging of performance transactions in *Hitting Town* and *Catch*, where characters' ambivalence intensifies their perception of their space and options. This hesitation also, arguably, dislocates their moral perspective. In both plays, the dislocation furnishes a mild fugue state in which characters defy personal and social taboos; bleak settings facilitate bleak choices. In 1975, intervention, sabotage, or reversal of the situation, are still options, surrender is a possibility, but assimilation a more distant prospect. The precinct and surveillance are still a source of fascination: a danger and a novelty.

Hitting Town and *Catch*

The concept of "uptake", navigating a hesitant expectation, arises in *Hitting Town* as the characters' persistent need to reinterpret the boundaries of private and public behaviour, in an environment with an emergent sense of being watched. Clare and Ralph, brother and sister, resume a suppressed flirtation when Ralph, a student in Birmingham, visits. Clare, at thirty, ten years older than Ralph and apparently in control, is uneasy, but there is no extended debate of the implications.[16]

In Poliakoff's subsequent plays, characters are typically incited, by an encounter with the unfamiliar, to re-interpret the familiar. Discovery of a place, an enigmatic individual or independent faction, challenges their assumptions and unconscious denials through their fixation with the strange and new. Sometimes, aided by an object or picture, the protagonist painstakingly decodes an image and reconstructs memory.[17] This recovery of truth and meaning in the landscape is, however, in *Hitting Town*, presented by dramatizing inner and outer landscapes of meaninglessness and loss in a period when the full implications of urban change were becoming apparent.

---

[15] Ibid., 51.
[16] Stephen Poliakoff, *Hitting Town & City Sugar*, originally published 1976. References here to Stephen Poliakoff, *Hitting Town & City Sugar* [Play Script] (London: Eyre Methuen, 1978).
[17] See Poliakoff: *The Tribe* (1998), *Close My Eyes* (1991), *Shooting The Past* (1990) and *Blinded by The Sun* (1996) for relationships between place, objects, memory and meaning.

Poliakoff states that:

> The set should be suggestive of an overall precinct-style environment, neon lit, in which Clare's room is the dominant part, a featureless nasty blank box. Other areas and the front stage can be used for the rest of the locations—walkway, precinct, snack bar, and disco—which can be suggested simply by concrete blocks etc., litter bins, and bright striking graffiti.[18]

This design, spare if literal, shows how the sophisticated functionality of composite sets illustrates both the limitations of the environment portrayed and the characters' own need to reinterpret even the apparently "real". No open, panoramic backdrop of cityscape is prescribed, only that which is close by: a bin, a concrete block. The staging itself implies limited perspective. Scene Two has a "walkway, represented by a concrete shelf, behind it the wall is covered in graffiti."[19] Poliakoff suggests the now common staging convention of condensing performance space by aligning minimalism with naturalism. Single objects and sparse settings at once establish mood and place. A virtue is made of the necessities of compact performance space by avoiding detailed representation. This creates a "shorthand" that evokes a dissonance between the exterior and interior life. The "box" of the urban flat is a thin defence against an implied unseen, unknowable, urban conflagration. Clare's agoraphobic responses, perhaps a reaction to her relationship with Ralph, are illustrated by her passive endurance of mysterious noise from the neighbouring flat.

Clare's first conversation with Ralph is his hoax obscene telephone call, a continued private joke, recalling that, in the 1970s, the anonymous call was a closer threat than hidden cameras, particularly in its objectification of women as trapped and *un*seen in the home. Ralph's intention, in wild speculation about the neighbour's activities, is to draw Clare out from her flat and the memory of a failed relationship with an unnamed man. The "not naming" of *real* threats is crucial; Ralph and Clare mostly converse obliquely, using the sights and sounds of the precinct variously as conduit, displacement and direct metaphor for spare, emotionally undernourished, lives:

> There's no escape. *(Louder)* There's one woman, you know, one *single, anonymous, lady,* who arranges all this muzak, produces it, by herself, she

---

[18] Poliakoff, *Hitting Town,* Introduction.
[19] Ibid., 9.

does, this is true! It just pours out of her, uncontrollably, tons and tons of it! A real madwoman. [...] There are three enormous warehouses of it. [20]

The narrative projects a sense of 1970s urban stasis rather than stimulus, evoking a growing skepticism toward the new environment; in *Catch*, characters do not identify and articulate the origins of such disappointment. In *Hitting Town*, the unsavoury restaurant, the disco with its "bubblegum music", is part of a new concrete wall against which Ralph struggles to extract a response. The inertia of the precinct prompts a compensatory opening up by Ralph of imaginative space; in *Catch*, this space is mainly characterized by territorialism and materialist desire. In *Hitting Town*, only the interior, imaginative, dimension seems both real and private. However, the desire for privacy is balanced by a desperation to be seen, and thus to exist, in a cityscape that cannot yet be fully interpreted, or ignored. Clare finally does choose: "When this music stops [...] I'm going to work" suggests for her a large step into reality. [21]

Private games as a response to a banal setting illustrate the problems of making connections any other way; Ralph fantasizes in order to challenge the environmental ignominy by mythologizing it. By contrast, characters in *Catch* display a sophisticated awareness of social transactions. Waiting for service from the uninterested waitress, Ralph jokes about the lack of nourishment; the plastic tomatoes, the rubbish deposited inside them and the "recipe" he can create from it all. Mixing crisps, brown sauce and the contents of their pockets, old sweets, tobacco, a piece of Mars Bar, tranquillizers, to a parody of TV-chef commentary, Ralph remarks that it is "about the only food you can get round here any more". Cutting open the plastic tomato-shaped sauce bottle, he reveals chewing gum, "half of a sardine ... lots of cigarette butts ... and a tooth!"[22] The significant mix of the inedible, rubbish, dregs and tranquillizers are, Ralph thinks, an insight into any town: "You can always tell a town by what's in its tomatoes. All its undesirables are pushed there. It spews out of them."[23]

Claire and Ralph's fixation is symptomatic of their inertia, the combination of claustrophobia and agoraphobia, and their inability to escape from the overly-familiar place whose detritus cannot be distinguished from that of any other town. For Ralph and Clare, the concrete jungle also obscures; they are babes in the wood, their incestuous relationship is reflected in the closed nature of their environment. They

---

[20] Ibid., 14.
[21] Ibid., 51.
[22] Ibid.,16.
[23] Ibid.

are, however, objectified by the pervasion of tinny muzak and radio noise. By the time *Catch* is written, the personal stereo and mobile have enabled the young to privatise and individualise their preoccupations; in *Hitting Town*, low-level noise imposes its own theme.

In *Hitting Town*, the environmental starkness reflects the characters' failed ambition. Nicola, the waitress obsessed with the disco karaoke, is a pale urban faerie who "hasn't seen daylight for weeks."[24] This is a morbid fascination with ersatz neon-lit glamour that appears in Poliakoff's other city-located dramas. It signifies not just urban sleaze, but a particularly lacklustre version, disconnected from its history and cultural roots of fairgrounds and arcades and appropriately represented here by a single neon strip. Imagination is reduced to titillation at the twin potentials of anonymity and surveillance; the dead eye of the camera, the pervert, or the bored waitress. Poliakoff has remarked that the atmosphere of "strained desolation" identified in his early works is "not their main subject, the chief centre of interest".[25] The "chief centre of interest" here is, perhaps, personal loss which is played out through urban displacement. The city "playground" is provincial. It is not the London of the 1960s, which is recognizable in its contemporary drama and cinema as a setting in which characters can challenge familiar landmarks and values. Leicester, in this portrayal, represents both the unfamiliarity and the over-familiarity of any provincial city, unremarkable yet strange. It might be watching, but more likely is not. The precinct provides Ralph and Clare's generation with neither stimulating urban mystique nor substance; it is equally inadequate in creating their fantasies and defining their realities. Instead they create an alternative imaginative space between the private and public.

Thirty years on, this lack is more culturally integrated, but the response is one of heightened awareness, faster pace and shorter concentration. In *Hitting Town*, in spite of Ralph's games, the dominant register is that of inertia. In *Catch*, the inertia is embedded, but overlaid with a more intense, and sometimes violent, response.

Hitting Town illustrates the 1970s awareness of how design had not only revolutionized the post-war landscape, but had become conceptually dominant: this assimilated "brutalism" is common to *Hitting Town* and *Catch.* Jean Baudrillard in "The Rise of the Object: The End of Culture— The Formal Liturgy of the Object" (1998) remarks of "The Consumer Society" that wealth makes people interact more with objects than with each other. Concepts such as "environment" and "ambience" are "more

---

[24] e.g. Poliakoff, *Blinded by The Sun.*
[25] Stephen Poliakoff, *Plays. Introduction* [Play Script] (London: Methuen Contemporary Dramatists, 1989), 1.

important now we associate less with other human beings."[26] Such a heightened relationship of self to environment has developed from being a threat in *Hitting Town* to being a commonplace in *Catch*. Socially, the "other" is more objectified, awareness of consequences numbed, viewpoint unsure and obsession with lifestyle enhanced, since Ralph's 1975 inventory of civic design and artifacts.[27]

The undermining of urban vitality identified, and perhaps romanticized, in 1974 by Jonathan Raban re-surfaces in the world of *Catch*. Here, development overlays some of the 1975 concrete, but the underpass remains. In *Catch*, the obsession with material goods, celebrity culture and image co-exist with fears of being "caught". Reality is a volatile and fragile state, frequently undistinguished from fantasy; the ultimate "never-knowing" in the gaze of the Panopticon. *Catch* portrays the advance, since 1975, of a new urban species: gangs whose innate egoist paranoia and random actions show decreasing awareness of personal or environmental perspective. Although not staged visually, the city image is mainly vertical; *Hitting Town* suggests overpasses and underpasses, walkways and stairs; *Catch* further extends physical levels as metaphors of both long-range and restricted view. In *Catch*, Claire, who "re-actualises" identities and confidence destroyed by theft, scans her clients from her Panopticon office "ivory tower" and her database (a new, immeasurable, dimension). The subway occupied by the gang is traversed nervously; from Clare to Claire the contradictory surveillance addiction of reliance and fear grows. Both characters intuit the shifting nature of surveillance, and a sense of impending disaster, whilst the gang in *Catch* simultaneously plays to, and denies the presence of, the camera. Comprehension and ignorance, seeing and not seeing, real and imaginary, are thus interchangeable; any threat from CCTV cameras is balanced by their randomness and ubiquity.[28] The gang prefers self-created images on phones; the all-seeing CCTV is now a blind God.

The idealism of open performance space, augmented by millennial optimism, has, by *Catch*, evaporated. In addition, the subsequently more playful postmodernism does not register on the street. Diminished perception of moral choice enhances the relevance of "uptake"; the self is reinvented, at once both free and caught, in the more sophisticated surveillance culture. Possible anarchy is, however, offset by an

---

[26] Jean Baudrillard, "The Consumer Society," in *Mass, Identity, Architecture*, 94–95.
[27] See Mark Ravenhill, *Shopping and F*****g* (London: Methuen, 1997).
[28] See April de Angelis and others, *Catch* [Play Script] (London: Oberon Modern Plays, 2006), 86.

underworld infrastructure, albeit one where values are a mythologized travesty. *Hitting Town's* expression of bewilderment now exists alongside characters' expectations; the spare staging in *Hitting Town* has become an integrated concept in *Catch*.   No set is described in the latter, but the constant textual presence of the "tower" and subway suggests that the audience now accepts the spare staging conventions, and is able to identify them with the subject portrayed. Separate representational space is now seen as an unnecessary distraction.

Summary

    Drama uniquely advances strategies for the revelation of truth in extremis and for the contemplation of dilemmas. Between 1975 and 2006, however, the ideal of moral choice upheld by classical dramatic structure has shifted to embrace the more subjective values of the sometimes disaffected individual, both perpetually observed and self-documented by mobile technologies.

    Hitting Town raised the growing visible/invisible paradox of urban society; surveillance and social disengagement implying an omnipresent judgement and disinterest, and a traditional romantic urban anonymity which gives way to alienation. *Catch* exemplifies the constant contemporary re-cycling of this 1970s sense of the lost opportunity of urban modernism; one generation strives to articulate it, but succeeding generations can only intuit and internalize the loss. *Catch* perpetuates the staging of uncertain boundaries and relativism in the new urban surveillance protocol, where what counts is whether or not the camera is live.

    Hitting Town and *Catch* illustrate the development in staging this perceptual shift. The ideal of dramatic "realism" has perhaps reached its limit for portraying an urban reality that has become too real, too fragmented, but also too banal to be easily accommodated in a structure assuming a linear narrative of catharsis and resolution. The personal and the internal has become a permanent, rather than initial and preparatory, site of action for drama. The dramatic "inciting incident" is suspended throughout both plays, creating a state of hyper-realistic tension, because the characters' engagement with a moral dilemma that usually delineates structured dramatic action and resolution is ambivalent. Where resolution occurs, it is less the outcome of revelation and decision than of a random act. The citizens are constantly diverted within the concrete jungle.

SEX IN THE SITTING ROOM:
RENEGOTIATING THE FASHIONABLE
BRITISH DOMESTIC INTERIOR
FOR THE POST-PERMISSIVE GENERATION

JO TURNEY

Design history frequently and rather narrowly understands the 1960s as an era in which design was at its most innovative and youthful, challenging convention and removing hierarchical boundaries relating to sex, sexuality, fashion and its objects.[1] Such an explosive description has, within the literature of design, left the 1970s as a post-coital decade that style forgot. Indeed, the seemingly garish patterns, man-made fibres and emphasis on kitsch sits uncomfortably with the Modernist doctrine, which informs much design history and discourse.[2] This essay aims to redress this rather short-sighted view, by suggesting that interior design during the 1970s period was the expression of a post-permissive generation's desire to be "modern".

By investigating critical and stylistic themes inherent in domestic interior design of the period, this discussion will demonstrate that the 1970s gave rise to innovative understandings of the home as well as the relationships and roles within. Central to this discourse is the exploration of the ways in which the notion of sensuality and sensual perception became a focus of interior design, and how this became manifest in domestic spaces, i.e. the tactile home. Using the domestic setting of *Abigail's Party* (dir. Mike Leigh, 1977) and advertisements for home furnishings as examples, the relationships between the self and its display will be explored. This paper aims to emphasise cultural, social, inter-

[1] Nigel Whiteley, *Pop Design: From Modernism to Mod* (London: Design Council, 1987).
[2] Paul Greenhalgh, ed., *Modernism in Design* (London: Reaktion Books, 1990); Penny Sparke, *An Introduction to Design and Culture in the Twentieth Century* (London: Routledge 1992); Jonathan Woodham, *Twentieth Century Design* (Oxford: Oxford University Press, 1997).

personal gender and style shifts hitherto marginalised, which sites women and the traditionally feminine space of the home as both consumer and consumed; both subject and object of consumer and sexual desire.

Interior design, as a profession and business in the 1970s, was booming in the UK. Universities had started to offer courses in interior design,[3] and designers started to work with new clients, primarily public institutions including hospitals, universities and offices, as well as shops, hotels and bars. These schemes tended to focus on open-plan, stylised architectural layouts, emphasising a design vogue for psychoanalytic approaches to the organisation of people and spaces. Design focus centred on the comfort of the user—both physical comfort and a sense of being at "ease"—which was addressed through adherence to colour theory, lighting, airiness and ergonomic or healthy furniture.[4] One might conclude that this approach extended the safety associated with the private arena of the home, to impersonal public environs, extending the Modernist design doctrine which promoted a fitness for purpose in objects and spaces. These, with a new emphasis on the comfort and well-being of the individual, paved the way for today's user-centred design.

Conversely, in terms of aesthetic, domestic interior design of the 1970s witnessed a seeming confusion of design motifs, styles, ideas and boundaries. Initially, this confusion and apparent lack of direction could be seen as symptomatic of, or a reaction to, the unstable cultural climate. The 1970s encapsulated social and cultural confusion, war and rebellion, economic decline (inflation was 27% in 1975) and environmentalism, and it fused the local with the global in unprecedented ways. The threat of potential social disarray exemplified by Watergate and the first resignation of a US president, the rise of trade unionism ("the winter of discontent" 1978-9) and impending strikes and accompanying shortages, the horrors of Cambodia and an increasing concern about world energy resources (the 1973 oil crisis) challenged the status quo as never before.[5] The future didn't look great, as the promise of post-war restoration failed to materialise to any extent. Reaction or resistance to such social instability, or the potential for chaos, was demonstrated by a turn towards that which offered stability, marked by increased worldwide conservatism and a fearful nostalgia for the past.

---

[3] An example of this is the three-year AIBD course at Trent Polytechnic, Nottingham, which was running in the early 1970s.
[4] Victor Papanek, *Design for the Real World* (London: Thames & Hudson, 1972).
[5] Christopher Booker, *The Seventies: Portrait of a Decade* (London: Allen Lane, 1980), 4.

A fear for the future and indeed the present left interior design somewhat out of place and time, seeking solace in the past, confused and continually seeking stability, as demonstrated by the eclecticism of the period. Post-modern philosophy and styling was emerging, i.e. fusing high cultural styles with popular cultural forms, and the past was opening a dressing up box full of styles, motifs, forms and references from which designers and home makers could find inspiration. Indeed, the period witnessed a whole host of style revivals; Arts and Crafts, Art Nouveau, Art Deco, to such an extent it appeared as if the whole twentieth century was being revisited. However, the period was not merely characterised by retro-gazing; the past was indeed revisited, but was juxtaposed with a futuristic acknowledgement of technology in the form of new materials, specifically synthetics.

The development of synthetics characterised the period; new, user-friendly surfaces, such as wipe-clean laminates, wallpapers and easy-to-wash soft furnishings became central to contemporary styles. Like technological innovation throughout the 20th century, new materials were introduced to the public in traditional formats, emphasising their similarity with existing natural forms, not just in terms of "look", but also in terms of "feel".[6] Therefore, new finishes and so on were advertised as if they were "the real thing", i.e. like leather, marble, wood, but cheaper in cost *not* appearance, democratising design and taste on a mass scale. Everyone now could afford the latest trends, even if they appeared derivative and nostalgic.

Simultaneously, the domestic was evolving into a space for sensory exploration, emphasising what has been called "the tactile home". This can be seen as an extension of wider socio-cultural shifts in attitudes and lifestyle, a letting go, or of letting one's hair down as a sign of the *Zeitgeist.*[7]

This desire to shake off the past, to be modern and express the self in less constrained ways was indicative of a continuation of a largely American Hippie counter-culture, which promoted self-exploration, sexual experimentation and new ways of being. Such expressions of the "self" were completely at odds with normative behaviour in British society,[8] and although one may not have been able to freely express oneself within these

---

[6] Adrian Forty, *Objects of Desire: Design and Society since 1750* (London: Thames & Hudson, 1986).

[7] Sam Binkley, *Getting Loose: Lifestyle Consumption in the 1970s* (Durham: Duke University Press, 2007), 10.

[8] Mike Leigh, quoted in Ray Carney and Leonard Quart, *The Films of Mike Leigh: Embracing the World* (Cambridge: Cambridge University Press, 2000), 96.

boundaries, one could encapsulate a sense of self, "ease" and being
modern through the purchase of goods, particularly those which were easy
to maintain, and luxurious in terms of style and tactility. Indeed, the
disparity and discourse between self and society became central to lifestyle
shopping and its promotion, particularly in relation to home furnishings.
This was demonstrated in two ways: an emphasis on "authenticity", and,
the expression of "experience".

The concept of the "authentic" took variant forms, each of which
emphasised a sense of freedom; freedom from the constraints of old social
hierarchies and attitudes, to the expression of personal freedoms of taste
and a sense of self. These can be generalised thematically as a move
towards the "natural", a laying bare, freedom from the constraints of
clothing and masking in all its forms including furnishings and surfaces.
Paradoxically, synthetics are unnatural, but were promoted as the opposite.
For example, in 1972, an advertising campaign for Arlington Plastics
(furnishing fabrics and wall-coverings) promoted the "naturalness" of
Arlan (a polyurethane leather-like fabric) as having "even more colours
and textures than you do" under which 9 photographs of eroticised
sections of a naked woman were presented. Featured were seductive, part-
open lips behind a phallic finger, a weeping (ejaculating) eye, bare
buttocks and an erect nipple, each of which emphasised a sexual
willingness. The synthetic surface here was not merely personalised and
individualised (it's just like *you*), but was sexualised, demanding intimate
touch and possession. It was also emotionalised—not only does the
laminate elicit touch, it also *feels*—and therefore is presented as a "living"
and therefore, natural, object of desire.[9] The inanimate was having life
breathed into it and that life was sexual, open, natural and available to
everyone.

The notion of the "natural" and "authentic" extended its remits to
include a Romantic and nostalgic approach to furnishings in terms of
styles and new materials. Craftsmanship, even where products were mass
produced, was promoted, emphasising the ways in which new materials
could imitate the old, but at a much lower price. For example, a vinyl
surface produced by Nairn in 1976, *Baroque*, was described as giving
furnishings "the classic finish". The advertising campaign depicted a man
in an apron proudly standing behind a traditional-style buttoned and

---

[9] Similarly, female nudity featured in other advertisements, demonstrating the
'naturalness' of synthetic products and surfaces for the home, including Arborite, a
laminates manufacturer, for whom a 1971 campaign included a photograph of 70
naked women in an overgrown field, each concealing their modesty with a sheet of
the company's product.

studded "leather" armchair, in what appears to be his workshop. He proclaims "this new upholstery takes me back to the time when you could afford to use leather", indicating that times had changed, but style and quality had not. Craftsmanship was still enduring, even in technologically dynamic and economically unstable times. Indeed, the marriage between new materials and methods of production with established expectations of what furniture should look like, was a real issue for manufacturers during a time when the market was becoming increasingly democratized. But consumer spending was seriously limited as a response to the recession and the country's entry into the Common Market.[10]

As a result, popular interior design elements emphasised a fusion of high cultural form with affordability, by reproducing aspects of older, aristocratic and luxurious taste and fusing it with modern technology, such as man-made fibres, plastics and wipe-clean surfaces, which emulated wealth and status. Consequently, synthetic floor tiling was produced to emulate grand mosaics or lavish marbles, whilst wallpapers, became textured, heavily decorated and coloured, referencing the décor of stately homes.[11] Style and design, it appeared, became an exercise in imitation of accepted "good" or high class taste, and a vehicle for the expression of contemporary technology. This might be construed as an early form of post-modernism, or indeed kitsch, in which the copy becomes subject to copying, the imitation is presented as the "authentic" and luxury is diffused on a wide scale through re-appropriation and reproduction.[12]

The notion of the reproduction is essential to an understanding of the way in which traditional patterns and styles continue to remain within the language of contemporary design of the 1970s. In essence, the ability to reproduce something which is ostensibly authentic, an original, highlights the object's desirability to contemporary designers and consumers: why bother to copy something which is ugly, outdated, or poorly designed? With this in mind, styles and motifs deemed suitable for reproduction had some kind of cultural value that related to the contemporary world, either through the communication of ideas and ideals, or by implying connoisseurship and an institutional understanding of taste.

---

[10] Tracey Potts, "Creating 'Modern Tendencies': The Symbolic Economics of Furnishing," in *Historicizing Lifestyle: Mediating Taste, Consumption and Identity from the 1900s to the 1970s*, eds. David Bell and Joanne Hollows, 161 (Aldershot: Ashgate, 2006).

[11] Examples include advertisements for Sanderson's wall-coverings and Flotex flooring.

[12] Judy Attfield, *Wild Things* (Oxford: Berg, 2000), 99–100.

Leonore Davidoff recognises this quest for the past in the present as a symptom of the alienation of the workforce and the rise in multi-national corporations, which turns the seemingly "static" arena of the home into an idealised state. In the 1970s, the idealised version of "home" ignited within its occupants, a need for "creative home-making", including "farmhouse cookery" (interestingly, a metaphor developed in the 1972 publication of the *Joy of Sex*[13] in which sexual activities were presented as a menu) "organic gardening", and "wine making" which were a suburban substitute for authenticity.[14] One might also suggest that the activity inherent in these forms of "authenticity" were responding to a desire to "get in touch" with the self and experience one's personal environment.

Indeed, although the decade appeared synonymous with a nostalgic yearning in terms of style, it was the immediacy of experience that fuelled interior design innovation. Experience was interpreted as a voyage of self-discovery, an interest in broadening one's horizons through travel overseas, cultural pursuits, as well as engaging in new sensations, exploiting the boundaries of the senses. Interiors became a site for the explosion of colours, patterns, textures, stimulating the senses to new and wider dimensions, akin to sexual pleasure.[15] Entry into the home became an adventure; a voyage of discovery that went beyond the realms of the mundane.

"Home" derives from Anglo-Saxon and Nordic languages, and is a term which refers not merely to a place, but to a state of mind, and it is from these origins that "home" as a place of intimacy and privacy emerges. Similarly, the cultural appropriation of the home as a feminine and feminised space—a consequence of Victorian biological determinism[16]—which gendered people, places and behaviours as a means of constructing social hierarchy, contributed to a symbolic correlation between woman and home.[17] The feminisation of the domestic interior

---

[13] Alex Comfort, *The Joy of Sex* (Ann Arbor: University of Michigan, 1972).

[14] Leonore Davidoff, *Worlds Between: Historical Perspectives on Gender and Class* (New York: Routledge, 1995), 65.

[15] Carl B. Holmberg, *Sexualities and Popular Culture* (Oxford: Sage Publications, 1998), 28.

[16] Penelope Brown and Ludmilla Jordanova, "Oppressive Dichotomies: The Nature/Culture Debate," in *A Cultural Studies Reader*, eds. Jessica Munns and Gita Rajan, 509–18 (London: Longman, 1995); Alison Ravetz, "A View From the Interior," in *A View From the Interior: Women and Design*, eds. Judy Attfield and Pat Kirkham, 190 (London: The Women's Press, 1995).

[17] Juliet Kinchin, "Interiors: Nineteenth Century Essays on the 'Masculine' and the 'Feminine' Room," in *The Gendered Object*, ed. Pat Kirkham, 12–29 (Manchester: Manchester University Press, 1996).

became manifest through the shapes, styles, forms, fabrics and motifs, as well as through the symbolic imagery that decorated it.[18] Floral design, for example, was seen to be an expression of feminine taste, rather than masculine culture, as the motifs were drawn from nature. Swathes of drapery were seen as representative of the drapes concealing the Classical Venus, or, from a Freudian perspective, the folds of female genitalia.[19] Therefore, referring to a rather crude series of binary opposites, the soft, rounded, draped, warm, natural and organic were essentially female, and were explicit in domestic interior design. In the 1970s, advertisements for seemingly mundane products such as floor coverings, furniture, crockery, and wallpaper, all extended the boundaries of this "feminine" taste by exploiting the concept of the female form through tactility; the feel of the product on the skin inviting one's toes, fingers and flesh to luxuriate in the warmth and quality of new surfaces. One might see this then as an extension of the female self, the tactile, soft, frivolousness, creating almost another body to be explored, experienced and touched by the inhabitants.

This extension toward the sensory was particularly significant in relation to changing concepts of femininity and the female body. Feminism, which was beginning to have an impact in relation to social equality, was combined with new personal empowerment surrounding concepts of pleasure and the sexual body. The publication of popularised texts such as: Germaine Greer's *The Female Eunuch* (1971), Erica Jong's *The Fear of Flying* (1973), J's *The Sensuous Woman* (1969), Marilyn French's *The Women's Room* (1974), and Shere Hite's *The Hite Report* (1976), emphasised the significance of sexual pleasure and the female orgasm amidst the middle classes.[20] Tabloid newspapers, on the other hand, such as *The Sun* and sex comedies like the *Confessions of...* series, focussed on sex as a bastion of working-class fun which could be enjoyed by men and women alike, as long as women weren't "frigid", lesbians, humourless feminists, ugly like Olive from *On the Busses*, or all four.

---

[18] Leonore Davidoff and Catherine Hall, "'My Own Fireside': The Creation of the Middle-Class Home," in *The Politics of Domestic Consumption*, eds. Stevi Jackson and Shaun Moores, 277–89 (Hemel Hempstead Harvester Wheatsheaf, 1995); Marianne Gullestad, "Home Decoration as Popular Culture: Constructing, Homes, Genders and Classes in Norway," in *The Politics of Domestic Consumption*, eds. Stevi Jackson and Shaun Moores, 321–35 (Hemel Hempstead: Harvester Wheatsheaf, 1995).

[19] Gen Doy, *Drapery: Classicism and Barbarism in Visual Culture* (London: I.B. Tauris, 2002), 98–138.

[20] Liz Stanley, *Sex Surveyed: 1949-94* (London: Taylor and Francis, 1995).

Such working-class fun must be protected from the onslaught of moral do-gooders and those wishing to deprive others of any sense of pleasure.[21]

This drive towards liberalism, which equally emphasised the sterility, snobbishness and standardisation of suburbia, was performed and lampooned in sex and television comedies of the period. Similarly, media stories of wife-swapping and Cynthia Payne's infamous luncheon voucher suburban sex parties in 1978 contributed to a disturbed and overtly sexual vision of "home", which voyeuristically suggested that taboo behaviour was taking place behind the net curtains.

Socio-cultural discussion of female sexual pleasure, combined with a desire for solace in a changing world, idealised by and manifested in the locale of the home, was representative of a *Zeitgeist* that embraced domesticity (including the female form) as tactile, sensual and sexual to be enjoyed by men and women alike. This was exemplified in the lifestyle marketing of domestic goods which intended to stimulate desire in a new way; this was less about "keeping up with the Jones's" and more about lust-induced longing. Consumer goods became associated firmly with desire, and by association, with fantasy "lifestyle" choices, stimulating desire, not just for the goods themselves, but for access to a world of fantasy and desirous experience.[22] In the 1970s this desire was both female and sexual, penetrating the domestic landscape to the extent that goods became extensions of the female body, and in some examples, had replaced it.[23]

Furniture, in advertising at least, took on female characteristics: sofas, dining room sets and the like were given women's names such as Ercol's *Melissa* 3-piece suite, whilst sofas like the Parker Knoll *Maxi* (1972) had arms that could "hold you close, in cosy two-seater intimacy" stating that "there's nothing more boring than being held in the same old way". The adverts humorously suggest staid domestic sexual relationships, intimating that if your wife is sexually unwilling, she can be replaced by the ever-available sofa, and intimacy can be obtained through the purchase of consumer goods. The reliance on *double-entendres*, very much part of

---

[21] Leon Hunt, *British Low Culture: From Safari Suits to Sexploitation* (London: Routledge, 1998), 26.

[22] Elizabeth Cowie, "Pornography and Fantasy Psychoanalytic Perspectives," in *Sex Exposed: Sexuality and the Pornography Debate*, eds. Lynne Segal and Myra McIntosh, 136 (London: Virago, 1992), quoted in Rebecca Arnold, *Fashion Desire and Anxiety* (London: I B Tauris, 2001), 71.

[23] Laminate manufacturer Arborite's advertising campaign (1972) used various product surfaces to provide a relief revealing a silhouette of a naked woman.

British popular culture and humour,[24] was further utilised in adverts such as Austin Suite's *Richmond* desk (1972) the strap-line of which read: "even without her drawers she's no pushover." This referenced popular conceptions of boss/secretary sexual relationships as well as animating the desk as a "saucy" woman who is in need of domination and control. The choice of home furnishings may have rested with women, but as feminism entered the mainstream and women were encouraged to look beyond the walls of domesticity, patriarchy remained firm.

Indeed, Bremworth's 1974 advertising campaign for the new *Bremworth Ram* carpet embodied the strap-line "The Bremworth Ram makes life much more colourful" by referencing the sexual potential of the product. In one advert, the carpet becomes synonymous with seduction, a player in a post-coital scenario. The image shows a woman's silver platform shoe, discarded by an open door, beyond which is a bed draped with an ostrich feather-trimmed negligée. The male figure appears in slightly ruffled clothing, lighting a cigarette. Adjacent to him is an opened cocktail cabinet. The rather literal allusion to both passionate sex with an available woman (frantic abandonment of erotic clothing) and post-coital behaviour (smoking) voyeuristically demonstrates the desirability of the carpet, but also emphasises more subtle gender relationships and the reinstatement of patriarchal values in the home. Indeed, the only figure is male, and, although alluded to in Cinderella-style referencing, the woman is absent. He is the seducer, and now, after sex, his partner, like her clothing, has been discarded. The balance of power is evident: the male is in control.

Historically women had been targeted as domestic consumers, but frequently in the 1970s advertisements were aimed at men, presumably as they held the purse strings for high-priced household goods. These advertisements emphasised the feminine attributes and sexiness of furnishings. The implication was "a sensual home means a sensual wife", moving the role of the woman to one of sexual rather than domestic, goddess; as part of the pleasure, rather than the utility, of the home. Alternatively, one can see the woman as commodified, an adornment or possession amongst many, existing for the pleasure of the male consumer.

Aspects of commodification and the sexualisation of the domestic interior are evidenced in the *mise en scène* of *Abigail's Party*, in which the open plan living/dining room of 13 Richmond Road plays not merely centre stage to the narrative, but also to the eclecticism of the 1970s middle-class domestic arena. Within this space, all of the senses are

---

[24] Hunt, *British Low Culture,* 34–56.

aroused. The merging of a wood floor, leather sofa, textured cushions, shag-pile rug, mood lighting, record player piping out aural seduction, cheese and pineapple on sticks requiring the consumption of a phallic explosion of flavours, and cigarette smoke (a further pleasure of the mouth) dominate the space. Indeed, Beverley's orgasmic swaying and smoking to Donna Summer's "Love to Love you Baby" (1975) in which she appears lost in the environment, and the over-blown domineering floral wallpaper, representative of a landscape of female genitalia, situates women as sensual extensions of the décor.

Roles of women were changing and domesticity no longer seemed as appealing as before. In *Abigail's Party*, Beverly exemplifies the social praxis where the domestic ideal meets the modern woman. Although married and living in an "ideal" home, she has no interest in domesticity (the new kitchen and appliances remain unused), or traditional roles (she doesn't fancy childbirth) preferring to revel in the acquisition of goods and the power of her own sexuality which she flaunts seductively at her neighbour's husband Tony. Beverley's perceived vacuousness acts metaphorically as a sign of her emptiness; she is a hollow vessel (childless) and is overly concerned with appearance, all surface and no substance, a "useless" adorned object, much like the rest of the bric-à-brac in the room. Her softly draped tangerine coloured dress and green eye-shadow co-ordinate with the ornaments and furnishings, whilst her ample bosom bursts forth from its low-cut constraint. She has put all her "goods on display"; she is an extension of her home and in turn is part of the furniture. As such, Beverley's shallowness encapsulates her out-of-placeness, which can be understood as symptomatic of women's contemporary condition; straddling a pre- and post-feminist existence, a woman who embodies pleasure and the sensory, yet is derided for this desire, constricted and bound by the traditional expectation and role of her sex.

For Beverley, and indeed the majority of representations of women and femininity within the domestic interior during the 1970s, an "ideal" home was located in the display of one's authentic self: an objective achieved through the consumption of goods. In itself, this was nothing new, women had historically been addressed as consumers. Yet by the 1970s, the "ideal" home, marriage and family were increasingly becoming a contemporary cabinet of curiosities, a form of propaganda, in which social change, frustration and suppressed desire, were literally "papered over" in order to maintain some sense of "normality". Indeed, as the narrative progresses, Beverley's isolation and distance from traditional norms of domesticity are obvious; as her emptiness becomes apparent, her home appears more cluttered, and consumer goods become substitutes for genuine emotion and sexual gratification. Women's pleasure it seemed, could only be validated and experienced through constructions of fantasy and advertising narratives, all of which were firmly controlled by a patriarchal sub-text.

In conclusion, it is possible to suggest that the 1970s, as a period of turbulent social and global issues, created a climate of instability and fear, and attempted to capture the essence of the nurturing sanctuary inherent in the definition of "home". Interior design responded by wallowing in a stylistic safety associated with the past, attempting to recreate more stable times through a nostalgic longing, with interior design merely an aspect of revivalism. The revival of past styles also became a vehicle for the mainstream absorption and acceptance of new materials and methods of production, a Trojan Horse for technological innovation, previously considered "cheap" and "poor" quality.

The praxis at which the traditional met the modern in terms of style was mirrored in the uncomfortable and transitory personal and inter-personal relationships within the domestic interior, and the frustrations of the expression of the self within rigid social structures and hierarchies. Fuelled by the Hippy ethos for a quest for self-discovery and "letting go", and a vogue for psychoanalysis, design and its advertising responded to unstable social discourse by exploring and capturing notions of the authentic and the experiential. The taboo of touch, a primary sensory urge, emerged as a means of loosening social constraint, which, when combined with more liberal approaches to sexual and sensual experimentation, explosively created the tactile home. Likewise, consumer goods proliferated, and were promoted as an extension of the physical or internal "authentic" self, thus representing actual or emulated lifestyle choice.

Equality, the mainstay of feminist discourse and politics, filtered into the mainstream and was, by the mid-decade *de jure*. Women, whose seemingly natural place within the home, as both producers and consumers, appeared increasingly dissatisfied with domesticity.[25] They were actively encouraged to look beyond their four walls,[26] and to experience power and pleasure in the workplace and in the bedroom.[27] As a result, traditional gender roles were disrupted and both women and men strove to bridge the distance between the responsibilities of the past and the potential of the modern.

---

[25] Ann Oakley, *The Sociology of Housework* (Oxford: Wiley Blackwell, 1974).

[26] Judy Giles, *The Parlour and the Suburb: Domestic Identities, Class, Femininity and Modernity* (Oxford: Berg, 2004), 142.

[27] Betty Friedan, *The Feminine Mystique* (New York: Dell Co., 1963).

The desire to be modern was problematic and expressed the anxieties of what was a period of transition. A fear for the future hindered an embracing of the new; attempts to break away from the past, both socially and stylistically, proved tentative, although widely promoted in the media and through lifestyle marketing. This disparity culminated in an emphasis on *surface* rather than real change, what appeared "natural" was "unnatural", and the modern merely the traditional in disguise. Sex did indeed come out from the closet, only to be swept under the shag-pile.

BIBLIOGRAPHY

The Angry Brigade 1967–1984. Documents and Chronology. London: Elephant Editions, 1985.

The Avengers: The Official Souvenir Magazine. London: Titan, 1998.

"Housing Primer." *Architectural Design* XXXVII (1967): 394–435

Aesthetics and Politics. Afterword by Fredric Jameson. Translated and edited by Ronald Taylor. London: NLB, 1977.

Agamben, Giorgio. *The Coming Community.* Translated by Michael Hardt. Minneapolis: University of Minnesota Press, 1993.

Aldiss, Brian, and David Wingrove. *Trillion Year Spree: The History of Science Fiction.* Thirsk: House of Stratus, 2001.

Alexandrian, Sarane. *Surrealist Art.* London: Thames and Hudson, 1996.

Allaby, Michael, and Peter Bunyard. *The Politics of Self-Sufficiency.* Oxford: Oxford University Press, 1980.

Allan, Stuart. *News Culture.* Buckingham: Open University Press, 2005.

Allaun, Frank. *Spreading the News.* Nottingham: Spokesman, 1988.

Altheide, David L. *Creating Reality: How TV News Distorts Events.* Beverly Hills: Sage, 1976.

Anderson, Lindsay. "Two Inches off the Ground." In *Never Apologise: The Collected Writings*, edited by Paul Ryan, 582–83 London: Plexus, 2004.

Anderson, Perry. "Components of the National Culture." *New Left Review* 50 (July–August 1968): 3–57.

—. *Considerations on Western Marxism.* London: Verso, 1979.

Apte, Mahadevhi. *Humour and Laughter: An Anthropological Approach.* Ithaca, London: Cornell University Press, 1985.

Ardis, Ann. "Staging the Public Sphere: Magazine Dialogism and the Prosthetics of Authorship at the Turn of the Twentieth Century." In *Transatlantic Print Culture 1880–1940: Emerging Media, Emerging Modernisms*, edited by Ann Ardis and Patrick Collier, 30–47. Basingstoke: Palgrave Macmillan, 2008.

Arnold, Dana, and Andrew Ballantyne. *Architecture as Experience: Radical Change in Spatial Practice.* London: Routledge, 2004.

Arnold, Rebecca. *Fashion Desire and Anxiety.* London: I.B. Tauris, 2001.

Attfield, Judy. *Wild Things.* Oxford: Berg, 2000.

Baistow, Tom. *Fourth-Rate Estate.* London: Comedia, 1985.

Baker, Phil. "Welcome to Big Biba." *The Art Book* 14, no. 4 (2007): 65.
Bakhtin, Mikhail. "Carnival and the Carnivalesque." In *Cultural Theory and Popular Culture*, edited by John Storey, 250–260. London: Prentice Hall, 1998.
Ballaster, Ros, and others. *Women's Worlds: Ideology, Femininity and the Woman's Magazine*. Basingstoke: Macmillan, 1991.
Barker, Hugh, and Yuval Taylor. *Faking It: The Quest for Authenticity in Popular Music*. London: Faber and Faber, 2007.
Barnes, Richard. *Mods!* London: Plexus, 1979.
Barnhurst, Kevin and John Neron. *The Form of News: A History*. London: The Guildford Press, 2001.
Barry, Angela. "Black Mythologies: The Representation of Black People on British Television." In *The Black and White Media Book: Handbook for the Study of Racism and Television*, edited by John Twitchin, 83–102. Stoke on Trent: Trentham, 1988.
Barthes, Roland. *Image/Music/Text*. New York: Hill and Wang, 1977.
Baudrillard, Jean. *Simulacra et Simulation*. Paris: Editions Galile'e, 1981.
—. "Simulations." In *Continental Philosophy*, edited by Richard Kearney. London: Blackwell, 1981.
—. "Transaesthetics." In *The Transparency of Evil: Essays on Extreme Phenomena*, translated by James Benedict, 14–19. London: Verso, 1993.
—. "Transeconomics." In *The Transparency of Evil: Essays on Extreme Phenomena*, translated by James Benedict, 26–35. London: Verso, 1993.
—. "Cool Memories III (1992–1995)." In *Mass, Identity, Architecture*, edited by Francesco Proto, 37–70. Chichester: Wiley-Academy, 2006.
—. "The Consumer Society." In *Mass, Identity, Architecture*, edited by Francesco Proto, 95–121. Chichester: Wiley-Academy, 2006.
Beckett, Andy. *When the Light Went Out: Britain in the 1970s*. London: Faber and Faber, 2009.
Benjamin, Walter. "Paris, Capital of the 19th Century," *New Left Review* 48 (March–April 1968): 77–88.
—. "The Work of Art in the Age of Mechanical Reproduction." In *Illuminations*, edited and introduced by Hannah Arendt, translated by Harry Zohn, 219–253. London: Fontana, 1973.
—. "The Work of Art in the Age of Mechanical Reproduction." In *Reflections*, edited by Peter Demetz, translated by Edmund Jephcott. New York: Schocken Books, 1986.
Berger, John. "The Moment of Cubism." *New Left Review* 42 (1967): 75–94.

—. *The Moment of Cubism and Other Essays.* London: Weidenfeld & Nicolson, 1969.

—. *Art and Revolution: Ernst Neizvestny and the Role of the Artist in the U.S.S.R.* London: Weidenfeld & Nicolson, 1969.

Berger, John, and others. *Ways of Seeing.* Harmondsworth: Penguin, 1972.

Berger, John. *G.* Harmondsworth: Penguin, 1976.

Berger, John. *The Success and Failure of Picasso.* 1965. London: Writers and Readers, 1980.

Bey, Hakim. "From TAZ: The Temporary Autonomous Zone." In *Cultural Resistance Reader*, edited by Stephen Duncombe, 113–18. London: Verso, 2002.

Biddle, Erika, Stephen Shukaitis and David Graeber, eds. *Constituent Imagination: Militant Investigations, Collective Theorizations.* Oakland, USA: AK Press, 2007.

Bignell, Jonathan, and Andrew O'Day. *Terry Nation.* Manchester, New York: Manchester University Press, 2004.

Billig, Michael. *Laughter and Ridicule: Towards a Social Critique of Humour.* London: Sage, 2005.

Binkley, Sam. *Getting Loose: Lifestyle Consumption in the 1970s.* Durham: Duke University Press, 2007.

Bish, Geoff. "The Manifesto." In *What Went Wrong*, edited by Michael Barratt Brown and Ken Coates, 187–206. Nottingham: Spokesman, 1979.

Bishop, Claire, ed. *Participation. Documents of Contemporary Art.* London: Whitechapel/MIT Press, 2006.

Blackburn, Robin. "A Brief History of New Left Review." *New Left Review.* http://www.newleftreview.org/?page=history.

Bolton, Roger. *Death on the Rock and Other Stories.* London: WH Allen, 1990.

Booker, Christopher. *The Seventies: Portrait of a Decade.* London: Allen Lane, 1980.

Born, Georgina. *Uncertain Vision: Birt, Dyke and the Reinvention of the BBC.* London: Vintage, 2004.

Bourdieu, Pierre. *Distinction: A Social Critique of the Judgment of Taste.* London: Routledge, 1979.

Bourne, Stephen. *Black in the British Frame: The Black Experience in British Film and Television.* London, New York: Continuum, 2001.

Bracewell, Michael. *England is Mine: Pop Life in Albion from Wilde to Goldie.* London: Flamingo, 1997.

—. *Re-make, Re-model: Art, Pop and Fashion and the Making of Roxy Music.* London: Faber and Faber, 2007.

Bradbury, Ray. *The Martian Chronicles (The Silver Locusts)*. London: Grafton Books, 1977.

Braunstein, Peter. "Disco." *American Heritage Magazine* 50, no. 7 (1999). http://www.americanheritage.com/articles/magazine/ah/1999/7/1999_7_43.shtml.

Breed, Warren. "Social Control in the Newsroom: A Functional Analysis." *Social Forces* 33 (1955): 326–55.

Brett, Guy. *Exploding Galaxies. The Art of David Medalla*. London: Kala, 1995.

Brook, James, Chris Carlsson and Nancy J. Peters, eds. *Reclaiming San Francisco: History, Politics, Culture*. San Francisco: City Lights, 1998.

Brown, Penelope, and Ludmilla Jordanova. "Oppressive Dichotomies: The Nature/Culture Debate." In *A Cultural Studies Reader*, edited by Jessica Munns and Gita Rajan, 509–18. London: Longman, 1995.

Callaghan, John. *The Retreat of Social Democracy*. Manchester: Manchester University Press, 2000.

Carmichael, Stokely. "Black Power." In *The Dialectics of Liberation*, edited by David Cooper, 150–174. Harmondsworth: Penguin, 1968.

Carney, Ray, and Leonard Quart. *The Films of Mike Leigh: Embracing the World*. Cambridge: Cambridge University Press, 2000.

Carruthers, Susan. "Reporting Terrorism: The British State and the Media, 1919–1994." In *War, Culture and the Media: Representations of the Military in 20th Century Britain*, edited by Susan Carruthers and Ian Stewart, 101–29. Trowbridge: Flicks,1996.

Caughie, John. "Broadcasting and Cinema 1: Converging Histories." In *All Our Yesterdays: 90 Years of British Cinema*, edited by Charles Barr, 189–205. London: BFI Publishing, 1986.

Caute, David. *The Occupation: A Novel*. London: André Deutsch, 1971.

Centre for Contemporary Cultural Studies. *The Empire Strikes Back: Race and Racism in 70s Britain*. London: Hutchinson, 1982.

Chandler, David P. Brother. *Number One: A Political Biography of Pol Pot*. Revised edition. Boulder, Colorado, Oxford: Westview Press, 1999.

Chapman, James. "Action, Spectacle and the Boy's Own Tradition in British Cinema." In *The British Cinema Book*, edited by Robert Murphy, 217–25. London: BFI Publishing, 2001.

Chibnall, Steve. *Making Mischief: The Cult Films of Pete Walker*. Guildford: FAB Press, 1998.

Christopher, John. *The Death of Grass*. London: Michael Joseph, 1956.

Chun, Lin. *The British New Left*. Edinburgh: Edinburgh University Press, 1993.

Clarke, David B., ed. *The Cinematic City*. London: Routledge, 1997.

Cleto, Fabio, ed. *Camp: Queer Aesthetics and The Performing Subject. A Reader*. Edinburgh: Edinburgh University Press, 1999.

Cleto, Fabio. "Pop Camp, Surplus Counter-Value, or the Camp of Cultural Economy. Introduction." In *Camp: Queer Aesthetic and the Performing Subject. A Reader*, edited by Fabio Cleto, 302–07. Edinburgh: Edinburgh University Press, 1999.

Clutterbuck, Richard. *The Media and Political Violence*. London: Macmillan,1981.

Cohen, Stanley. *Folk Devils and Moral Panics*. London: MacGibbon & Kee, 1972.

Cohn, Nik. *Awopbopaloobop Alopbamboo: Pop from the Beginning,* 194–210. London: Pimlico 1969.

Cohn, Nik. "Mods." In *The Sharper Word: A Mod Anthology,* edited by Hewitt Paolo, 137–43. London: Helter Skelter Books, 1999.

Comfort, Alex. *The Joy of Sex*. Ann Arbor: University of Michigan, 1972.

Conboy, Martin. *Tabloid Britain*. London: Routledge, 2006.

Conrich, Ian. "The Divergence and Mutation of British Cinema." In *Seventies British Cinema*, edited by Robert Shail, 25–35. London: Palgrave Macmillan, 2008.

Cooper, David. "Beyond Words." In *The Dialectics of Liberation*, edited by David Cooper, 193–202. Harmondsworth: Penguin, 1968.

Cork, Richard, and others. *Art for Whom?* London: Arts Council of Great Britain, 1978.

Corner, John. *Popular Television in Britain: Studies in Cultural History*. London: Macmillan, 1981.

Coult, Tony, and Baz Kershaw. *Engineers of the Imagination. The Welfare State Handbook*. London: Methuen,1990.

Coverley, Merlin. *Psychogeography*. Harpenden: Pocket Essentials, 2006.

Cowie, Elizabeth. "Pornography and Fantasy Psychoanalytic Perspectives." In *Sex Exposed: Sexuality and the Pornography Debate*, edited by Lynne Segal and Myra McIntosh, 132–54. London: Virago, 1992.

Craven, John, and Eric Rowan. *And Finally: Funny Stories from John Craven's Newsround*. London: BBC/Knight, 1983.

Creeber, Glen. *The Television Genre Book*. London: BFI, 2001.

Crisell, Andrew. *An Introductory History of Broadcasting*. London: Routledge, 1997.

Curran, James, and Colin Leys. "Media and the Decline of Liberal Corporatism in Britain." In *De-Westernizing Media Studies*, edited by

James Curran James and Myung-Jin Park, 221–36. London: Routledge, 2000.

Curran, James. "Different Approaches to Media Reform." In *Bending Reality*, edited by James Curran, 89–135. London: Pluto, 1986.

—. *Policy for the Press*. London: IPPR, 1995.

—. "Press Reformism 1918–98: A Study in Failure." In *Media Power, Professionals and Policies*, edited by Howard Tumber, 35–55. London: Routledge, 2000.

—. *Media and Power*. London: Routledge, 2002.

Curtis, Liz. "A Catalogue of Censorship 1959–1993." In *War and Words: A Northern Ireland Reader*, edited by Bill Rolston and David Miller, 265–304. Belfast: Beyond the Pale Publications, 1996.

—. *Ireland: The Propaganda War*. London: Pluto, 1984.

Curtis, William JR. *Modern Architecture since 1900*. Oxford: Phaidon, 1982.

Kemp, Daren. *New Age: A Guide*. Edinburgh: Edinburgh University Press, 2004.

Davidoff, Leonore, and Catherine Hall. "'My Own Fireside': The Creation of the Middle-Class Home." In *The Politics of Domestic Consumption*, edited by Stevi Jackson and Shaun Moores, 277–89. Hemel Hempstead: Harvester Wheatsheaf, 1995.

Davidoff, Leonore. *Worlds Between: Historical Perspectives on Gender and Class*. New York: Routledge, 1995.

Davies, Helen. "All Rock and Roll is Homosocial: The Representation of Women in the British Rock Music Press." *Popular Music* 20, no. 3 (2001): 301–19.

Day, Robin. *Grand Inquisitor*. London: Pan Books, 1990.

Dixon, Winston Wheeler. "The End of Hammer." In *Seventies British Cinema*, edited by Robert Shail, 14–24. London: Palgrave Macmillan, 2008.

Doy, Gen. *Drapery: Classicism and Barbarism in Visual Culture*. London: I.B. Tauris, 2002.

Doyle, Gillian. *Media Ownership*. London: Sage, 2002.

—. *Understanding Media Economics*. London: Sage, 2002.

Dyer, Geoff. *Ways of Telling: The Work of John Berger*. London: Pluto Press, 1986.

Dyer, Richard. "In Defence of Disco." *Gay Left* 19 (1979): 20–23.

—. "It's Being so Camp as Keeps us Going." In *Camp: Queer Aesthetic and the Performing Subject. A Reader*, edited by Fabio Cleto, 110–16. Edinburgh: Edinburgh University Press, 1999.

Ellen, Mark. "Amateur Hour." *The Word* 38 (2006): 82–88.

English, James F. *Comic Transactions: Literature, Humor and the Politics of Community in Twentieth-Century Britain*. Ithaca: Cornell University Press, 1994.

Epstein, Edward. *News from Nowhere: Television and the News*. New York: Random House, 1973.

Fishman, Mark. *Manufacturing the News*. Austin: University of Texas Press, 1980.

Flinn, Caryl. "The Deaths of Camp." In *Camp: Queer Aesthetic and the Performing Subject. A Reader*, edited by Fabio Cleto, 443–57. Edinburgh: Edinburgh University Press, 1999.

Forde, Eamonn. "From Polyglottism to Branding. On the Decline of Personality Journalism in the British Press." *Journalism* 2, no. 1 (2001): 23–43.

Forty, Adrian. *Objects of Desire: Design and Society since 1750*. London: Thames & Hudson, 1986.

Foucault, Michel. *Power/Knowledge. Selected Interviews and Other Writings 1972–77*, edited and translated by Colin Gordon. Brighton: Harvester Press, 1980.

—. *Essential Works 1954–84, Vol. 3*, edited by James D. Faubion, translated by Robert Hurley and others. London: Penguin, 2002.

Fowles, John. *The French Lieutenant's Woman*. Frogmore: Triad Panther, 1969.

Frampton, Kenneth. "A Conversation with Kenneth Frampton." In *October* 106 (2003): 35–58.

Freear, Andrew. "Alexandra Road: The Last Great Social Housing Project." *AA Files* 30 (1995): 35–46.

French, Marilyn. *The Women's Room*. New York: Deutsch, 1974.

Fried, Michael. "Art and Objecthood." *Art Forum* 5 (1967): 12–23.

Friedan, Betty. *The Feminine Mystique*. New York: Dell Co., 1963

Frith, Simon. "Afterword." In *After Subculture: Critical Studies in Contemporary Youth Culture,* edited by Andy Bennett and Keith Kahn-Harris, 173–78. Basingstoke: Palgrave, 2004.

Frith, Mark. *The Best of Smash Hits*. London: Sphere, 2006.

Frith, Simon, and Howard Horne. *Art into Pop*. London: Methuen, 1987.

Frith, Simon. "Introduction." In *Pop Goes the Culture*, edited by Craig McGregor. London: Pluto Press, 1984.

—. "Look! Hear! The Uneasy Relationship of Music and Television". *Popular Music* 21, vol. 3 (2002): 277–90.

Frith, Simon, David Muggleton and Rupert Weinzierl, eds. *The Post-Subcultures Reader*. Oxford: Berg, 2003.

Gans, Herbert. *Deciding What's News: A Study of CBS Evening News,*

NBC Nightly News, Newsweek and Time. New York: Random House, 1979.

Garnett, Mark. *From Anger to Apathy: The British Experience Since 1975*. London: Jonathan Cape, 2007.

Grindon, Gavin. "The Breath of the Possible." In *Constituent Imagination: Militant Investigations, Collective Theorizations*, edited by Erika Biddle, Stephen Shukaitis and David Graeber, 94–107. Oakland, USA: AK Press, 2007.

Gifford, Denis. *The British Film Catalogue. Vol. 1: Fiction Film 1895–1994*. London: Fitzroy Dearborn, 2001.

Giles, Judy. *The Parlour and the Suburb: Domestic Identities, Class, Femininity and Modernity*. Oxford: Berg, 2004.

Gilroy, Paul. *There Ain't No Black in the Union Jack: The Cultural Politics of Race and Nation*. London: Unwin Hyman, 1987.

Goddard, Peter, John Corner and Kay Richardson. "The Formation of World in Action: a Case Study in the History of Current Affairs Journalism." *Journalism* 2, no. 1 (2001): 73–90.

Goddard, Peter, John Corner and Kay Richardson. *Public Issue Television: World in Action, 1963–98*. Manchester University Press, 2007.

Golding, Peter, and Peter Elliott. *Making the News*. London: Longman, 1979.

Goodman, Geoffrey, and David Basnett. *Royal Commission on the Press: Minority Report*. London: Labour Party, 1997.

Gorman, Paul. *In Their Own Words: Adventures in the Music Press*. London: Sanctuary Publishing, 2001.

Graham-Dixon, Andrew. *A History of British Art*. London: BBC Books, 1996.

Grant, Barry Keith. "The Body Politic: Ken Russell in the 1980s." In *Fires Were Started: British Cinema and Thatcherism*, 2nd ed., edited by Lester D. Friedman, 182–194. London: Wallflower, 2006.

Green, Barbara. "Feminist Things." In *Transatlantic Print Culture 1880–1940*, edited by Ann Ardis and Patrick Collier, 66–79. Basingstoke: Palgrave Macmillan, 2008.

Green, Martin. "Nostalgia Politics." Review of Ragtime. *The American Scholar* 45 (1976): 841–45.

Greenhalgh, Paul, ed. *Modernism in Design*. London: Reaktion Books, 1990.

Greer, Germaine. *The Female Eunuch*. McGraw Hill, 1971.

Grogan, Emmett. *Ringolevio*. Edinburgh: Rebel Inc., 1999.

Grossberg, Lawrence. "The Media Economy of Rock Culture: Cinema, Postmodernity and Authenticity." In *Sound and Vision: The Music Video Reader*, edited by Simon Frith, 159–80. London: Routledge, 1993.

Gudmundsson, Gunter. "Brit Crit: Turning Points in British Rock Criticism 1960–1990." In *Pop Music and the Press*, edited by Steve Jones. Philadelphia: Temple University Press, 2002.

Guffy, Elizabeth E. *Retro: The Culture of Revival*. London: Reaktion, 2006.

Gullestad, Marianne. "Home Decoration as Popular Culture: Constructing, Homes, Genders and Classes in Norway." In *The Politics of Domestic Consumption*, edited by Stevi Jackson and Shaun Moores, 321–35. Hemel Hempstead: Harvester Wheatsheaf, 1995.

Habermas, Jürgen. *Legitimation Crisis*. London: Heinemann, 1976.

Hall, Stuart. "The Whites of their Eyes: Racist Ideologies and the Media." In *Silver Linings: Some Strategies for the Eighties*, edited by George Bridges and Rosalind Brunt, 28–52. London: Lawrence and Wishart, 1981.

Halloran, James, Philip Elliott and Graham Murdock. *Demonstrations and Communications: A Case Study*. London: Penguin, 1970.

Hamilton, John. *Beasts in the Cellar: The Exploitation Career of Tony Tenser*. Surrey: FAB Press, 2005.

Hampshire, James. *Citizenship and Belonging: Immigration and the Politics of Demographic Governance in Post-War Britain*. Basingstoke: Palgrave, 2005.

Hansen, Randall. *Citizenship and Immigration: the Institutional Origins of a Multi-Racial Nation*. Oxford: Oxford University Press, 2000.

Harper, Sue. "History and Representation: The Case of 1970s British Cinema." In *The New Film History: Sources, Methods, Approaches*, edited by James Chapman, Mark Glancy and Sue Harper, 27–40. Basingstoke: Palgrave Macmillan, 2007.

Harrison, Jackie. *Terrestrial TV News in Britain: The Culture of Production*. Manchester: Manchester University Press, 1999.

Harrison, Margaret. "Notes on Feminist Art in Britain 1970–77." *Studio International* 193, no. 987 (1977): 212–20.

Harrop, Martin. "The Press and Post-War Elections." In *Political Communications: The General Election of 1983*, edited by Ivor Crewe and Martin Harrop, 137–49. Cambridge: Cambridge University Press, 1983.

Harvey, Sylvia. *May '68 and Film Culture*. London: BFI, 1978.

Haslam, Dave. *Not Abba: The Real Story of the 1970s*. London: Fourth Estate, 2005.

Hay, James. "Piecing Together What Remains of the Cinematic City." In *The Cinematic City*, edited by David B. Clarke, 214-5. London: Routledge, 1997.

Hebdidge, Dick. *Subculture: The Meaning of Style*. London: Routledge, 1979.

Hebditch, Ian. "Weekend." In *The Sharper Word: A Mod Anthology*, edited by Hewitt Paolo, 132–36. London: Helter Skelter Books, 1999.

Heelas, Paul. *The New Age Movement*. London: Blackwell, 1996.

Hewison, Robert. *Culture and Consensus: England, Art and Politics since 1940*. London: Methuen, 1995.

—. *Culture and Consensus: England, Art and Politics*. London: Methuen, 1997.

—. *Too Much: Art and Society in the Sixties 1960–75*. London: Methuen, 1986.

Hewitt, Paolo, ed. *The Sharper Word: A Mod Anthology*. London: Helter Skelter Books, 1999.

Hewitt, Paolo. *The Soul Stylists: Forty Years of Modernism*. London: Mainstream, 2000.

Higson, Andrew. "A Diversity of Film Practices: Renewing British Cinema in the 1970s." *The Arts in the 1970s: Cultural Closure?*, edited by Bart Moore-Gilbert, 216–39. London: Routledge, 1994.

Hite, Shere. *The Hite Report: A Nation-Wide Study on Female Sexuality*. New York: Collier Macmillan, 1976.

Hodgart, Matthew. *Satire*. London: Weidenfeld and Nicolson, 1969.

Holland, Patricia. *The Angry Buzz*. London: I.B.Taurus, 2006.

Holmberg, Carl B. *Sexualities and Popular Culture*. Oxford: Sage Publications, 1998.

Home, Anna. *Into the Box of Delights: A History of Children's Television*. London: BBC Books, 1993.

Høst, Sigurd. "The Norwegian Newspaper System: Structure and Development." In *Media and Communication*, edited by Helge Ronning and Knut Lundby, 281–301. Oslo: Norwegian University Press, 1991.

Howes, Keith. *Broadcasting It: An Encyclopaedia of Homosexuality on Film, Radio and TV in the UK 1923–1993*. London: Cassell, 1993.

Hunt, Leon. *British Low Culture: From Safari Suits to Sexploitation*. London: Routledge, 1998.

Hyman, James. T*he Battle for Realism: Figurative Art in Britain during the Cold War 1945–60*. New Haven: Yale University Press, 2001.

Isherwood, Christopher. "The World in the Evening." In *Camp: Queer Aesthetic and the Performing Subject. A Reader*, edited by Fabio Cleto, 49–52. Edinburgh: Edinburgh University Press, 1999.

J. *The Sensuous Woman*, New York: Dell Publishing Co, 1969.

James, David E. "Cubism as Revolutionary Realism: John Berger and G." *Minnesota Review* 21 (1983): 92–109.

—. "Cubism as Revolutionary Realism: John Berger and G." Revised edition. In David E. James. *Power Misses: Essays Across (Un)popular Culture*, 48–69. London: Verso, 1997.

Jameson, Fredric. *Postmodernism, or, The Cultural Logic of Late Capitalism*. London: Verso, 1991.

Jencks, Charles. *The Language of Post-Modern Architecture*. London: Academy Editions, 1977.

—. *The Language of Post-Modern Architecture*. Revised and enlarged edition. London: Academy Editions, 1978.

Johnson, B.S. *Travelling People*. Letchworth: The Garden City Press, 1963.

Jones, Edward. "Fleet Road: A Critique." *Architectural Design* 8–9 (1978): 524–26.

Jong, Erica. *The Fear of Flying*. London: Signet, 1973.

Kael, Pauline. *5001 Nights at the Movies: Shorter Reviews from the Silents to the '90s*. London: Marion Boyars, 1993.

Kant, Immanuel. *Critique of Pure Reason*. Translated by Norman Kemp Smith. London: MacMillan, 1985.

Keane, Stephen. *Disaster Movies: The Cinema of Catastrophe*. London: Wallflower, 2001.

Keightley, Keir. "Reconsidering Rock." In *The Cambridge Companion to Rock and Pop*, edited by Simon Frith, 109–43. Cambridge: Cambridge University Press, 2001.

Kershaw, Baz. *The Politics of Performance: Radical Theatre as Cultural Intervention*. London, New York: Routledge, 1992.

Kester, Grant H. *Conversation Pieces, Community and Communication in Modern Art*. Berkeley: University of California Press, 2004.

Khan, Naseem. *The Arts Britain Ignores: The Art of Minorities in Great Britain*. London: Arts Council of Great Britain, 1976.

Kiddle, Catherine. *What Shall We Do With the Children?* Devon: Spindlewood, 1981.

Kiernan, Ben. *The Pol Pot Regime: Race, Power, and Genocide in Cambodia under the Khmer Rouge, 1975–79*. New Haven, London: Yale University Press, 1996.

Kinchin, Juliet. "Interiors: Nineteenth Century Essays on the 'Masculine' and the 'Feminine' Room." In *The Gendered Object*, edited by Pat Kirkham, 12–29. Manchester: Manchester University Press, 1996.

Klinger, Barbara. *Melodrama and Meaning: History, Culture and the Films of Douglas Sirk*. Bloomington: Indiana University Press, 1994.

Labour Party. *The People and the Media*. London: Labour Party, 1974.

Laing, Dave. "Anglo-American Music Journalism." In *The Popular Music Studies Reader*, edited by Andy Bennett, 333–43. London: Routledge, 2007.

Laing, Stuart. "The Politics of Culture: Institutional Change in the 1970s." In *The Arts in the 1970s: Cultural Closure?*, edited by Bart Moore-Gilbert, 29–56. London: Routledge, 1994.

Lambert, Gavin. *Mainly about Lindsay Anderson*. London: Faber, 2000.

LeMay, Curtis E. *Mission with LeMay: My Story*. Garden City, N.Y.: Doubleday, 1965.

Levy, Shawn. *Ready Steady Go: Swinging London and the Invention of Cool*. London: Fourth Estate, 2002.

Lindley, Richard. *Panorama: Fifty Years of Pride and Paranoia*. London: Politicos Publishing, 2002.

Lippard, Lucy. *Six Years: The Dematerialisation of the Art Object 1966–1972*. Berkeley: University of California Press, 1997.

MacInnes, Colin. *Absolute Beginners*. London: Alison & Busby, 2001.

Malia, Martin. *Russia Under Western Eyes: From the Bronze Horseman to the Lenin Mausoleum*. Cambridge, Mass., London: The Belknap Press of Harvard University Press, 1999.

Mallarmé, Stéphane. *Selected Poems*, translated by C.F. MacIntyre. Berkeley: University of California Press, 1957.

Marcuse, Herbert. "Liberation from the Affluent Society." In *The Dialectics of Liberation*, edited by David Cooper, 175–92. Harmondsworth: Penguin 1968.

—. *Eros and Civilization: A Philosophical Inquiry into Freud*. Boston: Beacon Press, 1955.

—. *One Dimensional Man: Studies in the Ideology of Advanced Industrial Society*. Boston: Beacon Press, 1964.

—. *The Aesthetic Dimension: Towards a Critique of Marxist Aesthetics*. London and Basingstoke: Macmillan, 1978.

Marx, Karl. *The Economic and Philosophic Manuscripts of 1844*, edited and introduced by Dirk J. Struik, translated by Martin Milligan. New York: International Publishers Co. Inc., 1967.

Massumi, Brian. "Translator's Forward: Pleasures of Philosophy." In Gilles Deleuze and Felix Guattari. *A Thousand Plateaus*, translated and foreword by Brian Massumi, ix–xvii. Minneapolis: University of Minnesota, 1987.

Matthews, Julian. "Cultures of Production: The Making of Children's News." In *Media Organization and Production*, edited by Simon Cottle, 131–45. London: Sage, 2003.

—. "A Missing Link? The Imagined Audience, News Practices and the Production of Children's News." *Journalism Practice* 2, no. 2 (2008): 265–80.

—. "Negotiating News Childhoods: News Producers, Visualized Audiences and the Production of the Children's News Agenda." *Journal of Children and Media* 3, no. 1 (2009): 3–18.

McAsh, Iain M. "After they cleaned up on Wimbledon Common… Can the Wombles Do The Same For The British Film Industry?," *Films Illustrated* 7, no. 73 (1977): 30–32.

McDonagh, Maitland. *Broken Mirrors/Broken Minds: The Dark Dreams of Dario Argento*. London: Kensington Books, 1994.

McGrath, John. *Loving Big Brother – Performance, Privacy and Surveillance Space*. London: Routledge, 2004.

McKay, Ron, and Brian Barr. *The Story of the Scottish Daily News*. Edinburgh: Canongate, 1976.

McLeod, Kembrew. "Abandoning the Absolute: Transcendence and Gender in Popular Music Discourse." In *Pop Music and the Press*, edited by Steve Jones, 93–113. Philadelphia: Temple University Press, 2002.

Medhurst, Andy. "Introduction: Situation Comedies." In *Black Images in British Television: The Colour Black*, edited by Therese Daniel and Jane Gerson, 15–21. London: British Film Institute, 1989.

—. *A National Joke: Popular Comedies and English Cultural Identities*. London, New York: Routledge, 2007.

Melly, George. *Revolt Into Style: The Pop Arts*. London: Penguin Books, 1970.

Menger, Pierre-Michel. *Profession Artiste*. Paris: Editions Textuel, 2005.

Meyer, Moe. *The Politics and Poetics of Camp*. London: Routledge, 1994.

Mills, Sara. "Smash Hits." *Media Magazine* 19 (2007): 53–54.

Mitchell, John. *Flickering Shadows: A Lifetime in Films*. Malvern Wells, Worcestershire: Harold Martin & Redman, 1997.

Moore-Gilbert, Bart. "Introduction: Cultural Closure or Post-Avantgardism?." In *The Arts in the 1970s: Cultural Closure?*, edited by Bart Moore-Gilbert, 1–28. London: Routledge, 1994.

—. *The Arts in the 1970s: Cultural Closure?* London: Routledge, 1994.

Morgan, Kenneth. *Callaghan: A Life*. Oxford: Oxford University Press, 1997.

Morrison, Grant. "A World of Miraculous Transformations." In *The Avengers Companion*, edited by Alain Carraze, Jean-Luc Putheaud and Alex J. Geairns, 21–22. London: Titan Books, 1997.

Mort, Frank. *Cultures of Consumption*. London: Routledge, 1997.

Muggleton, David. *Inside Subculture: The Postmodern Meaning of Style*. Oxford: Berg, 2000.

Mulholland, Gary. *This is Uncool: The 500 Greatest Singles since Punk and Disco*. London: Cassel, 2002.

Mulvey, Laura. *Visual and Other Pleasures*. Bloomington: Indiana UP, 1989.

Murdock, Graham, and Peter Golding. "For a Political Economy of Mass Communications." In *The Socialist Register 1973*, edited by Ralph Milliband and John Saville, 205–33. London: Merlin, 1974.

Nairne, Sandy, and Caroline Tisdall, eds. *Conrad Atkinson: Picturing the System*. London: Pluto Press, 1981.

Nancy, Jean-Luc. *The Inoperative Community*, edited by Peter Connor. Minneapolis: University of Minnesota Press, 1991.

Nixon, Sean. *Hard Looks: Masculinity, Spectatorship and Contemporary Consumption*. London: UCL Press, 1996.

Nowell-Smith, Geoffrey. "Editorial." *Screen* 18, no. 1 (1977): 5–8.

O'Connor, Alan, ed. *Raymond Williams on Television: Selected Writings*. London: Routledge, 1968.

O'Malley, Tom. *Closedown? The BBC and Government Broadcasting Policy, 1979–92*. London: Pluto, 1994.

Oakley, Ann. *The Sociology of Housework*. Oxford: Wiley Blackwell, 1974.

Oddey, Alison. "Different Directions: The Potentials of Autobiographical Space." In *The Potentials of Spaces – The Theory and Practice of Scenography and Performance*, edited by Alison Oddey and Christine White, 33–49. Bristol: Intellect, 2006.

—. *Re-Framing the Theatrical: Interdisciplinary Landscapes for Performance*. Basingstoke: Palgrave Macmillan, 2007.

Orbanz, Eva, and Klaus Wildenhahn. "Journey to a Legend and Back: The British Realistic Film." In *Granada: The First Twenty-Five Years*, 99–102. London: BFI, 1981.

Østbye, Helge. "Norway." In *The Media in Western Europe*, edited by Stubbe Ostergaard Bernt, 168–184. London: Sage, 1997.

Palmer, Jerry. *Taking Humour Seriously*. London, New York: Routledge, 1994.

Panitch, Leo, and Colin Leys. *The End of Parliamentary Socialism: From New Left to New Labour*. London: Verso, 1997.

Papanek, Victor. *Design for the Real World*. London: Thames & Hudson, 1972.

Parker, Roszika, and Griselda Pollock. *Framing Feminism*. London: Pandora, 1987.

Paul, Kathleen. *Whitewashing Britain: Race and Citizenship in the Postwar Era*. Ithaca, London: Cornell University Press, 1997.

Phillips, Gene D. *Ken Russell*. Boston: Twayne, 1979.

Plant, Sadie. *The Most Radical Gesture: Situationist International in a Postmodern Age*. London: Routledge, 1992.

Porter, Vincent. "The Context of Creativity: Ealing Studios and Hammer Films." In *British Cinema History*, edited by James Curran and Vincent Porter, 179–207. London: Weidenfeld and Nicholson, 1983.

Poster, Mark. "Introduction." In Jean Baudrillard. *Selected Writings*, edited and introduced by Mark Poster, 1–9. Oxford, Cambridge: Polity Press, 1988.

Potts, Tracey. "Creating 'Modern Tendencies': The Symbolic Economics of Furnishing." In *Historicizing Lifestyle: Mediating Taste, Consumption and Identity from the 1900s to the 1970s*, edited by David Bell and Joanne Hollows, 156–72. Aldershot: Ashgate, 2006.

Raban, Jonathan. *Soft City – What Cities Do To Us and How They Change The Way We Live, Think and Feel*. London: Hamish Hamilton,1974.

Railton, Daine. "The Gendered Carnival of Pop." In *Popular Music* 20, no. 3 (2001): 321–31.

Rancière, Jacques. *The Politics of Aesthetics*, translated and introduced by Gabriel Rockhill. London,New York: Continuum, 2006.

Rasmussen, Steen Eiler. *Towns and Buildings Described in Drawings and Words*. Cambridge, Massachusetts: Harvard University Press, 1951.

Ravenhill, Mark. *Shopping and F*****g*. London: Methuen, 1997.

Ravetz, Alison. "A View From the Interior." In *A View From the Interior: Women and Design*, edited by Judy Attfield and Pat Kirkham, 107–285. London: The Women's Press, 1995.

Rawlings, Terry. *Mod: A Very British Phenomenon*. London: Omnibus, 2000.

Richards, Huw. *The Bloody Circus*. London: Pluto, 1997.

Richardson, Tony. *Long Distance Runner: A Memoir*. London: Faber and Faber, 1993.

Rimmer, Dave. *Like Punk Never Happened: Culture Club and New Pop*. London: Faber and Faber, 1985.

—. *The Guinness Book of Hit Singles*. London: Guinness, 2006.

Robertson, Pamela, "What Makes the Feminist Camp?." In *Camp: Queer Aesthetic and the Performing Subject. A Reader*, edited by Fabio Cleto, 266–82. Edinburgh: Edinburgh University Press, 1999.

Roddick, Nick. "Only the Stars Survive: Disaster Movies in the Seventies." In *Performance and Politics in Popular Drama: Aspects of Popular Entertainment in Theatre, Film and Television 1800–1976*, edited by David Bradby, Louis James and Bernard Sharratt, 243–69. Cambridge: Cambridge University Press, 1981.

Ross, Andrew. *No Collar: The Humane Workplace and its Hidden Costs.* Philadelphia: Temple University Press, 2004.

Ross, Kristin. *May 68 and its Afterlives.* Chicago: University of Chicago Press, 2002.

Rowbotham, Sheila. "The Beginnings of Women's Liberation in Britain." In *The Body Politic: Women's Liberation in Britain, 1969–72*, edited by Michelene Wandor, London: Stage 1, 1972.

—. *A Century of Women: The History of Women in Britain and the United States.* London: Penguin, 1999.

Rowe, Marsha, ed. *Spare Rib Reader.* Harmondsworth: Penguin, 1982.

Rowland, Robert. "Panorama in the Sixties." In *Window on the Sixties: Exploring Key Texts of Media and Culture*, edited by Anthony Aldgate, James Chapman and Arthur Marwick, 154–182. London: I.B. Tauris, 2000.

Royal Commission on the Press. *Final Report.* London: HMSO, 1977.

Rubinstein, Ruth. *Dress Codes: Meanings and Messages in American Culture.* Boulder, San Francisco, Oxford: Westview, 1995.

Russell, Ken. *Fire Over England: The British Cinema Comes Under Friendly Fire.* London: Hutchinson, 1993.

Ryan, Paul. "Introduction." In *Never Apologise: The Collected Writings of Lindsay Anderson*, edited by Paul Ryan, 1–29 London: Plexus, 2004.

Saggar, Shamit. *Race and Politics in Britain.* London: Harvester Wheatsheaf, 1992.

Sanchez-Tabernero, Alfonso, and Alison Denton. *Media Concentration in Europe.* Manchester: European Institute for the Media, 1993.

Sandbrook, Dominic. *White Heat: A History of Britain in the Swinging Sixties.* London: Little Brown, 2006.

Sartre, Jean-Paul. *Nausea*, translated by Robert Baldick. Harmondsworth: Penguin Books, 1965.

Satin, Mark Ivor. *New Age Politics.* New York: Delta Books, 1976.

Savage, Jon. "The Enemy Within: Sex, Rock and Identity." *In Facing The Music: Essays on Pop, Rock and Culture*, edited by Simon Frith, 131–72. London: Mandarin, 1990.

—. "Tainted Love." In *Consumption Identity and Style*, edited by Alan Tomlinson, 153–71. London: Routledge, 1991.

—. *Teenage: The Creation of Youth 1875–1945*. London: Chatto & Windus, 2007.

Scannell, Paddy, and David Cardiff. *A Social History of British Broadcasting, 1922–1939*. Oxford: Blackwell, 1991.

Schatz, Thomas. *Hollywood Genres: Formulas, Filmmaking, and the Studio System*. Boston: Mcgraw-Hill, 1981.

Schlesinger, Phillip. *Putting Reality Together*. London: Methuen, 1978.

Selden, R. "Commitment and Dialectic in Novels by David Caute and John Berger." *Forum for Modern Language Studies* 11 (1975): 106–21.

Sennett, Richard. *The Uses of Disorder*. New York: Alfred A. Knopf, 1970.

Sexton, Jamie. "Televérité Hits Britain: Documentary, Drama and the Growth of 16mm Filmmaking in British Television." *Screen* 44, no. 4 (2003): 429–444.

Seymour-Ure, Colin. *The British Press and Broadcasting since 1945*. Oxford: Blackwell, 1996.

Shail, Robert, ed. *Seventies British Cinema*. London: British Film Institute, 2008.

Sheridan, Simon. *Keeping The British End Up: Four Decades of Saucy Cinema*. Richmond: Reynolds & Hearn, 2001.

Shouse, Eric. "Feeling, Emotion, Affect." *M/C Journal* 8, no. 6 (2005). http://journal.media-culture.org.au/0512/03-shouse.php.

Shuker, Roy. *Understanding Popular Music*. London: Routledge, 2001.

Shute, Neville. *On the Beach*. London: Heinemann, 1957.

Sigel, Leon V. *Reporters and Officials: The Organization and Politics of Newsmaking*. Massachusetts: Health and Company, 1973.

Sillars, Stuart. "Is it Possible for Me to Do Nothing as My Contribution? Visual Art in the 1970s." In *The Arts in the 1970s: Cultural Closure?*, edited by Bart Moore-Gilbert, 259–80. London: Routledge, 1994.

Sivanandan, Ambalavaner. *A Different Hunger: Writings on Black Resistance*. London: Pluto, 1982.

Smith, Anthony. "Television Coverage of Northern Ireland." In *War and Words: A Northern Ireland Reader*, edited by Bill Rolston and David Miller, 22–37. Belfast: Beyond the Pale Publications, 1996.

Smith, Justin. "Glam, Spam and Uncle Sam: Funding Diversity in 1970s British Film Production." In *Seventies British Cinema*, edited by Robert Shail, 67–80. London: BFI/Palgrave Macmillan, 2008.

Solomos, John. *Race and Racism in Britain*. Basingstoke: Macmillan, 1987.

Sontag, Susan. "Notes On Camp." *Partisan Review* 31, no. 4 (1964): 515–30.

—. "Notes On 'Camp'." In *Camp: Queer Aesthetic and the Performing Subject. A Reader*, edited by Fabio Cleto, 52–65. Edinburgh: Edinburgh University Press, 1999.

—. "Notes on Camp." In *Camp: Queer Aesthetics and the Performing Subject*, edited by Fabio Cleto, 53–65. Ann Arbor: University of Michigan Press Ann, 1999.

Sounes, Howard. *Seventies: the Sights, Sounds and Ideas of a Brilliant Decade*. London: Simon and Schuster, 2006.

Sparke, Penny. *An Introduction to Design and Culture in the Twentieth Century*. London: Routledge 1992.

Sparks, Colin. "Concentration in the UK National Press." *European Journal of Communication* 10 (1995): 195–97.

Speight, Johnny. *For Richer, For Poorer: A Kind of Autobiography*. London: BBC, 1991.

—. "If There Weren't Any Blacks You'd Have to Invent Them." In Johnny Speight. *Three Plays*. London: Oberon, 1998.

Spencer, Ian R.G. *British Immigration Policy Since 1939: The Making of Multi-Racial Britain*. London: Routledge, 1997.

Spicer, Andrew. "The Production Line: Reflections on the Role of the Film Producer in British Cinema." *Journal of British Cinema and Television* 1, no.1 (2004): 33–50.

Stanley, Liz. *Sex Surveyed: 1949–94*. London: Taylor and Francis, 1995.

Stevenson, Deborah. *Cities and Urban Culture. Cultural and Media Studies*. Berkshire: Open University Press, 2003.

Stevenson, Randall. *The British Novel since the Thirties: An Introduction*. Athens: University of Georgia Press, 1986.

Stimpson, Blake, and Gregory Sholette. *Collectivism after Modernism: The Art of Social Imagination after 1945*. Minneapolis: University of Minnesota Press, 2007.

Strachan, Robert and Marion Leonard. "Journalistic Practices." In *The Continuum Encyclopedia of Popular Music of the World. Volume 1: Media Industry and Society*, edited David Horn, 253–57. London: Continuum 2003.

Street, John. *Mass Media, Politics, and Democracy*. Basingstoke: Palgrave, 2001.

Sweetman, Paul. "Tourists and Travellers? 'Subcultures', Reflexive Identities and Neo-Tribal Sociality." In *After Subculture: Critical Studies in Contemporary Youth Culture*, edited by Andy Bennett and Keith Kahn-Harris, 79–93. Basingstoke: Palgrave, 2004.

Thomas, James. *Popular Newspapers, the Labour Party and British Politics.* Abingdon: Routledge, 2005.

Thomas, Peter. "The Struggle for Funding: Sponsorship, Competition and Pacification." *Screen* 47, no. 4 (2006): 461–67.

Thompson, Hunter S. *Fear and Loathing in Las Vegas.* London: Flamingo Modern Classics, 1971.

Thompson, Kristin, and David Bordwell. *Film History: An Introduction.* London: McGraw-Hill, 1994.

Thompson, Noel. *Political Economy and the Labour Party.* London: UCL Press, 1996.

Tolkien, J. R. R. *The Lord of the Rings.* London: George Allen & Unwin, 1955.

Tracey, Michael. *In the Culture of the Eye: Ten Years of Weekend World.* London: Hutchinson, 1983.

Tuchman, Gay. *Making News: A Study in the Construction of Reality.* New York: The Free Press, 1978.

Tunney, Sean. *Labour and the Press.* Brighton: Sussex Academic Press, 2007.

Tunstall, Jeremy. *Newspaper Power.* Oxford: Oxford University Press, 1995.

Turner, Alwyn. *Crisis? What Crisis?* London: Aurum Press, 2008.

Twiggy. *Twiggy: An Autobiography.* St Albans: Mayflower, 1976.

Venturi, Robert. *Complexity and Contradiction in Architecture.* New York: Museum of Modern Art, 1966.

Venturi, Robert, Denise Scott Brown and Steven Izenour. *Learning from Las Vegas: The Forgotten Symbolism of Architectural Form.* Cambridge, MA: MIT Press, 1977.

Wagg, Stephen. "'One I Made Earlier': Media, Popular Culture and the Politics of Childhood." In *Come on Down: Popular Media Culture in Postwar Britain*, edited by Dominic Strinarti and Stephen Wagg, 150–78. London: Routledge, 1992.

Walker, Alexander. *National Heroes: British Cinema in the Seventies and Eighties.* London: Harrap, 1985.

—. *Hollywood, England: The British Film Industry in the Sixties.* London: Harrap, 1986.

Walker, John A. *Crossovers: Art into Pop/Pop into Art.* London: Comedia, 1987.

Walker, John. *Left Shift: Radical Art in 1970s Britain.* London: I.B. Tauris, 2002.

Walters, Peter. "The Crisis of 'Responsible' Broadcasting: Mrs Thatcher and the BBC." *Parliamentary Affairs* 42, no.3 (1989): 380–98.

Wandor, Michelene. *Once a Feminist: Stories of a Generation*. London: Virago, 1990.

Watkin, David. *Morality and Architecture*. Oxford: Clarenden Press, 1977.

Watkins, Gordon, ed. *BFI Dossier 15: Tonight*. London: BFI, 1982.

Weight, Richard. *Patriots: National Identity in Britain 1940–2000*. London: Pan/MacMillan, 2003.

Wheen, Francis. *Strange Days Indeed: the Golden Age of Paranoia*. London: Fourth Estate, 2009.

White, Cynthia. *Women's Magazines 1693–1968*. London: Michael Joseph, 1970.

White, David M. "The Gatekeeper: A Case Study in the Selection of News." *Journalism Quarterly* 27 (1950): 383–94.

Whiteley, Gillian. *Radical Mayhem: Welfare State International and its Followers*. Exhibition Catalogue. Burnley: MidPennine Gallery, 2008.

Whiteley, Nigel. *Pop Design: From Modernism to Mod*. London: Design Council, 1987.

Wickham-Jones, Mark. *Economic Strategy and the Labour Party*. New York: St. Martin's Press, 1996.

Widgery, David. *Preserving Disorder*. London: Pluto Press, 1989.

Williams, Raymond, and Michael Orrom. *Preface to Film*. London: Film Drama, 1954.

Williams, Raymond. *Culture and Society*. London: Chatto and Windus, 1958.

—. "Culture is Ordinary." In *Conviction*, edited by N. Mackenzie, 74–92. London: MacGibbon and Kee, 1959.

—. *Marxism and Literature*. Oxford: Oxford University Press, 1977.

Wilson, David. "O Lucky Man." *Sight and Sound* 42, no. 3 (1973): 126–29.

Wilson, Elizabeth. *Only Halfway to Paradise: Women in Postwar Britian, 1945–1968*. London: Tavistock Publications, 1980.

Wilson, Sandy. *I Could Be Happy*. London: Joseph, 1975.

Winship, Janice. *Inside Women's Magazines*. London and New York: Pandora, 1987.

Wolfe, Tom. *New Journalism*. New York: Picador, 1975.

Wood, Linda. *British Films 1971–1981*. London: BFI Publishing, 1983.

Woodham, Jonathan. *Twentieth Century Design*. Oxford: Oxford University Press, 1997.

Wyndham, John. *The Day of the Triffids*. London: Michael Joseph, 1951.

Yarrow, Megan. "Gimme Some Truth: The Documentary Films of John Pilger." *Screen Education* 41 (2005): 42–48.

CONTRIBUTORS

Dave Allen is Principal Lecturer at the University of Portsmouth. Before he was an academic he was a Mod. He grew up in 1960s Britain as a huge fan of popular music and more broadly popular culture, and by the late 1960s he was a professional musician. He has continued to perform, broadcast and write about popular music, but since the mid-1970s he has also been a teacher of the visual arts. For many years, his main research work (including his doctorate) was in visual pedagogy. In the last few years he has turned to research and teaching popular music, particularly the 1960s. His publications include work on the Woodstock Festival, the British Blues scene, and an extensive study of popular music in Portsmouth in that decade.

Peri Bradley is Associate Lecturer in Film and TV at Southampton Solent University and University of Southampton. She was part of the 1970s British Film project group at University of Portsmouth and co-organiser with Professor Harper of the conference in July 2008. She has chapters included in Sorcha Ni Fhlainn (ed.) *Dark Reflections, Monstrous Reflections: Essays on the Monster in Culture* (2006), and Paul Newland (ed.) *Don't Look Now: British Cinema in the 1970s* (Intellect, 2010). She is also contributing archival work for Sue Harper and Justin Smith (eds.) *British Film Culture in the 1970s: the Boundaries of Pleasure* (Edinburgh University Press).

Anthony Dunn is a Visiting Principal Lecturer in English at Portsmouth University. His main research interests are in British and American Modernism and Post-War British Theatre. He has published essays on Henry James, D. H. Lawrence, Ezra Pound, Alan Bleasdale and Howard Barker, as well as on more general topics such as the evolution of Cultural Studies and British theatre in the 1980s. He is at present writing a full-length study of the life and work of Wolf Mankowitz.

Dr Sue Evans is currently Associate Lecturer with The Open University and the University of Portsmouth in Creative Writing, particularly fiction and playwriting. Her research interests include: the subversion of realism and dramatic structure by women and feminist playwrights in late twentieth-century theatre; feminist dramatisation of interiority, and developments in the staging of realism in contemporary theatre writing. She has recently contributed to the National Association of Writers in Education publication *Writing in Education* and has reviewed for *Writernet.*

Kirsten Forkert is a PhD student at Goldsmiths, University of London. Her research is concerned with working conditions in the arts, and explores relationships between social and cultural policy. She has also written on cultural policy, cultural activism and the politics of education. In addition, she is an activist and is involved in trade union politics, campaigns and social centres.

Laurel Forster is Senior Lecturer in Media Studies at the University of Portsmouth. Her research interests include women's literature, history and cultures. She has published articles on the work of modernist writer May Sinclair, co-edited *The Recipe Reader* (Ashgate, 2003) with Janet Floyd, and contributed chapters which explore relationships between media forms, representations of women (often in domestic contexts), and literary and cultural theories. Her involvement with the Portsmouth AHRC 1970s project has led to articles on feminism, television and magazines of the decade. She is currently working on a longer study of feminist magazines.

Adrian Garvey lectures in film at Birkbeck, University of London, and is currently writing a book on Hollywood melodrama of the 1940s. He is also the author of 'Pre-Sold to Millions: British Sitcom Films of the 1970s', in Paul Newland (ed.), *Don't Look Now: British Cinema in the 1970s* (Intellect, 2010).

Tim Gough leads the third year Design Studio 2 at Kingston University School of Architecture and Landscape, UK, and lectures in the history and theory of architecture. He is partner in Robertson Gough, an artist-architect collaborative based in London. His recent research interests include phenomenology, the work of Gilles Deleuze, and the Roman baroque. Published papers include *Let us Take Architecture* (publication and symposium at the Wordsworth Trust with artist Lucy Gunning, May 2007); *Non-origin of Species – Deleuze, Derrida, Darwin*, essay in the journal *Culture and Organisation*, Issue 4 December 2006; and *Defiguration of space*, an essay in *Figuration-Defiguration*, edited by Atsuko Onuki and Thomas Pekar, published by Iudicum Verlag, Munich (Germany) 2006.

Sue Harper is Emeritus Professor of Film History at the University of Portsmouth. She has written a range of articles on British cinema, and her books include: *Picturing the Past: the Rise and Fall of the British Costume Film* (BFI, 1994); *Women in British Cinema: Mad, Bad and Dangerous to Know* (Continuum, 2000); *British Cinema of the 1950s: the Decline of Deference* (OUP, 2003) with Vincent Porter; and *The New Film History* (Palgrave, 2007) with James Chapman and Mark Glancy. Her forthcoming books include *British Film Culture in the 1970s: the Boundaries of Pleasure* (with Justin Smith) and *Beyond the Archive*. Sue was Principal Investigator of the Arts and Humanites project at Portsmouth on British cinema in the 1970s.

Stephen Hill has been Head of Media at Burgate School since 2004; he is also affiliated with Bournemouth Media School where he has taught Media Theory and supervises student research. He has just completed a PhD on the music press at the University of Winchester and has previously published on *Q* and *The Face* in *Popular Music History* (2006). In addition to this Stephen writes for *Media Magazine*; recent articles include pieces on the magazine industry (2005), the history of music video (2006), film and censorship (2008), Marxism and global media (2009) and television drama (2009).

John Izod is Professor of Screen Analysis in Film, Media and Journalism at the University of Stirling. University archivist Karl Magee has worked at the Chester Beatty Library, the National Archives of Ireland and the Mitchell Library in Glasgow. Prior to moving to Stirling, project archivist Kathryn Mackenzie worked at Glasgow Caledonian University on the Scottish Trades Union Congress Archive. Isabelle Gourdin, is a PhD candidate and has worked as a lecturer at The Robert Gordon University.

Keith M. Johnston is Lecturer in Film and Television Studies at the University of East Anglia. His recent publications include *Coming Soon: Film Trailers and the Selling of Hollywood Technology* (McFarland 2009) and "Ealing's Colour Aesthetic: *Saraband for Dead Lovers*" (*Journal of British Cinema and Television* 6.3). His research interests include cross-media phenomena such as The Wombles, as well as British cinema and television more widely. He has a particular interest in how the British film industry reacted to technological changes such as colour and 3-D.

Adam Locks is Senior Lecturer/Programme Coordinator in Media Studies at the University of Chichester, and specializes in horror cinema and representations of extreme bodies. He is co-editing a book with Niall Richardson entitled *Flex: Critical Readings in Bodybuilding*, (Routledge 2010) and researching another with Adrian Smith on the career of British horror director Norman J. Warren.

David McQueen recently submitted his PhD thesis "BBC TV's Panorama 1987-2004: conflict coverage and the 'Westminster consensus'" at Bournemouth University. He is currently a researcher on the 'No Such Thing as Society Project' under Patricia Holland, and teaches part-time at Bournemouth University. His research interests include news and current affairs, war reporting, politics and democracy, the history of the BBC and the political economy of the media. He is the author of *Television: A Media Student's Guide* (Arnold 1999).

Julian Matthews is a Lecturer in the Department of Media and Communication at the University of Leicester. He is Editor of the Communication and Media Section of the international journal *Sociology Compass* and is Convenor of the British Sociological Media Study Group. His research interests include the production of news journalism and its representations of health, the environment and other social problems. He has published work in a range of academic journals.

Gavin Schaffer is Senior Lecturer in Modern European History at the University of Portsmouth. He is the author of *Racial Science and British Society 1930-62* (Palgrave 2008) and co-editor of *The Lasting War: Society and Identity in Britain, France and Germany after the Second World War* (Palgrave 2008) with Monica Riera. He is presently writing a new book on race relations and the BBC in the nineteen sixties and seventies.

Rochelle Simmons is a Senior Lecturer in English at the University of Otago, Dunedin, New Zealand. Her research interests include contemporary literature and film. She has published articles on Michael Ondaatje, John Berger, and various topics concerning New Zealand Cinema and she is currently writing a book on John Berger and the visual.

Dr Andrew Spicer is Reader in Cultural History in the Faculty of Creative Arts, University of the West of England. He has published numerous journal articles and chapters in collections on British cinema and two monographs: *Typical Men: The Representation of Masculinity in Popular British Cinema* (I. B. Tauris 2003) and *Sydney Box* (MUP 2006). He is currently engaged on a two-year AHRC-funded project to catalogue and interpret the Michael Klinger Papers housed at UWE, part of a wider investigation into the changing historical role of the film producer.

Gwilym Thear is currently finishing his PhD on apocalyptic narratives in British culture at the school of Journalism, Media and Cultural Studies at Cardiff University. His research interests include apocalypticism, narrative psychology, 1970s culture and temporality.

Sean Tunney is Principal Lecturer in Journalism and News Media at Roehampton University. A former newspaper and Web journalist, he published a modern history of media policymaking and partisan politics, *Labour and the Press* (Sussex Academic Press 2007). He has recently co-edited the book *Web Journalism* (Sussex Academic Press, 2009) with Garrett Monaghan, an international collection analysing Web reporting, journalistic blogging and the role of citizen journalism.

Jo Turney is course leader for the Investigating Fashion Design, MA course at Bath Spa University. She is the co-author of *Floral Frocks* (Antique Collectors Club 2007) with Rosemary Harden, and is the sole author of *The Culture of Knitting* (Berg, 2009). Her main interests include fashion and textiles since 1970, and everyday approaches and appropriations of dress, particularly in relation to anti-social behaviour and masculinity. She has also published widely on contemporary textile crafts practice and critical theory.

Gillian Whiteley is Lecturer in Critical and Historical Studies at Loughborough University School of Art and Design. Her research interests focus on trans-disciplinary practices within socio-political contexts, from cultural activism and artists' collectives in the 1960s to contemporary practice. Her publications include *Telling Stories: Countering Narrative in Art, Theory and Film* (Cambridge Scholars Publishing 2009) with Jane Tormey, and a forthcoming book, *Junk: Art and the Politics of Trash* (I. B. Tauris). Also see www.bricolagekitchen.com

INDEX

1. General Index
2. Index of Media Titles

1. General Index

2. Index of Media Titles: Film, Television, Magazines, Journals, Radio, Theatre and Songs